Law and Division of Power in the Crimean Khanate (1532–1774)

The Ottoman Empire and Its Heritage

POLITICS, SOCIETY AND ECONOMY

Edited by

Suraiya Faroqhi
Boğaç Ergene

Founding Editor

Halil İnalcık (d. 2016)

VOLUME 65

The titles published in this series are listed at *brill.com/oeh*

Law and Division of Power in the Crimean Khanate (1532–1774)

With Special Reference to the Reign of Murad Giray (1678–1683)

By

Natalia Królikowska-Jedlińska

BRILL

LEIDEN | BOSTON

Cover illustration: The tuğra of Khan Murad Giray from the oath-letter (şartname) sent to Tsar Fedor III in 1682 (RGADA, f. 123 "Snoshenia Rossii s Krymom", op. 2, no. 64, fol. 1). Reproduced by courtesy of the Russian State Archives of Early Acts in Moscow (RGADA).

Library of Congress Cataloging-in-Publication Data

Names: Krolikowska-Jedlińska, Natalia, author.
Title: Law and division of power in the Crimean Khanate (1532-1774): with special reference to the reign of Murad Giray (1678-1683) / by Natalia Krolikowska-Jedlińska.
Description: Leiden ; Boston : Brill, 2019. | Series: The Ottoman Empire and its heritage ; Volume 65 | Based on author's thesis (doctoral - Uniwersytet Warszawski, 2010) issued under title: Law and division of power : a study on the reign of Murad Giray. | Includes bibliographical references and index.
Identifiers: LCCN 2018041884 (print) | LCCN 2018042949 (ebook) | ISBN 9789004384323 (E-book) | ISBN 9789004366534 (hardback : alk. paper)
Subjects: LCSH: Justice, Administration of--Crimean Khanate--History--17th century. | Justice, Administration of--Crimean Khanate--History--17th century.
Classification: LCC KKY4891.A197 (ebook) | LCC KKY4891.A197 K76 2019 (print) | DDC 349.47/10903--dc23
LC record available at https://lccn.loc.gov/2018041884

Typeface for the Latin, Greek, and Cyrillic scripts: "Brill". See and download: brill.com/brill-typeface.

ISSN 1380-6076
ISBN 978-90-04-36653-4 (hardback)
ISBN 978-90-04-38432-3 (e-book)

Contents

Appendices

Preface

The idea that law reveals the differences between societies and the changes in their social structure has been recognized since Antiquity (e.g., Greek comparisons of various types of *politeia*). Eminent European scholars, from Charles Montesquieu to Max Weber, stressed the importance of law as the source of our knowledge of societies. Contemporary anthropologists developed their analyses based on the studies of law, because—as Sally Humphreys stated—"law is, in all societies, one of the most explicit, concrete and institutionalized cadres of ethno-sociological discourse".[1]

This book takes up two main and related issues: the structure of power in the Crimean Khanate and the legal position and activity of its ruler and the various groups who were his subjects. The practice of the *kadıasker* court and a district court, described below, reveals how the khans used the judicial administration to communicate with their subjects. Throughout the study, we encounter various individuals, some seeking justice before the courts, others brought there by the authorities. The characterization of the khanate's law and its origins constitutes a vital part of this book, which focuses on comparing the legal practices revealed in court registers with those embedded in the legal systems of the Mongols (derived from the Golden Horde) and the Ottomans (derived from Islam).

The Chronological Scope of the Research

The chronological scope of this study was determined by the availability of sources. The tragic history of the Crimean Khanate and the Tatar nation in the nineteenth and twentieth centuries greatly reduced the number of extant documents. In the present study, I focus on two chronological periods.

The first one, which is utilized for discussing general data about the Crimean structure of power and law, covers the period between the reforms of Sahib Giray (1532–51) and the Peace of Küçük Kaynarca (1774). The historical materials I study in this book show that Sahib Giray laid the foundations for the mixed Ottoman-Golden Horde judicial and administrative system of the khanate. Its core institution consisted of the khan, his council, his first deputy known as the *kalga*, the *kurultay*, and the four to six *karaçı beğ*s; this institution

1 S. Humphreys, "Law as Discourse," *History and Anthropology* 1 (1985): 241–265

functioned until the introduction of the Russian protectorate over the khanate in 1774.

The second period, which encompasses the reign of Murad Giray (1678–83), enables us to engage in an in-depth study based on the judicial court registers. Before moving on, it is necessary to explain the use of these two chronological periods. My choice to use data from an extended period for detailed research of a shorter period raises two important methodological questions. First, is it possible to draw information on the core institutions of the khanate from sources written over a period of almost 250 years, and does this information allow us to understand, in general, how these institutions functioned in the last quarter of the seventeenth century? Second, why have I chosen to focus this in-depth study on the reign of Murad Giray?

In addressing the first question, a caveat is in order regarding the comprehensiveness of my descriptions of the core institutions. The present study aims to characterize the general features of the khanate's internal policy on the basis of sources dating to the period between 1532 and 1774, whereas the in-depth research includes a basic statistical analysis of the court registers during the reign of Murad Giray. We would argue that studying the *sicil*s must be preceded by research covering the broader period of the history of the khanate, in order to present a coherent general description of the most important Crimean institutions and their officials. This is necessary because we lack a reliable description of the majority of these institutions and officials. We can demonstrate this point with the example of the office of the khan's vizier. In contrast to the Ottoman Empire, there is no single study devoted to this institution in any time period; we do not have a list of officials appointed to this office, nor do we have any reliable research on their origins, education, family connections, career paths, wealth, households, not to mention their prerogatives and role in domestic and foreign policy. Most of what we know about this office comes, thus far, from studying the lives of Sefer Gazi Ağa, Subhan Gazi Ağa, and Islam Ağa, the three most powerful viziers from the mid-seventeenth century, who were relatively well-described by contemporary Crimean and foreign sources. This is not to claim that we have a comprehensive study of any of the three reputed viziers. Yet, there is sufficient data in the chronicles, and in diplomatic sources, to reconstruct some of the most important points in their careers. Perhaps the Crimean court registers remain the unique source from which we can find detailed data on their family connections, the relations within their households, and their wealth. Yet, it is difficult to understand references to particular individuals or institutions mentioned in the court registers, without reference to the khanate's political system. We would argue that, given the present state of research and bearing in mind the limited sources on Crimean history, even a general description of the khanate's institutions requires us to use all available narrative and diplomatic sources dating to the period between the reforms of Sahib Giray and the Peace of Küçük Kaynarca. We do not intend to imply that the political culture of the khanate was static. On the contrary, we expect relations between power-holders such as the ruler, his council, his heirs apparent, the nobles, and the diet to have evolved. Again, the office of the khan's vizier could serve as an example of these changes. It was only introduced at the end of the sixteenth century, while the most powerful known officeholders were active in mid-seventeenth century. When the sources report subtle or even important changes in the khanate's political system, we have noted them in the present study. Nevertheless, we acknowledge that this does not demonstrate the evolution of the khanate's political and judicial institutions. Hopefully, further research on the Crimean court registers will allow scholars to pursue research in this direction and add to our understanding of the changes among power-holders in the khanate.

Having said this, let us address the second question: why have we opted to focus this in-depth research on the rule of Murad Giray? We would argue that his short reign, which coincides with a turning point in European international relations, contains features characteristic of the preceding and the following time periods. The changes in European policy caused by the Vienna campaign in 1683 greatly affected the khanate's position in its relations with its Christian neighbors. These changes also influenced Crimean-Ottoman relations, which shifted toward strengthening Ottoman patronage over the khanate. The increased Ottoman pressure on the khanate was related to the new, active northern policy of the Sublime Porte. Murad Giray was the last Crimean khan to handle Ottoman diplomatic relations with Moscow.

This is not to say that Murad Giray acted as an independent ruler. The shifts in the relations between various players on the international scene are discussed briefly in Chapter 1. Here we would like to mention that until Murad Giray's reign, the Sublime Porte left the branch of its international policy concerning Muscovy in the khan's hands, in recognition of his right, as a descendant of the Golden Horde. For the same reason, the Russians had been paying tribute to the khans for more than two hundred years. Murad Giray was the last khan to receive it. After the Treaty of Karlowitz (1699), the tsar openly challenged the Tatar claim of sovereignty over his state. Dispatching Russian envoys directly to Istanbul was a visible sign of Moscow's independence from Bahçesaray, while the Crimean khans were no longer powerful enough to reassert their rights. With the ongoing strengthening of Russian power in the Black Sea region, the Tatar rulers became increasingly dependent on the Ottomans. As a result, they had to desist from conducting their own policy in the north.

We should consider, to what extent did the change in the international position of the khanate affect its internal policies? Was the year 1683 a cataclysmic event in the internal affairs of the most important figures in the khanate? In this work, we demonstrate that the most important groups in the khanate, for example, the khan, his household and his officials, the *karaçı beğ*s and the *mirza*s, preserved the core of their rights throughout the period between the reforms of Sahib Giray (1532–51) and the Peace of Küçük Kaynarca (1774). Yet, a certain shift of power took place. The international situation weakened the position of the khan. This fact must have had some repercussions on his relations with the Nogays and the *karaçı beğ*s, who became, by the eighteenth century, very difficult to control. Nonetheless, we must keep in mind that in the sixteenth and seventeenth centuries the vassals also rebelled against the khans. Admittedly, the reality of the eighteenth century made such actions less dangerous for possible rebels. Their chance of success, i.e., of deposing an unpopular khan and replacing him with another one, was higher than in previous centuries, but the patterns of rebellions against the khans remained almost unchanged from the sixteenth to the eighteenth centuries.

In sum, we acknowledge the danger of constructing a general picture of the core institutions based on sources written over a period of 250 years. Nonetheless, we believe that the similarities between the core institutions of the khanate from the sixteenth to the eighteenth centuries allow us to use it as a backdrop for more in-depth research on the reign of Murad Giray based on the court registers. We hope that more in-depth studies on other Crimean *sicil*s will follow, and comparisons between these results and the conclusions of the present study can be undertaken. This is certainly a unique way to learn whether, and perhaps in what direction, the practice of law in the khanate evolved.

The availability of sources is yet another reason to focus on the period of Murad Giray. We discuss this problem in detail in the second part of the introduction. Now, we would like to mention that the Crimean court registers dating back to the reign of Murad Giray contain entries from the *kadıasker* court, district courts, and the records of proceedings before the khan's council. Thus, *sicil*s from this relatively short period offer us insight into the day-to-day practice of three judicial fora. An unusual register (*defter*) from Kefe province, which was located in Sofia and dates to the year 1682–83, was another factor in our choice of this period.

Outline of the Book

The emphasis of this study is on the relations between the khan and his various subjects. I concentrate on the division of power within the khanate and aim to understand these relationships by describing the administration of justice in the khan's *kadı* courts.

The study is composed of an introduction and five chapters. In the introduction I discuss the manner in which the Crimean Khanate has been described over the course of time. As the study concerns Crimean law, I also summarize Mongol law. Finally, the introduction provides general information on the sources I have utilized.

Chapter 1 provides a historical background and discusses the way in which Murad Giray was depicted in the Crimean chronicles. This analysis of his early life prior to ascending the throne; his character; and his domestic and foreign policy with special emphasis on the Second Vienna campaign in 1683 as described by these sources, brings us closer to understanding why the Crimean chroniclers differed so widely in their assessments of Murad Giray.

Chapter 2 concentrates on the position of the khan, as gleaned from the court registers and narrative sources. We describe the limitations of his power as a judge and lawgiver, and the means he used to rule and control his subjects. The dignities reserved for the Giray dynasty and the offices held by the khan's subordinates are also discussed, but only members of the khan's council. The chapter ends with an analysis of twenty-three cases judged at the khan's council during the reign of Murad Giray; this brings us closer to understanding the judicial functions of the institution.

Chapter 3 covers the position of Crimean nobles. This group was by no means homogenous; for this reason, we discuss the differences between the two major sub-groups. This chapter of the study provides data, mostly extracted from narrative sources, regarding the origins, rights, and duties of the Crimean nobles. Here, from two micro studies based on the court registers, we present a portrait of two main groups of nobles who appeared in the sharia courts. The first micro study depicts the more powerful group, who were known as *karaçı* nobles (members of the *karaçı* families), and presented cases in the sharia courts. The second micro study focuses on the less influential group of nobles, non-*karaçı* nobles. The way they used the courts is described on the example of the Yaşdağı family.

In Chapter 4, I present the characteristics of the provincial courts, as the crucial means of the khan's control over society; this chapter is comprised of two main sections. The first begins with analysis of the origins, education, and career prospects of the Crimean *kadı*s. It then focuses on the court personnel (*naib*s, *katib*s, case witnesses, *zabit*s, *beytülmal*s, *konakçı başı*s, and *pencik emini*s) and their relations with the district judge. The second section deals with the limitations of the judicial power of the provincial *kadı*s and their subordinates. I characterize the *kadı*'s competitors among the local administration (*muhtesibs*, *serdars*, *nakıbüleşrafs*) and the members of the *divan* (the mufti, the *karaçı beğs*). Finally, I examine whether the *kadı*'s judicial power was limited by the competence of the khan's council and autonomous jurisdiction of non-Muslims. The approaches in chapters 2 and 4 might be described as state-centric, as they focus on the vital political and judicial institutions of the khanate.

In Chapter 5 I focus on the khanate's law and its users. First, I address the laws applied in the khanate. Then, I present information on the social, economic, and geographical characteristics of the court clients. We hope that these analyses of their identity will bring us closer to understanding who stood a chance of success in the Crimean sharia court. We also discuss the types of disputes brought to the law courts and the practices of dispute resolution. Finally, in this chapter I focus on the Ottoman subjects who used the courts in the khanate. It includes a micro study centered on the inhabitants of the judicial district (*kaza*) of Mangub, in the province of Kefe. The issues listed above enable us to more deeply understand the questions that are central to this study: the division of power in the khanate and the law applied within its borders.

The five chapters are followed by a conclusion and four appendices containing data such as:

1. transliteration, translation, and facsimile of the order issued by Khan Canibeg Giray in 1612;
2. transliteration, translation, and facsimile of a case judged at the khan's council;
3. cases judged by the council of Murad Giray (1678–82); and
4. a list of officials mentioned in the court registers dating back to Murad Giray's reign.

Acknowledgments

As is often the case with first books, the present study started as my dissertation. I owe thanks to many people who have guided, discussed, questioned, and encouraged my work during my PhD studies. First, I want to express my warmest gratitude to my supervisor, Dariusz Kołodziejczyk. I thank him for his moral, intellectual, and practical support over many years. Thanks to his help, I was able to discuss my results and study with the leading scholars in the field.

I have benefited enormously from the guidance of Svetlana Ivanova (University of Sofia), Henryk Jankowski (Adam Mickiewicz University in Poznań), Maria Kalitzin (Bulgarian Academy of Science), Tadeusz Majda (University of Warsaw), Michael Ursinus (University of Heidelberg), Fehmi Yilmaz (Medeniyet University in Istanbul), and Andrzej Zakrzewski (University of Warsaw). Special thanks are due to my hosts at the Moscow State University, Mikhail Meier and Svetlana Kirilina, and to my host at the University of Cambridge, the late Christopher Bayly, for the warm welcome they extended during my scholarships. Of the many others whose assistances were of utmost importance to my research, I would like to thank Meinolf Arens, Kate Fleet, Rossitsa Gradeva, Tetiana Grygorieva, Colin Imber, Maria Ivanics, Galina Ivanova, Gabor Kármán, Denise Klein, Kirill Kochegarov, Maryna Kravets, Włodzimierz Mędrzecki, Osman Özgüdenli, Milena Petkova, Aleksandra Porada, Tomasz Szwaciński, Hacer Topaktaş, Ahmet Üstüner, Olga Vasil'eva, Asparuh Velkov, and Michał Wasiucionek. Additionally, I benefited from discussions with my teachers and colleagues from the Institute of History and the Institute of Oriental Studies of the University of Warsaw.

Several institutions supported the research for this book. Scholarships from the Turkish government supported me during my stay in Ankara and Istanbul, while the German Academic Exchange Service (Deutscher Akademischer Austausch Dienst) covered the costs of my stay at the University of Heidelberg (2007–08). I am also grateful to the COST Office for granting me a Short-Term Scientific Mission at the University of Cambridge (2008) and to the Polish National Programme for the Development of Humanities (2012–16) for covering the expenses of archival research in Rome and Istanbul.

I want to express my gratitude to the following institutions where research for this project was done: Haus-, Hof- und Staatarchiv in Vienna, the Centre for Islamic Studies (İslam Araştırma Merkezi) in Istanbul, Ismail Gasprinsky Republican Crimean Tatar Library in Simferopol, the Main Archive of Early Acts in Warsaw, the Oriental Department of the Bulgarian National Library 'St. Cyril and Methodius' in Sofia, Propaganda Fide Historical Archives in Rome,

Russian National Library in St. Petersburg, and the Russian State Archives of Early Acts in Moscow.

Separate thanks go to the editors of the *Ottoman Heritage* series, and to the reviewers of the book manuscript.

Finally, and most importantly, I thank my dear family who encouraged and guided me over many years and enabled me to pursue my scholarly interests.

Illustrations

Figures

Tables

Abbreviations

ACTA	*Acta Sacrae Congregationis*
AGAD	Archiwum Główne Akt Dawnych [Main Archives of Early Acts, Warsaw]
AKW	Archiwum Koronne Warszawskie [Crown Archives of Warsaw]
APF	Propaganda Fide Historical Archives in Rome
BSOAS	*Bulletin of the School of Oriental and African Studies*
CMRS	*Cahiers du monde russe et soviétique*
*EI*²	*Encyclopedia of Islam* (second edition)
Fondo Lettere	*Fondo Lettere e decreti della Sacra Congregazione e biglietti di Mons. Segretario*
HHStA	Haus-, Hof- und Staatsarchiv [Vienna]
HJAS	*Harvard Journal of Asiatic Studies*
HUS	*Harvard Ukrainian Studies*
IA	*Islam Ansiklopedisi*
IJMES	*International Journal of Middle East Studies*
ITUAK	*Izvestiia Tavricheskoi Uchenoi Arkhivnoi Komissii* [Proceedings of the Taurida Learned Archival Commission]
JESHO	*Journal of the Economic and Social History of the Orient*
KH	*Kwartalnik Historyczny*
NBKM, Or. Dept.	Oriental'ski Otdel Narodnoi Biblioteki Imieni Sv. Sv. Kirilla i Mefodiia [Oriental Department of Bulgarian National Library 'St. St. Cyril and Methodius]
ÖNB	Österreichische Nationalbibliothek [Austrian National Library]
ORRNB	Rossiiskaia Natsional'naia Biblioteka in St. Petersburg [Russian National Library in St. Petersburg, Oriental Manuscript Division of the Russian National Library (Otdel Rukopisev Rossiiskoi Natsionalnoi Biblioteki)]
PSB	*Polski Słownik Bibliograficzny*
RGADA	Rossiiskii Gosudarstvennyi Arkhiv Drevnikh Aktov [Russian State Archives of Early Acts, Moscow]
SC	*Scritture referite nei Congressi*
SOCG	*Scritture originali referite nelle Congregatione*
ZOOID	*Zapiski Imperatorskogo Odesskogo Obshchestva Istorii i Drevnostei* [Proceedings of the Imperial Odessa Society for History and Antiquities]

Note on Place Names, Proper Names, and Transliteration

Place Names

In Eastern Europe place names cause significant trouble because they reflect past and present ethnic and political conflicts. As the states' frontiers have changed dramatically over the last four centuries, the decision about whether to uphold the historical place names used in the described period or follow the contemporary names has become a political issue. In the case of states that no longer exist, such as the Crimean Khanate, the problem is particularly complex. We cannot lose sight of the fact that Tatar and Turkish place names in the Crimea were changed in accordance with imperialistic Russian, and then Soviet policy. In 1784, tsarist officials returned to some ancient Greek place names, in an effort to underline the classical heritage of the Russian Empire. Thus, the Crimea was included in the newly created Tauridian Province, while the most important cities were given ancient Greek names, for example, Feodosia replaced Kefe, and Gözleve became Evpatoria. Yet, the tsarist policy was modest in scale, in comparison to that of the Soviets. In the wake of the deportation of the Crimean Tatars in 1944, almost all Tatar and Turkish place names on the peninsula were changed.[1] This time, the new names had no reference to the pre-Tatar names. Some of the new place names were given in honor of Russian and Soviet heroes,[2] but the majority of them seem to have been given in haste from an agriculture textbook. To sum up, the newly introduced place names in the Crimea were products of state propaganda rather than a reflection of the language and culture of the local inhabitants of non-Tatar and non-Turkish origins.

For these reasons, I resolved the issue of place names as follows:

a. Standard English place names are preferred, where they exist (e.g., Warsaw or Istanbul);
b. contemporary place names are used to refer to settlements outside the historical boundaries of the Crimean Khanate, for instance, Chyhyryn or Varaždin; and

---

1 H. Jankowski, *A Historical-Etymological Dictionary of Pre-Russian Habitation Names of the Crimea* (Leiden and Boston, 2006).

2 B.G. Williams, *The Crimean Tatars: The Diaspora Experience and the Forging of a Nation* (Leiden and Boston 2001), 404.

c. historic place names are used for places that were situated in the Crimean Khanate (including Nogay steppes) and in the Kefe province of the Ottoman Empire. These are written in the forms most frequently recorded in the Crimean court registers (from the years 1678–83) and the Kefe *defter* (from the year 1682–83). As they were written in the Arabic script, there are some ambiguities concerning their transliteration. The Crimean Tatars did not pronounce words uniformly. It is possible to distinguish two main forms: Oghuz in the southern part of the peninsula and Kipchak in the north. The Oghuz forms seem to be very close to the Ottoman Turkish pronunciation. As the Crimean court registers were written in Ottoman Turkish, in cases where it was unclear how to pronounce a place name, we preferred Ottoman Turkish forms.

Proper Names and Terms

Likewise, the Ottoman Turkish forms of proper names are used, for example, 'Giray' instead of its Kipchak form 'Kerey.' We also use the Ottoman Turkish forms of Arabic names, e.g., 'Mehmed' instead of the Arabic form 'Muḥammad' or the Kipchak form 'Memet.'

Legal and administrative terms also cause trouble. Most of the terms used here existed in Ottoman Turkish. In these cases, the Ottoman Turkish form is preferred. Foreign terms are given in italics.

Transliteration

Modern Turkish spelling is used in cases of words which were recorded in Arabic script and which occur in Ottoman Turkish (Türkçeİngilizce. Redhouse Sözlüğü). Therefore, the long vowels in words of Arabic and Persian origins are not indicated. The majority of the Turkish letters are pronounced as in English, with the exception of the following:

c sounds like English *j*
ç sounds like English *ch*
ğ is silent and lengthens the proceding vowel
ı sounds like *u* in *radium*
ö sounds like German *ö*
ş sounds like English *sh*
ü sounds like German *ü*.

We follow the Library of Congress system of transliteration from Russian to English.

Concordance of Frequently Mentioned Place Names

Ottoman-Turkish name	Contemporary name in Russian
Akkerman	Belgorod
Ak Mescid	Simferopol
Bahçesaray	Bakhchesaray
Eski Kırım	Staryi Krym
Ferahkerman / Or Kalesi	Perekop
Gözleve	Evpatoria
Kara Su	Belogorsk
Kefe	Feodosia
Kerç	Kerch
Mangup	Mangup
Özü	Ochakov

Glossary

acemî oğlans	conscripts who joined the janissaries
ahırcı başı	head stableman
akçe	a small silver coin minted in the Ottoman Empire and in the Crimean Khanate; also known as *sim akçesi*
altun (*altun-i şerif*)	a gold coin minted in the Ottoman Empire
askeri	a subject of the khan who has tax immunity (as opposed to a member of the *reaya*)
atalık	a tutor of the male members of the Giray dynasty
beylik	land that could not be sold or given; land that could not be divided among the members of the clan, but remains in the ownership of the whole clan under the administration of the head of the clan
beytülmal emini	a treasury officer whose responsibilities covered various matters related to financial administration and security
bölükbaşı	an officer in the janissary corps
cadırcı başı	head tent keeper
çaşnigir başı	head taster
cebeci	armourer
cizye	polltax payable by nonMuslims enjoying the protection of an Islamic ruler
defterdar	finance director
divan	a council presided over by the khan or his deputy in the khanate
dönüm	a unit of land measurement (ca. 940 square metres)
ferman	an order issued by the khan, the sultan, or their highest officials
fetva	a nonbinding legal opinion issued by a mufti
guruş	a large silver coin, initially of Western origin, since the eighteenth century also minted by Ottoman sultans; in the seventeenth-century Crimea, the Dutch *leeuwendaaler* was known as '*esedi guruş*' while the Spanish real as '*riyal guruş*'
hacı	a pilgrim to Mecca
han	bazaar
Hanafi	one of the four schools of Islamic law; the Hanafi school prevailed in the khanate

haraç	(a) a land tax (tribute) payable from territories conquered in a holy war; or (b) a term used (incorrectly) to describe the *cizye*
khatib	a preacher who gave the Friday *hutba*
kilerci başı	chief/head of the larder
halife	a junior clerk
hazinedar	a treasurer
hutba	a sermon delivered during the Friday prayer, in which the preacher mentions the ruler's name
hüccet	a title deed
iltizam	tax farms auctioned to the highest bidders for a determined period
imam	the prayer leader in the mosque
kadı	a judge; in addition to his judicial and notarial responsibilities, this official carried out various administrative functions
kadıasker	an 'army judge'; the title of the chief judge in the Crimean Khanate; in contrast to the Ottoman Empire, there was only one *kadıasker* in the khanate. The *kadıasker* was a member of the ruler's council and resided in the capital city of Bahçesaray. (In the *sicil*s they are referred to as *kadı bi-l asker* or *kadı bi-l-cünd.*)
kalga	in the Crimean Khanate, he was the heir apparent and the first deputy of the khan
kanun	secular law issued by the Ottoman sultan; it supplemented or at times even superseded Islamic religious law
kapıkulu	'slave of the Porte'; a term borrowed from the Ottoman Empire to refer to the khan's slave servitors who perform various functions in the state administration
*karaçı beğ*s	in Mongolian, the term *karaçı* means a 'servant,' or a 'retinue member.' In the Crimean Khanate, it was the title of the heads of the most powerful noble families (hereafter '*karaçı* families'). The *karaçı* families traced their origins back to the Golden Horde. They owed their elevated status to their economic and military power. They were headed by *beğ*s, who extended a great influence over the khanate's policy and held significant power within its borders. The *karaçı* families were juxtaposed to the heads of less important noble families (hereafter 'non-*karaçı* noble families').

katib	a scribe
kaza	a judicial district
kaymakam	(a) a head official, or (b) a deputy (substitute) of the khan or *kalga* (in the Ottoman Empire, a deputy of the grand vizier)
kethüda	a warden, steward, man of affairs
konakçı	a billeting officer
kul	see *kapıkulu*
kurultay	a general diet in a successor state of the Golden Horde
ma'ruz	a statement, petition
matrakçı başı	a head swordsman, a janissary officer
medrese	a higher college often attached to a mosque
mezheb	one of the four Sunni schools of law
mirahor	an equerry
miri	a state property, as opposed to private (*mülk*) property
mirza	a title confirming noble status
mubaşır	a special emissary
mufti	a jurist; a person with authority to issue a legal opinion (*fetva*)
muhtesib	a market inspector
müderris	a teacher in an Islamic school (*medrese*)
mülk	private property as opposed to state (*miri*) property
mürasele	judge's letter of appointment
mütevelli	an administrator of a pious foundation
muhzır	a summons official
nahiye	a judicial subdistrict; in the Ottoman Empire these were administered by *naib*s
naib	a deputy judge
nakıbüleşraf	a marshal of the descendants of the Prophet
Nakşbendi	a dervish order founded in the fourteenth century; it was very popular in the Ottoman Empire
nazır	a superintendent
nöker	a client of a member of the ruling dynasty or a mighty noble family in the Crimean Khanate
nuraddin	the second deputy of the khan in the Crimean Khanate
odabaşı	a lower officer in the janıssary corps
para	a silver coin minted in the Ottoman Empire
pencik emini	an official responsible for collecting the tax named *pencik*, which was imposed on the sale of slaves

reaya	lit., 'flock'; a tax-paying subject of the khan (as opposed to an *askeri*, who who was exempt from taxes)
sekban	in the Crimean Khanate a member of the regular military unit directly subordinate to the khan or the *kalga*; their formation was patterned, to some extent, on the janissary corps, hence, in Crimean sources, they were also called 'janissaries'
serasker	lit., 'the head of troops'; in the eighteenth century, this was the title of the khan's deputies who were appointed to supervise and command the Nogay hordes
serdar	commanderinchief (e.g., of a garrison)
seyyid	a descendant of the Prophet Muhammad
sharia	Islamic religious law
*sicil*s	judicial registers kept by *kadı*s
silahdar	a weapon master
siyaset	administrative justice
soyurgal	(a) a money grant, or (b) a grant of immunity from the interference of government officials in land belonging to the beneficiary or in crown land bestowed upon the beneficiary
şeyh	(a) a senior member of a *derviş* order, or (b) a head of a craft guild
tapu tax	an entry fee collected from the new occupant of a plot, paid in exchange for the title to the land
ta'zir	a discretionary punishment
Tat ağası	an official dealing with the affairs of the Tats, a people who inhabited the southern coast of the Crimea; their ethnic origins are poorly understood
timar	an assignment of income, whose holder owed some sort of service
topçu	a gunner
türbedar	a keeper of a mausoleum or a cementary
ulan (*oğlan*)	a nobleman's title that confirms his kinship with the royal family in the Crimean Khanate
ulema	a member of the religious and legal elite
usta	a master in a craft guild
vekil	a legal agent
vizier	a minister of the khan and a member of his council
vakf	a pious foundation; the revenues are assigned by the founder

yalı ağası	an official of the khan; he dealt with the Bucak Nogay Horde
zabit	a member of the military class; he performed various police duties
zimmi	nonMuslims living in an Islamic state and enjoying its protection

Introduction

1 Historiography of the Crimean Khanate

In this section, I briefly review the most important studies on the Crimean Khanate. I focus on two genres: general works on the khanate and monographs strictly related to its domestic history. In the literature review, I also include studies on Crimean-Tatar foreign policy, which provide us with vital insight into the khanate's domestic relations. Because of its institutional focus, the present study elaborates on the Golden Horde origins of Crimean political traditions and on the Ottoman influence that shaped their development in the early modern period. I do not engage in an extensive analysis of historical writings from the Golden Horde and Ottomans, as these are relatively well described in contrast to the khanate. Rather, these are briefly discussed in the sections in which they were used. A unique exception was made for the historiography of Chingisid law, namely, the studies concerning the *Yasa*, because the importance of the evolution of the understanding of this crucial term in modern historiography.

1.1 *The* Yasa

François Petis de la Croix (1622–95) was the first European author who defined the *Yasa* as the written code of law promulgated by Chingis Khan, probably at the *kurultay* (general diet) in the year 1205.[1] Although no copy of the *Yasa* survived to the time of Petis de la Croix, he believed that the code could be reconstructed on the basis of various narrative sources. His work contains, therefore, a list of supposed prescriptions of the *Yasa*. Eminent scholars, for instance, George Vernadsky[2] and Valentin Riazanovsky,[3] who drew their theories from medieval sources, such as the writings of al-Maqīzī, Rashīd al-Dīn, al-ʿUmarī, Bar Hebraeus, and al-Juwaynī, followed the idea of Petis de la Croix and strove to improve his reconstruction of the *Yasa*. The *Secret History of the Mongols*,[4] which is not very descriptive on this subject, was used less extensively.

1 François Petis de la Croix, *The History of Genghizcan the Great* (London, 1722); the original French edition entitled *Histoire du Grand Genghizcan* was published by the son of Francois de la Croix, also named Francois de la Croix (Paris, 1710). Later scholars corrected Petis de la Croix and dated the promulgation of the *Yasa* to the year 1206.

2 G. Vernadsky, "The Scope and Contents of Chingis Khan's Yasa," *HJAS* 3 (1938): 337–360.

3 V. Riazanovsky, *Fundamental Principles of Mongol Law* (Bloomington, IN, 1965), 83–91.

4 F.W. Cleaves (ed.), *The Secret History of the Mongols* (Cambridge, MA, 1982).

 | DOI:10.1163/9789004384323_002

Information about the *Yasa*, therefore, comes mainly from sources written by Muslims or compiled in Muslim countries from the thirteenth to the fifteenth centuries. European scholars were so determined to extract every possible piece of information about the *Yasa* that they paid little attention to critically analyzing the sources they utilized. Hence, the reconstructions of the *Yasa* were carried out with little consideration of the chronological order of sources and their dependence on each other. The personal feelings of medieval authors, who may have resented the customs of their conquerors, were not discussed in depth.

These serious drawbacks led David Ayalon to reexamine the abovementioned sources. He aimed to determine the authenticity of the passages concerning the *Yasa*, and also discussed the medieval authors' attitudes toward the Mongol conquest in order to establish whether they may have purposely distorted information concerning the *Yasa*. His analysis demonstrates that al-Maqrīzī, al-ʿUmarī, and Bar Hebraeus were strongly dependent on al-Juwaynī. The reliability of al-Juwaynī was also questioned. Although Ayalon discarded all but one source used previously for the reconstructions of the *Yasa*, he did not disprove the entire idea of a written code of law dating back to the period of Chingis Khan. Although he acknowledged that even the medieval authors did not claim to have seen a written copy, he attempted to explain this fact, by arguing that access to the sacred texts, such as *Yasa*, must have been very limited.[5]

The studies of David Morgan offer a new approach to the problem of the *Yasa*. He distinguishes the *Yasa*, defined as the customary Mongol law, from the *Great Yasa*, i.e., the code of law promulgated by Chingis Khan. Morgan asks whether "the Great Yasa existed at all? And if did, was it written down, its contents known and enforced?"[6] He denied the existence of the *Great Yasa*, because "there are difficulties, possibly insuperable difficulties, in establishing the nature and contents of the Mongol Yasa, its associations with Chingis Khan himself, or even whether it ever existed as a written, coherent, enforceable code of laws."[7] Nonetheless, medieval authors may truly have believed in its existence. Morgan's study also focuses on the role played by the *Yasa* in the

5 D. Ayalon, "The Great Yasa of Chingiz Khan: A Reexamination," *Studia Islamica* 33 (1971): 97–140; 34 (1971): 151–180; 36 (1972): 112–158; 38 (1973): 107–156.

6 D.O. Morgan, "The Great Yasa of Chingiz Khan and Mongol Law in the Ilkhanate," *BSOAS* 49 (1986), 168.

7 Ibid., 172. In 1993, Anatoly Khazanov associated the *Yasa* with Chingis Khan but limited its contents almost exclusively to military matters; Anatoly Khazanov, "Muhammad and Jenghiz Khan Compared: The Religious Factor in the World Empire Building," *Comparative Studies in Society and History* 35, no. 3 (1993), 464.

post-Chingisid states. He states that for medieval Mongols, the *Yasa* was the symbol of Chingis Khan's glory and the period of "pure" social relations.

Denise Aigle has studied the reception of the *Yasa* among the Mongols. She started by re-examining medieval sources and concluded that medieval authors, the majority of whom were not Mongols, did not distinguish the state law promulgated by the khans (*jasaq*) from the customary law (*yosun*). Thus, the term *Yasa* was used in to refer to both, and therefore, it is very difficult to derive information from medieval sources about the new legal order enforced by Chingis Khan. Aigle, nevertheless, examined the branches of law in which the precepts of the *Yasa*, *jasaq* or *yosun* were applied. Her analysis also revealed that our knowledge about Mongol law is limited to the branches that were perceived as important by medieval authors, i.e., those related to military matters and some family matters, along with particular types of crimes, such as witchcraft, poisoning, incorrect ablutions, and adultery.[8]

To conclude, the articles of Morgan and Aigle constitute a turning point in the scholarly approach to the *Yasa*. Their reassessments of this term led them to deny any connection between it and the written code of Chingis Khan. Scholars in the field now refer to the *Yasa* as denoting the body of laws governing the social and legal behavior of the Mongols and, to some extent, their non-Mongol subjects. Although in the Golden Horde and its successor states it was believed that the *Yasa* had been promulgated by Chingis Khan, it should rather be viewed as a body of law consisting of customary and state law, a body that preceded Chingis Khan and continued to evolve even after his death. Modern researchers also accepted another idea of Morgan and Aigle, i.e., the importance of in-depth studies of the *Yasa* in the post-Chingisid states. Important reflections on these subjects can be found in the works of Revren Amitai,[9] George Lane,[10] and Anne Broadbridge.[11]

1.2 *Studies on the Domestic History on the Khanate*

In early modern Europe, the Tatars attracted moderate attention. Notwithstanding a few short descriptions, published as early as the first half of the sixteenth century, the khanate, not surprisingly, was much less interesting for popular readers than, for example, the Ottoman Empire, which was described

8 D. Aigle, "Le grand *jasaq* de Gengis-khan, l'empire, la culture mongole et la shari'a," *JESHO* 47 (2004), 31–79.

9 R. Amitai, *The Mongols in the Islamic Lands: Studies in the History of the Ilkhanate* (Aldershot and Burlington, 2007), 1–10, 15–43.

10 G. Lane, *Daily Life in the Mongol Empire* (London, 2006).

11 A. Broadbridge, *Kingship and Ideology in the Islamic and Mongol Worlds* (Cambridge, 2008).

in detail already in the sixteenth century.[12] Equally detailed writings about the Crimea did not appear before the second half of the eighteenth century. The first scholarly history of the khanate, written by Joseph von Hammer-Purgenstall [Purgstall], appeared just after the end of the Crimean War. It was based on a variety of sources, not only European chronicles.[13] Twenty years later, Vasilii Smirnov wrote a detailed study of the khanate up to the eighteenth century, his synthesis remains unsurpassed. Smirnov, unlike Hammer-Purgenstall, used Crimean chronicles extensively.[14] Thus, he had access to the texts written from the Crimean perspective. Nonetheless, he shared the earlier author's conviction that the khanate was a vassal state of the Ottoman Empire, and that the khans obediently executed the sultan's will.[15]

The nineteenth-century interest in the Crimea motivated scholars to publish the first editions of documents produced by the khanate. First, we must mention an edition prepared by Vladimir Vel'aminov-Zernov and Huseyn Faizkhanov[16] that contains treaties and letters sent by Crimean dignitaries to the Polish-Lithuanian Commonwealth and Muscovy between the sixteenth and eighteenth centuries. The edition they published also contains a few lists of Crimean dignitaries who received customary "gifts" (*tiyiş*) from neighboring states. The documents were published in almost faultless Arabic script.[17] Special mention must be made of the studies of Fedor Lashkov, who appended numerous translations of documents written by khans and their officials.[18] These documents, which were prepared for publishing by Murat Bey Biarslanov,

12 See, for example, the letters of Ogier Ghiselin de Busbecq (the ambassador of Ferdinand I) to the Sublime Porte in the 1550s; O.G. Busbecq, *The Turkish Letters of Ogier Ghiselin de Busbecq* (Oxford, 1927).

13 J. Hammer-Purgenstall, *Geschichte der Chane der Krim unter Osmanischer Herrschaft vom 15. Jahrhundert bis yum Ende 18. Jahrhundert* (Vienna, 1856).

14 V. Smirnov, *Krymskoe khanstvo pod verkhovenstvom Otomanskoi Porty do nachala XVIII veka* (St. Petersburg, 1887).

15 The titles of the studies by Smirnov and Hammer-Purgenstall reflect the same attitude.

16 S. Faizov, "Znachenie nasledia Husaina Faizkhanova v oblasti krymsko-tatarskoi arkheografii dla izuchenia istorii Krymskogo yurta i russko-krymskikh otnoshenii," *Faizkhanovskie chtenia* 2 (2005), 146–151.

17 H. Faizkhanov and V. Vel'aminov-Zernov (eds.), *Materialy dla istorii krymskogo khanstva izvlechenyia po rasporazheniu Imperatorskoi Akademii Nauk, iz Moskovkogo Glavnago Arkhiva Ministerstva Inostrannykh del* (St. Petersburg, 1864).

18 F. Lashkov, "Istoricheskii ocherk Krymsko-tatarskogo zemlevladeniia," *ITUAK* 21 (1894): 59–89; 22 (1895): 35–81; 23 (1895): 71–117; 24 (1896): 35–71; 25 (1896): 29–88; F. Lashkov, "K voprosu o kolichestve naseleniia tavricheskoi gubernii v nachale 19 stoletiia," *ITUAK* 53 (1916): 158–176; F. Lashkov, "Sbornik dokumentov po istorii krymsko-tatarskogo zemlevladeniia," Part 1—*ITUAK* 22 (1895), 82–115; Part 2—*ITUAK* 23 (1896), 118–129; Part 3—*ITUAK* 24 (1896), 72–137; Part 4—*ITUAK* 25 (1896), 154–158; Part 5—*ITUAK* 26 (1897),

complemented the works of Lashkov on land tenure and the administration of the khanate. Separately, Biarslanov published a study containing a few documents extracted from the *sicil*s.[19] His translations were by no means flawless. By 1918, Nikolai Ivanovich Vesolovskii, a reputed Russian orientalist and archeologist, pointed out some of his errors in translation, some of which resulted from a lack of understanding of certain words and others from his rendering of *sicil* records.[20] These drawbacks notwithstanding, the publications of Biarslanov and Lashkov are of great importance for the present study, because they remain unique, and the only generally correct publications of Russian translations of numerous documents registered in the Crimean *sicil*s. In addition to the *sicil*s, Lashkov used diplomatic sources, from which he published translations of some Crimean-Muscovite treaties from the sixteenth and seventeenth centuries.[21]

To conclude, nineteenth-century historiography evolved from popular writings about the Crimean Peninsula to scholarly works that treated the Crimean Khanate as a specialized field of study. This change of focus saw the publication of numerous works covering not only diplomatic relations between the khanate and its neighboring states, but also some vital studies of its internal history. Yet, we must also emphasize that the majority of the works were written by researchers of Russian, Ukrainian, and Polish origin. The authors were brought up in traditions, according to which their respective fatherlands had formed the bulwark of Christendom (*antemurale christianitatis*). Nineteenth-century Polish, Ukrainian, and Russian nationalists pictured the Tatars as "others," who "wallowed in Christian blood." Moreover, they vaunted their fatherlands' past victories over the khanate. These facts affected Russian, Polish, and Ukrainian studies, which should be used with a great deal of caution.

24–154; F. Lashkov, "Statisticheskaia svedeniia o Kryme, soobshchennyia kaimakamami v 1783 godu," *ZOOID* 14 (1886): 91–156.

19 M. Biarslanov (trans.), "Vypisi iz kadiaskerskago sakka (knigi) 1017–1022 g. khidzhry (1608/9–1613 g. khr. liet.) khraniashchagosia v arkhive Tavricheskago gubemskago pravleniia," *ITUAK* 8 (1889), 41–51; 9 (1890), 68–70; 10 (1890), 74–78.

20 N.I. Vesolovskii, "Ob izdanii kadiaskerskogo sakka," *ITUAK* 54 (1918), 276–278.

21 *Pamiatniki diplomaticheskikh snoshenii Krymskago khanstva s Moskovskim gosudarstvom v XVI i XVII v.v., khraniashchiesia v Moskovskom Glavnom Arkhive Ministerstva Inostrannykh Diel*, ed. F. Lashkov (Simferopol, 1891). Documents concerning the khanate can also be found in nineteenth-century editions of diplomatic sources from neighboring states, most notably Muscovy, Poland, and Lithuania; see W. Kazimirski (ed.), *Documents sur les rapports diplomatiques de l'ancienne Russie avec les puissances étrangères et notamment la Crimée* (St. Petersburg, 1884–98); K. Pułaski (ed.), "Machmet—Girej chan Tatarów perekopskich i stosunki jego z Polską (1515–1523)," in *Szkice i poszukiwania historyczne*, series 2 (St. Petersburg, 1898).

In the twentieth century, Crimean studies further developed, along with the increased interest in Oriental studies typical for this period. This interest stemmed from a growing appreciation of non-European societies, and from new scholarly trends. The political changes that led to the emergence of new independent states in Eastern Europe, especially after WWI and again after the fall of Communism, enabled scholars from smaller nations to focus on their own histories and the relations of their ancestors with the Crimean Khanate. The emergence of modern Turkey, whose government acted as a patron of Muslim minorities in neighboring states, also resulted in numerous Turkish studies on the Crimean Khanate. I discuss the problem of their reliability below. It is also worth mentioning that with the disintegration of communism, the Tatars themselves were allowed to study their own history, and this led to a certain number of publications in Tatarstan and Ukraine.[22]

Our survey of the modern historiography on domestic Crimean history begins with Vladimir Syroechkovskii's study entitled "Mehmed Giray and His Vassals."[23] This classical work concerning the khanate's structure of power focuses on the reign of Mehmed I Giray (1515–23) and is based mainly on Russian diplomatic correspondence and reports. The limited number of sources from this period forced Syroechkovskii to use later sources dating to the end of the sixteenth century and even to the seventeenth century. Thus, the study's conclusions were extrapolated, to some extent, on the later period. The author's aim was to identify the various groups of the khan's subjects and define their social status. He describes the Giray princes, the judicial court officials, aristocratic families, other noble members of the Crimean *kurultay* (general diet), and the ulema. Syroechkovskii's study demonstrates that nobles in the khanate did not, by any means, form a monolith; rather they could be divided into two main groups, i.e., the aristocratic clans of Mongol origin, and the khan's service *beğ*s. The differences within these two groups seem to be less clear. Because of a variety of terms used by Russian diplomats and their divergent descriptions, even Syroechkovskii, in his detailed analysis, could not extract more information from these sources. It is clear, however, that members of aristocratic noble families exercised great influence on the khan's policy.

22 See, for example, the study by Oleksa Haivoronskii, *Pobediteli dvukh materikov* (Simferopol, 2007–09); and Narimaan Seyyityahya, "Voennye deistvia v Krymu v 1735–1736 gg," *Qasevet* 33 (2008), 40–49.

23 Vladimir Syroechkovski, a Soviet scholar who specialized in oriental studies, enjoyed the relatively liberal atmosphere during the first half of the 1930s, then died in the Great Purge, cf. Vladimir Syroechkovskii, "Mukhammed-Gerai i ego vassaly," *Uchenye zapiski Moskovskogo Gosudarstvennogo Universiteta im. M.V. Lomonosova* 61, 2 (*Istoria*) (1940), 3–71.

Moreover, to some extent, they could influence the Ottomans. The murder of Mehmed I Giray by the Nogay *mirza*s seems to have happened at the heyday of their power. As Syroechkovskii concludes, Khan Sahib Giray tried to balance the power of the Mongol clans by introducing Ottoman administrative practices and by supporting other groups, for example, the Giray princes and the service *beğ*s.

Barbara Forbes Manz[24] and Halil Inalcık[25] briefly addressed the khanate's structure of power in the first half of the sixteenth century. Manz analyzed Russian and Lithuanian diplomatic sources concerning the khanate's history between the year 1466, when Mengli I Giray ascended to the throne, and the end of the reign of Saadet Giray in 1532. Her study discusses the influence of the aristocratic clans on the khanate's policy. She argues that they were too weak and much too torn by inner conflicts to maintain their powerful positions in relation to the khan, the princes, and the service *beğ*s. Manz underscores that "in many ways service and clan begs had similar careers and fairly equal power."[26] According to her, both groups led important diplomatic missions and took equal part in the khan's council. There is no evidence that the *beğ*s of aristocratic clans, who had certain military strength, performed more important tasks during the campaigns than did the service *beğ*s. Yet, the latter could not marry into the Giray dynasty. The author's idea to focus on similarities rather than differences between these two groups is quite interesting. Nonetheless, it is worth asking to what extent her theory may be a consequence of her choice of sources, the majority of which consisted of Russian-Crimean diplomatic correspondence. Muscovite diplomatic sources may have exaggerated the role played by families of service *beğ*s, because one of them, i.e., the Yaşlav family, oversaw the Crimean relations with Muscovy. The Russians, whose non-Yaşlav contacts were limited, tended to overestimate the real power of this group of the khan's subjects. Moreover, Manz questions the reliability of some sources that suggested a higher status for aristocratic clans than the service *beğ*s.[27]

---

24 B.F. Manz, "The Clans of the Crimean Khanate," *HUS* 2 (1978), 282–309.

25 H. Inalcık, "The Khan and the Tribal Aristocracy: The Crimean Khanate under Sahib Giray I," *HUS* 3–4 (1979–80), 445–466.

26 Manz, "The Clans," 293.

27 E.g., Manz notes the diplomatic treaties between the khanate and Muscovy that demonstrated the social hierarchy of various groups of the khan's vassals. Manz quotes the letter of Crimean malcontents sent to Saadet Giray in ca. 1523, and refers to *Le Khanate de Crimée dans les Archives du Musée du Palais de Topkapı* but cited the pagination incorrectly (pp. 332–333 instead of pp. 106–110). See A. Bennigsen, et al. (eds.), *Le khanat de Crimée ans les Archives du Musée du Palais de Topkapı* (Paris, 1978).

Halil Inalcık's study, which concerns the reign of Sahib Giray (1532–51), returns to Syroechkovskii's idea of a hierarchy between the khan's vassals. According to Inalcık, the *beğ*s of the aristocratic clans (*karaçı*) had a higher status than the service *beğ*s, but lower than the members of the Giray dynasty. The author perceived the service *beğ*s as the khan's clients (*nöker*), whose position had much in common with the clients of the aristocratic clans. Sahib Giray was by no means a weak ruler. He strengthened his position by reforming the state administration and army, supporting his service *beğ*s and clergy, and by dealing skillfully with the Ottoman Empire. Seeking allies among the aristocratic clans seems to have played a vital role in his domestic policy too. But conflict with one of the clans cost him his throne and his life. Inalcık's study is based mainly on Crimean and Ottoman sources, but he also used, to some extent, European diplomatic correspondence.

This is, perhaps, the proper place to introduce the study of Carl Max Kortepeter.[28] Even though his main purpose was to describe how the Ottomans shaped their relations with their vassals and neighbors in the second half of the sixteenth century, he also offers an inspiring study of the reign of Gazi II Giray (1588–96; 1597–1608). His study is based on European and Ottoman sources. Kortepeter demonstrates that the balance of power between the khan, the Sublime Porte, and the aristocratic clans, which acted at cross purposes during this period, determined the khanate's policy. Moreover, the diverging aims of the Ottomans and some of the Crimean clans made it possible, on the one hand, for Gazi II Giray to seize enough power to control his vassals, and, on the other hand, for him to engage in more independent policies toward the Ottomans. Kortepeter also discusses the subject of the Tatars' role in Ottoman military campaigns. Caroline Finkel[29] and Mustafa H. Evracı[30] touched on this last issue as well.

Alan Fisher's monograph, published in 1978, appears to have been the first modern study covering the whole history of the khanate.[31] He stresses the Ottoman's influence on the inner relations of the Crimeans as an important policy determinant. Fisher also points to the evolution of the degree to which the khanate was dependent on the Ottomans between the late fifteenth century and the end of the eighteenth century. He questions the view that the

28 C.M. Kortepeter, *Ottoman Imperialism During the Reformation: Europe and the Caucasus* (London, 1972).

29 C. Finkel, *The Administration of Warfare: The Ottoman Military Campaigns in Hungary, 1593–1606* (Vienna, 1988).

30 M.H. Evracı, "The Role of the Crimean Tatars in the Ottoman-Safavi War (1578–1639)," *Historical Yearbook* 4 (2007), 153–160.

31 A. Fisher, *The Crimean Tatars* (Stanford, 1978).

Tatars were servile vassals of the Sublime Porte throughout the period. They conducted a separate foreign policy, which sometimes differed from that of the Ottomans. Fisher elaborates on this subject in numerous articles covering political, social, and financial aspects of their mutual relations.[32] He also discusses the Ottoman presence in the Crimean Peninsula. This subject has also been treated by Mihnea Berindei, Mikhail B. Kizilov,[33] and Gilles Veinstein.[34] Finally, Yücel Öztürk produced a detailed study on Kefe province up to the end of the sixteenth century.[35]

An edition of documents entitled *Le Khanat de Crimée dans les Archives du Musée du Palais de Topkapı*, which was published by Alexandre Bennigsen, Peter Naili Boratav, Dilek Desaive, and Chantal Lemercier-Quelquejay, sheds more light on the Ottoman's influence in the Crimea. This volume consists of French translations (full or abridged) along with a synopsis of about 200 documents preserved in the Topkapı Museum.[36] The archives in the Topkapı house the majority of the known correspondence between Ottoman and Crimean dignitaries.[37] These documents include valuable commentaries that contribute to our understanding of the khanate's domestic and foreign relations.

32 A. Fisher, *Between Russians, Ottomans and Turks: Crimea and Crimean Tatars* (Istanbul, 1998); A. Fisher, *A Precarious Balance: Conflict, Trade, and Diplomacy on the Russian-Ottoman Frontier* (Istanbul, 1999).

33 M.B. Kizilov, "The Black Sea and the Slave Trade: The Role of Crimean Maritime Towns in the Trade in Slaves and Captives in the Fifteenth to Eighteenth Centuries," *International Journal of Maritime History* 17, no. 1 (2005), 211–235.

34 M. Berindei and G. Veinstein, "La presence Ottomane au sud de la Crimée et en mer d'Azov dans la premiére moitié du XVIe siècle," *CMRS* 20 (1978), 399–465.

35 Y. Öztürk, *Osmanlı Hakimiyetinde Kefe: 1475–1600* (Ankara, 2000).

36 The documents are followed by a valuable critical apparatus that provides us with biographical notes on select Crimean khans and on a few other important persons. Appendices also contain a foldout genealogy of the Giray dynasty, a chronology of the khans' reigns and their *kalgas* and *nuraddins*, and a glossary of Ottoman, Mongol, and Slavic terms. This critical apparatus should be used along with remarks made by Victor Ostapchuk ("The Publication of Documents on the Crimean Khanate in the Topkapı Sarayı: New Sources for the History of the Black Sea Basin," *HUS* 6, no. 4 (1982), 500–528) and Zygmunt Abrahamowicz ("Comments on Three Letters by Khan Islam Gerey III to the Porte (1651)," *HUS* 14, no. 1 (1990), 139–143). In another review article, Victor Ostapchuk listed errors and omissions in the translations of the documents from fifteenth to the seventeenth century and offered his own suggestions for their translations; Ostapchuk, "The Publication of Documents on the Crimean Khanate in the Topkapı Sarayı: The Documentary Legacy of Crimean-Ottoman Relations," *Turcica* 19 (1987), 247–276.

37 The correspondence between khans, princes, *beğ*s of the *karaçı* clans, Ottoman sultans and governors constitutes the majority of the volume. There are also a few atypical documents, e.g., Bohdan Khmelnytsky's letter to the sultan in Bennigsen, et al. (eds.), *Le khanat de Crimée*, 191–195.

The volume covers the period between 1453 and 1790.[38] It does not offer the same wealth of information for every khan's reign. There are no documents, for example, from the period between 1654 and 1692, and unfortunately, the reign of Murad Giray took place during that time. The gap is only partly filled by Halil İnalcık's study, which covers roughly the same period (1640s–1710s) and discusses how the titles used in the diplomatic correspondence between Muscovy, the Sublime Porte, and the khanate reflected their changing power relations.[39]

The works introduced up to this point focus on political history. Until the 1990s, social and economic aspects of the khanate's history attracted less scholarly attention. Until 2014, this increase in interest resulted from two reasons. First, political changes in the former Soviet republics enabled the Tatars in the Crimea and in Tatarstan to begin to research their own history. The cultural institutions of the Crimean Tatars, such as the Library of Ismail Gasprynsky in Bahçesaray, collect materials on the history of the peninsula. The library holds photocopies from the microfilms of sixty-one Crimean court registers. Information on the whereabouts of this collection was popularized by Halil İnalcık, who authored a short article providing transliterations and analyses of nineteen records registered in the *sicils*.[40] This study encouraged numerous Turkish scholars to work on the history of social and economic life in the Crimea. Second, the opening of archives and libraries in Russia gave both local and foreign scholars access to the whole collection of the Crimean court registers. Until recently, there were numerous researchers working on these, e.g., Ömer Bıyık,[41] Ahmed Cihan,[42] Recep Çiğdem,[43] Maryna Kravets,[44] Zeynep

38 The volume also includes material for the reigns of Şahbaz Giray (1787–89) and Baht Giray (1789–92), whom the Ottomans appointed as the khans of Kuban.

39 H. Inalcık, "Power Relationships between Russia, the Crimea and the Ottoman Empire as Reflected in Titulature," in *Passé turco-tatar. Présent soviétique. Études offertes à Alexandre Bennigsen* (Paris, 1986).

40 H. Inalcık, "Kirim Hanlığı Sicilleri Bulundu," *Belleten* 140 (1996), 170–189.

41 Unfortunately, his PhD thesis, "Crimea under Ottoman Rule (1600–1774)," submitted to Ege University in Izmir in 2007, was not available to me.

42 A. Cihan and F. Yılmaz, "Kırım Kadi Sicilleri," *Islam Araştırmaları Dergisi* 11 (2004), 131–176.

43 R. Ciğdem, "Crimes Threatening Bodily Integrity (Assault and Battery): A Legal Analysis of Four Cases from the Judicial Registers of the Bakchisaray/Crimea Law Court," *Ankara Üniversitesi Hukuk Fakültesi Dergisi* 54, no. 1 (2005), 61–71; R. Ciğdem, "Khul or Dissolution of Marriage by a Woman: A Historical Background and Two Cases from the Bakchisaray/Crimea Court," *Dokuz Eylül Üniversitesi İlahiyat Fakültesi Dergisi* 21 (2005), 95–115; R. Ciğdem, "The Judicial Registers of the Bakchisaray/Crimea Law Court: A Study of Murder Crimes," *Hamdard Islamicus* 28, no. 4 (2005), 41–53.

44 M. Kravets, "From Nomad's Tent to Garden Palace: Evolution of a Chinggisid Household in the Crimea," *Toronto Studies in Central and Inner Asia* 7 (2005), 47–60; and M. Kravets,

Özdem,[45] Ahmed N. Turan,[46] Fırat Yaşa,[47] Fehmi Yılmaz;[48] I also utilized them extensively.[49] Unfortunately, there are still very few completed and published studies. Among these, several provide insight into vital aspects of socio-economic life in the khanate, and these deserve to be mentioned. For instance, the articles of Maryna Kravets focus on the institution of the khan's palace with a special emphasis on the origins and role of slaves in the ruler's household. Fırat Yaşa's dissertation on socio-economic life in the khanate in the third quarter of the seventeenth century also brings up the question of slavery in the khanate. Based on fifteen court registers, he offers valuable insights into the everyday activities and lifestyles of the inhabitants of Bahçesaray.[50] Zeynep Özdem has examined the socio-economic life of another Crimean city, namely Kara Su. Her monograph is based on four Crimean court registers (nos. 25, 33, 47, and 65) dating to the period from 1683 to 1744. The author analyzes the city's administration, its organization of trade, and the daily lives of its inhabitants. She selects and summarizes a large number of cases, mostly concerned with

---

"Blacks Beyond the Black Sea: Eunuchs in the Crimean Khanate," in *Slavery, Islam and Diaspora*, ed. B.A. Mirzai, I.M. Montana, and P.E. Lovejoy (New York, 2009), 21–36.

45 Z. Özdem, *Kırım Karasubazar'da Sosyal Ekonomık Hayat* (*17. Yüzyil Sonlarından 18. Yüzyil Ortalarına Kadar*) (Ankara, 2010).

46 A.N. Turan, "Sudebnyie reiestry krymskovo khanstva (posle ich obnaruzheniia)," *Kultura narodov prichernomoria* 30 (2002), 90–93; and A.N. Turan, "Kırım Hanlığı Kadı Sicilleri Hakkında Notlari," *Türk Kültürü İncelemeleri Dergisi* 9 (2003), 1–16.

47 F. Yaşa, "Kırım Hanlığı'nda Köleliğin Sosyal ve Mali Boyutları," *Gaziantep University Journal of Social Sciences* 13, no. 3 (2014), 657–669; and F. Yaşa, "Bahçesaray (1650–1675)," PhD diss. (University of Sakarya, 2017).

48 F. Yılmaz, "On Sekizinci Yüzyılın İkinci Yarısında Kırım'da Gayrimüslimler," *Osmanlı Araştırmaları* 33 (2009), 237–268. Yılmaz is preparing a catalogue of the Crimean court register, which is provisionally entitled *Kırım Hanlığı Kadi Sicilleri Kataloğu* (publication forthcoming).

49 N. Królikowska, "Crimean Crime Stories: Homicide and Bodily Harm Cases During the Reign of Murad Giray (1678–1683)," in *The Crimean Khanate Between East and West*, ed. D. Klein (Wiesbaden, 2012), 109–123; N. Królikowska, "Sąd rady chańskiej w czasach Murata Gireja (1678–1683)," in *Studia z dziejów i kultury ludów tureckich. Badania polskich turkologów prezentowane podczas I i II Konferencji Turkologicznej: Poznań 2007 i Warszawa 2008* (Warsaw, 2013), 161–171; N. Królikowska, "Praworządny jak Tatarzyn?—stosunki prawne w Chanacie Krymskim na podstawie miejscowych ksiąg sądowych z XVII i XVIII wieku," *Czasopismo Prawno-Historyczne* 65, no. 1 (2013), 121–142; N. Królikowska, "Ród Jaszławskich przed sądem chana Murada Gireja. Przyczynek do dziejów mirzów krymskich," in *Od Ałtaju po Syberię*, ed. E. Siemieniec-Gołaś and J. Georgiewa-Okoń (Cracow, 2010), 115–120; N. Królikowska-Jedlińska, "Social Standing, Living Conditions and Religiosity of Slaves from the Territory of the Commonwealth in the Crimea in the 17th Century," in *Osmanlı Devletinde Kölelik: Ticaret–Esaret–Yaşam*, ed. Z. Güneş Yağcı, F. Yaşa, and D. İnan (Istanbul, 2017), 269–296.

50 Yaşa, "Bahçesaray (*1660–1675*)."

administrative and commercial matters. Fehmi Yılmaz discusses the material framework within which the non-Muslims lived in the Crimea in the 1770s. He carefully analyzes the information recorded in two real estate registers left by non-Muslims who emigrated from the Crimea after the Treaty of Küçük Kaynarca (1774).[51]

This short list of valuable studies clearly demonstrates both the need for further research based on this body of sources and its great potential for future studies on the history of the Black Sea region. It goes without saying that research should be conducted on the whole collection preserved in St. Petersburg, to avoid inexplicable gaps in the database; these gaps characterize numerous articles that are based solely on photocopies of the sixty-one registers preserved in the Gasprinsky Library.[52] It is only when the rich collection of the Crimean court registers is exploited that the history of the khanate can be written properly.

I conclude this section with the mention of Nicole Kançal-Ferrari's study of art history, which provides a detailed description of the khan's palace in Bahçesaray. Her study was by no means an easy task. According to the investigation conducted in the introduction, the residency was completely destroyed and rebuilt several times. Nonetheless, the author embarks on a fascinating study to determine the origins and meaning of every detail of architecture and visual art. Clearly, the khan's palace was modeled on the Topkapı Palace; it was a miniature and less elaborate version. The author's in-depth knowledge of Ottoman architecture as well as literature on the Crimean Khanate enabled her to explain how the building was created and what the functions of the various rooms were. To sum up, Nicole Kançal-Ferrari's study brings us closer to understanding everyday life in the khan's court.[53]

1.3 *Studies on the Khanate's Foreign Relations as a Source of Information on its Domestic History*

My brief survey of studies focused on the khanate's foreign policy begins with research on Russian-Tatar relations. The first modern study that directly addresses the problem of Russian-Crimean relations, rather than discussing them as a factor of Russian policy toward the Ottoman Empire,[54] was written by Aleksei Novoselski in the late 1940s. He points out that dignitaries of

51 These registers (nos. 119 and 120) are included in the collection of the Crimean *sicils* in the Russian National Library in St. Petersburg.

52 See, for example, Turan, "Kırım Hanlığı"; and Yaşa, "Kırım Hanlığı'nda."

53 N. Kançal-Ferrari, *Kırım'da Kalan Miras. Hansaray* (Istanbul, 2005).

54 This attitude characterizes the study of Nicolai Smirnov, which appeared two years before Novosielski's book, see N. Smirnov, *Rossia i Turtsia v XVI–XVII vv.* (Moscow, 1946).

the khanate were able to conduct their own foreign policy, which sometimes even opposed Ottoman interests, for example during the Astrakhan campaign in 1569.[55] Yet, apart from Novoselski's book, for over forty years after World War II, Soviet historians produced only minor studies on the subject. It was only in the late 1980s that Giennadii Sanin again raised the issue of the history of Russian-Crimean relations. His study deals with the mid-seventeenth century.[56] To quote a comment by Alan Fisher, Sanin asserted "that Russian and Ukrainian achievements and Crimean Tatar and Ottoman failures were all positive developments for the future of East Europe."[57] He did not perceive the Crimean Khanate as an independent state, with its own tasks and political goals. With such a traditional approach, Sanin produced a study whose conclusions seem to be borrowed from imperial Russian historiography and justified the Soviet policy toward the Tatars. He did not consult the works of Alexandre Bennigsen and Chantal Lemercier-Quelquejay, which offer a different perspective of Crimean-Russian relations.[58] Nonetheless, Sanin's study is worth reading, for the valuable data he extracted from the still relatively unexplored Russian archives. The period between the fall of communism in Russia in the 1990s and the second annexation of the Crimea in 2014 has been marked by a new approach. In studies of such contemporary scholars, like Anna Khoroshkevich or Aleksandr Vinogradov, the khanate was treated as a partner equal to Muscovy. Both historians focus on the earlier period of the Crimean-Russian relations. Khoroshkevich studied their evolution from the alliance against the Great Horde in the 1470s to the military conflict in 1521. The author, who utilized not only numerous European sources, but also some translations of Oriental works, depicted Russian-Crimean relations against a broader Eastern European background. Khoroshkevich emphasizes that the Tatars pursued their own policy toward Muscovy, one that did not always coincide with that of the Ottomans. In addition, she discusses economic and social relations

55 A. Novoselski, *Borba Moskovskogo gosudarstva s tatarami v pervoi polovine XVII v.* (Moscow, 1948).

56 G. Sanin, *Otnoshenia Rossii i Ukrainy s krymskim khanstvom v seredine XVII veka* (Moscow, 1987).

57 A. Fisher, "G.A. Sanin, Otnoshenia Rossii i Ukrainy s krymskim khanstvom v seredine XVII veka, Moskva 1987 [The Relations of Russia and Ukraine with the Crimean Khanate in the Middle of the Seventeenth Century, Moscov, 1987] (Book review)," *American Historical Review* 95, no. 2 (1990), 546.

58 Cf. A. Bennigsen and C. Lemercier-Quelquelay, "La Moscovie, L'Empire Ottoman et la Crise Successoriale de 1577–1588 dans le Khanat de Crimée. La Tradition Nomade Contre le Modèle des Monarchies Sédentaires," *CMRS* 14 (1973), 453–487; C. Lemercier-Quelquelay, "Les Expéditions de Devlet Giray contre Moscou en 1571 et 1572 d'après Documents des Archives Ottomanes," *CMRS* 13 (1972), 555–583.

between the two neighboring states extensively.[59] Vinogradov's study covers the period between 1552 and 1574. These twenty years, according to the author, constituted a turning point in Russian-Crimean relations. After the early 1570s, the khanate could no longer seriously threaten Muscovy, which had learned how to defend itself against the Tatars. Vinogradov describes Russian-Crimean relations in the context of the First Northern War (1700–21) and the Ottoman policy in the Black Sea region. His study also contains valuable data on the internal policy of the khanate, as Vinogradov sees the northern policy of the Tatars as an outcome of endless negotiations conducted between the khans, their most important dignitaries, and aristocratic clans.[60] For the last quarter of the seventeenth century, specifically for 1682, we have at our disposal Kirill Kochegarov's excellent study of relations between Russia, Poland-Lithuania, and the khanate.[61] Based on detailed reports of the Russian envoys on the peninsula, the study provides information on the court of Khan Murad Giray.

Dariusz Kołodziejczyk[62] discusses four hundred years of diplomatic relations between the khanate and its second northern neighboring state—the Polish-Lithuanian Commonwealth.[63] His extremely interesting study is divided into three parts, which are organized chronologically. The first part provides the reader with a basic chronology of more than four-hundred years of diplomatic relations. The second part, which deals with the evolution of chancery forms, the typology, composition, and contents of instruments of peace, and the procedure of peace-making, also provides valuable data. By focusing

---

59 A. Khoroshkevich, *Rus i Krym. Ot soiuza k protivostoianiu. Konets XV- nachalo XVI vv.* (Moscow, 2001).

60 V. Vinogradov, *Russko-krymskie otnoshenia. 50-e-vtoraa polovina 70-kh godov XVI veka* (Moscow, 2007); V. Vinogradov, "Rod Sulesha vo vneshnei politike Krymskogo khanstva vtoroi poloviny XVI v," in *Turkologicheskii Sbornik. 2005—Turskie narody Rossii i velikoi stepi* (Moscow, 2006), 26–72.

61 K. Kochegarov, "The Moscow Uprising of 1682: Relations between Russia, the Crimean Khanate, and the Polish-Lithuanian Commonwealth," in *The Crimean Khanate Between East and West (15th–18th Century)*, ed. D. Klein (Wiesbaden, 2012), 59–73.

62 D. Kołodziejczyk, *The Crimean Khanate and Poland-Lithuania. International Diplomacy on the European Periphery (15th–18th Century): A Study of Peace Treaties Followed by Annotated Documents* (Leiden and Boston, 2011).

63 In the early modern era, the diplomacy of the Polish Kingdom and the Great Duchy of Lithuania is generally divided into two periods. During the first, which lasted till the Union of Lublin in 1569, the states had separate international policies; they only shared a ruler. A common foreign policy was stipulated only after the Union of Lublin, which created a united Polish-Lithuanian state. Diplomacy was overseen by the Polish-Lithuanian Diet. In practice, foreign relations with the khanate were executed by Polish rather than by Lithuanian dignitaries.

on Crimean diplomatic procedures, he covers an area that had not been well studied in comparison to Polish-Lithuanian procedures. The third part consists of the instruments of peace, which he has published in the original languages dating back to the years from 1463 to 1742. Documents written in more exotic languages (i.e., Khwarezmian Turkish, Crimean Turkish, Ottoman Turkish, Ruthenian, and Polish) are accompanied by English translations, in contrast to the documents preserved in commonly known languages like Latin or Italian. Finally, Kołodziejczyk's book contains an updated historiographical sketch of the literature on diplomatic relations between the khanate and Poland-Lithuania.

Studies on relations between the Crimean Khanate and other European states provide important data on the changing power relations at the Crimean court. One of the most valuable studies was prepared by Josef Matuz; his work consists of an edition of letters sent by the highest Crimean dignitaries (men and women) to the Danish kings.[64] Karl V. Zetterstéen has edited a catalogue of Turkish, Tatar, and Persian documents preserved in the Swedish National Archives; these include information about a variety of Crimean Tatar correspondents with Swedish kings and queens.[65] Elżbieta Święcicka focuses on Crimean letters sent by the khans' wives and Giray princesses to the Swedish rulers.[66] Maria Ivanics and Sándor Papp touched on some aspects of the khanate's diplomatic relations with the Habsburg monarchy[67] and Transylvania,[68] while Gilles Veinstein studied French-Crimean relations.[69] Articles written by

64 J. Matuz (ed.), *Krimtatarische Urkunden im Reichsarchiv zu Kopenhagen* (Freiburg, 1976).

65 K.V. Zetterstéen, *Türkische, tatarische und persische Urkunden im Schwedischen Reicharchiv* (Uppsala, 1945).

66 E. Święcicka, "The Diplomatic Letters by Crimean Keräy Ladies to the Swedish Royal House," *Rocznik Orientalistyczny* 55 (2002), 57–90.

67 M. Ivanics, "Posolstva krymskikh tatar pri Venskom dvore v 1598–1682 gg. (iz istorii krymsko-tatarskoi diplomatii XVI-XVII vv.)," in *Turcica et Ottomanica. Sbornik statei v chest' 70-letia M.S. Meiera*, ed. I.V. Zaitsev, S.F. Oreshkova (Moscow, 2006), 226–237.

68 M. Ivanics, "Formal and Linguistic Peculiarities of 17th Century Crimean Tatar Letters Addressed to Princes of Transylvania," *Acta Orientalia Academiae Scientiarum Hungaricae* 29, no. 2 (1975), 213–224; M. Ivanics, "Macaristan'daki Kırım Tatarlarına Ait Vesikaları," in *VIII. Türk Kongresi II. Cilt'den Ayrıbasım* (Ankara, 1981), 423–426, 1049–1053; M. Ivanics, "Der Bündnisplan zwischen dem Chan Gazi Giray II. und dem Fürsten Sigismund Báthory aus dem Jahre 1598," in *Hungarian-Ottoman Military and Diplomatic Relations in the Age of Süleyman the Magnificent*, ed. G. Dávid and P. Fodor (Budapest, 1994), 183–198; S. Papp, "Die Inaugurationender Krimkhane durch die Hohe Pforte (16.–18. Jahrhundert)," in *The Crimean Khanate Between East and West* (Weisbaden, 2012), 75–90.

69 G. Veinstein, "Missionaires Jésuites et agents français en Crimée au début du XVIIIe siècle," *CMRS* 10, nos. 3–4 (1969), 414–458; G. Veinstein, "Les Tatars de Crimée et la second election de Stanislas Leszczyński," *CMRS* 11, no. 1 (1970), 24–92.

Roumiana Mihneva, which concern the political history of Eastern Europe, also include notes on relations between the khanate and the Danubian principalities.[70] Vasile Mihordea discusses the "gifts" sent by Moldavia and Walachia to the khanate and the Tatars' raids of their territories.[71]

Is the Crimean Khanate a growing field of research? Recent years have witnessed a continuing interest in the history of the Crimean Khanate. Research in this field reached a new phase after the political changes of 1990s that resulted in the opening of the Russian archives and new questions into the imperial Soviet paradigm of the khanate as "a parasite" of the Slav nations. The outlook of many historians, therefore, has changed. For this reason, perhaps we can anticipate more studies on the relations between the Crimean Khanate and its neighbors. Yet, the domestic history of the khanate merits even more complex research. Exploring this part of the khanate's history will enable us to use the khanate as a fascinating example in various types of comparative studies. The khanate should be of interest to scholars studying Islamic influences on pre-Islamic governmental systems. The example of the khanate should also be used in comparative studies that concern the formation of the Eastern European state system. As noted, the number and scope of available studies has left many thus far unexamined issues. The whole collection of the Crimean *sicil*s along with numerous Crimean chronicles still need the kind of detailed research that cannot be conducted by a single scholar.

The decree of the Presidium of the USSR Supreme Soviet released in 1967, which absolved the Crimean Tatars of the charges of mass betrayal during World War II,[72] allowed their return to their homeland after 1989, protected their rights in the Ukrainian state till 2014, and facilitated field research in the peninsula. Although there are still very few archeological excavations related to the history of the khanate, those conducted in Bahçesaray and its surroundings constitute a good starting point. Until the recent Russian annexation of the peninsula, many researchers hoped that future, extensive field research would increase the number and types of available sources.

---

70 R. Mihneva, "The Muscovite Tsardom, the Ottoman Empire and the European Diplomacy (Mid-Sixteenth to the End of Seventeenth Century)," *Études Balkaniques* 34, nos. 3–4 (1998), 99–128; R. Mihneva, "The Muscovite Tsardom, the Ottoman Empire and the European Diplomacy (End of Sixteenth Century—Beginning of Eighteenth Century (on the 'Center' 'Periphery' and 'Europe' in the Transition to Modern Times)), Part 2." *Études Balkaniques* 36, no. 3 (2000), 41–54.

71 V. Mihordea, "Raportuile Moldavei şi Ţării Româneşti cu Tătarii în secolele XVI–XVIII," *Revista de Istoria* 32, no. 6 (1979), 1069–1095.

72 Williams, *The Crimean Tatars*, 421.

2 Sources

2.1 *Crimean Court Registers* (şer'iye sicilleri) *as Historical Sources*

The importance of *sicil*s, the records of the proceedings of sharia courts, has long been recognized by scholars of Ottoman history. Numerous studies covering various aspects of the social, economic, and political history of the Ottoman Empire demonstrate that the *sicil*s are a treasure trove of information.[73] The material accrued in the court registers complement that of other Ottoman sources.

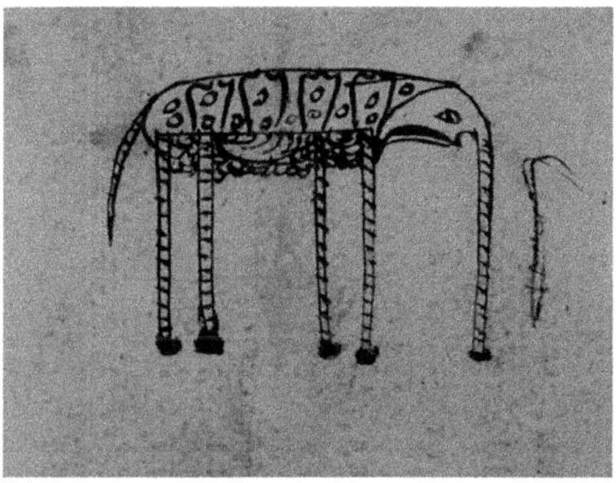

FIGURE 1
An elephant from the Crimean court register no. 24 (ORRNB, Fond 917, defter 24/51a)

73 Over the last fifty years numerous scholars have based their studies on the *sicil*s, for example, R. Jennings, "Women in the Early 17th-Century Ottoman Judicial Records: The Shari'a Court of Anatolian Kayseri," *JESHO* 18 (1975), 53–114; H. Gerber, "Social and Economic Position of Women in the Ottoman City, Bursa, 1600–1700," *IJMES* 12 (1980), 231–244; A. Marcus, *The Middle East on the Eve of Modernity: Aleppo in the Eighteenth Century* (New York, 1989); N. Abacı, *Bursa Şehri'nde Osmanlı Hukuku'nun Uygulanması (17. Yüzyıl)* (Ankara, 2001); H. Canbakal, *Society and Politics in an Ottoman Town: Ayntab in the 17th century* (Leiden and Boston, 2006); B. Ergene, *Local Court, Provincial Society and Justice in the Ottoman Empire: Legal Practice and Dispute Resolution in Çankırı and Kastamonu (1652–1744)* (Leiden and Boston, 2003); L. Peirce, *Morality Tales: Law and Gender in the Ottoman Court of Aintab* (London, 2003); F. Zarinebaf, *Crime and Punishment in Istanbul, 1700–1800* (Berkeley, 2010); R. Gradeva, "On the Judicial Functions of Kadi Courts: Glimpses from Sofia in the Seventeenth Century," *Wiener Zeitschrift zur Geschichte der Neuzeit* 5, no. 2 (2005), 15–43; S. Ivanova, "The Divorce between Zubaida Hatun and Esseid Osman Aga: Women in the Eighteenth-Century *Shari'a* Court of Rumeli," in *Women, the Family, and Divorce Laws in Islamic History*, ed. A. Sonbol (Syracuse, NY, 1996), 112–125. In addition, an increasing number of *sicil*s have been published over the last two decades, for example,

N. Abacı (ed.), *The Ottoman Judges and Their Registers: The Bursa Court Registers B-90/295 (Dated AH 1081/AD 1670–1671)*, parts 1–2 (Cambridge, MA, 2007); M.A. Yediyıldız, S. Maydaer, and İ. Oruçoğlu (eds.), *A153 Nolu Bursa Şeri'ye Sicili* (Bursa, 2010); I. Sak (ed.), *47 Numeralı Konya Şeri'ye Sicili (1128–1129/ 1716–1717). Transkrypsiyon ve Dizin* (Konya, 2006); M. Âkif Aydın (ed.), *İstanbul Kadı Sicilleri* (Istanbul 2008–12); and M. Kurz, *Das sicill aus Skopje. Kritische Edition und Kommentierung des einzigen vollständig erhalten Kadiamtsregisterbandes* (sicill) *aus Üsküb (Skopje)* (Wiesbaden, 2003).

The data preserved in the *sicil*s are particularly important for Crimean history. The collection of 121 court registers is the only remaining source that was produced by the Crimean administration and that covers an extensive period of the khanate's history (1608–1783).[74] The Crimean *sicil*s are similar to Ottoman registers in many ways. Therefore, it is helpful to note some of the general features of this type of source before dealing with the particularities.

The content of a *sicil* reveals the work of judges and their auxiliary staff. Court records contain two types of documents: records of the proceedings of the sharia courts (*hüccet, i'lams, ma'ruz, mürasele*), and various types of documents sent to judges from central or provincial officials. The ratio between the two types of entries depended on the local circumstances in which they were produced.[75]

The records of proceedings consist mainly of two types of documents, i.e., documents (*hüccet*s) and written judgments (*i'lam*s). The first are the records of hearings, which were entered into registers at the request of plaintiffs. The second differ from *hüccet*s, as they contain the evidence used in the case and the sentences of the *kadı*s. An examination of *sicil*s from various parts of the Ottoman Empire and the Crimean Khanate reveals a certain degree of standardization in the recording of court proceedings. The introductory formulae are followed by data concerning plaintiffs and defendants or, in the case of contracts, the two parties. Usually descriptions of litigants contain indications about their religion. The formulae often reveal their social background, residential affiliation (the names of their villages and sometimes also the names of the judicial districts in which they lived), and occupation as well. The following part of the entries consists of the spoken record. It opens with the plaintiff's statement or accusation, followed by the response of the other party. As oral testimony played a crucial role in the Islamic/Ottoman court procedure, the entries usually contain the "voices" of the parties, edited by court writers. Moreover, this part also includes information about other evidence used in the court. We should not, however, expect every entry to end with the *kadı*'s sentence. With the exception of *i'lam*s, the entries seldom contain verdicts, as this was not a required part of the formal registration of a case. Instead, we encounter formulae such as, "after the legal confirmation, everything that happened was written at their [litigants] request" or "the present record was

74 This collection is preserved in the Russian National Library in St. Petersburg (Oriental Manuscript Division of the Russian National Library [Otdel Rukopisev Rossiiskoi Natsionalnoi Biblioteki, hereafter ORRNB]), Fond 917. It contains 119 court registers and two registers of real estate left by Christians who emigrated from the Crimean Peninsula prior to the year 1778; Yılmaz, "On Sekizinci."

75 I. Tamdoğan, "Sulh and the 18th Century Ottoman Courts of Üsküdar and Adana," *Islamic Law and Society* 15, no. 1 (2008), 58–59.

written in accordance with what happened." Therefore, the kinds of sentences pronounced by the judges and the punishments meted out to the culprits are often unclear. The date and the witnesses (*şuhudülhal*, lit., 'witnesses of the event') were recorded in the closing part of the document.[76] The witnesses in the cases, who are discussed in detail in Chapter 1, are the persons presented in the court, not only to attest to the authenticity of the proceeding, but also to verify the work of the court. These witnesses, recruited from the members of local communities, testified to the truth of the registered documents.

We must exercise caution when using court records as sources. First, as Dror Ze'evi points out, the *sicil*s are similar to other types of sources; they are "complex webs of meaning, in which a social *reality*, a series of specific biases, contemporary codes and symbols, styles and tropes of writing, the interventions of copiers and editors, all blend inextricably to form a written source."[77] It is of the utmost importance to understand that records of the hearings were not precise accounts of what was said or happened in the court, but were formulated by court scribes, who used formularies taken from a special branch of literature called the science of stipulations (*ilmu'ş-şurut*).[78] The court scribes adopted or simply filled prepared forms with the data of a given case. The *sicil*, as Boğaç Ergene observes, is nothing more than a translation of a particular legal performance into a formal and immensely formulaic language. The characteristics of individual performances are left out (for example, body language, or expressions). The quotations of individuals involved in the proceedings are rarely the words they actually used, rather their statements were translated into the official language of the legal system.[79] This is easy to observe in the case of the Crimean Khanate, where, if we took the court registers at face value, we would conclude that the whole population spoke Ottoman Turkish in

76 A. Akgündüz, *Şer'iye Sicilleri* (Istanbul, 1988); K. Çiçek, "*Zimmi*s (non-Muslims) of Cyprus in the Sharia Court: 1110/39 A.H./ 1698–1726 A.D.," PhD diss. (University of Birmingham, 1992); K. Hegyi, "The Terminology of the Ottoman-Turkish Judical Documents on the Basis of the Sources from Hungary," *Acta Orientalia Academiae Scientiarum Hungaricae* 18, nos. 1–2 (1965), 191–203.

77 D. Ze'evi, "The Use of Ottoman Sharī'a Court Records as a Source for Middle Eastern Social History: A Reappraisal," *Islamic Law and Society* 5, no. 1 (1998), 37.

78 In the Ottoman Empire, guide books were adapted for the needs of court officials. However, there were numerous differences among the documents from the various court registers and in the different periods; this would indicate that the Ottomans used a variety of formularies. Moreover, they changed these forms as necessary. Nonetheless, toward the end of the seventeenth century, the language of the court documents crystallized and became far more uniform in the Ottoman lands; J.A. Wakin, *The Function of Documents in Islamic Law* (Albany, NY, 1972), 1–70.

79 Ergene, *Local Court*, 130.

court, while in fact, there are almost no Tatar words and grammatical constructions recorded in the *sicil*s.

Second, many researchers working on the Ottoman *sicil*s are mesmerized by entries that prove that the court defended the rights of the poor against the notables. In the 1970s and 1980s, leading scholars in the field, for example, Ronald Jennings and Abraham Marcus, elaborated on the relative "fairness" of the courts. More recent research conducted by Leslie Peirce and Fariba Zarinebaf challenges this optimistic perception of the sharia courts. Instead, they underline that characteristics such as gender, social status, and religion significantly influenced an individual's chances of having a fair trial. In their recent book, Bogaç Ergene and Metin Coşgel call attention to the fact that without a sophisticated quantitive analysis, we have no data by which to assess the impartiality of the court. Based on the *sicil*s from Kastamonu in the late seventeenth and eighteenth centuries, Ergene and Coşgel they conducted

> a systematic analysis in order to answer questions such as the following: Who went to court? How often? For what purpose? Whom did these parties encounter or engage with as allies and adversaries? Who won and lost litigations? What types of litigations? And, how might these patterns have changed over time?[80]

The same scholars, building on the earlier research of Ergene,[81] call attention to the fact that the court's own archive in Kastamonu and Çankırı did not serve an evidentiary function.[82] Ergene connects this fact with *kadı* rotation, which most probably increased the number of individuals who had access to the court archives, and thus the chance of its contamination. Numerous words or even whole entries in the registers are crossed out, while some words and sentences were corrected by unknown people, which put into question whether the final version of the text was written down by an authorized clerk fulfilling the *kadı*'s orders.

The Crimean *sicil*s, 121 volumes in all, are preserved in the Russian National Library in St. Petersburg.[83] Sometime prior to 1799, Mehmed Ağa, the last Crimean *kadıasker*, surrendered the collection to the Russian authorities. It

80 M. Coşgel and B. Ergene, *The Economics of Ottoman Justice: Settlement and Trial in the Sharia Courts* (Cambridge, 2016), 32–33.

81 B. Ergene, "Evidence in Ottoman Courts: Oral and Written Documentation in Early-Modern Courts of Islamic Law," *Journal of the American Oriental Society* 124, no. 3 (2004), 471–491.

82 Coşgel and Ergene, *Economics of Ottoman Justice*, 237.

83 One more *sicil* from the court of Kara Su (1752–53) is housed in the Museum of History and Literature in Yalta. This *sicil* was not available to me; Turan, "Kırım Hanlığı."

was kept in the archives of the governor of Simferopol till 1905, when it was sent to the Imperial Public Library in St. Petersburg.[84] The collection contains *sicil*s of the *kadıasker*, the *kadı*s of main Crimean cities (Bahçesaray, Kara Su, Gözleve), and a few registers with unidentified territorial affiliations. The content of these last *sicil*s indicates that they were also prepared in district courts. Fehmi Yilmaz discovered that some district court registers only contain entries of cases adjudicated by the *naib*s.[85] In addition, two registers of non-Muslims who emigrated from the Crimea after 1774 are also included in the collection. The first regular entries of the *sicil*s date to the year 1608, but the registers do not constitute a continuous series. This very fact indicates that only a part of the Crimean *sicil*s has survived to our times. The reason these particular volumes have been preserved remains unclear; it may be purely coincidental. The content of the *sicil*s from the reign of Murad Giray is discussed in detail in Chapter 5, where we provide only general information on the proportion of the various types of cases recorded in this period. The two largest groups of entries concern money related to contracts and disputes, while divisions and registrations of inheritances also constitute a substantial part of the *sicil*s. Other types of cases concerning family matters, pious endowments, manumissions, murder, and assault were brought to the court less frequently. We seldom encounter documents issued by the central and provincial Tatar administration. The latter group consists of orders (called *yarlığ* or *ferman*) issued by the khan or the *kalga*, as well as one certificate (*tezkere*) of the *kalga*'s *kaymakam*. There is one privilege (*berat*) from Sultan Mehmed IV that was registered in the Crimean *sicil*s during the reign of Murad Giray.[86] The whole collection of the Crimean court registers contains fifteen documents issued by Ottoman sultans and officials in the period between 1604 and 1738.[87]

Since the in-depth section of this study covers the reign of Murad Giray, basic statistical analysis is based on three registers written during this period. The oldest of them, register no. 22, comprises documents recorded on 99 pages

84 O. Vasil'eva, "Krymsko-Tatarskie Rukopisnye Materialy v otdele rukopisei Rossiiskoi Natsional'noi Biblioteki," *Vostochnyi Sbornik* 5 (1993), 37–45.

85 I wish to thank Fehmi Yılmaz for sharing with me his finding during our meeting in November 2016. His remarks on the *naib* registers will be published in the catalogue of the Crimean court registers (*Kırım Hanlığı Kadi Sicilleri Kataloğu*), which is forthcoming.

86 The document dated 13 Sefer 1094/11 February 1683 regulated the collection of the *tapu* tax and *öşr* (tithe) from the province of Kefe. The *berat* was probably recorded in the *kadıasker* register because the sultan granted the revenue from these taxes from the districts between Balaklava and Bahçesaray to the khan (ORRNB, Fond 917, *defter* 23b/212b/1).

87 ORRNB, Fond 917, *defter* 1/19a/3, 1/11b/1, 1/54a/1, 4/77a/1, 19/87a/1, 22/4a/8, 23b/212b/1, 26/66b/1, 27/91a/6, 27/133b/4, 28/25b/3, 34/19b/1, 34/19b/3, 57/77a/1, 60/59b/1.

between Cemazil I 1087/February–March 1677 and Şevval 1089/November–December 1678. On the endpaper and the last page, we also find a few later records. The most recent comes from the year 1115/1703–04.[88] The regular entries begin with the statement that it was the official judicial register, in which "the learned scholar Ibrahim, the military judge of the victorious khan, Selim Giray Khan, son of Bahadır Giray Khan was on duty. It was registered in the month of Zilhicce of the year 1087 [February–March 1677]."[89] With the change on the Crimean throne, Ibrahim must have lost his post. In spring 1678, Hasan Efendi, son of Şeyh Cafar Efendi, is recorded as the *kadıasker* of the new khan, Murad Giray.[90] Apparently, the appointment of the new *kadıasker* triggered changes to the staff in the court. The *katib*s who served during the time of Ibrahim were no longer recorded among the case witnesses (*şuhudülhal*).[91] Instead, we encounter *katib* Abdulbaki, whose name is mentioned frequently in register no. 22 and in register no. 23b.[92] His name appears for the first time in a case recorded at the beginning of May 1678.[93] This individual, Katib Abdulbaki, is crucial to the identification of register 23 (parts a and b) as a *sicil* of the *kadıasker*. We know that both registers 22 and 23 were products of the same chancellery because entries were written in Abdulbaki's handwriting, with his name mentioned among the case witnesses in register 23, combined with the fact that the mention of his name begins with records dating to the same month in which the regular entries in register no. 22 (Şevval 1089/16 November–14 December 1678) ended.[94] Several other writers worked next to Abdulbaki. We know the

88 ORRNB, Fond 917, *defter* 22/endpaper.

89 This opening formula was published, in part, by Ahmed Cihan and Fehmi Yılmaz. They read the title of Ibrahim as *el-kâdi* instead of *el-kadı bi'l-cünd*. The latter term was used interchangeably with *kadıasker*, and also means "the judge of the army." It should be emphasized that Ahmed Cihan and Fehmi Yılmaz are familiar with the title *el-kadı bi'l-cünd*, and read it properly elsewhere in the Crimean registers, see Cihan and Yılmaz, "Kırım Kadi Sicilleri," esp. 141, 147, 151; ORRNB, Fond 917, *defter* 22/1a/1.

90 Since the record contains only the year (1089/1678–79), in order to date it more precisely I used information from the nearest available record, which was dated 12 Rebi I 1089 (4 May 1678), see ORRNB, Fond 917, *defter* 22/68b/5 and 22/70b/2.

91 See, for example, the *katib*s Huseyn and Ebussuud, whose names were recorded when Ibrahim was the *kadıasker*: ORRNB, Fond 917, *defter* 22/55b/4 and 22/61b/4.

92 Register no. 23 is divided into two parts, which are catalogued in ORRNB, Fond 917, *defter* 23a and *defter* 23b. The chronologically earlier Part 23b consists of 124 pages, while Part 23a consists of 130 pages. Presumably, the original register 23 was split into halves because its binding was too weak to hold 254 pages together. The fact that the last page is damaged may indicate that the register remained without a cover for some time.

93 Since the record only lists the year 1089 (1678–79), I used the data from the next case, which was 12 Rebi I 1089 (4 May 1678), see, ORRNB, Fond 917, *defter* 22/70b/1–2.

94 See, for example, the following entries: ORRNB, Fond 917, *defter* 23b/1a/4–5, 23b/5a/1,4, 23b/5b/1–3.

names of a few of them, because they are listed among the case witnesses (Seyyid Ali Monla, Can Ahmed, son of Hüsam Hacı, Adil or Seyyid Gazi).[95] The rest, whose names do not appear in the registers, can only be distinguished by shifts in calligraphic and narrative style; these shifts are visible between successive entries, but contain no information on the identity of the *katib*.[96] Partial information on the writers and numerous undated entries make it difficult to reconstruct precisely how *sicil*s of the *kadıasker* were produced. Register nos. 22 and 23 offer only a few indications on the subject. After the appointment of Hassan Efendi, 2,273 entries were recorded in these two registers. It seems that the majority of them were written down as the results of court sessions in the period between the month of Rebi I 1089/23 April–22 May 1678 and the month of Receb 1093/5 July–4 August 1682.[97] Until July/August 1682, the entries were recorded every month, which meant that court sessions were held at least once a month. Since the exact dates of the entries are rarely included, it is hard to establish whether records written down in the same month, or in the same ten days of a month, were the results of one or more court sessions. The only longer gap in the regular entries follows the records registered on 243 pages of *defter* no. 23 in the month of Receb 1093/5 July–4 August 1682. The next dated record was written in the second ten days of the month of Rebi I 1095/27 February–7 March 1684.[98] Presumably, the following thirty-two entries, which were rather chaotically registered on the last ten pages, are also from the first half of the year 1684.[99] Thus, these entries date to the reign of Hacı Giray Khan, who ruled after the deposition of Khan Murad Giray in autumn 1683. It is hard to explain why the last ten pages were left blank in 1682, and then used to record a few entries two years later. Perhaps these ten pages, along with the endcovers of numerous other Crimean registers, were used in later periods to save paper, which was a precious commodity.

The third register used for basic statistical analysis begins with the opening formula that states that it was produced during the reign of Murad Giray Khan, when Ibrahim was *kadı* of the district of Kara Su. The formula is dated 1 Ramazan 1094/24 August 1683.[100] The first thirty-five pages contain 253 entries from the period between 1 Ramazan 1094/24 August 1683 and 15 Sefer 1095/2 February 1684, when *kadı* Ibrahim was replaced by the appointee of the new ruler Hacı Gıray. The regular entries in autumn 1683 and winter 1683–84 bear witness to the fact that the court functioned without disturbance during the Vienna campaign and the interregnum following the deposition of Murad Giray. Both

95 ORRNB, Fond 917, *defter* 23b/22a/4, 23b/23b/4, 23b/33b/1, 23b/48b/423b/50b/2–3.
96 ORRNB, Fond 917, *defter* 23b/23b/45a/2, 23b/46b/5–6.
97 ORRNB, Fond 917, *defter* 23a/243b/7.
98 ORRNB, Fond 917, *defter* 23a/244a/2.
99 ORRNB, Fond 917, *defter* 23a/244a/2 to 23a/253b/3.
100 ORRNB, Fond 25, *defter* 25/1a/1.

district *kadıs* of this period relied on the help of Abdulbaki, who performed the functions of both *katib* and *naib* at least until 5 Zilkade 1094/14 October 1684.[101]

Register no. 24 from the district of Bahçesaray, which contains, for the most part, entries from the first reign of Selim I Giray (1671–78), also merits our attention. It begins with a formula dated to the first ten days of Cemzil I 1088/2–11 July 1677, and states that the register was created during the reign of Selim I Giray, when Ebussuud, son of Mehmed, was the *kadı* of Bahçesaray. Then, there is a statement affirming that it is the register of the sub-district of the court of Bahçesaray ("mahkeme-i muta'allika nahiyesi sicillatıdır").[102] We also learn that the entries were registered by Mustafa Efendi. The beginning formulae are followed by regular entries recorded between Cemzil I 1088/2–11 July 1677 and the second ten days of Şaban 1088/9–19 October 1677.[103] Near the end of the register, on the first day of Rebi I 1090/12 April 1679, we encounter a formula introducing Musalli Efendi as the new *kadı*.[104] There is no information on the *naib* parallel to the one above, related to Mustafa Efendi. The last four folios of the register contain twenty-six entries exclusively concerning matters related to family and money, and a list of fixed prices (*narh*), which I have translated in Chapter 4. Because the number of entries that date to the reign of Murad Giray is very limited, we are unable to analyze it for any reliable basic statistical analysis of this register, which we could compare with data extracted from the abovementioned nos. 22, 23a and b, and 25.

My research is based on the cases brought before the Crimean courts. It is essential to understand who is referred to in these fora. While it is usually clear if the litigants are Muslims or non-Muslims, their social background is not directly identified in the court entries. Thus, distinguishing various social groups among the litigants is not simple; we discuss this in detail in Chapter 5. Here, following the approach of numerous researchers on the Ottoman studies, we propose to divide the Muslim litigants in the Crimean courts based on their honorific titles, which we have grouped into the following title-based categories:

(a) members of the Giray dynasty (khan, sultan, *hani*)
(b) nobles (*beğ, mirza, emeldeş, ulan*)
(c) members of the administrative and military elite (*ağa, beşe*)
(d) members of the religious elite (*çelebi, efendi, hoca, şeyh, dede, seyyid*)

101 The entry was written on the last page of the register (ORRNB, Fond 25, *defter* 25/120a/1). Since the following register from Kara Su has not survived, it is unclear whether Abdulbaki continued to work in the court.

102 The formula was partially transcribed by Fehmi Yılmaz and Ahmed Cihan (Cihan and Yılmaz, "Kırım Kadi Sicilleri," 149); ORRNB, Fond 917, *defter* 24/1a/2.

103 The last precise data was written in the following entry: ORRNB, Fond 917, *defter* 24/114a/1.

104 ORRNB, Fond 917, *defter* 24/116a/3.

(e) common people (who have no titles other than the honorific title *hacı*/*hacıye* for men/women who had performed the pilgrimage to Mecca).[105]

2.2 *Other Handwritten Documents in Ottoman Turkish and European Languages*

The unusual *defter* (land register) of Kefe province, which dates to 1094/1682–83, provides vital social, economic, demographic, and toponymic data and is a key source for this book.[106] The register was prepared shortly before the second siege of Vienna, most likely to give the Ottomans new sources of income. In contrast to typical Ottoman land registers, this *defter* reveals nothing about taxes. Instead, it contains unusually detailed data about various types of land owned by individuals. It lists the following information: the name of settlements and their location in the provincial administration, the names of the owners of real estate in each settlement, and the type and amount of land owned. In contrast to previous land surveys,[107] in 1682/83, the surveyors started by measuring the individual land of every landholder. The Kefe *defter* resembles the registers from the vicinity of Edirne, dated 1669/70,[108] from Crete and from the smaller Aegean islands (1670/71).[109] These few registers, instead of maintaining the older trends and providing a general record of the land and

105 Coşgel and Ergene demonstrate that in Kastamonu the title *hacı* indicated that the person had considerable wealth. They analyzed how being a pilgrim affected trial outcomes and observed that the pilgrim status translated into a higher likelihood of success in court against common Muslims without titles (Coşgel and Ergene, *Economics of Ottoman Justice*, 55, 296–303).

106 Oriental Department of Bulgarian National Library 'St. St. Cyril and Methodius' in Sofia [Hereafter, NBKM, Or. Dept.], Fond D737, fols. 1–68.

107 Öztürk describes the sixteenth-century Ottoman *tapu tahrir defter*s of Kefe; see Öztürk, *Osmanlı Hakimiyetinde Kefe*.

108 S. Parveva, "Rural Agrarian and Social Structure in the Edirne Region During the Second Half of the 17th Century," *Études Balcaniques* 3 (2000), 55–90.

109 On these registers and on the debate concerning the "new Ottoman system" of taxation introduced in the late seventeenth century, see M. Greene, "An Islamic Experiment? Ottoman Land Policy on Crete," *Mediterranean Historical Review* 11 (1996), 60–78; Greene, *A Shared World: Christians and Muslims in the Early Modern Mediterranean* (Princeton, NJ, 2000), 22–25; E. Gülsoy, *Girit'in Fethi ve Osmanlı Idaresinin Kurulması, 1645–1670* (Istanbul, 2004); E. Kermeli, "Caught in Between Faith and Cash: The Ottoman Land System of Crete, 1645–1670," in *The Eastern Mediterranean under Ottoman Rule: Crete, 1645–1840*, ed. A. Anastasopoulos (Rethymno, 2008), 17–48; E. Kolovos, "Beyond 'Classical' Ottoman Defeterology: A Preliminary Assessment of the Tahrir Registers of 1670/1671 Concerning Crete and the Aegean Islands," in *The Ottoman Empire, the Balkans, the Greek Lands: Towards Social and Economic History*, ed. E. Kolovos, P. Kotzageorgis, S. Laiou, and M. Sariyannis (Istanbul, 2007), 201–235.

population,[110] list the land possessions of each landowner using the formula: "the land of A, son of B." The clerks recorded the types of land (fields, gardens, pastures, vineyards, etc.) and the number of *dönüm*s within the boundaries of each village. Toward the end of the seventeenth century, similarities between the Aegean and Edirne registers ignited a debate on reforming the taxation system. Many scholars, such as Molly Greene, Ersin Gülsoy, Eugenia Kermeli, and Elyas Kolovos discussed the possible advantages of the "new system" (e.g., it made it easier to collect lump sum payments, it reflected the development of legal rights on land) and the effects it had on the structure of land ownership. I believe that a detailed analysis of the Kefe *defter* would bring us closer to understanding these significant changes in Ottoman fiscal policy, but it is difficult to address this issue in the scope of the present study; such a topic merits a separate monograph.

I frequently invoke various handwritten documents in Ottoman Turkish and European languages, which are preserved in the Main Archives of Early Acts in Warsaw (hereafter, AGAD), the Russian State Archives of Early Acts in Moscow (hereafter, RGADA), the Oriental Department of Bulgarian National Library 'St. Cyril and Methodius' in Sofia (hereafter NBKM, Or. Dept.), the Haus-, Hof- und Staatsarchiv in Vienna (hereafter, HHStA).

The Propaganda Fide Historical Archives in Rome (hereafter, APF) are of particular value for the study of Crimean history. It houses letters exchanged between missionaries sent to the Crimea and their correspondents in the Sacred Congregation for the Propagation of the Faith, to which both sides attached a variety of documents.[111] The oldest letter related to the Crimea dates from 1624, when the first Dominican mission headed by Emiddio Portelli d'Ascoli

110 These "classical" *defter*s written in the second half of the seventeenth century were examined by J. Blaškovič, "Ziemie lenne (hass) namiestnika Nowych Zamków w latach 1664–1685," *Rocznik Orientalistyczny* 45 (1977), 83–92; and also examined by D. Kołodziejczyk (ed.), *The Ottoman Survey Register of Podolia (ca. 1681) Defter-i Mufassal-i Eyalet-i Kamaniçe* (Cambridge, MA, 2004).

111 Data from the following archival fonds were used: 1—*Acta Sacrae Congregationis* (hereafter, ACTA) containing the minutes of the monthly meetings of cardinals and other members of the congregation, the reports of the most important officials of the congregation and the resolutions taken by members from the years 1677–1725 and 1737; 2—*Scritture originali referite nelle Congregatione* (hereafter, SOCG) containing documents used as a basis for discussion during the monthly meetings dating to the years 1620–1725; 3—*Scritture referite nei Congressi* (hereafter, SC), which groups the documents referred to during the weekly meetings. Although the congregation considered this material less important than the documents preserved in SOCG archival fonds, modern historians have praised the SC archival fonds as a treasure-trove of information with regard to the daily lives of missionaries. In the present study, I used the materials dating to the years 1620–1725; 4—*Fondo Lettere e decreti della Sacra Congregazione e biglietti di Mons. Segretario* (hereafter, Fondo

set off to the city of Kefe.[112] Over the next thirty-five years, Emiddio and other priests serving on the peninsula authored many letters and reports containing abundant data on the khanate and its neighboring polities.[113] The death of the prefect Raymund Charzewski in 1658 marks the end of the permanent Dominican mission on the peninsula.[114] For the next fifty years, the Crimea witnessed numerous attempts to establish a new Catholic mission. Eventually, in 1710, one was founded by the French Jesuits.[115]

2.3 *Narrative Sources*

Narrative sources written by the Tatars, Ottomans, and Europeans have proven to be a mine of information for historians of the Crimea. Their authors provide us with abundant, though often contradictory, accounts of the khanate's history and institutions. It is clear that the writers were not equally well-informed, and also apparent that they wrote for a variety of reasons and to satisfy the interests of different groups of readers. Often, they harbored strong feelings on the subjects they described. Their personal beliefs could lead them to distort

---

Lettere) containing copies of letters sent by the secretaries of the congregation informing it of its decisions for the years 1622 to 1678.

112 Raymund Lorenz and Abrosius Eszer published a number of important studies on their activity, cf. R. Loenertz, "Le origini della missione secentesca dei Domenicani in Crimea," *Archivum Fratrum Praedicatorum* 5 (1935), 261–288; A. Eszer, "Giovanni Giuliani da Lucca O.P. Forschungen zu seinem Leben und zu seinen Schriften," *Archivum Fratrum Praedicatorum* 37 (1967), 353–468; Eszer, "Die *Beschreibung des Schwarzen Meeres und der Tatarei* des Emidio Portelli d'Ascoli O.P.," *Archivum Fratrum Praedicatorum* 42 (1972), 199–249; Eszer, "Missionen in Randzonen der Weltgeschichte: Krim, Kaukasien und Georgien," in *Sacra Congregationis De Propaganda Fide Memoria Rerum 1622–1972*, ed. J. Metzler, vol. 1, Part 1: 1622–1700, 650–679 (Rome, 1971); Eszer, "Missionen im Halbrund der Länder zwischen Schwarzem Meer, Kaspisee und Persischem Golf: Krim, Kaukasien, Georgien und Persien," in *Sacra Congregationis De Propaganda Fide Memoria Rerum 1622–1972*, ed. J. Metzler, vol. 2: 1700–1815, 421–462 (Rome, 1971); Eszer, "Neue Forschungen zur Geschichte der II. Krim-Mission der Dominikaner (1635–1665)," *Archivum Fratrum Praedicatorum* 41 (1971), 181–239.

113 For the published reports of the Dominicans, see E.D. [correctly P.] d'Ascoli, *Descrittione del mare Negro et della Tartaria*, ed. N. Dashkevich, in *Chtenia v Istoricheskom Obshchestve Nestora Letopisca* (Kiev, 1891), 5:1–46; Giovanni da Lucca, "Opisaniie perekopskikh i nogaiskikh tatar, cherkesov, mingrelov i gruzin Zhana da-Liuka," ed. P. Yurchenko, *ZOOID* 11 (1879): 473–493.

114 Eszer, "Neue Forschungen," 214.

115 The Propaganda Fide Historical Archives in Rome (hereafter, APF), ACTA, vol. 82, fols. 503r–504v; vol. 89, fols. 39v–40v, 459; SC, Bessarabia, Crimea, Moscovia (1679–1856), fols. 12–14, 16, 20–21; Józef Andrzej Gierowski, "Krym w Polityce Wersalu w latach 1704–1709," in *Węgry–Polska w Europie Środkowej. Historia-Literatura. Księga pamiątkowa ku czci Profesora Wacława Felczaka*, ed. A. Centarowicz, C.G. Kiss, and I. Kovács (Cracow, 1997), 86–92; Veinstein, "Missionaires Jésuites."

the facts or include outright fiction in their works. In order to give the reader a better understanding as to why certain authors described recorded events in a particular way, below I present the most important information about the authors. A better knowledge of the authors enables us to filter the information presented in their works.

I begin the survey with the texts of the most important Crimean chronicles.[116] The first preserved chronicle was written soon after the death of Sahib Giray (1553), while the last one was finished in 1811. There is a gap of over 250 years between them. At the beginning of the period, the Crimean Tatars burned the suburbs of Moscow and put an end to the Astrakhan campaign of the Ottomans; by the end of the eighteenth century, the territory of the khanate had become a Russian province. It is clear to see that these chronicles were written in vastly different times and for different reasons. Yet, as different as these texts are, they share one vital similarity. As Alan Fisher has persuasively argued, the authors, be they Ottoman or Tatar, presented "both historical and ideological justifications for considering the Crimean Khanate as a separate state—a state under Ottoman suzerainty, yet with its own institutions that bore traces of the khan's Central Asian heritage that had been received directly from Jengiz Khan."[117] In line with this remark, Denise Klein convincingly demonstrates, with the example of "The History of Mehmed Giray" (an unpublished chronicle), the frustration of the Crimean elite with the Ottoman policy toward the khanate.[118] In view of these statements, it is reasonable to exercise great caution in using these kinds of sources, especially for understanding Ottoman-Tatar relations and Ottoman influence on Tatar domestic policy.

The "History of Khan Sahib Giray,"[119] the oldest preserved Crimean chronicle, was authored by Bedr ed-Din Mehmed, son of Mehmed Kaysunizade Nidam Efendi, known as Remmal Hoca. He arrived in the khanate from the Ottoman Empire in 1532, as a member of the retinue of Khan Sahib Giray. He finished his chronicle and panegyric in 1553, after the tragic death of his patron. The

116 For further information about the historiography of the Crimean Khanate, see Mehmed Bursalı, *Osmanlı Zamanında Yetişen Kırım Müellifleri* (Ankara, 1990); N. Seyyityahya, "Istoricheskaia proza w krymskotatarskoi literature XV–XVIII vv.," PhD diss. (Crimean University, Simferopol, 2005); I. Zaitsev, *Krymskaia istoriograficheskaia traditsia XV–XIX vekov* (Moscow, 2009).

117 Fisher, *Crimean Tatars*, 35.

118 D. Klein (ed.), *The Crimean Khanate Between East and West (15th–18th Century)* (Wiesbaden, 2012), 138–139.

119 For the French translation of this chronicle, see Özalp Gökbilgin (ed.), *Tarih-i Sahib Giray Han* (Ankara, 1973); in the text, I refer to this work by my translation of the title used by the editor.

writing was commissioned by the khan's daughter, Nur Sultan. The chronicler, who was an eyewitness to the events he described, created a lively and fascinating picture of the reign of this great khan, who started to introduce new administrative institutions patterned on those of the Ottomans. The chronicle, which depicts a society torn by tensions and conflicts between the khan and his vassals, is perhaps a unique source, in that it provides a detailed description of the seminal reforms of Sahib Giray from the perspective of an eyewitness. Remmal Hoca, who, along with the khan, took part in the campaigns of Sultan Suleyman ('the Lawgiver') as well as in Tatar raids of Circassia, also provides additional details on the foreign policy of his master.[120] For all these reasons, the chronicle remains one of the most important sources of the history of the Crimean Khanate in the first half of the sixteenth century.[121]

Abdullah, son of Rizvan Paşa, who wrote the second oldest Crimean chronicle, was also of Ottoman origin. His father was governor of Kefe. The author dedicated his writing, dated about 1638, to the Ottoman *kaymakam*, Musa Paşa. Abdullah's writing provides basic data about the reigns of fourteen khans from Mengli I Giray to Inayet Giray (1468–1637). He is particularly well-informed about events dating to his lifetime, the 1620s and 1630s. The Latin script transliteration of the chronicle was published fifty years ago by Ananiasz Zajączkowski. His edition also contains a French translation made in 1737 by a *jeune de language*,[122] Mr. Delaunay.[123]

A good deal of information on the mid-seventeenth century khanate is contained in "The History of Islam Giray Khan" of Hacı Mehmed Senai.[124] The author, who was of Tatar origin, served as a secretary of the khan and a district judge. His chronicle was most probably commissioned by the khan's vizier Sefer Gazi Ağa. It covers the years 1648–49 and was finished in 1651. The author describes the Tatar raids of the Polish-Lithuanian Commonwealth during the Cossack uprising of Bohdan Khmelnytsky in detail. Hacı Mehmed Senai based

120 The facsimiles of two of the seven extant manuscripts have also been published, cf. S.I. Menger, *Tarih-i Sahib Giray Han* (Istanbul, 2000).

121 For the significance of the chronicle see, for example, V. Ostapchuk, "Crimean Tatar Long-Range Campaigns: The View from Remmal Khoja's History of Sahib Gerey Khan," in *Warfare in Eastern Europe, 1500–1800*, ed. B.J. Davies (Leiden and Boston, 2012), 147–171.

122 In early modern France, interpreters trained in the languages of the Levant (Turkish, Persian, Arabic, and others) were referred to as *jeunes de langues*. Their training included studies in Paris and Istanbul.

123 A. Zajączkowski (ed.), *La chronique des steppes kipchak: Tevārīh-i Dešt-i Qipčak du XVIIe siècle* (Warsaw, 1966).

124 The Ottoman Turkish text of this chronicle (written in Arabic script) was translated into Polish. See Hacı Mehmed Senai z Krymu, *Historia chana Islama Gireja III*, ed. Zygmunt Abrahamowicz (Warsaw, 1971).

his writing on his own observations and on eyewitness accounts. He also used official materials, those accessible to high officials of the khanate.

A particularly important source for Crimean history in the two last decades of the seventeenth century is "The History of Mehmed Giray" written by Derviş Mehmed Giray, son of Mubarek Giray. As the father of Khan Murad Giray was also named Mubarek, one may presume that the chronicler may have been the khan's brother. The entire chronicle of Mehmed Giray covers the years 1683–1703. It is the only extant detailed description of the second siege of Vienna written by a Tatar. According to Richard Kreutel, the chronicle of Mehmed Giray contains no new facts about the campaign. In fact, Kreutel emphasizes its oversimplifications and intentional distortions of facts, which enabled the author to praise Murad Giray and severely criticize Kara Mustafa Paşa. Moreover, Kreutel states that the unsophisticated language of the chronicle distinguishes it from contemporary high literature addressed to the Ottoman elites and lends it a more popular flavor.[125] Zygmunt Abrahamowicz disagrees with Kreutel on some aspects. He points out that the chronicle not only demonstrates the Crimean view on the Ottoman military campaigns in Europe in the 1680s, but also provides vital information about the relations between Murad Giray and his subjects. Of all the known Muslim sources, Mehmed Giray best explains the reasons Kara Mustafa Paşa insisted on deposing Murad Giray after the Vienna defeat.[126]

For historians of the eighteenth-century Crimea, "The essence of history" of Abdulgaffar el-Kırımi[127] has proven to be a mine of information. The author was a nobleman, born into the family of Kiyat from the village of Safa Kongrat; he traced his origins to Alaçıoğlu Mamay Beğ and his wife Biysulu, who was a

125 R. Kreutel (ed.), "Osmanische Berichte über Kara Mustafa's Feldzug gegen Wien, Walter Sturminger zum 70. Geburstag," *Die Welt des Islams* 12 (1969–70), 196–227.

126 Zygmunt Abrahamowicz translated a part of the chronicle concerning the reign of Murad Giray and Hacı II Giray, see Z. Abrahamowicz (ed.), *Kara Mustafa pod Wiedniem. Źródła muzułmańskie do dziejów wyprawy wiedeńskiej 1683 roku* (Cracow, 1973), 25–27; 309–322. The German translation of Markus Köhbach only covers the period of Murad Giray; see M. Köhbach (ed.), "Der Tarih-i Mehemmed Giray—Eine Osmanische Quelle zur Belagerung Wiens durch die Türken im Jahre 1683," *Zeszyty Naukowe Uniwersytetu Jagiellońskiego. Prace Historyczne* 75 (1983), 137–164. The only extant copy of Mehmed Giray's chronicle is preserved in the Österreichische Nationalbibliothek [hereafter, ÖNB] in Vienna (catalogue number H.O.86).

127 The transliteration of the chronicle has been published; see Abdulgaffar Kyrymi, *Umdet al-akhbar*, ed. Derya Derin Paşaoğlu (Kazan, 2014). "The essence of history" is my English translation of the title used by the editor.

daughter of Canibeg, a khan of the Golden Horde (d. 1357).[128] Abdulgaffar was a man of extensive interests, he was active as a judge, a secretary of the khan, and a special envoy in various diplomatic missions. He was much esteemed by his contemporary kinsmen as well as foreigners.[129] Nonetheless, most information concerning Abdulgaffar comes from several short notes in his chronicle. The first note mentions him as a participant in the Prut campaign (1711)[130] and the last one dates to the reign of Selim II Giray (1743–48), when Abdulgaffar was exiled from the Crimea to the particularly inhospitable fortress of Soğucak.[131] The author, as an eyewitness of and participant in the events he describes, left us a fascinating picture of the collapsing Crimean Khanate. His writing, which begins with Chingis Khan, also provides interesting data for researchers on the early history of the Tatars.[132]

"The Seven Planets" written by Seyyid Mehmed Riza[133] is recognized as the most reliable and the extensive chronicle of the Crimean Khanate. Its author, who lived in the second half of the eighteenth century, was a member of the

128 Until very recently, Abdulgaffar el-Kırımi [also Kyrymi] was considered a member of the Şirin family, cf. F. Babinger, *Die Geschichte der Osmanem und ihre Werke* (Leipzig, 1927), 270; Bursalı, *Osmanlı Zamanında*, 33; B. Kellner-Heinkele, "Who Was 'Abdulghaffar el-Qirimi? Some Notes on an 18th Century Crimean Tatar Historian," *Journal of Asian History* 32, no. 2 (1998), 145–156; M. Ivanics, "Die Şirin. Abstammung und Aufstieg einer Sippe in der Steppe," in *The Crimean Khanate between East and West*, ed. D. Klein (Weisbaden, 2012), 27–44. Based on the research of Derya Derin Paşaoğlu and the study of Nariman Seyyityahya, we now know that Abdulgaffar el-Kırımi came from the Kiyat family, see Abdulgaffar Kyrymi, *Umdet al-akhbar*, 123, 128; N. Seyyityahya, "Uchebnyi iz Karasu Abdul'gaffar Kyrymi i ego istoricheskoe cochinienie," in *Choban-zade. Sbornik materialov I krymskoi mezhnunarodnoi konferentsii. Belogorsk (Karasubazar), 23–25 maja 2012* g., ed. A.R. Emirov (Simferopol, 2013), 222–242.

129 Said Giray Sultan praised his honor and wide knowledge, also in "specialistic sciences." He maintained that Abdulgaffar had no equals in terms of education in the khanate; see B. Kellner-Heinkele (ed.), *Aus den Aufzeichnungen des Sa'id Giray Sultan. Eine zeitgenössische Quelle zur Geschichte des Chanats der Krim um die Mitte des 18. Jahrhunderts* (Freiburg im Breisgau, 1975), 226–227. Charles Peysonnel, the French consul in Bahçesaray, mentioned that "a Tatar, named Hadji Gaffar Efendi, who resided at Carasou, one of the principal cities of the Crimea, has composed, in Turkish verse, a short history of all the khans of Little Tartary, who succeeded each other since the time of Ginghiz Khan. In 1757, he, with the utmost politeness, presented me with a copy gratis"; see C. Peysonnel, *Strictures and Remarks on the Memoires of Baron de Tott* (London, 1786), 68–69.

130 Abdulgaffar Kyrymi, *Umdet al-akhbar*, 166–172.

131 Soğucak was an Ottoman fortress on the eastern coast of the Black Sea, on the territory of the present city of Novorossiysk, Abdulgaffar Kyrymi, *Umdet al-akhbar*, 128.

132 D. DeWeese, *Islamization and Native Religion in the Golden Horde: Baba Tükles and Conversion to Islam in Historical and Epic Tradition* (University Park, PA, 1994), 352–366.

133 "The Seven Planets" is the English translation of the title used by the editor; see Mirza Kazembeg (ed.), [*Seyyid*] *Muhammad Riza, Essebüsseyyar ili sem' planet soderzhavshchii*

Afifi family, which was known for its literary figures. In the sixteenth century, the Afifis left Bukhara for the khanate, where they were granted lands in the villages of Kipçak and Başı Beğ. Seyyid Mehmed Riza's career was connected to the fate of his cousin, the *kadıasker* Feyzullah Efendi. The last Afifi was a protégé of Mengli II Giray, who probably commissioned Riza's work. When the khan was deposed in 1739, Riza left the khanate for the Ottoman Empire, where he worked as a mullah in various cities and districts (Niş, Diyarbekir,[134] Bursa, Üsküdar). According to a note in one of the manuscripts of Riza's chronicle, he completed his work when Hacı Mustafa Efendi Tabukçu was appointed *reis efendi*[135] for the second time, i.e., in May–June 1744.[136] The title of Riza's chronicle refers to the seven khans whose reigns he extensively studied: Mengli I Giray (1466–67; 1469–74; 1478–1515), Sahib Giray (1532–51), Devlet I Giray (1551–77), Gazi II Giray (1588–96; 1597–1608), Bahadır Giray (1637–41), Hacı Selim I Giray (1671–78; 1684–91; 1692–99; 1702–04), and Mengli II Giray (1724–30; 1737–40). The author based his work on his own observations, but also on other chronicles that have not survived to our times. Since the nineteenth century, the chronicle has been mined for facts. Its part concerning the reign of Murad Giray includes stories that are not attested to by any other sources; in fact, some of them seem to be fictional. "The Seven Planets" was published in the early nineteenth century by Mirza Kazembeg.[137]

The memoirs of Said Giray, son of Khan Saadet III Giray, merit special attention for their personal character. The most valuable part of the chronicle concerns the author's reflections on the Nogays, among whom he was placed as the khan's deputy (*serasker*) in Yedisan in 1750s. Said Giray left a moving picture of a well-educated Tatar prince sent away from the civilized world to the Nogays, barbarous vassals he was unable to control. His memoirs also contain accounts of the outstanding individuals of his time, for example, the ulema of the contemporary Crimean Khanate. Although this work has not been published, its content is discussed in detail by Barbara Kellner-Heinkele.[138]

---

istoriu krymskikh khanov ot Mengli Girej Khana pierwogo do Mengli Girej Khana vtorogo t. e. s 871/1466 po 1150/1737 (Kazan, 1832).

134 According to Ilya Zaitsev, there is some question about whether Seyyid Mehmed Riza was a *kadı* in Diayarbekir, see Zaitsev, *Krymskaia istoriograficheskaia*, 102.

135 In the eighteenth-century Ottoman Empire, the *reis efendi* was a high official in charge of foreign affairs.

136 N. Seyyityahya, "Proiskhozhdenie Seiida Mukhammeda Rizy (k voprosu o meste ego 'Semi planet' sredi proizvedenii krymskoi istoricheskoi prozy XVIII veka)," *Kultura Narodov Prichernomora* 44 (2003), 35–41.

137 On the preserved manuscripts, see Zaitsev, *Krymskaia istoriograficheskaia*, 107–112.

138 Kellner-Heinkele (ed.), *Aus den Aufzeichnungen*.

The last Crimean chronicle, "The Rose Bush of the Khans or the History of the Crimea," was written by Halim Giray Sultan after the Russian annexation.[139] Its author (1772–1823) spent his entire adult life in the Ottoman Empire. His chronicle contributes little to our knowledge of Crimean history before the 1740s. His account of that period mirrors previously mentioned writings, for instance, the chronicle of Mehmed Seyyid Riza. Yet, his description concerning the 1760s and 1770s sheds light on this turning point in the history of the khanate. According to Alan Fisher, his severe criticism of the irresponsibility of the elite members of that time had a great impact on the nineteenth-century Crimean Tatar movement.[140]

In contrast to the abovementioned chroniclers, Khachatur, who authored a chronicle covering the years from 1615 to 1658, was a non-Muslim, an Armenian priest from Kefe. He focuses on the fate of his own kinsmen living in the Crimea in the turbulent times of Canibeg Giray and Mehmed III Giray. Yet, his interests were by no means limited to the everyday life of his community. He kept track of international events in the Black Sea region and in Eastern Europe as well. His chronicle describes the everyday life of common people, but also includes notes on the most important political events.[141]

At this point, it is useful to briefly note another text, which for many years was considered yet another Crimean chronicle from the eighteenth century. "The History of the Tatar Khan and the Lands of Dagestan, Muscovy, and the Kipçak Steppe" was attributed to Kefevi Ibrahim Efendi.[142] Its text is quite unusual compared with other Crimean chronicles. It contains a surprisingly deep understanding of the past and contemporary situation in Eastern Europe and in the Black Sea region. Kefevi stressed that Moscow posed a threat to the independence of its neighboring states, including the Crimean Khanate, and noted that the latter could remain independent only in the close alliance with the Ottoman Empire. Such a deeply meaningful account, along with the author's extensive knowledge of contemporary Russian diplomacy, led Ilya Zaitsev to

139 "The Rose Bush of the Khans or the History of the Crimea" is the English translation of the title used by the editor. See Halim Giray, *Gülbünü Hanan yahud Kırım Tarihi*, ed. A. Ilmi (Istanbul, 1870); Halim Giray, *Gülbünü Hanan yahud Kırım Tarihi/Rozovyi kust khanov ili istoriia Kryma*, ed. A. Ilmi (Simferopol, 2004); Halim Giray, *Gülbünü Hânân (Kırım Hanları Tarihi)*, ed. B. Günay, A. Başer, A. Günaydın (Istanbul, 2013).

140 Fisher, *Between Russians*, 89–90.

141 E. Schütz (ed.), "Eine armenische Chronik von Kaffa aus der ersten Hälfte des 17. Jahrhunderts," *Acta Orientalia Academiae Scientiarum Hungaricae* 29, no. 2 (1975), 133–186.

142 "The History of the Tatar Khan and the Lands of Dagestan, Muscovy, and the Kipçak Steppe" is the English translation of the title used by the editor. See Kefeli Ibrahim Efendi, *Tevarih-i Tatar Han ve Dagistan Moskov ve Deşt-i Kıpçak Ülkelerinindir*, ed. Ibrahim Otar (Istanbul, 2005).

believe that the chronicle was a twentieth-century fabrication.[143] Recently, Uğur Demir's discovery proved that the text was a much earlier falsification made by Claude Alexandre, Comte de Bonneval, known as Humbaraci Ahmed Paşa. The French renegade wrote it to support the Ottoman cause during the war with Russia in the years 1736–39.[144]

Among the most valuable narrative sources, we must mention the account of Evliya Çelebi (1611?–84?), who Robert Dankoff praised for his openness and great curiosity, even enthusiasm, for meeting new people and traveling through unknown countries.[145] This most famous Ottoman traveler visited the Crimean Khanate twice.[146] Evliya's account is of great importance to the present study, as he described the political system of the khanate and made detailed reports about every village he visited.[147] His account also helps us to understand the Ottoman perception of the Tatars.[148]

143 Ilya Zaitsev also argues that the language of the chronicle is far too modern for an eighteenth-century writing; see I. Zaitsev, "'Istoria tatarskih hanov, Dagestana, Moskvy i narodov Desht-i Kipchak' Ibrahima b. Ali Kefeli," in *Desht-i Kipchak i Zolotaia Orda v stanovlenii kultury evraziiskih narodov* (Moscow, 2003), 95–102.

The chronicle has been published twice: Kefeli Ibrahim, *Tevarih-i Tatar Han*; and Kefeli Ibrahim Efendi, *Tevarihi Tatar Han ve Dagistān, Moskov ve Deşt-i Kıpçak Ülkelerinindir*, ed. Seyyid Ahmed Kırımlı (Pazarcık, 1933). There is also a rather rough Polish translation, cf. Abdullah Zihni Soysal (ed. and trans.), *Z dziejów narodów Kaukazu, Nadczarnomorza, Krymu, Moskwy i Polski* (Warsaw, 1935).

144 U. Demir, "Muhayyel bir Kirim Tarihçisi Kefevî Ibrahim Efendi ve Humbaracıbaşi Ahmed Paşa'nin Rusya'ya Dair Raporu," *Türkiyat Mecmuası* 24 (2014), 23–32, 28.

145 R. Dankoff, *An Ottoman Mentality: The World of Evliya Çelebi* (Leiden and Boston, 2004), 20–38.

146 Evliya Çelebi, *Tam Metin Seyahatnâme*, vol. 7. ed. Mümin Çevik (Istanbul, 1985). The importance of Evliya Çelebi's accounts are clear: numerous editions comprising parts of or the whole text have been translated. For another complete edition based on the original text, see Y. Dağlı and S.A. Kahraman (eds.), *Evliya Çelebi Seyahatnamesi*, 10 vols. (Istanbul, 2008). I also used the heavily annotated translation of his account concerning travel through the Crimea that is included in the Polish edition; A. Abrahamowicz, A. Dubiński, and S. Płaskowicka-Rymkiewicz (trans.), *Księga podróży Ewliji Czelebiego (Wybór)* (Warsaw, 1969).

147 Numerous scholars have pointed out that Evliya's account is not necessarily reliable in terms of the number of objects and places he describes. He was also accused of patterning villages and their social and administrative organization on "ideally" organized Ottoman settlements. He tended to refer to books he had not read and quote inscriptions and descriptions of places he had not seen. Nevertheless, his writing is recognized as a very important part of Ottoman narrative literature.

148 On the Ottoman perception of the Tatars, see D. Klein, "Tatar and Ottoman History Writing," in *The Crimean Khanate Between East and West (15th–18th Century)* (Wiesbaden, 2012), 125–146.

Another narrative source of vital importance is the *Description from the Year 1669*.[149] In 1669, Khan Mehmed IV Giray sent an envoy, Mustafa Ağa, to the Danish king, Frederick III. During his stay in Copenhagen, a Danish clerk asked the envoy to describe the current political situation and main state institutions of the khanate. The clerk wrote down the information he collected in German and entitled his report, *Description from the Year 1669*. Unfortunately, the description contains numerous misspellings and some facts are unintentionally distorted. This should come as no surprise, as the author had very limited knowledge of the Crimean Khanate. Moreover, it seems that he was only able to communicate with Mustafa Ağa with the help of an interpreter. Despite these drawbacks, the report provides us with one of the most detailed descriptions of everyday life in the khan's palace. Finally, it contributes to our knowledge about the staffing of the Crimean offices.

In addition to the sources above, we must introduce narrative sources written by Europeans, though it is beyond the scope of the present book to discuss the ways in which the Tatars were described in European sources. For this reason, we limit ourselves to a few remarks that may be valuable to properly understand the most commonly used sources.

We propose to divide the European accounts on the Crimean Khanate into three main groups: (1) diplomatic reports written for the use of state administration, (2) travelogues of private individuals, composed for the amusement of their readers, and (3) in-depth descriptions of the khanate made by diplomats and targeted at officials and readers from cultured classes.

Diplomatic reports seem to be less prone to deliberate distortion of the facts than travel literature. The delivery of an accurate account was one of the aims of official missions. Diplomats, who rarely knew either Ottoman or Tatar languages, frequently brought interpreters with them to aid in their contacts with the local elite. With the help of interpreters, diplomats could speak with the most influencial Crimean officials and the khan himself. Diplomats, who were frequently suspected of spying, were subject to various restrictions, which limited the scope of their activity. If the Tatars had unfriendly relations with a given European ruler, his envoys might face imprisonment, as we know from the example of a few Polish and Russian diplomats. In such unfavorable circumstances, they were unlikely to offer valuable eyewitness accounts on the social and political institutions of the khanate. We should point to another drawback of diplomatic reports. As their authors associated themselves with the highest circles in the Crimean Khanate, they rarely described the daily lives

149 J. Matuz (ed.), "Eine Beschreibung des Khanats der Krim aus dem Jahre 1669," *Acta Orientalia (Havniae)* 28 (1964), 129–151.

of common local people. In the present study, we have used the diplomatic reports of the following authors: Ivan Sudakov, a Muscovite envoy to the Crimean Khanate in the years 1587–88;[150] Ławryn Piaseczyński, a Polish nobleman and envoy to the Crimean Khanate in the years 1601–03;[151] Ambrosii Lodizhenski and Petr Danilov, Muscovite envoys to the Crimean Khanate in 1613;[152] Vasilii Mikhailovich Tiapkin and Nikita Zotov, Muscovite envoys to the Crimean Khanate in 1680–81;[153] Nazar Melnikov and Fedor Martynov, Muscovite envoys to the Crimean Khanate in 1682;[154] Nikita Tarakanov and Petr Burtsov, Muscovite envoys to the Crimean Khanate in 1682–83;[155] Kiril Khlapov and Timotei Protopopov, Muscovite envoys to the Crimean Khanate in 1683;[156] Vasilii Aitemiriev, a Muscovite envoy to the Crimean Khanate in 1692–95;[157] and Xavier Glavani, a French consul in Bahçesaray in the 1720s and the 1730s.[158] With exception of Piaseczyński and Glavani, these reports were written by the Russian envoys. The tsar's representatives were carefully chosen for diplomatic missions to the Crimea. Usually, the job was given to two types of men, experienced diplomats, such as Vasilii Tiapkin or Nikita Tarakanov, or high-ranking clerks like Nikita Zotov or Petr Burtsov.

---

150 F. Lashkov (ed.), "Stateinyi spisok moskovskogo poslannika v Krym Ivana Sudakova v 1587–1588 godu," *ITUAK* 14 (1891), 43–80.

151 Ł. Piaseczyński, "Trzy poselstwa Ławryna Piaseczyńskiego do Kazi Gereja chana perekopskich Tatarów," ed. K. Puławski, *Przewodnik Naukowy i Literacki* 39 (1911), 135–145, 244–256, 358–366; 467–472, 553–566, 645–660, 756–768, 845–864, 945–960. A high-ranking clerk in the Polish Crown Chancellary, Piaseczyński was considered an expert on the Crimean Khanate.

152 A.A. Sergeyev (ed.), "Posolstvo Ambrosiia Lodyzhenskago i podiachago Petra Danilova v Krym v 1613 godu (k 300-letnemu iubileiu Tsarstvuiushchago Doma Romanovykh", *ITUAK* 50 (1913), 7–56.

153 N. Murzakevich (ed.), "Spisok s stateinago spiska velikago gosudaria ego tsarskago velichestva poslannikov," *ZOOID* 2 (1850), 558–658.

154 RGADA, Fond 123, *Posol'skii prikaz. Krymskie dela*, op. 1, no. 67, fols. 24–94; Fond 123, op. 1, no. 68, fols. 37–38.

155 RGADA, Fond 123, *Posol'skii prikaz. Krymskie dela*, op. 1, no. 71, fols. 55–104.

156 RGADA, Fond 123, *Posol'skii prikaz. Krymskie dela*, op. 1, no. 72, fols. 1–562.

157 A.I. Markievich (ed.), "Spisok s stateinogo spiska podiachago Vasilia Aitemirieva, posyl'annogo v Krym s predl'ozheniiem mirnykh dogovorov (7200/1692–7203/1695)," Part 1, *ZOOID* 18 (1895): 1–47; Part 2, *ZOOID* 19 (1896): 1–58.

158 Xavier Glavani was in the service of Marquis de Villeneuve, the French ambasador in Istanbul (1728–41). There, he met Mengli II Giray, who was appointed the Crimean khan in 1729. Before his departure to the Crimea, Mengli Giray offered Glavani a post as his personal doctor. France eagerly supported the proposal, as it was a perfect opportunity to place a French diplomat at the khan's court. For the next decade, Glavani served as both a doctor and a French consul in Bahçesaray. For more on Glavani, see G. Veinstein, "La révolte des mirza tatars contre le khan 1724–1725," *CMRS* 12, no. 3 (1971), 327–338.

In contrast to diplomats, private individuals moved in rather less exalted circles. They tended to be more interested in the description of day-to-day life and the natural environment than in the contemporary political situation. Unfortunately, in case of the Crimea, such travelogues only date back to the second half of the eighteenth century. Moreover, with the exception of Nikolaus Ernst Kleemann, their authors visited the peninsula only after the Russian annexation. Therefore, they described the Crimea in the process of changes initiated by Russian administrative and social reforms. As some of them were the tsar's employees, they responded favorably to the new policy conducted by Russian officials and described it as the peaceful modernization of the backward Tatar society. Such a view was rooted in Enlightenment theories that extolled the European mission in non-European societies.[159] In the present study, I used the accounts of the following authors: Nikolaus Ernst Kleemann, a merchant who visited the Crimea in the years 1770–71;[160] Elizabeth Craven, an English gentlewoman who traveled through Europe, Russia, and the Crimea to Constantinople in 1785–86;[161] Peter Simon Pallas, a member of the Russian Academy of Sciences, whose description of the Black Sea region has long been recognized as one of the most reliable sources for the history of this territory;[162] Maria Guthrie, an Englishwoman-savant from the end of the eighteenth century who worked as the directress of the Imperial Convent for the Education of the Female Nobility of Russia, and who visited the Crimea in 1795–96;[163] Mary Holderness, a well-educated middle-class Englishwoman who resided in Kara Göz in the Crimean Peninsula (1816–20).[164]

Finally, there are a few accounts written by diplomats that are similar to the travelogues written by private individuals. These authors depicted the government, natural enviroment, culture, and the way of life of the natives in detail. The writings of such author-diplomats mentioned below contain complete descriptions of the khanate: Wenclaw Mikołajewicz from Mojszagoła, also known as Michalon Litwin, a Lithuanian nobleman sent as an envoy to the

159 I. Kamps and G. Singh (eds.), *Travel Knowledge: European "Discoveries" in the Early Modern Period* (New York, 2001).

160 N. Kleemann, *Voyage de Vienne à Belgrade et à Kilianova,* (Neuchatel, 1780); K.S. Jobst, *Die Perle des Imperiums. Der russische Krim-Diskurs im Zarenreich* (Konstanz, 2007), 88–92.

161 E. Craven, *A Journey Through the Crimea to Constantinople* (Dublin, 1786; reprint New York, 1970).

162 P.S. Pallas, *Travels Through the Southern Provinces of the Russian Empire* (London, 1803).

163 M. Guthrie, *A Tour Performed in the Years 1795–6 through the Taurida, or Crimea* (London, 1802).

164 M. Holderness, *Notes Relating to the Manners and Customs of the Grim Tatars* (London, 1821).

Crimean Khanate in 1542–43;[165] Marcin Broniewski, a Polish nobleman sent as an envoy to the Crimean Khanate in 1578, 1587, and 1592;[166] Charles Peysonnel, the French consul in Bahçesaray in 1753–57;[167] Aleksander von Golz, a Prussian envoy to the Crimean Khanate in 1761;[168] and François de Tott, the French consul in the Crimean Khanate in 1767–69.[169]

Many researchers of travel history have noted that authors typically referred to previously written travelogues rather than produce original descriptions. Often, earlier travelogues were treated as a kind of "travel guide." Maria Guthrie, for instance, compared almost every place she visited in the Crimea with relevant passages written by earlier travelers, such as Elizabeth Craven and Peter Simon Pallas.[170] Moreover, the origins and the education of the authors determined the way in which they described far-away countries and their descriptions of the Crimea. These authors were inspired by and well-read in classical literature. Passages concerning the ancient glory of Taurida were compared to the barbarous conduct of the Tatars and noted along with remarks on the "righteousness" of simple nomads; this exemplified the influence of their classical education. Such attitudes are clearly visible in the sixteenth-century accounts written, for example, by Michalon Litwin or Marcin Broniewski. This also characterizes the eighteenth-century descriptions authored, for instance, by Peter Simon Pallas or Marie Guthrie. For these reasons, European descriptions of the Crimea should be cautiously filtered when used.

---

165 J. Ochmański, "Michalon Litwin i jego traktat o zwyczajach Tatarów, Litwinów i Moskwicinów z połowy XVI wieku," *KH* 83, no. 4 (1976), 765–783; N. Kalachov (ed.), "Desiat otkrytkov razhnoobraznogo istoricheskogo soderzhaniia (iz sochinieniia) Mikhalona Litvina 'O pravakh tatar, litovcev i moskvitian,'" in *Arkhiv istoriko-iuridicheskikh svedenij otnosiavshikh do Rossii*, ed. S.D. Shestov (Moscow, 1854), 2–77; Michalon Litwin (Mykolas Lietuvis), *O pravakh tatar, litovcev i moskvitian*, trans. V. Matuzova, ed. A. Khoroshkevich (Moscow, 1994).

166 S. Albrecht, "Die 'Tartariae Descriptio' des Martinus Broniovius. Enstehung und Wirkung eines Gesandtenberichts aud dem Krimkhanate," in *The Crimean Khanate Between East and West (15th–18th Century)*, ed. D. Klein (Weisbaden, 2012), 149–168; K. Chodynicki, "Marcin Broniewski," *PSB* 2:461–462 (Warsaw, 1925); M. Broniewski, *Tartariae Descriptio* (Cologne, 1595); M. Broniewski, "Opisanie Kryma," *ZOOID* 6 (1867), 333–365; M. Broniewski, *Tartariae Descriptio: Opis Tatarii*, trans. E. Śnieżewska, ed. M. Mączyńska (Łódź, 2011).

167 C. Peysonnel, *Traité sur le commerce de la mer noire* (Paris, 1787).

168 T. Mundt, *Krim-Girai, Khan of the Crimea* (London, 1856).

169 F. Tott, *Mémoires sur les Turcs et les Tatares*, 2 vols. (Amsterdam, 1784); English edition = *Memoirs of the Baron de Tott on the Turks and the Tatars* (London, 1785); Polish edition = *Opisy Turków i Tatarów* (Warsaw, 1791).

170 Guthrie, *A Tour Performed*, 61.

CHAPTER 1

Murad Giray and His Times

1 The Context of the Crimean Khanate Ruled by Murad Giray

The short reign of Murad Giray (1678–83), son of Mubarek Giray Sultan, coincided with a groundbreaking period in the relations between the Ottoman Empire and its European neighbors. The new khan replaced Selim I Giray, who was deposed by the Ottomans as a result of the defeat of the Ottoman-Crimean army during the first siege of Chyhyryn (1677). This unsuccessful campaign was linked to the northeastern policy of the Sublime Porte. The Ottomans were deeply concerned with the Polish-Russian truce of Andrushovo in 1667. The agreement sanctioned the division of Ukraine into two parts, i.e., the Left Bank Ukraine, ruled by Hetman Ivan Samoilovich, who recognized Russian patronage, and the Right Bank Ukraine, ruled from Chyhyryn by Hetman Petro Doroshenko, who in 1667 still recognized Polish suzerainty. Moreover, the Polish-Lithuanian Commonwealth had to agree to other territorial concessions to achieve peace with Muscovy. To sum up, the Truce of Andrusovo strengthened the position of Muscovy vis-à-vis the Polish-Lithuanian Commonwealth. For this reason, it posed a threat to the Ottoman's Crimean policy of maintaining a balance of power between the two northern states. The peace, therefore, changed the political situation in the Black Sea region unfavorably for Bahçesaray and Istanbul. Moreover, the Ottomans and the Tatars were faced, once again, with the problem of the raids by the Cossacks, who were no longer involved in the Polish-Russian conflict. Doroshenko, however, preferred to become an Ottoman vassal, and thus have a new chance to unite the Ukrainian territories divided between Moscow and Warsaw, rather than pillage Turkish and Tatar territories. The Ottoman sultan, who formally accepted Doroshenko as his vassal in 1669, was well aware that the Cossacks could be very dangerous allies if not properly handled. The Ottomans could not give the task of commanding them to the Crimean Khanate, the Cossacks' former rival in the Black Sea region. The Tatars, even if they had been trusted, were not powerful enough to control the Cossacks. According to Dariusz Kołodziejczyk, the supervision of the new vassal was an important reason for the Ottoman conquest of Podolia (1672).[1] In 1676, the Ottoman Empire and the Polish-Lithuanian Commonwealth concluded the Armistice

1 Kołodziejczyk (ed.), *The Ottoman Survey Register*, 3–5.

 | DOI:10.1163/9789004384323_003

of Zhuravno, which ensured the Ottoman possession of Podolia till 1683. The truce enabled the Sublime Porte to go to war with Muscovy over control of the Right Bank Ukraine in 1677. The Ottoman army only succeeded in conquering the most important fortress of the region, i.e., Chyhyryn, at the end of the second campaign (autumn 1678). This victory hastened the end of the war and the Ottoman-Russian peace that was concluded in Bahçesaray in 1681. The negotiations resulted in two documents: a treaty between Murad Giray and Tsar Fedor Alekseevich, and the khan's *temessük*[2] containing provisions of the future Ottoman-Russian treaty. According to the traditional pattern, the conditions of the latter were first negotiated and ratified by the khan. Then, the Crimean ruler sent the aforementioned *temessük* to the grand vizier, who in turn presented it to the sultan for approval. The Ottoman ruler issued another document to confirm his acceptance of the provisions negotiated by the khan. Subsequently, Russian envoys arrived in Istanbul to ask the sultan to issue a formal *'ahdname*,[3] in accordance with the Tatar-Russian agreement stipulated in Bahçesaray. Eventually, Mehmed IV issued the demanded instrument of peace, which consisted of provisions negotiated in Bahçesaray, with some minor additions.[4]

The Treaty of Bahçesaray (1681) prolonged the period of relative peace in the Black Sea region, a peace that began after the second siege of Chyhryn and lasted until 1683. In that year, Murad Giray participated in a new Ottoman campaign, which culminated with the second siege of Vienna. Both the Ottomans and the Tatars tried to name the person responsible for the catastrophe. The Ottoman grand vizier, Kara Mustafa Paşa, pointed at the Crimean khan. Ottoman chroniclers expressed diverging opinions on the subject.[5] Accounts given by Crimean authors provide quite different information on this event. The manner in which Crimean chroniclers presented the reign of Murad Giray suggests that they harbored strong feelings on the subject. Before moving into a detailed analysis of the diverse images of the khan presented by Crimean

2 In Ottoman chancery language, *temessük* referred to a note about state affairs; it was usually sent from a lower official to a higher one.

3 In the Ottoman chancery, the term *'ahdname* referred to a treaty unilaterally granted by the Ottoman sultan to a foreign ruler.

4 C.B. O'Brien, "Russia and Turkey, 1677–1681: The Treaty of Bakhchisarai," *Russian Review* 12, no. 4 (1953), 259–268; Smirnov, *Rossia i Turtsia*, 165–168; *Polnoe sobranie zakonov rossiiskoi imperii* (St. Petersburg, 1830), 2:290–292, 389–392.

5 While Cebeci Hasan Esiri (a participant of the Vienna campaign, his dates of birth and death remain unknown), and Defterdar Sarı Mehmed Paşa (1656?–1717) blamed Murad Giray, Huseyn Hezarfen (ca. 1611–1691/2) maintained that the grand vizier was responsible for the defeat. Silahdar Mehmed Ağa (1654–1720) condemned both the khan and the grand vizier for the unsuccessful campaign; see Abrahamowicz (ed.), *Kara Mustafa*, 157–159, 219, 252, 298.

historians, we first present how Murad Giray was perceived by three European diplomats.[6]

The first account was written by Jan Gniński, a Polish envoy to the Sublime Porte in the years 1677–78. He met Murad Giray in Istanbul at the beginning of 1678, when the latter was appointed khan. The Polish envoy thus witnessed the khan's first political acts prior to his departure to the Crimea (on 27 February 1678). In Gniński's writings, the khan appears as a reasonable and cautious statesman, who had a realistic outlook on the khanate's place in international diplomacy. This realism is clearly visible in his stance during the Polish-Ottoman negotiations that preceded the Treaty of Gniński in 1678. When Gniński asked Murad Giray to persuade the Ottoman grand vizier to return two frontier fortresses (Bar and Medzhybizh) to the Poles, the khan rejected the request, as he was fully aware that his position was not influential enough to persuade the Ottomans to soften their policy toward the Polish-Lithuanian Commonwealth.[7]

The Russian envoys to the Crimean Khanate in the years 1680–81, Vasilii Tiapkin and Nikita Zotov, shared Gniński's view of Murad Giray and presented the khan as a reasonable statesman. We should note that their mission was by no means an easy or pleasant task. The Tatar-Russian negotiations started cordially, but tensions soon developed. Subsequently, the envoys were imprisoned for a few weeks. Despite these difficulties, their report gives evidence of the substantive negotiations led by the khan and his officials. Moreover, Tiapkin and Zotov draw our attention to the khan's authority and the respect his vassals had for him. The envoys also provide us with information about the outward appearance of the khan, whom they portrayed as an impressive person. Murad Giray, according to their description, was a tall and handsome middle-aged man with dark hair and a well-grown beard. During his audience with the Russian envoys, he was dressed in red and green clothes of very good quality; these were designed in a mixed Turkish-Tatar style.[8]

2 Murad Giray as Viewed by Crimean Chroniclers

In contrast to the two European descriptions, the authors of the Crimean chronicles, such as Mehmed Giray, Mehmed Seyyid Riza, Abdulgaffar el-Kırımi,

---

6 Kazembeg (ed.), [*Seyyid*] *Muhammad Riza*, 184–186; Abdulgaffar Kyrymi, *Umdet al-akhbar*, 147; Halim Giray, *Gülbünü Hânân* (ed. Günay, Başer, and Günaydın), 71; Köhbach (ed.), "Der Tarih-i Mehemmed Giray," 157.

7 F. Pułaski (ed.), *Źródła do poselstwa Jana Gnińskiego wojewody chełmińskiego do Turcyi w latach 1677–1678* (Warsaw, 1907), 64–80, 298–301.

8 Murzakevich (ed.), "Spisok s stateinago spiska," 568–658, esp. 583–584.

and Halim Giray, differed in their opinions on Murad Giray. Below we discuss the descriptions of these chroniclers in matters such as Murad Giray's life prior to his reign, his internal policy, his foreign policy, his character, and finally, his role in the Vienna campaign. These sections are followed by an attempt to understand the ambiguities that we encounter in these descriptions.

2.1 *Murad Giray's Life Prior to His Reign*

"The Seven Planets" of Seyyid Mehmed Riza contains the most detailed description of Murad Giray's life before he ascended to the throne. The khan was a son of Mubarek Giray Sultan, who spent his life in Yambol[9] as one of the Giray princes supported and controlled by the Ottoman Empire. After his father's death, Murad Giray was cared for by his uncle Rezmi Bahadır Giray. According to the chronicler, his other uncle Mehmed IV Giray (1654–66) appointed him as his *nuraddin*.[10] After the deposition of Mehmed IV Giray, Murad Giray spent twelve years in a village near Yambol.

Riza states that Kara Mustafa Paşa designated Murad Giray as khan in the month of Zilhicce 1088/Jan.–Feb. 1678. Murad Giray appointed Tohtamış Giray, a son of his uncle Safa Giray, as his *kalga* and Saadet Giray, son of Kırım Giray, as his *nuraddin*. Unfortunately, other chroniclers did not add to our knowledge about Murad Giray's life prior to his ascendance to the throne.

2.2 *Murad Giray's Domestic Policy*

The chronicles provide us with just two stories about Murad Giray's domestic policy. Our description begins with a fascinating anecdote written by Mehmed Seyyid Riza. It concerns the reign of Murad Giray shortly before he set out on the Vienna campaign. According to the chronicler, the ruler decided to replace the sharia with Mongol law. Instead of calling the chief judge '*kadıasker*' (a title etymologically linked to Arabic), the khan named a new official *töre başı*, and gave him judicial control over the khanate.[11] This official was to be responsible

9 Yambol (Tk. Yanbolu) is a town in Southeastern Bulgaria. In the Ottoman Empire it was the center of the judicial district (*kaza*) situated in the Özü province (*eyalet*). Deposed Crimean khans and other Giray princes were sent there to live comfortable lives under Ottoman control. For the Sublime Porte, they, as well as their relatives settled on the island of Rhodes, constituted a reserve of potential Crimean khans, *kalgas*, and *nuraddins*. When needed, they could replace insubordinate Tatar dignitaries.

10 The table of the khans, *kalgas*, and *nuraddins* included in the edition of documents *Le khanat de Crimée* erroneously lists Murad Giray, the brother of Mehmed IV Giray, as the khan's *nuraddin*. Actually, this post was held by the future khan Murad Giray (1678–83), who was a nephew of Mehmed IV Giray; Bennigsen, et al. (eds.), *Le khanat de Crimée*, 364.

11 This title consists of two Turkish words: the term *töre* referred to Chingisid law while *baş* means "a head." The term composed of these two words, combined in a typical Turkish

for applying the Chingisid law (*töre-i cingiziyye*). Seyyid Mehmed Riza states that the khan perceived the sharia as a means by which the Ottomans maintained their influence over the khanate; therefore, he sought to gain independence from the Ottoman Empire by eliminating the sharia. Riza describes Murad Giray's reforms as short-lived. The khan was forced to cancel them as a result of the protests of his subjects, who remained dissatisfied with the newly introduced norms and prescriptions. Vani Mehmed Efendi, a famous derviş and the favorite preacher of Sultan Mehmed IV, played an important role in the khan's decision to return to the Islamic law.[12]

Abdulgaffar el-Kırımi's account was much shorter than that of Riza. His notes on the internal policy of the khan are limited to brief complaints about the ruler's attitude toward the Şirins, the most influential aristocratic family in the Crimea. In the eyes of the chronicler, a client of the Şirins, Murad Giray did not think highly of them and favored the Mansurs, the second most powerful family. The chronicler underlines that the Mansurs, in comparison to the Şirins, were only partly settled on the peninsula, while another branch inhabited the Nogay Steppes. As a result of the khan's policy, which was aimed at putting more power into the hands of "uncivilized" nomads, Abdulgaffar el-Kırımi reported that the Crimea was not at peace.[13] If Abdulgaffar el-Kırımi's story is factual, this probably means that Murad Giray, like numerous predecessors, tried to pit the two most important *karaçı* families against each other. Not much earlier, in 1667, at the request of Adil I Giray, the Mansurs played an important role in punishing the Şirins, who had refused to take part in a military campaign against Muscovy.[14]

---

construction, means "the head of the Chingisid law," i.e., "the head judge of the Chingisid law." Interestingly, in the sixteenth century, the chief military judge of the khanate was titled not only *kadıasker*, but also *hakim-i cünd-i hani*, i.e., "the judge of khan's army." The latter title consists of words of Arabic and Mongol origin; see the letter from Tengri Kutlu(?) (the *hakim-i cünd-i hani*) to the Polish king, Zygmunt August sent on 17 June 1572; Archiwum Główne Akt Dawnych [i.e., Main Archives of Early Acts, Warsaw; henceforth AGAD], Archiwum Koronne Warszawskie [i.e., Crown Archives of Warsaw; henceforth AKW], Dz. tatarski, k. 65, t. 68, no. 644, fol. 2. In seventeenth-century court registers, we encounter two forms of the title: *kadı bi'l-cünd* and *kadı bi'l-asker* (ORRNB, Fond 917, *defter* 22/1a/1, *defter* 34/ab/1).

12 Kazembeg (ed.), [*Seyyid*] *Muhammad Riza*, 188–189. Possible reasons for the reform described by Seyyid Mehmed Riza were discussed by R. Pochekaev. He believes that it was meant to strengthen the position of the khanate in relation to the Ottoman Empire; see R. Pochekaev, "Kırım Hanı Murat Giray'ın Adli Reformu," *Belleten* 75 (2011), 571–578.

13 Abdulgaffar Kyrymi, *Umdet al-akhbar*, 147.

14 Abrahamowicz, Dubiński, and Płaskowicka-Rymkiewicz (trans.), *Księga podróży Ewliji Czelebiego*, 356–361; Evliya Çelebi, *Tam Metin Seyahatnâme*, 617–622. It is noteworthy that Abdulgaffar elKırımi's description of Adil Giray's reign is also very short and negative. The

In light of these two brief cases, it becomes clear that Murad Giray was perceived by the next generations of Tatars as a ruler who tried, by the means at his disposal, to strengthen his power in relation to the Ottomans and his own most powerful vassals. Seyyid Mehmed Riza and el-Kırımi do not credit him with political intuition or knowledge of his own people. Their stories reveal a picture of a power-hungry ruler who destabilized the social order. His attempt to bring about a return to Mongol law was directed against the Islamic/Ottoman influence in Tatar society. In addition, the support of the semi-nomadic Mansurs threatened the settled way of life exemplified by the "civilized" Şirins.

Mehmed Giray, the only author who witnessed Murad Giray's reign, left us a very different description. He depicted Murad Giray as a righteous and wise ruler admired by his subjects.[15]

2.3 *Murad Giray's Foreign Policy*

Until the Vienna campaign, the chronicles only inform us about one aspect of Murad Giray's foreign policy: his relations with Muscovy. This is understandable, as these relations constituted the most important field for Murad Giray's diplomacy.

Seyyid Mehmed Riza blamed the short-tempered ruler for the loss of Crimean control over Ottoman-Russian relations. According to the chronicler, Murad Giray, who was offended by a Russian envoy, ordered the envoy publicly humiliated by making him ride on a donkey. Halim Giray likewise stated that Muscovite rulers had maintained diplomatic relations with Ottoman sultans through the mediation of Crimean khans until the reign of Murad Giray. Because the khan insulted a Russian envoy, the tsar sent his diplomats directly to the sultan.[16] The last part of this story seems to have been copied from Seyyid Mehmed Riza. Interestingly, neither Riza nor Halim Giray claim that Tiapkin or Zotov was tortured. Yet, Kirill Kochegarov underlines that, according to the report of the mission of Nikita Tarakanov and Petr Burtsov in 1682–83, the latter was put on a special instrument of torture called "the wooden-mare" by the *nuraddin*, Saadet Giray. The treatment of the two Muscovite envoys remains disputed in Russian historiography. The issue was only recently revisited by Kirill Kochegarov, who claims that the report of Burtsov and Tarakanov is reliable. Yet, Kochegarov points out that whatever the behavior of the *nuraddin*,

---

chronicler states that the khan did not have sound judgment. For this reason, he relied on his vizier, İslam Ağa for guidance in all state affairs. From the description of the preceding reign of Mehmed IV Giray, we learn that elKırımi severely criticized the said vizier (Abdulgaffar Kyrymi, *Umdet al-akhbar*, 144–145).

15 Köhbach (ed.), "Der Tarih-i Mehemmed Giray," 157.

16 Halim Giray, *Gülbünü Hânân* (ed. Günay, Başer, and Günaydın), 71.

Murad Giray refused to break the truce with Muscovy in 1683 when the Polish envoy asked for support in retaking the Left Bank Ukraine.[17] It seems clear, therefore, that the khan had no interest in a conflict with Muscovy in 1683. The report of Burtsov and Tarakanov only confirms the *nuraddin*'s inappropriate behavior. It remains unclear whether the khan authorized the torture of the Russian envoy. Unfortunately, the chronicle of Abdulgaffar el-Kırımi does not broaden our knowledge on Murad Giray's policy toward Muscovy, as the author offers no comment on the subject.

Mehmed Giray's account again contradicts those of the other chroniclers. He praises Murad Giray for the proper way in which he handled relations with Muscovy. The prince states that out of respect for the khan, the tsar sent him *haraç* for three years and then continued to pay the yearly tribute.

We might reasonably ask why Seyyid Mehmed Riza and Halim Giray differed from Mehmed Giray in their opinion on the khan's policy toward Muscovy. Perhaps, it relates to the time in which they wrote their chronicles. In the second half of the eighteenth century, when Seyyid Mehmed Riza completed his work, Russia had become the greatest threat to the Crimean Khanate. The chronicler, therefore, tried to understand the reasons for the change in the khanate's relations with a former tributary state. He clearly held Murad Giray responsible for losing control over Russian-Ottoman relations and, as a consequence, of losing the upper hand in diplomatic relations with Muscovy. As Murad Giray was the last khan to receive the annual payment from Moscow, it is clear why Seyyid Mehmed Riza searched for the origins of the change in precisely that period. Perhaps, Seyyid Mehmed Riza included the incident of the Russian envoy being forced to ride a donkey, because it was less humiliating for the Tatar writer than acknowledging Russian military ascendancy and the khanate's decline. Ascribing blame on a stupid act left some hope for the future. It is noteworthy that Seyyid Mehmed Riza's chronicle was most probably designed to raise the Tatars' spirit by praising their independent and strong khans. Halim Giray likely included the story because, as many others, he simply copied it from Seyyid Mehmed Riza's chronicle.

Two additional factors may have conditioned Mehmed Giray's description of Tatar-Russian relations. First, he generally had a good opinion of Murad Giray's reign. One might perceive the Bahçesaray Treaty of 1681 as a success of Tatar diplomacy. Mehmed Giray, therefore, simply included in his chronicle the facts that spoke in favor of Murad Giray. It is not clear what he knew about

17 K. Kochegarov, "The Moscow Uprising of 1682: Relations Between Russia, the Crimean Khanate, and the Polish-Lithuanian Commonwealth," in *The Crimean Khanate Between East and West (15th–18th Century)*, ed. D. Klein (Wiesbaden, 2012), 59–73.

the Istanbul Treaty of 1700 and its consequences. His description of the beginning of Devlet Giray's reign (1699–1702) is limited to the khan's arrival, his appointments of dignitaries, and his conflicts with family members and vassals. We cannot exclude the possibility that he might not have properly understood the meaning of the khan's exclusion from the mediation between the Russians and Ottomans. Perhaps he did not mention the treaty in his chronicle because he regarded it as an unimportant event and a temporary solution.[18] Second, as Denise Klein points out,

> for the Tatar prince, history writing was an exercise undertaken primarily in order to secure the continuity of the khan's authority and power in a precarious political situation. The author obviously conceived his history as part of a discourse on the state of the Crimean Khanate and the Ottoman Empire.[19]

Klein underlines that Mehmed Giray severely criticized the Ottomans for their interference in the internal policies of the khanate, and their negligence of the Tatar's vital interests in the international arena. The Treaty of Karlowitz was a vivid example of such an attitude. Thus, the Tatar historian could turn a blind eye to the errors of Murad Giray because he believed the Ottoman policy in the north to be the key destructive factor.

2.4 *Murad Giray's Character*

The Crimean chroniclers also differed in their opinions on Murad Giray's character. While Seyyid Mehmed Riza and Abdulgaffar el-Kırımi left rather negative descriptions, Mehmed Giray praised his cousin's personality.

Seyyid Mehmed Riza described Murad Giray as a violent person and a heavy drinker.[20] We must bear in mind that the accusation of alcohol abuse not only

---

18 Mehmed Giray, *Tarih-i Mehemmed Giray*, ÖNB, H.O.86, 104–107. Admittedly, it should be stressed that later chroniclers, for example Abdulgaffar el-Kırımi, Seyyid Mehmed Riza, and Halim Giray, do not provide any real insight into the Istanbul Treaty, although they certainly saw its long-lasting consequences.

19 Klein, "Tatar and Ottoman History Writing," 139.

20 This problem has been discussed by V. Smirnov, who points out that twice in one letter Murad Giray reminded the tsar not to forget to send him vodka. Yet, the Russian envoys in Bahçesaray, who, as noted, prepared very detailed reports, did not allude to the khan as an alcoholic; cf. Smirnov, *Krymskoe khanstvo*, 605–606. We cannot know whether the diplomats had not heard about a drinking problem, or whether they considered drinking vodka as perfectly common behavior not only in their own country, but also in the khanate. From various sources, we learn that Tatars used to drink a lot of *boza* (a beverage made of

raised the issue of his sobriety and judgment, but also his piety. Nonetheless, Seyyid Mehmed Riza admitted that the khan was able to control this weakness. As in the story he related about Murad Giray's attempts to introduce Chingisid law, Murad Giray returned to the Islamic path following the advice of a religious authority. This time, he was guided by a Crimean *şeyh* from Kaçı, whose name was not recorded.[21] In sum, Seyyid Mehmed Riza did not entirely condemn the khan's character. He maintained that the ruler was able to change his wrong decisions when admonished by pious men. Still, the story with the Russian envoy makes it clear that Seyyid Mehmed Riza doubted whether the khan could make proper and responsible decisions on his own. Apparently, the chronicler did not have a high opinion of Murad Giray's intelligence and political intuition.

Halim Giray's description of Murad Giray also contains a passage about a humiliated Russian envoy, which speaks unfavorably about the khan's character. In contrast to Seyyid Mehmed Riza, Halim Giray embellished his brief chapter about Murad Giray with compliments on his generous and kind nature. Still, a comparison with sections about other Crimean khans reveals that the chronicler often included similar remarks in reference to other Crimean rulers. His praises tell us more about his idea of the image of an ideal Islamic ruler than about Murad Giray's character.

Abdulgaffar el-Kırımi did not include his own opinions on the khan's character. Nevertheless, he portrayed him in a rather pejorative way; his short description of Murad Giray's reign consists solely of the story of the aggrieved Şirins and the catastrophe of the Vienna campaign.

In contrast to the above chroniclers' opinions, Mehmed Giray admired Murad Giray for his piety, military skills, and political decisions, which secured his subjects a favorable peace with Russia and economic prosperity. A reader must conclude that the ruler he presents was an intelligent person. In his cousin's view, Murad Giray also possessed self-control, as he calmly accepted his deposition.

As noted, two divergent descriptions of Murad Giray's character were maintained to the end of the eighteenth century. It is hard to reconcile Seyyid Mehmed Riza's or Abdulgaffar el-Kırımi's image of the khan with that of Mehmed Giray. The khan's determination and bravery may be the only commonalities and central aspects of his image. We can be certain that no chronicler ever described him as indecisive or a coward.

---

fermented millet); see Abrahamowicz, Dubiński, and Płaskowicka-Rymkiewicz (trans.), *Księga podróży Ewliji Czelebiego*, 296–297; Evliya Çelebi, *Tam Metin Seyahatnâme*, 360.

21 Kazembeg (ed.), [*Seyyid*] *Muhammad Riza*, 184.

2.5 *Murad Giray's Role in the Vienna Campaign and His Deposition*

The chroniclers that were critical toward Murad Giray's deposition commented on the second siege of Vienna, but only briefly. Seyyid Mehmed Riza states that

> Sadrazam Kara Mustafa Paşa did with Murad Giray exactly the same as with Selim Giray, i.e., he sent numerous letters to the sultan in which he shifted the blame for the defeat onto the khan. [Through these letters] he caused the deposition of the khan in Şevval 1094 [Sept.–Oct. 1683].[22]

Interestingly, Seyyid Mehmed Riza did not express his opinion on Murad Giray's role in the Vienna campaign. We cannot know what his comparison of the khan's deposition to that of Selim I Giray may have meant. Seyyid Mehmed Riza explicitly praised the latter. For this reason, the analogy between the two depositions may be a favorable characterization of Murad Giray. Perhaps indirectly, Seyyid Mehmed Riza did not consider him guilty of the defeat in Vienna. Yet, the comparison to Selim I Giray seems obvious. The latter reigned directly before Murad Giray and was deposed because of the Ottoman-Tatar failure during the first siege of Chyhyryn (1677).

Abdulgaffar el-Kırımi and Halim Giray openly criticized Murad Giray's role in the Vienna campaign. The former blamed the khan for the defeat, and also stated that Murad Giray was deposed for his negligence in this Ottoman campaign.[23] Halim Giray notes that Murad Giray was deposed in the vicinity of Varaždin[24] because he failed to carry out his responsibilities toward the Ottoman Empire.[25]

Mehmed Giray, who took part in the Vienna campaign, praised Murad Giray's military skills. He states that the infidels trembled with fear before the khan. For the chronicler, there is no doubt who was responsible for the defeat in 1683: Kara Mustafa Paşa postponed attacking the city because he did not want to share the booty with the janissaries.[26] Apparently, the grand vizier

---

22 Kazembeg (ed.), [*Seyyid*] *Muhammad Riza*, 184–186.

23 Abdulgaffar Kyrymi, *Umdet al-akhbar*, 147.

24 Varaždin was an important fortress in the valley of Drawa River. The Ottomans never conquered it from the Habsburgs, though they plundered its surroundings several times.

25 Halim Giray, *Gülbünü Hânân* (ed. Günay, Başer, and Günaydın), 71.

26 Mehmed Giray was not the only chronicler to state that the delay in storming Vienna was a result of financial, not military reasons. A Jewish chronicle from Buda, written by Issack ben Zalman Schulhof after the year 1688, attributes the following to Kara Mustafa Paşa: "Se occuperemo la città sarà preda dei soldati e verrà disperso, cosicché il sultano

hoped that Vienna would surrender to him. According to Islamic law, the army had the right to pillage a city if it was captured in battle. As a result, the vizier's decision, against the good advice of the khan, brought dishonor to the entire Muslim army. The delay, as Mehmed Giray correctly reported, enabled the Polish king and the German emperor to capture the hills near Vienna and attack the Muslims. Although the Tatars fought bravely against the infidels, they could not hold off the enemy.

Kara Mustafa Paşa desperately wanted to find a scapegoat for the defeat. He blamed the khan and proposed that he be deposed. The khan's vassals opposed it and swore to be faithful to him even against the order of the Ottoman grand vizier. Except for the treacherous Hacı Giray Sultan, no other member of the ruling dynasty accepted Kara Mustafa Paşa's proposition to be khan of the Crimean throne. Yet, Murad Giray did not oppose the vizier's will, because according to Mehmed Giray, he held a much more pessimistic view of his vassals' loyalty. According to the chronicler, he stated: "Until now the Crimean people have never been seen to remain faithful to their oath and to keep their promise."[27] Apparently the khan thought that his vassals' support was unreliable. The ruler who was not backed by the Porte could expect a rebellion by his vassals. Murad Giray appears to have thought that he could not control his own state, therefore he chose safe retirement in Rumelia. Denise Klein's important remarks contribute to our understanding of this chronicle. As she points out, Mehmed Giray held a very pessimistic view of the khans' ability to shape domestic and foreign policy of the khanate at the turn of the eighteenth century. As she convincingly demonstrates, the chronicler perceived the Crimean khans of the period as powerless rulers who faced dethronement if they displeased the Ottomans or their own noble vassals.[28]

---

non ne riceverà per nulla o ne avrà soltanto una minima parte. Perciò é meglio per noi se per ora non ricorrememo all'assalto, afffamando invece la città con l'assedio e, quando il peso della fame graverà su di essa, ci si sottometterà, consegnandosi nelle nostre mani e offrendoci anche gli antichi tesori e un grande riscatto, e tutto ciò finirà nelle tesorerie del sultano"; I. Schulhoff, *Megilat Oven*, ed. and trans. P. Agostino (Rome, 1982), 35. Zygmunt Abrahamowicz also studied the financial aspects of the second siege of Vienna and suggested that Kara Mustafa Paşa deliberately postponed the storming of the city to avoid its pillage; Z. Abrahamowicz, "Tło polityczne i ekonomiczne wyprawy wiedeńskiej Kary Mustafy," *Kwartalnik Historyczny* 90 (1983), 21–54.

27 Köhbach (ed.). "Der Tarih-i Mehemmed Giray," 157.

28 D. Klein, *'Das Chaos der Welt' Ein krimtatarischer Blick auf die Zeit um 1700* in *Şehrâyîn*, ed. Y. Köse with of T. Völker (Wiesbaden, 2012), 157–172.

2.6 *Murad Giray—A Pious Muslim Warrior (gazi) or a Drunken Troublemaker?*

It is clear that the Crimean chroniclers viewed Murad Giray in much different ways. The reasons for such diverse opinions merit further deliberation. As noted, the differences between the chronicles might result from the times in which they were written. There is a difference of over fifty years between Mehmed Giray's chronicle and that of the other three. While Mehmed Giray was an eyewitness to the events he described, the latter three relied on oral traditions and written sources, some of which have not survived to our time. It seems that Mehmed Giray's chronicle was not used as a source by other chroniclers.

It is not altogether clear how the three later chroniclers chose which stories to include in their descriptions. In the case of Abdulgaffar el-Kırımi,[29] his loyalty to the Şirin family seems to have been his primary interest. Seyyid Mehmed Riza's rather negative account of Murad Giray is a mystery, as it is clear that his chronicle aimed to extol the strong and independent Crimean rulers, and it would seem that Murad Giray had such qualities. We can gain some insight into Halim Giray's chronicle from a remark by Alan Fisher on this historical writing. He states that it is

> the best known of the Tatar histories or chronicles to deal with Crimean affairs independently of Ottoman events.... Halim Giray's book is understandably bitter towards the Russians, the Ottoman government, and also those of his Tatar brothers who worked hard for the *separatism* and independence until the last half of the eighteenth century.[30]

If Halim Giray took Seyyid Mehmed Riza's notice about Murad Giray's aspirations for independence from the Ottomans seriously, it is understandable that he would depict the khan in a rather unfavorable way.

Whether the khan attempted to restore Mongol law merits further research. The Russian diplomatic sources, the *sicil*s of *kadıasker* (April/May 1678–Aug. 1682) and those of the judge of Kara Su (Aug. 1683–Feb. 1684) give no hint that the khan carried out such a reform. The *sicil*s prove that the *kadıasker* or the *kadı* of the most important commercial city of the khanate performed their

29 El-Kırımi's description indicates that the Şirins' conflict with Murad Giray was present in their oral tradition. Yet, neither Mehmed Giray nor the Russian diplomats confirmed its existence. On the contrary, these sources indicate that the khan and the vassals were on good terms; Murzakevich (ed.), "Spisok s stateinago," 631–635.

30 Fisher, *Between Russians*, 80.

usual duties, with the exception of the period between August 1682 and August 1683. This period is not covered by the court registers and was exactly when the reform was supposed to have taken place. However, we must remember that—according to Seyyid Mehmed Riza—Murad Giray was brought to his senses by the sultan's religious adviser; it would have taken time for him to learn the reform and then travel across the Black Sea. We would argue that the continuous and perfectly standard entries in the Kara Su district court register constitute a convincing argument that contradicts Seyyid Mehmed Riza's account. If we imagine, however, that this court register had not survived to our times, we would be obliged to ask numerous questions, such as, what would Murad Giray gain by such a radical reform? Did Chingisid law give the khan a stronger position than the sharia did? Why would Murad Giray limit his reforms to the judicial system? Was its control key to the power in the khanate? Did he not already control the khanate's judicial administration, which was patterned on Ottoman practices? Finally, how did the Tatars define the Chingisid law in the second half of the seventeenth century? This book takes up the issues of the khan's control over the judicial system of the khanate and the relation between sharia and Chingisid law.

To sum up, the chroniclers provide us with two conflicting images of Murad Giray, for some, he was an irresponsible violent ruler, while for others, he was an ideal khan. We would argue that the former, fully expressed by Seyyid Mehmed Riza and copied, to some extent, by Halim Giray, includes at least one story, namely on the introduction of Mongol law, which may be a distortion of the facts. The other image, drafted by Mehmed Giray, appears to be more reliable, but we must bear in mind remarks made by Denise Klein, that the chronicle was "intended as a contribution to the political and moral discourse in a time of crisis."[31] A few existing non-Crimean sources, such as Polish and Russian diplomatic reports, reveal the picture of a responsible ruler who had a very realistic vision of the khanate's modest importance in Europe and its dependence on the Ottomans. Because of that, he went along with Ottoman northern policy. In 1678, he took part in the second Chyhyryn campaign. Then, he concluded peace with Muscovy, although he was displeased with the Russian control over the Left Bank Ukraine, and he encouraged the Cossacks to conduct anti-Russian policies.[32] Yet, he did not risk another military conflict with Muscovy. Perhaps the story of the *nuraddin*'s torture of Tarakanov indicates that some members of the Crimean elites would rather have conducted a less peaceful policy. Nonetheless, Murad Giray remained at peace with Muscovy until the

31 Klein, "Tatar and Ottoman History Writing," 143.

32 Kochegarov, "The Moscow Uprising of 1682," 70.

second siege of Vienna. Presumably, five years of peace on the northern border allowed the khan to center his attention on domestic policy. The entries in the Crimean court registers confirm that during his reign Murad Giray maintained the administrative structure that delivered justice and protected order in his state. In 1683, when Kara Mustafa Pasha blamed him for the Vienna defeat, the khan again acted very reasonably. He accepted his deposition and left the Crimean throne for a safe retirement in Rumelia.

CHAPTER 2

The Household, Deputies, and the Council of the Khan

> The Great Padishah of the Great Horde, the Great Yurt, the Crimean Land, the Kipchak Steppe, innumerable Tatars and uncountable Nogays, numerous tens of thousands [tümens] of the Right Side and the Left Side, of the Tats, Tavgaçes, and Mountain Circassians—illustrious, grand, victorious, and fortunate Murad Giray Khan, may he be blessed…[1]

In the letter his vizier sent to Moscow, Murad Giray was depicted as a powerful ruler of numerous peoples and vast territories. As a member of the Giray dynasty, which traced its descent back to Chingis Khan's older son Djochi, he was a legitimate sovereign of the Tatars. The Mongol origin was essential to the Girays' claim to the Chingisid heritage; it enabled them to secure the dignified position of the Crimean khan for the family members. The tradition, however, led to certain limitations to the khan's power. He was expected to recognize the rights of aristocratic clans to take an active role in state government and to control their own territories. The *beğ*s, in theory, had the same authority in the lands of their clans as the khan had in his proper domain. In daily life, there were only two symbols of the khan's sovereignty over the whole khanate's territory—the right to mint his own coins and to have his name pronounced during the Friday prayer. So, in order to increase their power within their own domains, the khans tried to reshape the socio-political structures dominated by the nobles and inherited from the Golden Horde by introducing institutions patterned on the Ottoman administration. Apparently, the Crimean rulers hoped that this would enable them to become fully sovereign rulers.

In the present Chapter I focuse on the khan's palace, his central and provincial officials, and his servants. I also describe the judicial prerogatives of various branches of the khanate's administration and pay special attention to the court administered by the khan's council. I also discuss the households of the *kalga* and *nuraddin*, the two most important Tatar dignitaries.

Saadet I Giray and Sahib Giray, who spent years at the court of Sultan Suleyman I ('the Lawgiver'), started to reshape the khan's position on the Ottoman model. These reforms of the ruler's household constituted the first step in

1 RGADA, Fond 123, *Posol'skii prikaz. Krymskie dela*, op. 3, no. 212.

 | DOI:10.1163/9789004384323_004

strengthening his power. Maryna Kravets's study on this institution describes it as having a mixture of Golden Horde and Ottoman elements. It is likely that this evolution toward a more Ottomanized form was gradual. The founding of the khan's palace and capital in Bahçesaray, which was attributed to Sahib Giray, constituted an important step in this process. The khan adopted the so-called "harem system," marked by the separation of inner, women's quarters from outer, men's part of the household.[2] Our knowledge about Sahib Giray's palace is limited, since archeological excavations are still unfinished. It is clear, however, that it was divided into mens' and womens' quarters. The life of the court was organized around courtyards.[3] The palace was inhabited by the khan and his family and was surrounded by numerous officials and servants. From the narrative accounts and court records we learn their names and functions. The report of Kiril Khlapov and Timotei Protopopov, the Muscovite envoys to Murad Giray in 1683, contains a list of gifts sent to approximately 200 Crimean officials and dignitaries who did not belong to the Giray dynasty.[4] They were divided into thirty-seven groups, whose members received various gifts of furs and money. The grouping criteria are not completely clear. The *karaçı beğ*s were mentioned separately from other officials. Affiliation with the court of the khan, the *kalga* or the *nuraddin* constituted an important factor in the description of other officials. They were referred to as "people close to the khan/*kalga*/*nuraddin*," "the khan/*kalga*/*nuraddin*'s people," or "the members of the khan's inner retinue." A few groups were not affiliated with any of the three dignitaries of the Giray.[5] The report indicates that the *kalga* and *nuraddin* had separate households, which were dwarfed by that of the khan. Others, such as the *karaçı beğ*s, who were not members of the Giray dynasty, also supported households. The last ones are discussed in Chapter 3. The khanate, therefore, was a state based on a model of extended households. Its center consisted of the khan's household, which, in addition to the ruler, included the royal family, the courtiers, and the government apparatus.

2 Kravets, "From Nomad's Tent," 49; Glavani's report indicates that the harem was not entirely closed to the khan's male guests. He described his visit to see Mengli II Giray, who was eating breakfast in his harem; Veinstein, "Les Tatars de Crimée," 35.

3 Kançal-Ferrari, *Kırım'da Kalan Miras*, 64–66.

4 There are two versions of this, one in Russian in the Cyrillic alphabet and one in Ottoman Turkish, with elements of Crimean Tatar, in the Arabic alphabet.

5 Judging by their titles, they were nobles or the khan's officials. The status of the first group remains unclear. They could be those dependent on the Girays or any of the ruling families; RGADA, Fond 123, *Posol'skii prikaz. Krymskie dela*, op. 4, no. 72, fols. 491–576v.

1 The Khan's Household

1.1 *The Khan's Family*

The khan's household combined Ottoman and Golden Horde elements. Kravets states that

> in several important aspects—architectural features of the harem, seclusion of the harem's inmates, employment of eunuchs, and the harem's internal routine—the khan's household appears to follow closely the Ottoman example. Yet in other features of their life, such as the composition of the royal family, choice of marriage partners, and status of the dynastic ladies, the Crimean ruling family remained remarkably distinctive from the Ottomans. This cultural resilience stemmed mainly from the Gereys' Chinggisid legacy.[6]

In the early khanate, the Girays, as a Chingisid dynasty, enjoyed higher prestige than did the young Ottoman dynasty. Over the course of time, however, the sultans raised the prestige of their dynasty, which came to outrank that of the Girays. Leslie Peirce points out that "with the consolidation of empire, the sultan began to claim a preeminence that dictated a disdain for alliances with lesser powers."[7] As early as the end of the fourteenth century, the Ottoman dynasty "had come to practice reproduction through concubinage to the exclusion of reproduction through legal marriage" with Christian or Muslim princesses.[8] Since the reign of Sultan Suleyman I ('the Lawgiver'), they discontinued the practice of marrying the female relatives of their political partners. The Girays, in contrast to the Ottomans, continued to intermarry with their most important vassals, for example, with the Şirins, the Mangıts/Mansurs[9] and the most influential officials. Moreover, the Girays concluded marriages with the families of Circassian *beğ*s, whom they regarded as their vassals. According to Samuel Proski, a Polish emissary to the Ottoman-Crimean camp near

6 Kravets, "From Nomad's Tent," 52.

7 L. Peirce, *The Imperial Harem: Women and Sovereignty in the Ottoman Empire* (Oxford, 1993), 29–31.

8 Peirce, *Imperial Harem*, 29–31.

9 Ilya Zaitsev's short study on the Giray dynasty offers us data on the Girays' marriages with the Şirins, Mangıts, Seceuts, Kungrats, and with the *seyyids* in the fifteenth and sixteenth centuries; I. Zaitsev, "The Structure of Giray Dynasty (15th–16th Centuries: Matrimonial and Kinship Relations of the Crimean Khanate)," in *Kinship in the Altaic World: Proceedings of the 28th Permanent International Altaistic Conference*, Moscow, 10–15 July 2005, ed. E.V. Boikova and R.B. Rybakov (Wiesbaden, 2006), 341–353.

Chyhyryn in 1678, the eldest son of Murad Giray was absent during the siege because he went to Circassia to marry a daughter of one of the local *beğ*s.[10] The Crimean khans also continued the Mongol custom of levirate marriages.[11] Giving away Giray princesses to their vassals, as Peysonnel's description suggests, enabled the khans to interfere in the clans' inner relations. The French consul reported that the khans used to choose poor members of the ruling families as future in-laws. By giving a princess a considerable dowry, the khan raised the status of her husband, who remained dominated by his wife.[12] The Giray women held two state offices: that of *ana biyim* and *uluğ biyim* (*uluğ hani*), designated for the mother or stepmother of the ruling khan and for the first wife or the eldest Giray princess.[13] The women administered the land that was assigned to their offices. Peysonnel relates that petitioners used to speak with their female masters' legal agents (*vekil*s) near the "Tchoukour" Gate[14] in the harem wall.[15] From the time of Murad Giray, the court registers confirm that the women authorized their agents to take care of the financial and criminal matters of their subjects and slaves.[16]

The extent of the influence of Giray women on state policy merits further deliberation. It is worth asking whether the khans' consorts supported the policies of their clans, or rather, acted in the interests of their royal husbands and sons. It is clear that the Giray women did not exercise as much power as the consorts and female relatives of the Ottoman sultans. Although the former exchanged diplomatic correspondence[17] and received gifts from neighboring

---

10 Pułaski (ed.), *Źródła do poselstwa*, 368.

11 Lane, *Daily Life*, 227.

12 Peysonnel depicted the tragic fate of a Şirin *mirza* who married a daughter of Devlet II Giray (1699–1702, 1708–13). The poor nobleman, almost like Melek Ahmed Paşa in Evliya Çelebi's description, had to wait every evening at the foot of the princess's bed, asking for permission to sleep with her; see Peysonnel, *Traité sur le commerce*, 2:251. For Evliya Çelebi's description of his uncle's nuptial misfortunes, see Evliya Çelebi, *The Intimate Life of an Ottoman Statesman: Melek Ahmed Pasha (1588–1622) as Portrayed in Evliya Çelebi's Book of Travels*, trans. R. Dankoff (Albany, NY, 1991), 233.

13 Peysonnel, *Traité sur le commerce*, 2:321; Święcicka, "The Diplomatic Letters," 59.

14 Evliya Çelebi also mentioned a gate leading directly to the harem (Abrahamowicz, Dubiński, and Płaskowicka-Rymkiewicz (trans.), *Księga podróży Ewliji Czelebiego*, 276; Evliya Çelebi, *Tam Metin Seyahatnâme*, 350–351). Its location remains unclear. As the southern walls of the palace are bordered by a stream named Çürük Su, it is possible that Peyssonel misspelled the gate's name. If so, it might have been situated in the southern part of the harem.

15 Peysonnel, *Traité sur le commerce*, 2:260.

16 For example, the *ulu biyim* of Murad Giray paid blood money to the family of certain Bülbül Ali, who was killed by her slave; ORRNB, Fond 917, *defter* 23a/224b/1.

17 For translations of the letters sent by the *ana biyim* and the *uluğ hani* (*ulu biyim*) of Murad Giray to Leopold I and his wife, see HHStA, Türkei I, Turcica 150 (1680, Jänner-Juni), fols. 75–78; for the letters of Giray ladies to the Swedish queen, Christina, see Święcicka, "The Diplomatic Letters," 68–75.

states,[18] their actual role in foreign policy seems to have been limited. Only a few were described by their contemporaries as the khan's advisers; among them are, for example, Ayşe Sultan, the wife of Devlet I Giray (1551–77)[19] or Emine Sultan Biyim, the wife of Mehmed IV Giray (1642–44; 1654–66).[20] Sometimes they acted as mediators between the khans and the Giray princes who were exiled or imprisoned in foreign countries. Han Tokai, for instance, negotiated with Tsar Fedor I and Tsaritsa Irina on behalf of her son Murad Giray Sultan and his wife, who escaped to Russia. In 1593, after Murad Giray's death, Han Tokai and Gazi II Giray asked the tsar to allow the widow to return to the khanate. Until the 1560s, the Giray women even received Russian envoys, who bowed and presented them with gifts sent by the tsar. From 1564 onward, the women ceased to hold audiences themselves, because, as one envoy reported, it was no longer customary. The royal women started to communicate with envoys through their servants.[21] This fact demonstrates that the Giray princesses had adopted the Muslim custom of female seclusion. Nonetheless, they still took part in foreign policy.[22]

The impact of Giray women on the khanate's internal affairs was not extensively discussed by native and foreign observers. Perhaps the royal women did not wield enough power to interest the diplomats. Kravets suggests that the modest influence of the Giray women on state matters might reflect the khan's relatively weak position. Their close contact with the khan apparently did not secure them real political significance.[23] Other members of the khan's family did not automatically play an important political role either, rather, their influence was limited by, among other factors, relatively modest incomes and their competition with other Girays. Yet, the story of the imprisonment of Father Innocent of Malta in 1636 demonstrates that the Giray women could influence domestic policy.

From the correspondence of the Dominican missionaries, we learn about a sexual scandal involving one of the fathers, namely, Innocent Felici of Malta and a woman from the Italo-Circassian community from Fotsala,[24] who was

18 For gifts sent by the Russian tsar to the mother, four wives, and three sisters of Murad Giray in 1683, see RGADA, Fond 123, *Posol'skii prikaz. Krymskie dela,* op. 4, no. 72, fols. 491–493.

19 A.M. Nekrasov, "Zhenshchiny khanskogo doma Gireev v XV–XVI vv," in *Drevneishie gosudarstva vostochnoi Evropy*, ed. T.M. Kalinina (Moscow, 2000), 213–221.

20 A.Z. Soysal, "Emine Sultan Biyim," *Emel* 52 (1969), 37–38.

21 Nekrasov, "Zhenshchiny khanskogo," 213–221.

22 The female members of the Giray dynasty have not received much scholarly attention. Nur Sultan, the powerful wife of Mengli I Giray, constitutes an exception, see M. Berezhkov, "Nur-Sultan, tsaritsa krymskaia. Istoriko-biograficheskii ocherk," *ITUAK* 27 (1897), 1–17.

23 Kravets, "From Nomad's Tent," 54–55.

24 A seventeenth-century Ottoman register of Kefe province dated 1682 is one of the sources confirming that Fotsala, or Focciola as it was called by the brothers, was indeed inhabited

a milk-sister of one of the khan's wives.[25] Father Innocent Felici of Malta was already on the peninsula in 1625.[26] At the beginning of his mission, he served the local Catholics.[27] During next years, he must have gained the trust of the khan's court, since he was sent as an interpreter of the Tatar envoy to Vienna in 1633.[28] In a letter sent in August 1636, Father Innocent Felici of Malta described to the French Ambassador in Istanbul, Philippe de Harlay the count de Césy, that his fellow missionary Anthony of Flanders[29] was accompanied by a merchant called Mathew (an inhabitant of a village Fotsala), who accused him before the khan's vizier of engaging in an extramarital affair with a local woman for last eight years. After making this allegation, Anthony testified that Father Innocent Felici of Malta embezzled 10,000 sequins given by the emperor in Vienna for a new church.[30] The accused missionary stated that because an accusation of illicit sex was a criminal act, Father Innocent Felici was imprisoned in the home of the khan's captain of musketeers ("un sequestro in casa d'un capitano d'archebugieri del chan con bona custodia"). His friends did not leave him, and he was immediately released, thanks to the intervention of the first wife of the khan ("son stato subito fatto libero p[er] ordine della soltana moglie p[ri]ma del p[re]sente chan").[31] Accusations against Father Innocent

---

by people of mixed Italian (Genovese)-Circassian origins. Here they are called simply "Circassians." See the entry "Fotsala" in Jankowski, *A Historical-Etymological Dictionary*, 475–476; and the *defter* of Kefe province from the year 1682 preserved in the NBKM, Or. Dept., Fond D737, fol. 25v. The Italian missionaries used the name Focciola cf. APF, SOCG, vol. 104, fol. 255v.

25 For the story of Innocent Felici of Malta, see also Natalia Królikowska-Jedlińska, "Foreigners in Front of the Crimean Khan's Courts in the Seventeenth and Eighteenth Centuries," *International Crimes and History: Annual International and History Journal* 16 (2015), 145–149.

26 See the letter of Innocent Felici to Francesco Ingoli, the secretary of the congregation, sent from Messina dated 8 January 1625, APF, SOCG, vol. 209, fol. 496r.

27 In the early modern period, the Catholics in the Crimea could be divided into two main groups: people of mixed Italian (Genovese)-Circassian origins, who retained the religious beliefs of their ancestors, and slaves or war prisoners brought to the peninsula by the Tatars during raids or military campaigns against neighboring Christian states.

28 The letter of Innocent Felici to Francesco Ingoli, the secretary of the congregation, dated 15 October 1633; APF, SOCG, vol. 73, fols. 269r–270r.

29 For more on Anthony of Flanders (Antonio Fiandrese or Antonio Fiandrini) see Eszer, "Giovanni Giuliani da Lucca," 411–414; R. Matthee, "Poverty and Perseverance: The Jesuit Mission of Isfahan and Shamakhi in Late Safavid Iran," *Al-Qantara* 36, no. 2 (2015), 463–501.

30 From Ludovico Carrera's letter dated 29 May 1637 we know that Innocent Felici went to Istanbul to collect money sent there, most probably, from the Habsburgs ("il P[ad]ré Innocentio é andato a Constantinopoli p[er] pigliarli certi denari venuti da Germania"); APF, SOCG, vol. 106, fol. 323r.

31 In his very brief description of this scandal, Ambrosius Eszer, whose source of knowledge was the same letter from Innocent to the French ambassador, stated that the concubine of Innocent accused him in front of the khan's wife (Eszer, "Neue Forschungen," 183).

Felici of Malta were to be judged by a *kadı* from the khanate, although the village of Fotsala was situated in the province of Kefe.[32] During the trial, neither Anthony of Flanders nor Matthew could confirm that they had actually seen the defendant having illicit sex with the woman in question. Thus, the *kadı* strongly reprimanded both of them, and threatened to flog them for making serious, but groundless, accusations. The *kadı* likely warned Anthony of Flanders and Matthew that a false accusation of unlawful sexual intercourse (*kazf*) is a very serious offense in Islamic law. According to the Hanafi school, it incurs a punishment of eighty lashes and the lifelong removal of the right to testify.[33] The accusers attempted to defend themselves by saying that they believed that the khan's vizier, who was well aware of the emperor's donation, insisted on incarceration of Father Innocent. It seems that the missionary believed the vizier was sympathetic toward him. Eventually, the *kadı* and the khan's wife ordered the Dominican father to cease his relationship with the woman. Father Innocent Felici of Malta accepted this and declared that from that time onward they would live separately ("La soltana poi et il giudice per causa della continua mia familiaritá con questa donna, mi sforzanno per fa mia total liberatione ... p[er] honestar la med[esi]ma donna"). Eventually, he was set free.[34] The congregation decided to recall Father Innocent Felici of Malta to Italy, where his good command of Ottoman Turkish was in great demand, to help publish books for the missionaries serving in the Ottoman Empire.[35]

In addition, immediately after the scandal, Father Ludovico Carrera, who joined the mission in 1635, confirmed the version of events as described by

---

I believe that the letter clearly states that she used her influence to help the missionary for the sake of the local woman, who was her milk-sister.

32 As we see in Chapter 5, the inhabitants of the Ottoman province of Kefe used the *kadıasker* court as frequently as the inhabitants of the most populous districts of the khanate.

33 *Kazf*, designed to prevent slanderous accusations, is a *hadd* crime, which means it has a fixed punishment in the sharia, see R. Peters, *Crime and Punishment in Islamic Law: Theory and Practice from the Sixteenth to the Twenty-first Century* (Cambridge, 2005), 63–64; E. Semerdjian, *"Off the Straight Path": Illicit Sex, Law and Community in Ottoman Aleppo* (Syracuse, NY, 2008), 7, 20–21, 126–127; B. Tuğ, *Politics of Honor in Ottoman Anatolia: Sexual Violence and Socio-Legal Surveillance in the Eighteenth Century* (Leiden and Boston, 2017), 179–180.

34 The letter of Innocent Felici of Malta to Philippe de Harlay, comte de Césy, the French Ambassador in Istanbul, dated 30 August 1636, APF, SOCG, vol. 106, fols. 335r–337v. We learn the identity of the addressee from a summary of the letter made by a clerk working in the congregation, see APF, SOCG, vol. 106, fol. 334.

35 The secretary of the congregation to Angelo Petricca, the patriarchal vicar in Istanbul, dated 29 April 1637; APF, Fondo Lettere, vol. 17, fol. 91r-v; On the patriarchal vicar in Istanbul see C.A. Frazee, *Catholics and Sultans: The Church and the Ottoman Empire 1453–1923* (Cambridge, 1983), 97.

Father Innocent Felici of Malta.[36] Letters of both abovementioned missionaries as well as correspondence sent by other Dominicans provide evidence of the serious conflicts within their small community. The letters of Ludovico Carrera contain the most severe accusations addressed toward three of his co-missionaries: Anthony of Flanders, Reginaldo Paolini, and Giovanni of Lucca. He depicted them as corrupt drunkards who slept with local women and were involved in the trade of Christian slaves.[37] In 1636, he seemed to hold Innocent Felici in high in esteem. Yet, four years later, he expressed the hope that Innocent Felici would never return to the Crimea, because the woman from Fotsala complained before the khan and the Polish envoy that the missionary had abandoned her with two sons.[38] Leaving aside these fascinating issues, we should stress that the case of the court hearing of 1636 indicates the ways in which it was influenced by politics. Father Innocent Felici confessed that he regained his freedom not only because of the lack of evidence, but also because of the elevated status of his woman friend and her close contacts with the first wife of the khan.

1.2 *The Khan's Palace Servants and Central Officials*

The earliest Crimean chronicle, which describes the reign of Sahib Giray, provides evidence on the Crimean political institutions. Some of these were patterned on Ottoman institutions. Remmal Hoca depicted the khan as presiding over a council of hereditary clan leaders and officials appointed by the ruler. The officials bore the same titles as the members of the Ottoman sultan's council. Later sources confirm this composition of the khanate's administration, whose members were referred to by titles of Golden Horde or Ottoman origin.

1.2.1 Social Origins of Palace and Central Officials

Members of the ruler's household belonging to the Giray dynasty were surrounded by numerous officials and servants. Kravets noticed that the khans

---

36 Letters of Ludovico Carrera to Francesco Ingoli, the secretary of the congregation, dated 9 August 1635 and 12 August 1636; APF, SOCG, vol. 135, fols. 483r–484r; APF, SOCG, vol. 135, fols. 480r–481v.

37 See the two letters of Ludovico Carrera to Francesco Ignoli, the secretary of the congregation, dated 12 July 1636, 12 and 21 August 1636; APF. SOCG, vol. 135, fols. 486r–487r, 480r–481v, 485.

38 Ludovico Carrera's letter to Francesco Ignoli, the secretary of the congregation, dated 16 October 1640, APF, SOCG, vol. 62, fol. 193. The Polish envoy sent to the Crimea in 1640 was Krzysztof Dzierżek, a well-known diplomat (Kołodziejczyk, *Crimean Khanate and Poland-Lithuania*, 151). In 1642, Anthony of Flanders warned the congregation that Innocent Felici should not be allowed to return to the Crimea, because the local Catholics would not accept him (Anthony of Flanders to Francesco Ignoli, the secretary of the congregation, 29 August 1642; APF, SOCG, vol. 123, fol. 1r).

adopted the slave-household institution, which was typical for great Muslim families.[39] In such a household, relatively few members were legally free. Being a slave of a prominent master, however, did not necessarily indicate a low social position. Such slaves enjoyed prestige and considerable wealth compared to free but poor subjects. The slaves' proximity to their powerful masters secured them a high social status. Yet, the masters could exercise absolute power over their servants and officials. In the case of the Crimean khans, we have limited knowledge about the origins of their officials and servants. Data preserved in various sources indicate that they came from very different social groups, i.e., from ruling families, the Girays' noble clients,[40] common Muslim and non-Muslim subjects, ulema families, and slaves. It is beyond the scope of this study to determine the ratios of these groups in the khan's administration. The models of career development remain under-researched as well. We should approach the study of this subject by the prosopographical method. The works of Norman Itzkowitz,[41] Metin Kunt,[42] Suraiya Faroqhi,[43] and Madeline Zilfi,[44] to mention only a few, demonstrates the utility of this method for the study of various branches of the Ottoman administration. Yet, in the case of the Crimean Khanate, there are no known registers containing the names of officials and the outlines of their careers. Therefore, we use a few cases of famous Crimean officials who are well-described in narrative sources.

For example, Sefer Gazi Ağa, the famous vizier (1644–46, 1647–64), came from a middle-rank noble family. He started his career as the equerry (*mirahor*) of Hüsam Giray, the *kalga* of Khan Inayet Giray (1635–37). The tragic death of Hüsam Giray forced Sefer Gazi Ağa to look for another patron. He became the vizier of Islam Giray when the prince was nominated to the post of *kalga* by his brother, Bahadır Giray (1637).[45] After the latter's death, Islam III Giray was exiled to Rhodes and Sefer Gazi Ağa followed his patron. When Islam Giray

39 Kravets, "From Nomad's Tent," 49.

40 The following passage from the account of Marcin Broniewski reveals more about the training of young nobles: "Illos etiam qui ex insigniori et nobiliori Tartarica iuventute delecti sunt, mensibusque alternis in aula eius versantur, et cum idonei efficiuntur, iisdem dignitatibus honorantur, perpetuo alit"; see Broniewski, *Tartariae Descriptio*, 15.

41 N. Itzkowitz, "Eighteenth Century Ottoman Realities," *Studia Islamica* 16 (1962), 73–94.

42 M. Kunt, *The Sultan's Servants: The Transformation of Ottoman Provincial Government (1550–1650)* (New York, 1983).

43 S. Faroqhi, "Social Mobility and the Ottoman 'Ulema in the Sixteenth Century," *IJMES* 4 (1973), 204–218.

44 M.C. Zilfi, "The Ilmiye Registers and the Ottoman Medrese System Prior to the Tanzimat," in *Contributions à l'histoire économique et sociale de l'Empire ottoman*, ed. J.-L. Bacqué-Grammont and P. Dumont (Leuven, 1983), 309–327.

45 Kazembeg (ed.), [*Seyyid*] *Muhammad Riza*, 171.

became the khan in 1644, he appointed Sefer Gazi Ağa as his vizier.[46] The statesman held this office throughout Islam Giray's reign and the reign of the next khan, Mehmed IV Giray (1654–66). But by 1664, relations between the ruler and his minister had worsened to such an extent that the khan ordered the execution of Sefer Gazi Ağa. But before he died, the famous statesman managed to secure the future influence of his family. His daughter Zeyneb married the future khan Adil I Giray (1666–71).[47] Already in 1666, Sefer Gazi Ağa's son Islam Ağa, who was exiled after his father's execution, returned to the Crimea to be the vizier of the new khan, Adil I Giray. Islam Ağa served as the khan's vizier for less than two years. At the beginning of 1668, the khan ordered Islam Ağa's execution and confiscated his property under pressure from the Şirins and Mangıts, whose influence Islam Ağa had tried, but failed to marginalize.

Subhan Gazi Ağa, another eminent Crimean vizier from the second half of the seventeenth century, had noble origins, too.[48] From a case concerning the posthumous division of his property we learn that his son Huseyn Gazi Ağa was the gatekeeper (*kapı ağası*) of the *nuraddin* in 1680. Subhan Gazi Ağa's three other sons, Timur Gazi Beğ, Osman Mirza, and Derviş Mirza, were mentioned without reference to any office.[49] Nonetheless, the eighteenth-century Crimean chronicles reveal that Subhan Gazi Ağa's descendants played important political roles well after the vizier's death.[50]

The chronicle of Said Giray constitutes a treasure trove of information concerning family relations between various branches of the Crimean elite. With regard to Bahadır Ağa, the vizier of Halim Giray (1756–58), Said Giray mentioned that the vizier's father had also held the post of the vizier to Khan Saadet III Giray (1717–24), the father of Khan Halim Giray. Said Giray also noted that Bahadır Ağa's brother was a treasurer (*hazinedar*) during Halim Giray's reign.[51]

Some of the khan's officials might have come from the clients of the ruling families. For example, Abdulgaffar el-Kırımi, whose career began in the service of the Şirins,[52] held various offices in the state administration. He was a judge in the domain of the *kalga* and the khan's secretary. At Murad Giray's court, his chief gatekeeper, Murad Gazi Ulan, also seems to have come from a noble family.[53]

46 Kazembeg (ed.), [*Seyyid*] *Muhammad Riza*, 169–171.
47 Matuz (ed.), "Eine Beschreibung des Khanats," 136–137.
48 ORRNB, Fond 917, *defter* 23a/205a/2.
49 ORRNB, Fond 917, *defter* 23b/70a/1; ORRNB, Fond 917, *defter* 23a/205a/1.
50 Abdulgaffar Kyrymi, *Umdet al-akhbar*, 187; Kellner-Heinkele (ed.), *Aus den Aufzeichnungen*, 195–197.
51 Kellner-Heinkele (ed.), *Aus den Aufzeichnungen*, 96–97.
52 Abdulgaffar Kyrymi, *Umdet al-akhbar*, 128.
53 ORRNB, Fond 917, *defter* 23b/121b/3.

Members of ulema families were appointed as Crimean muftis, *kadıasker*s, and *kadı*s. We have data about eleven fathers of twenty-three *kadıasker*s registered in the Crimean *sicil*s. The titles of ten of them indicate that they were from among the ulema.[54] From thirty-three district *kadı*s (twenty-six of Bahçesaray and seven of Kara Su), the fathers of nineteen were from the religious elite.[55] The fathers of three *kadı*s bore no title and in eleven cases the names of the fathers were not registered.

Said Giray provides detailed information about the family connections of judges and muftis in the 1750s. He describes Mehmed Efendi from the Kaçı family; he was the chief mufti of Khan Halim Giray. His son Feyzullah Efendi was appointed as *kadıasker* by the same ruler. Said Giray also notes that the office of the *kadı* of Bahçesaray was held by Mehmed Efendi, son of *muderris* Osman Efendi, who was from the ulema. The Çuyunçu family from Kefe was another example of an ulema family with a long tradition. Its members held the offices of the *kadı* of the *kalga*, the *kadı*s of Ferahkerman and Akkerman, and the *kadı*s of the Nogay Hordes of Cemboyluk and Yedisan. From this, it is clear that, as in the Ottoman Empire,[56] family connections were helpful for a judicial career in the khanate. Nonetheless, people from outside the religious elite could also obtain important judicial positions; for example, we know that Ebussuud Efendi, who was the *kadıasker* of Selamet II Giray (1740–43) and Arslan Giray (1748–56) probably originated from the Tatar nobility.[57]

The most important judicial offices were also offered to judges who made at least a part of their career outside the khanate or Kefe province. From the Ottoman sultan's order, dated on 5 February 1641, we know of the death of Mevlana

---

54 ORRNB, Fond 917, *defter* 4/1a/1; *defter* 20/1a/1; *defter* 21/1a/1; *defter* 23/245a/1; *defter* 26/1a/1; *defter* 27/1a/1; *defter* 28/1a/1; 29/74a/1; *defter* 30/1a/1; *defter* 42/2a/1; *defter* 43/1a/1; *defter* 45/1a/1; *defter* 56/1a/1; *defter* 63/1a/1; *defter* 76/1a/1; *defter* 81/1a/1; *defter* 82 and 83/covers; *defter* 86/1a/1; *defter* 90/1a/1; *defter* 91/1a/1; *defter* 94/1a/1; *defter* 98/1a/1; *defter* 101/1a/1.

55 ORRNB, Fond 917, *defter* 11/1a/1; *defter* 16/1a/1; *defter* 17/31a/1; *defter* 18/1a/1; *defter* 18/55a/1; *defter* 25/1a/1 and 25/36a/1; *defter* 53/1a/1; *defter* 60/1a/1; *defter* 65/33b/1; *defter* 67/1a/1; *defter* 69/15a/1; *defter* 78/1a/1; *defter* 89/cover; *defter* 95/1a/1; *defter* 96/1a/1; *defter* 97/1a/1; *defter* 99/1a/1.

56 Many researchers have convincingly argued that high-ranking Ottoman ulema became a privileged social group that passed their elevated status on to sons or sons-in-law. See, for example, B. Ergene and A. Kaygun, "Spouse Selection and Marital Mobility in the Ottoman Empire: Observations from Eighteenth-Century Kastamonu," *Historical Methods* 45, no. 1 (2012), 10–12; C. Imber, *Ebu's-su'ud: Islamic Legal Tradition* (Edinburgh, 1997), 8–19; B. Tezcan, "The Ottoman *Mevali* as Lords of the Law," *Journal of Islamic Studies* 20, no. 3 (2009), 383–407; M.C. Zilfi, "Elite, Circulation in the Ottoman Empire: Great Mollas of the Eighteenth Century," *JESHO* 26, no. 3 (1983), 318–364; Zilfi, *The Politics of Piety: The Ottoman Ulema in the Post-Classical Age (1600–1800)* (Minneapolis, 1988).

57 M. Kemper, A. von Kügelgen, and D. Yermakov (eds.), *Muslim Culture in Russia and Central Asia from the 18th to the Early 20th Centuries*, ed. M. Kemper (Berlin, 1996), 279–296.

Abdullah Efendi, who was a Crimean *kadıasker* and the former *kadı* of Aleppo.[58] Our sources do not reveal more details about his career.[59] Therefore, we do not know whether he was born as a subject of the sultan or was a Tatar in Ottoman service who returned home to take up a lucrative job.

It was possible to switch between the military-administrative and the religious-judicial branch of the khan's administration. For example, the khan's vizier Islam Ağa, mentioned above, was replaced by the former *kadıasker*, Murtaza Ali Ağa in 1667–68.[60] Mustafa, the *kadıasker* during the reign of Hacı II Giray (1683–84), had the title of *ağa*, which indicates that he had held some military-administrative functions during his career. Nicolas Kleemann, a merchant who sought justice from the court, appeared before Kırım Giray's kaymakam, who simultaneously held the post of the Crimean chief mufti.[61]

It is difficult to recognize officials who were slaves.[62] It is clear that harem officials, like the eunuchs, were legally non-free. According to the *Description from the Year 1669*, eunuchs were so expensive that they could only be found in the khan's court. Adil Giray, for instance, had fifteen eunuchs.[63] As Kravets

58 The sultan granted Mevlana Abdullah Efendi's son the same income from the *cizye* tax collected in Kefe province as the deceased judge had received during his life; NBKM, Or. Dept., Fond 310A, arkh. ed. 252, no. 2.

59 He is not mentioned in *Sicill-i Osmani*, the voluminous biographical dictionary of Ottoman dignitaries; this might indicate that his career in the Ottoman Empire was not particularly noteworthy.

60 F. Kluczycki (ed.), *Acta Historica res gestas Poloniae illustrantia* (Cracow, 1880), 1:324, 353–355; Matuz (ed.), "Eine Beschreibung des Khanats," 145.

61 Kleemann, *Voyage de Vienne à Belgrade*, 90.

62 The testaments of the khan's officials could reveal their status as slaves or freed slaves. According to the Hanafi school, if a testator had been manumitted, his former owner had the right to a share of his estate. If the khan was the former owner of the deceased, a part of the latter's inheritance belonged to the treasury. For example, the property of a certain childless woman named Perizade, the daughter of Abdullah, was divided equally between her husband, Dilaver son of Abdullah, and Murad Giray (ORRNB, Fond 917, *defter* 23b/119b/4). This fact demonstrates that the husband was not the sole heir, and that the khan had the right to a share of the inheritance, as he was the former owner of Perizade. Therefore, the division of Perizade's estate was done strictly according to the Sunni rules of inheritance (cf. Syed Ameer Ali, *Personal Law of the Mahommedans: Mahommedan Law Compiled from Authorities in the Original Arabic*, vol. 2, *Containing the Law Relating to Succession and Status* (Calcutta and Simla, 1929), 67–69. Unfortunately, the court register nos. 22, 23 (a and b), 25, 26, and 27 do not contain testaments of the officials who were active during Murad Giray's reign. Nonetheless, we find some data about their predecessors during the first reign of Selim I Giray (1671–78). For example, Abdulkerim Ağa, the *defterdar* in that period, left his property to his family members and pious endowments, only. This indicates his freeborn status. The testament was registered during the second reign of Selim I Giray (1684–91); ORRNB, Fond 917, *defter* 27/30b/1.

63 Matuz (ed.), "Eine Beschreibung des Khanats," 141–142.

demonstrated, black eunuchs were brought from the Ottoman Empire.[64] The khan's clerks, who were of Christian origin, also came into the ruler's service as slaves; two examples include Jakub Fereng, who met the Polish envoy Ławryn Piaseczyński at Gazi II Giray's court in 1603,[65] and Islam Beğ Cegielski, who worked for Mehmed IV Giray.[66] The khans, who organized regular raids of Polish, Russian, and Caucasian territories, acquired slaves during raids. From the court registers, it is clear that the Girays owned a considerable number of slaves. Yet, there is little information about the khanate's system of training newly enslaved people. It seems that the khans did not maintain a palace school similar to that of the Ottoman sultans. This fact raises the question of whether or not the khan had at his disposal slaves properly trained for high state offices.

The court registers and the reports of Muscovite envoys, the most detailed sources on the reign of Murad Giray, rarely provide us with data concerning the social origins of the khan's central and palace officials. Thus, the list of key officials and palace servants who were active during the reign of Murad Giray has only incomplete data about their origins. We know names and sometimes the titles of officials, as listed below.

It is clear that persons with titles such as *beğ*, *ulan*, or *efendi* were not slaves. In other cases, we cannot determine their status. The officials may have been recorded by their names and functions only because it sufficed for their identification. That is, it did not necessarily imply their slave status. The khan or the *nuraddin*, if they constituted a party in a case, were also recorded by name and title.[67] In just two cases, we know the names of the officials' fathers. The first one, Ali Ağa, the father of the vizier Mehmed Ağa, seems to have been a military-administrative official. In the second case, *silahdar* Mehmed Ağa is described as the son of Abdullah. Such a patronymic suggests a slave origin because the name 'Abdullah,' which means God's servant, was typically assumed as the patronymic of slaves who converted to Islam. Nonetheless, it is not a conclusive argument that they were former slaves, as free-born individuals also bore this name.

To conclude, the palace servants and key officials of the khan came from a variety of social origins. We should point out that, in contrast to the Ottoman Empire, the most important positions, such as the vizier, could be held by the

64 Kravets, "From Nomad's Tent," 52; Kravets, "Blacks Beyond the Black Sea," 21–36.

65 Piaseczyński, "Trzy poselstwa Ławryna Piaseczyńskiego," 760.

66 See the letters sent by Islam Beğ Cegielski to the Polish chancellor, Mikołaj Prażmowski, in the 1660s; AGAD, AKW, Dz. tatarski k. 61, t. 57, no. 199; k. 61, t. 82, no. 224; k. 61, t. 102, no. 244; k. 61, t. 140, no. 283.

67 ORRNB, Fond 917, *defter* 23b/7b/1; *defter* 125a/1.

TABLE 1 List of central officials and palace servants during the reign of Murad Giray

Office	Name of the officeholder
Vizier	Mustafa Ağa, son of Ali Ağa,[a] replaced by Ahmed Ağa[b]
Mufti	Abubekir Efendi,[c] Huseyn Efendi[d]
Kadıasker	Hasan Efendi[e]
Defterdar	Kutlu Şah Ağa[f]
Hazinedar (treasurer)	Sadık Ağa[g]
Katib (scribe) of the khan's council	Mustafa Efendi[h]
Atalık (tutor)	Abdulfatah[i]
Ahırcı başı (head stableman)[j]	no name
Balcı başı (head administrator of honey)	Ahmed Ağa[k]
Çadırcı başı (head tent keeper)	Mustafa[l]
Çaşnigir (head taster)	Mustafa Ağa[m]
Kilerci başı (head larder)	Mustafa Ağa[n]
Imam of the khan	Mehmed Efendi[o]
Kapıcı başı	Murad Gazi Ağa[p] (also titled *ser-i bevvab* Murad Gazi Ulan)[q]
Kethüda-i bevvaban (deputy of the gatekeepers)	Abdulaziz[r]
Mirahor (equerry)	Timur Gazi Beğ,[s] Veli Şah Beğ,[t] *mirahor* Bekir Mirza Ağa, [son of] Suleyman Ağa[u]
Silahdar (weapon master)	Mehmed Ağa, son of Abdullah[v]

a ORRNB, Fond 917, *defter* 22/78b/1.
b ORRNB, Fond 917, *defter* 23b/6a/2.
c ORRNB, Fond 917, *defter* 23b/6a/2.
d ORRNB, Fond 917, *defter* 23a/192b/1.
e ORRNB, Fond 917, *defter* 22/68b/5.
f ORRNB, Fond 917, *defter* 23b/6a/2.
g ORRNB, Fond 917, *defter* 23b/6a/2; ORRNB, Fond 917, *defter* 23b/121b/3.
h ORRNB, Fond 917, *defter* 22/78b/1.
i ORRNB, Fond 917, *defter* 23b/123a/5.
j The official was also entitled *aktacı beğ;* Kellner-Heinkele (ed.). *Aus den Aufzeichnungen*, 99.
k ORRNB, Fond 917, *defter* 23a/175b/4; the title *balcı başı* or *balçı başı* could be translated as "the head administrator of honey." Perhaps his duties were related to the administration of the tribute called "honey money" paid by the Danubian principalities to the khan.

l ORRNB, Fond 917, *defter* 23a/193b/5.
m ORRNB, Fond 917, *defter* 23a/223b/3; in ORRNB, Fond 917, *defter* 26/63b/1.
n ORRNB, Fond 917, *defter* 23a/191a/1.
o ORRNB, Fond 917, *defter* 23a/185a/1 and 2.
p ORRNB, Fond 917, *defter* 23a/204b/1.
q ORRNB, Fond 917, *defter* 23b/126b/3.
r ORRNB, Fond 917, *defter* 22/78b/1.
s ORRNB, Fond 917, *defter* 23b/6a/2.
t ORRNB, Fond 917, *defter* 23b/85a/1.
u ORRNB, Fond 917/*defter* 23b/92b/2.
v ORRNB, Fond 917, *defter* 23a/125a/4.

khan's noble clients. This fact is of the utmost importance to our study, as it indicates that the nobles, as the khan's officials, were of great significance to the administration of the khanate. In this matter, the khans did not rely entirely on professionally trained slaves.

1.2.2 The Khan's Palace Servants

The distinction between courtiers and key officials is not clear. The khan ruled his domain and, to some extent, the whole state, through his court and through the members of his council who he appointed. Arguably, certain officials were mainly responsible for organizing the daily affairs of the palace. This group consisted of *aktacı başı* (head stableman), *atalık* (tutor), *çadırcı başı* (head tent keeper), *çaşnigir* (head taster), *kapıcı başı* (head gatekeeper), *kilerci başı* (head larder), *hazinedar* (treasurer), the khan's imam, *mirahor* (equerry), and *silahdar* (weapon master), and numerous eunuchs, pages, and domestic servants.[68] The majority of the palace posts were introduced by Saadet I Giray.[69] Various sources from the sixteenth through the eighteenth centuries list the same offices, thus, we can see that the palace organization remained stable over time.

68 The *Description from the Year 1669* provides us with some information on the khan's domestic servants. Although the data on their number should be treated with caution, the part concerning their types and functions seems to be reliable. From this source we learn that the ruler used to drink his morning coffee in the women's quarters before eight o'clock. He was accompanied by 100 Circassian girls. Then, on his way to the council, the ruler passed the courtyard, in which numerous *sipahis*, janissaries, pages, and other servants were gathered. After the council, which usually finished around ten o'clock, the khan used to have a morning meal. This time he was accompanied by 150 Slavic and 100 Abkhazian female slaves. The courses were served by the palace pages. The ruler, however, ate his meal alone. No one was invited to share it with him (Matuz (ed.), "Eine Beschreibung des Khanats," 142–144).

69 Syroechkovskii, "Mukhammed-Gerai," 60.

Courtiers had no formal political authority, but could nonetheless, through the khan, influence state policy. Their informal political power is less visible than the public decisions made by the members of the khan's council. Courtiers could influence the khan's orders by providing him with information selectively and by advising him. Moreover, the khan entrusted them with missions unrelated to their formal duties at the court. For instance, Vasilii Tiapkin and Nikita Zotov mentioned that Murad Giray used his *atalık* in diplomatic missions.[70] Yet, we should remember that, in contrast to Ottoman sultans, it was common for khans to interact with their dignitaries, various officials, vassals, and subjects. The Crimean rulers differed from Ottoman sultans; they attended their council and commanded their armies. In consequence, the courtiers constituted only one of several groups who could gain the khan's ear. Emiddio Portelli d'Ascoli describes the khan's court as informal; therefore, it was relatively easy to gain access to the ruler. Shortly after his arrival to the Crimea in 1625, the Dominican missionary traveled to Bahçesaray to ask for an audience before the khan. Mehmed III Giray did not keep Emiddio waiting—he received him immediately after he made the request. When the Dominican father entered the council room, he saw the khan, with a cheerful face, accompanied by his courtiers. The ruler shook his hand and inquired about his health. Then, Mehmed III asked his guest to sit down on the cushions on the floor. As soon as the ruler understood that Emiddio was not used to sitting on the floor, he ordered that a chair be brought for him. Afterward, out of politeness, the khan asked a few questions about Italy. Then he started a religious discussion with his guest.[71] Just over two years later, Emiddio visited Mehmed III a second time. Again, he obtained an audience without delay and engaged in a long religious discussion with the khan, who was surrounded by the *kalga*, the *nuraddin*, dervishes, *hoca*s, and noblemen.[72] Emiddio's depiction of the khan's informal behavior stands in contrast to accounts of the sultan by European travelers. Thomas Dallam, for example, who reconstructed the organs gifted by Elizabeth I to Mehmed III, encountered the sultan in a very intimate way, in comparison to the experiences of other Europeans. Yet, his description of a concert he gave for the ruler in the private quarters in the Topkapı palace is evidence of the author's great fear of the ruler and the lack of any direct conversation between

70 Murzakevich (ed.), "Spisok s stateinago," 579.

71 Emiddio Portelli d'Ascoli's letter to Francesco Ignoli, the secretary of the congregation, dated 15 December 1625; APF, SOCG, vol. 209, fols. 528r–530r.

72 Emiddio Portelli d'Ascoli's letter to Francesco Ignoli, the secretary of the congregation, dated 29 February 1628; APF, SOCG, vol. 147, fols. 272r–275r.

them. The sultan communicated with Dallam through his servants.[73] Certainly, we should keep in mind Rhoads Murphey's comments, that the sultan could not "withdraw himself from engagement with his court for long, as any prolonged period of disengagement seriously weakened his position as patron and overlord."[74] Yet, it is also clear that the right to approach the khan was granted more swiftly and with less formality than it was to the Ottoman sultan. Perhaps this relatively easy access to the khan, combined with the fact that the Crimean rulers were less powerful than the sultans, were indications that the khan's courtiers did not exercise as much power as their Ottoman counterparts.

1.2.3 The Khan's Key Officials

The khan presided over the state council and selected the majority of its members. Their functions were patterned on Ottoman officials. The council members made administrative and, to some extent, political decisions concerning foreign and domestic policy.[75]

According to Evliya Çelebi, the khan's religious and judicial officials had a higher rank than the others on the council.[76] The mufti, the foremost religious authority in the khanate, sat on the ruler's right side. However, according to Peyssonel, the mufti held a slightly less prestigious place, being seated on the right side after the royal dignitaries and the Şirin *beğ*.[77] The mufti was superior in rank to other ulema in the khanate. Like the Ottoman muftis, he issued only non-binding legal opinions on religious questions (*fetvas*). Because of his special relationship with the ruler, his *fetvas* influenced state policy. On numerous occasions, the khan and his vassals and subjects sought the mufti's approval for political or administrative acts.[78] A *fetva* issued by the mufti could even justify the deposition of a khan.

The *kadıasker*, according to Evliya, sat on the left side of the khan. This dignitary was the chief judge of the khanate. He presided over his own court, which ruled on cases from the whole of the khanate's territory. As a member of the

73 J.T. Bent (ed.), *Early Voyages and Travels in the Levant* (New York, 1943), 70–71; G. MacLean, *The Rise of Oriental Travel: English Visitors to the Ottoman Empire, 1580–1720* (New York, 2004), 3–47.

74 R. Murphey, *Exploring Ottoman Sovereignty: Tradition, Image and Practice in the Ottoman Imperial Household, 1400–1800* (Auckland, 2008), 154.

75 We discuss the territorial boundaries of the central officials in the sections concerning relations between the khan and the *kalga*, *nuraddin*, and *karaçı* families.

76 Abrahamowicz, Dubiński, and Płaskowicka-Rymkiewicz (trans.), *Księga podróży Ewliji Czelebiego*, 276–278; Evliya Çelebi, *Tam Metin Seyahatnâme*, 349.

77 Peysonnel, *Traité sur le commerce*, 2:259.

78 ORRNB, Fond 917, *defter* 22/78b/1; ORRNB, Fond 917, *defter* 89/47b/1; Markievich (ed.), "Spisok," 48–49.

khan's council and the chief judge, he was present when the sharia court convened at the *divan*.[79] While I discuss twenty-three cases judged by the khan's council during the reign of Murad Giray in detail in a subsequent section, here we should note that these cases were recorded in the *sicil*s of the *kadıasker*. Thus, it would seem that he and his staff were in charge of formulating the records of these hearings and writing them down in the *sicil*s. Yet another duty of the *kadıasker* involved administering justice during the military campaigns commanded by the khan. It remains unclear to what extend he influenced the staffing of judicial posts. From Peyssonel's description, we know that the *kadıasker*'s ability to choose *kadı*s in the territories of the *kalga*'s domain and in the *beylik*s was limited.[80] Yet, presumably, his opinion mattered to the khan, who designated other Crimean judges, including those of the most important cities such as Bahçesaray, Gözleve, and Ferahkerman.

The khan's vizier was another member of the council. This office was introduced by Gazi II Giray during his first reign (1588–96). Halim Giray noted that Gazi II Giray appointed one of his servants, Ahmed Ağa, as the chief minister of his court. He gave him a title *baş ağa* (*baş vezir*). Later such an official was called *han ağası*.[81] As the ruler's deputy, he was responsible for military, administrative, and foreign policy. Research on Polish–Tatar relations led Dariusz Kołodziejczyk to conclude that the role of the viziers in internal and foreign policy in the mid-seventeenth century was on the rise. Kołodziejczyk adds that the two most powerful viziers of this period, namely Subhan Gazi Ağa and Sefer Gazi Ağa, "acted as the khan's advisors, corresponded with foreign monarchs and chancellors, and led Tatar troops on campaigns."[82] Ahmed Ağa, who was the vizier of Murad Giray from at least May/June 1679, took an active part in Tatar internal and foreign policy. We know from the report of Vasilii Tiapkin, the Russian envoy in 1680–81, that he found himself under a great deal of pressure to hand the tsar's letter over to Ahmed Ağa instead of the khan. Since this letter was addressed to the khan, the Russian side could not agree to this. Eventually, they reached an agreement: Tiapkin left the tsar's letter in the headquarters and visited Ahmed Ağa before the official audience given by Murad

79 Two entries recorded in 1678 indicate that the hearing took place in front of the sharia court convened at the *divan* (*'akd-i meclis-i şer' ol-*; ORRNB, Fond 917, *defter* 22/78b/1; *defter* 23b/6a/2).

80 Peysonnel, *Traité sur le commerce*, 2:259.

81 „Emakdârlarından Ahmed Ağa'yı kethüda ve vekîl ma'nâsına *Baş Ağalık* ünvanıyla sâhib-i ihtişâm eyledi. Ba'de'z-zamân hidmet-i merkûmede istihdâm olunanlar *Han Ağası* ünvanıyla be-nâm olmışlar"; Halim Giray, *Gülbünü Hânân* (ed. Günay, Başer, and Günaydın), 46.

82 Kołodziejczyk, *Crimean Khanate and Poland-Lithuania*, 490.

Giray. The vizier demanded that Tiapkin explain not only why he had refused to hand over the tsar's letter to the khan, but also why he had not brought an answer to the khan's letter, sent previously to the head (*diak*) of the Posol'skii Prikaz.[83] Clearly, Ahmed Ağa treated the *diak* as an official of equal rank. In the case of the Habsburg monarchy, which abolished the position of first minister after Prince Wenzel Lobkowitz, Ahmed Ağa, like his predecessor Mehmed Ağa, sent official letters to the president of the Imperial Council of War (*Hofkriegsrat*), Count Raimondo of Montecuccoli.[84] After the latter's death in October 1680, the vizier corresponded with Prince Herman of Baden-Baden, who succeeded Montecuccoli in the council (*Hofkriegsrat*).[85] Usually, the khan's vizier considered the chancellor his counterpart, as in the case of Poland-Lithuania and Denmark.[86] In financial matters, the khan relied on the *defterdar* and *hazinedar*, who, in addition to the vizier and *kadıasker*, performed executive functions. There was also a scribal service, in which scribes and minor administrative officials prepared materials for discussions and performed minor diplomatic negotiations. From the diplomatic accounts, we know that the most important among these scribes were the *kethuda* of the khan's council, the *kapıcı başı*,[87] and the *katib*.

83 Murzakevich (ed.), "Spisok s stateinago," 580–582. See also an undated letter from Ahmed Ağa to "our brother, the deputy of the king of Muscovy and the white prince" (*Moskov kıralı bolgan Ak biynin vekili kardaşımızga*); RGADA, Fond 123, *Posol'skii prikaz. Krymskie dela*, op. 3, no. 212. On the tsars addressed as "white tsars" or "white grand princes," see M. Khodarkovsky, *Russia's Steppe Frontier: The Making of a Colonial Empire, 1500–1800* (Bloomington, IN, 2002), 41–45, 243.

84 The Italian translation of the letter written by Mehmed Ağa to Count of Montecuccoli, 24 March 1679 (HHStA, Türkei I, no. 149, fols. 20–21); the Italian translation of the letter written by Ahmed Ağa to Count of Montecuccoli, 1680 (HHStA, Türkei I, no. 149, fol. 81).

85 The Italian translations of the letters written by Ahmed Ağa to the prince of Baden-Baden in 1681 and 1682 (HHStA, Türkei I, no. 149, fols. 44, 88).

86 See, for example, the letter of the vizier Sefer Gazi Ağa to the Polish chancellor Mikołaj Prażmowski, 14 September 1664 (AGAD, AKW, dz. Tatarskie, k. 61, t. 111, no. 253, fol. 2); Ahmed Ağa to the Danish chancellor Friedrich Ahlefeldt, 1682? (Matuz (ed.), *Krimtatarische Urkunden*, 244–247). Ahmed Ağa also sent two letters to the Swedish "prime minister" in 1681 and 1682 (Zetterstéen, *Türkische, tatarische*, 117–125). The letters were likely received by Count Bengt Oxenstierna, who in 1680 was appointed president of the chancellary college, which acted as the Swedish foreign ministry (A.F. Upton, *Charles XI and Swedish Absolutism, 1660–1697* (Cambridge, 1998), 94).

87 The chief gatekeeper (*kapıcı başı*), who was in charge of keeping order in the presence of the sovereign, was often mentioned in the diplomatic correspondence. For instance, the khan's secretary, Islam Beğ Cegielski, notified his Polish correspondent that the *kapıcı başı* had hit the Russian envoy with his staff several times and called him "a Jewish dog" during the audience before the khan. The diplomat was punished for not speaking truthfully to the sovereign ("Kapudzi Basza kilka razy laską dał przez łep temuż ich posłowi, gdy

2 The *Kalga*

2.1 *The* Kalga *and His Officials*

In the Crimean Khanate, the post of the *kalga*, the first deputy of the khan, dates to the second reign of Mengli I Giray (1478–1515).[88] During the reign of Murad Giray, the title of *kalga* belonged to Tohtamış Giray. In 1681, the Russian envoys described him as follows:

> Kalga Tohtamış Giray Sultan is a middle-aged man of medium height and corpulent [figure]. His face and eyes are light-colored, and his medium-sized beard is ginger. He speaks confidently. He wears a red cloth caftan lined with sable fur, a cloth cap in the Tatar style; he sits on a barracan sofa leaning on golden barracan pillows.[89]

Tohtamış Giray, when he held the post of *kalga*, resided in Ak Mescid.[90] In the 1660s, Evliya Çelebi described the *kalga*'s palace as a less impressive version

---

poselstwo odprawował, mówiąc tak, iż ty nieprawdę mówisz żydowski psie"; Islam Beğ Cegielski to the Polish chancellor, Mikołaj Prażmowski, 29 July [1664], AGAD, AKW, dz. tatarskie, k. 61, t. 140, no. 283, fol. 5.

88 Inalcık discusses the etymology of the word *kalga* and the origins of this rank, see H. Inalcık, "Kalgay," *IA*, 6:505–522 and Joseph Matuz, "Qalga," *Turcica* 2 (1970), 101–129.

89 Murzakevich (ed.), "Spisok s stateinago," 586.

90 Murzakevich (ed.), "Spisok s stateinago," 641; it is not clear when Ak Mescid became the seat of the *kalga*. During the reign of Mehmed I Giray (1515–23) and at the beginning of that of Sahib Giray (1532–51), the *kalga*'s domain seems to have been organized around Ferahkerman. It also covered a part of the steppes to the north of the fortress (Syroechkovskii, "Mukhammed-Gerai," 20; Gökbilgin (ed.), *Tarihi Sahib Giray Han*, 21–22/157–158; the first number refers to the Ottoman text of the chronicle, while the second refers to its French translation). In the seventeenth century, the *kalga* already resided in Ak Mescid. For instance, Devlet Giray, the *kalga* during the second reign of Canibeg Giray (1628–35), sent letters to the Russian tsar, which were written in the *kalga*'s palace and in the Akmescid palace (Faizkhanov and Vel'aminov-Zernov (eds.), *Materialy dla istorii*, 34, 64). The foundation of the *kalga*'s new residence might have been caused by Sahib Giray's state reforms. The khan, who modernized the fortress of Ferahkerman, was likely to take control over "the gate to the Crimea." Hence, Ak Mescid might have constituted a compensation for the *kalga*. According to Marcin Broniewski, Ferahkerman, referred to as Perekop in the Polish sources, was administrated by the khan's official who was called the *beğ* of Perekop ("Oppidum obscurum … quasi reguli, seu supremi domini Palatinum, quem illi Begum, seu Perecopensem omnium vocitant"); see Broniewski, *Tartariae Descriptio*, 4. The Polish envoy's account can be corroborated by the letter of a certain Mustafa, the *beğ* of Ferahkerman from the year 1572; AGAD, Archiwum Koronne Królewskie, dz. Tatarski, k. 65; t. 14, no. 590. The foundation of the *kalga*'s new residence also might have been inspired by the construction of Sahib Giray's new palace in Bahçesaray. Nonetheless, it should be noted that Remmal Hoca, who twice mentioned Ak Mescid in his chronicle, did not refer to it as the seat of the *kalga*; cf. Gökbilgin (ed.), *Tarihi Sahib Giray Han*, 31/171, 135/266.

of the khan's residence in Bahçesaray. It was organized around one courtyard with *sekbans*' quarters,[91] with a kitchen on one side and a mosque on the other.[92] The administrative center of the *kalga*'s domain encompassed the central-eastern part of the peninsula.

The *kalga* ruled his domain through a council that consisted of various officials. Peysonnel left a detailed description of the *kalga*'s administration. The French consul pointed out that the *kalga* was the most important dignitary after the khan. The *kalga* could replace the khan at the head of the Crimean army and acted as a regent after the ruler's death. In his domain, he had the same authority over his subjects as the khan did in his territory; this was in line with Turkic state tradition of appanages. The household of the *kalga* included two female dignitaries: the *ulu hani* and the *ana biyim*. Presumably, their responsibilities were similar to those of their counterparts in the khan's court. The *kalga* appointed his own officials, i.e., his vizier, *defterdar*, *divan efendi*, and *kadı*, all of whom participated in his council, which was modeled on that of the khan. The council acted as the supreme court for subjects from the *kalga*'s domain. It judged criminal cases and could even condemn an individual to death. However, the *kalga* could not implement the death penalty, as such a sentence had to be confirmed by the khan's council. The subjects of the *kalga* had the prerogative to appeal from his council court to the khan's court.[93]

On many points, Peysonnel's description, which dates to the mid-eighteenth century, is in agreement with earlier, but less extensive or less systematic sources. Many writers reported, like the French consul, that the *kalga* was the most important dignitary after the khan.[94] Peysonnel's second observation, which concerned the titles of the *kalga*'s women dignitaries, cannot be confirmed in any other writing. There is no other data indicating the existence of such posts for women in the *kalga*'s domain. Nonetheless, we should mention that the *kalga*'s mother, wives, and daughters were given gifts by Russian envoys exactly like the women of khan were. This indicates that they held important positions in the *kalga*'s household and this fact might have confused the French consul.

Peysonnel's third and fourth observations concern the *kalga*'s authority within his domain. He states that the *kalga* ruled through his council. For the times of Murad Giray, we know that the members of the council consisted

---

91 In the Kara Su court register, we find a reference to an office of the *emin* of the *kalga*'s janissaries; this may indicate that such a military formation remained at the prince's disposal; ORRNB, Fond 917, *defter* 25/25a/3.

92 Abrahamowicz, Dubiński, and Płaskowicka-Rymkiewicz (trans.), *Księga podróży Ewliji Czelebiego*, 301–302; Evliya Çelebi, *Tam Metin Seyahatnâme*, 374–375.

93 Peysonnel, C. *Traité sur le commerce*, 2:253.

94 See, for example, Broniewski, *Tartariae Descriptio*, 14; d'Ascoli, *Descrittione*, 24; Matuz (ed.), "Eine Beschreibung des Khanats," 146; the report of a Dominican missionary, Rajmund Chorzowski dated 1649, SOCG, vol. 210, fols. 502r–505r, Tott, *Mémoires*, 1:405.

of the *ağa*,[95] *defterdar*,[96] *divan katibi*,[97] *kadı*,[98] *kethüda*,[99] and other palace officials like the *balçı başı*,[100] *çaşnigir*,[101] *hazine yazıcı*,[102] *kapıcılar kethüdası*,[103] *küçük hazinedar*,[104] and *mirahor*.[105]

Peyssonel also discussed the khan's control over the *kalga*'s domain. According to his description, the ruler's influence was limited to certain aspects of administering justice. The khan did not give the *kalga* two important rights that were linked to the sovereign's power: the right of capital punishment and the right to act as a judge for all subjects.

From this, we can reflect on the khan's judicial influence in the Ak Mescid district. The *kadıasker* court registers confirm that individuals from this territory brought various types of cases to the *kadıasker* court. There, inhabitants of the *kalga*'s domain registered sales contracts concluded with individuals from their own district[106] as well as from other parts of the peninsula, or[107] asked the *kadıasker* to resolve more complicated financial cases between them and the khan's officials. For example, Şah Mirza Beğ, son of Rahmet Ali from the Ak Mescid district, accused Ömer Ağa, son of Hacı Mehmed from the Ferahkerman district of not keeping watch over his slave (*kozak*).[108] It seems that the plaintiff expected the defendant, who was in charge of the prison in Ferahkerman, to keep the above-mentioned slave there. Ömer Ağa acknowledged that the slave was missing, but denied that he belonged to the plaintiff. It seems that the latter lost the case when two witnesses confirmed the defendant's testimony.[109]

The inhabitants of the *kalga*'s domain also ruled on family matters in the *kadıasker* court. For instance, Mustafa Monla, son of Hacı Dost Mehmed from

---

95 RGADA, Fond 123, *Posol'skii prikaz. Krymskie dela*, op. 3, no.72, fol. 566v.

96 Defterdar Şah Mirza Ağa; ORRNB, Fond 917, *defter* 22/91a/8.

97 RGADA, Fond 123, *Posol'skii prikaz. Krymskie dela*, op. 1, no.72, fol. 566v.

98 Abdulfatah Efendi was the *kadı* of the *kalga* during the reign of Murad Giray; ORRNB, Fond 917, *defter* 22/72a/8. He could rely on help of his *naib*, Veliş Efendi; ORRNB, Fond 917, 22a/90a/4 and 5.

99 RGADA, Fond 123, *Posol'skii prikaz. Krymskie dela*, op. 1, no.72, fol. 566v.

100 RGADA, Fond 123, *Posol'skii prikaz. Krymskie dela*, op. 1, no.72, fol. 566.

101 Ibid.

102 Ibid.

103 Ibid.

104 RGADA, Fond 123, *Posol'skii prikaz. Krymskie del*, op. 3, no.72, fol. 566v.

105 Mirahor Bekir Mirza Ağa, [son of] Suleyman Ağa; ORRNB, Fond 917, *defter* 23b/92b/6.

106 Ümme Gülsem, through her legal agent, sold a piece of land to certain Mehmed, son of Abdullah, ORRNB, Fond 917, *defter* 23a/195b/3.

107 Ahmed, son of Emretullah from the Ak Mescid district, requested that Hacı Mehmed's wife from the Çorgun district pay off her debts; ORRNB, Fond 917, *defter* 23b/36a/3.

108 In the Crimean court registers, the Turkic term *kazak* was used to describe a male slave. The term was adopted into Slavic language as *kozak*, and then into English as 'Cossack.'

109 ORRNB, Fond 917, *defter* 23b/15a/2.

Ak Mescid, bestowed an allowance (*nafaka*) on his underage son. The latter lived in Bahçesaray with his mother Rafiya, daughter of Ali, who had divorced Mustafa Monla and renounced any financial claims to her former husband four years earlier.[110] Mustafa Monla apparently chose to register his donation in the capital, because his son lived there.

Cases involving only inhabitants of Ak Mescid were also recorded in the *kadıasker sicil*s. For example, Kazay Dede, son of Ali Çelebi, stated before the *kadıasker* court that he had divorced his wife Melik Han and that they had divided their property in front of the *kadı* of Ak Mescid, where they had been living. The woman corroborated her ex-husband's statement. It is not clear why the parties decided to reaffirm the sentence of the district *kadı* in the *kadıasker* court.[111] Inhabitants of Ak Mescid figured in criminal cases, too. For example, Ayşe, daughter of Molaş Sufi, from the Ak Mescid district, sent her agent to the capital to clear herself of charges. Seyyid Mehmed Monla, son of Kara Mehmed from the Bahçesaray district, held her responsible for the actions of her slave, who he said had thrown a stone at him.[112] Individuals from the Ak Mescid district also had their cases heard by the court convened at the khan's council. For example, Halil Çelebi claimed blood money from Hasan, son of Osman Beşe, and Abbas, son of Halil, who killed the plaintiff's son Ibrahim.[113]

To sum up, 102 inhabitants from Ak Mescid registered as parties in cases brought to Murad Giray's courts in Bahçesaray. They constitute 3.6 percent of the litigants. The statistics show that they sought the ruler's justice in various types of cases as often as the subjects of other regions did.[114] It is striking that they seldom referred to previous cases or brought witnesses. The court certificate (*hüccet*) of the *kalga*'s *kadı* is mentioned in just one case.

Alas, besides Peysonnel's description, we do not have any specific data on cases that judges at the *kalga*'s council heard. Perhaps if a case was heard at the council of the *kalga*, the hiring took place before the members of the *kalga*'s council. Given the lack of evidence in the *kadıasker* registers and the absence of *sicil*s from Ak Mescid, we do not know whether the *kalga* indeed sent individuals condemned to capital punishment to Bahçesaray. In the cases

110 ORRNB, Fond 917, *defter* 23a/167a/1.

111 ORRNB, Fond 917, *defter* 23b/96a/2. For more on divorce in Islamic law and seventeenth-century Ottoman practice, see O. Düzbakar, "Divorce and Types of Divorce at the End of Seventeenth-Century Bursa," *Journal of Family History* 41, no. 2 (2016), 118–130.

112 ORRNB, Fond 917, *defter* 23a/196a/2.

113 ORRNB, Fond 917, *defter* 23a/179a/1 and 2.

114 The inhabitants of Ak Mescid brought various types of cases to the *kadıasker* court, in the following proportions: contracts including family matters—43 percent; financial disputes including family matters—47 percent; murder and assault—8 percent; theft and usurpation—1 percent.

from the Ak Mescid district, which were recorded and resolved in the khanate's capital, the plaintiffs never requested the death of the culprits who murdered their relatives. From what we know, the aggrieved parties were always satisfied with the blood money.

2.2 *The* Kalga *and the Kara Su District's Administration*

While the preserved *kadıasker* registers say little about the *kalga*'s judicial responsibilities, the Kara Su *sicil*s from the year 1684 offer us interesting data about his administrative activities. The court register contains six orders from Hacı II Giray, ten orders from his *kalga*, Devlet Giray, and a certificate (*tezkere*) issued by the *kalga*'s *kaymakam*.[115] The data concern Kara Su, the boundaries of which are unclear, as various narrative sources place it inside or outside the *kalga*'s domain. Evliya Çelebi, for example, stated that it covered the territory between Kerç in the east and Ak Mescid in the west. In the south, it bordered Kefe province. Thus, the Ottoman traveler described Kara Su as a city within the *kalga*'s domain. Yet, the fact that the lands of three or four Crimean *karaçı* families were located within these defined borders, i.e., between Ak Mescid and Kerç, casts some doubt on the reliability of Evliya's account.[116] Two Dominican missionaries who visited the city in the seventeenth century provided different descriptions of the issue. While Ludovico Carrera noted that Kara Su was a city of the khan ("…mi retrovo in una cità detta Carasou. Cità del Kan, dove habbitano molti Polachi e Russi…"),[117] Rajmund Charzewski clearly stated that it was administrated by the *kalga* ("hac sola quia non a Principis Tartarorum gubernatione, sel a Soltan Galga").[118] Since the narrative sources indicate that Kara Su may or may not have been in the *kalga*'s domain, for the purpose of the following analysis we presumed that the city was a kind of condominium shared by the *kalga* and the khan. This would mean that the khan's power was greater in Kara Su than in the *kalga*'s domain, while the *kalga*'s influence in Kara Su demonstrates the minimum degree of power he might have exercised in his domain. His prerogatives in Kara Su might constitute a starting point to

115 ORRNB, Fond 917, *defter* 25/112b/4, 25/112b/6, 25/113a/5, 25/113b/1, 25/114a/2, 25/114b/1, 25/115a/1; 25/115a/2; 25/115a/3; 25/115a/4 25/115a/5, 25/115a/6, 25/115b/2, 25/116b/2; 25/117a/1; 25/117b/2.

116 Abrahamowicz, Dubiński, and Płaskowicka-Rymkiewicz (trans.), *Księga podróży Ewliji Czelebiego*, 301–302; Evliya Çelebi, *Tam Metin Seyahatnâme*, 374–375.

117 Ludovico Carrera's letter to Francesco Ignoli, the secretary of the congregation dated 21 August 1636 (APF, SOCG, vol. 135, fol. 485v).

118 Rajmund Charzewski, also known as Raymund of St. Casimir, was a Polish father of the Dominican Order, and the head of the mission in the Crimea (1649–60?). For his description of Kara Su, see his report from the mission, which arrived in Rome in 1655 (APF, SOCG, vol. 210, fol. 502v).

establish the extent of his power in his own domain. The Kara Su court registers thus enable us to understand the role of a provincial court in coordinating various levels of the administration.

The abovementioned orders, issued by the khan and the *kalga*, regulated different aspects of daily life in the Kara Su district. The dignitaries addressed their writings to various provincial officials. The khan and the *kalga* seem to have agreed to rule the province in harmony. Their orders were frequently addressed to the same officials. If the orders concerned the same matters, they contained in majority unanimous or similar regulations.

Both Giray dignitaries intervened in a wide range of economic problems in Kara Su. The khan and the *kalga*, for example, protected the interests of local merchants, who complained against unfair competition from Armenian tradesmen from the Ottoman Empire. The orders of these dignitaries also concerned taxes. We thus learn that they shared the income derived from tax collection in the district of Kara Su.[119]

The khan and the *kalga* specified judicial procedures that applied to distinct groups of their subjects. While Hacı II Giray regulated the court proceedings concerning the military class,[120] the *kalga* secured the special treatment of the descendants of the Prophet (*seyyids*) who happened to be culprits in one case.[121] He also intervened on behalf of a certain Mehmed Mirza[122] by ordering that a merchant who was the *mirza*'s client be released from prison.[123]

119 In the *yarliğ* dated 16 Rebi II 1095/2 April 1684, Hacı II Giray appointed his merchant Moşe as the only collector of *cizye* tax due for the year 1095/1683–84 from his subjects and from the subjects of the Ottoman sultan. The khan forbade the *kadıs* of Kara Su and Gözleve from interfering in the tax collection (ORRNB, fond 917, *defter* 25/115a/4). We know about the taxes collected by the prince from the *tezkere* of Mustafa Ağa, the *kaymakam* of the *kalga*. This document dated on 8 Zilhicce 1094/28 November 1683 states that the *kaymakam* sent a servant to Kara Su to collect the following taxes: *haraç, ketan öşri, odun akçesi* (ORRNB, fond 917, *defter* 25/120a/2). As I discuss in Chapter 5, in this case *haraç* should be identified as *cizye*.

120 See the *yarliğ* of Hacı II Giray dated Muharrem 1096/8 December 1684–6 January 1685 concerning the appointment of *odabaşı* Ibrahim as the deputy commander in Kara Su (Kara Su'da Ibrahım odabaşı serdarlık hizmeti içın vekil nasb edüp). Ibrahim was supposed to investigate the conduct of the janissaries, *cebecis*, *kul oğlus*, *acemî oğlans*, and *topçus*. If any of them committed a crime, the deputy brought them to the court and punished them after the hearing; ORRNB, fond 917, *defter* 25/112b/6.

121 Kalga Devlet Giray Sultan informed the *kadı* of Kara Su that Seyyid Muharrem Efendi, the head of the *seyyids* (*nakibü 'leşraf*) appointed Seyyid Emir Abbas as his local deputy. The *kalga* also ordered that the *seyyids* wgi broke the law, had the right to be detained by their head. The *yarlığ* was dated Rebi I 1095/17 February–17 March 1684; ORRNB, fond 917, *defter* 25/114a/2.

122 Mehmed Mirza was most probably a son of the former vizier, Sefer Gazi Ağa; ORRNB, fond 917/*defter* 25/115a/3.

123 See the *yarliğ* of Kalga Devlet Giray Sultan (ORRNB, fond 917, *defter* 25/115a/5).

Moreover, the khan and the *kalga* restricted which social groups could settle in the city. They prevented the Circassians and Nogays from living in Kara Su. Finally, the two Giray dignitaries tried to solve the problem of billeting traveling officials and troops in the city. The khan and the *kalga* restricted the number of those with this privilege and regulated how the burden should be divided among the inhabitants.[124]

The appointments of various officials constituted another subject of the orders issued by these two dignitaries. The khan selected the military commander, his deputy, and one of his officers, while the *kalga* appointed the head and the warden (*kethüda*) of the *reaya* (i.e., common subjects obliged to pay taxes). The *kalga* also exercised certain control over the military officials. In 1684, Devlet Sultan, for instance, ordered one of the janissary officers to keep order in one of the city bazaars. It is unclear who had the right to appoint the *kadıs* of the districts situated within the *kalga*'s domain. An order of Canibeg Giray indicates that, in general, the khan had the right to appoint and depose the district *kadıs*.[125] It would be interesting to know whether or not the khan consulted with the *kalga* about his personal decisions in cases in the *kalga*'s domain and in the Kara Su district.

2.3 *The Limits of the* Kalga*'s Authority within His Domain*

A number of the issues brought up in the abovementioned orders provide us with a panorama of the roles of the khan and the *kalga* in the administration of Kara Su. The present section focuses on the *kalga*'s competencies within the provincial administration. The above evidence shows that the *kalga* took an active part in governing and the daily life of the district. He made decisions in the same matters as the khan. He exercised a certain control over the judicial and military administration. Its members, however, were appointed by the khan. We should note that the *kalga* derived income from his domain in the same way as the khan did from his land, i.e., by levying various taxes from Muslims as well as non-Muslims. The *cizye* was collected directly by the *kalga*'s officials. According to the Hanafi school of Islamic law, this tax belonged to the sovereign, who should redistribute it to the benefit of the Muslim community. Yet, with the ruler's permission, the individuals who undertook holy wars

---

124 The *sicil*s of Kara Su contain two *yarliğ*s concerning this subject. Khan Hacı II Giray, who issued the earliest one in 1684, attempted to regulate who could be asked to billet soldiers and in what circumstances. Sixty years later, Kalga Şahin Giray also addressed this issue, stipulating who could obtain lodgings in the city and who could settle there; ORRNB, fond 917, *defter* 25/115b/2, *defter* 65/34b/1.

125 See the *yarliğ* of Khan Canibeg Giray to the Crimean *kadıs* dated 1612 (ORRNB, fond 917, *defter* 1/71b/1).

could collect this tax directly.[126] The khan's concession on behalf of the *kalga*, who was often in charge of military campaigns against the infidels, would be in perfect accordance with the religious requirements related to the *cizye*. Thus, the fact that the *kalga* collected this tax directly does not necessarily imply his independence from the khan.

2.4 *Recapitulation: The* Kalga*'s Prerogatives in His Domain*

A Giray prince appointed to the office of *kalga* was assigned a part of the khanate's territory with the capital in Ak Mescid. The *kalga* exercised a certain autonomy within his domain. He controlled it through the officials whom he had appointed. Their titles, patterned on those of the khan's officials, indicate that they might have had similar competencies. If so, the *kalga* controlled through them the political, financial, and to some extent, also the judicial aspects of the local inhabitants. The orders recorded in the Kara Su court registers confirm that even in this territory the *kalga* made important decisions in all of these fields. We can only speculate about the extent to which the *kalga* took over, in his domain, the responsibilities and privileges exercised by the khan in other parts of the khanate. Obviously, certain rights were reserved exclusively for the khan; these included the right to mint one's own coins, to have one's name invoked in the Friday prayer, to dispense capital punishment in the khanate, and to allow every subject from the *kalga*'s domain to appeal to the khan's court in Bahçesaray, and if Peysonnel was correct, to implement capital punishment.

3 The *Nuraddin* and His Officials

The post of *nuraddin*, the second deputy of the khan, dates to the year 1579. As Muzaffer Ürekli pointed out, the rank of the second heir apparent of the khan was created by Mehmed II Giray (1577–84) for his son, Saadet Giray. The ruler could not appoint his son as *kalga* because he was obliged to offer this rank to his eldest living male relative, in this case, to his brother Alp Giray. In order to elevate his son's position, he created a new post, that of the second deputy.[127] Perhaps this decision was designed to strengthen the position of the khan's son, in order to secure him the throne in the future.

126 Imber, *Ebu's-su'ud*, 119.

127 The etymology of the word *nuraddin* and the origins of this rank are discussed in Muzaffer Ürekli, *Kırım Hanlığının Kuruluşu ve Osmanlı Himayesinde Yükselişi* (Ankara, 1989), 74–77. He based his description on the accounts of Seyyid Mehmed Riza (see Kazembeg (ed.), *[Seyyid] Muhammad Riza*, 103) and (Halim Giray, *Gülbünü Hânân* (ed. Günay, Başer, and Günaydın), 43).

No clear evidence is offered about the *nuraddin*'s domain. We learn about his various residencies in the sixteenth through the eighteenth centuries. Josef Matuz specified that there were three of them and these were in Süren, Kaçı, and Bahçesaray.[128] Nicole Kançal-Ferrari's research on the *nuraddins*' diplomatic correspondence demonstrates that in the years from the 1640s to the 1680s they often resided in Kaçı.[129] Her results are confirmed by the chronicle of Mehmed Senai, which suggests that in the mid-seventeenth century, Kaçı was the customary residence of the *nuraddins*.[130] However, the author of the *Description from the year 1669* stated that the *nuraddin* resided in Süren.[131] Moreover, in 1681, the *nuraddin* gave the Russian envoys, Vasilii Tiapkin and Nikita Zotov, a formal audience in the village of Bulganak, on the Bulganak river.[132] The same envoys described "the gardens on the Kaçı [river]" as the khan's residence.[133] Around the 1750s, the *nuraddin* lived in the khan's capital and had no palace in the countryside.[134] The *nuraddin*'s lack of a permanent residence might be explained by the relatively late establishment of this post. The khan, who had limited sources of income, might have been reluctant to permanently bestow an extended part of his domain on the *nuraddin* and authorize him to hold his own court. According to the Crimean tradition, Mehmed II Giray created the new rank to balance the power of the *kalga*. Surely he did not aim to create another rival to his throne. Perhaps, he promoted his trustworthy son so that he would have an alternative military commander to the *kalga*. Granted the rank of the khan's second deputy, the *nuraddin* enjoyed the right to participate in the khan's council, to use the appopriate titulature, and to receive a relatively high income. His exalted position was also confirmed by his right to maintain direct diplomatic correspondence with foreign rulers.[135]

---

128 Matuz (ed.), *Krimtatarische Urkunden*, 5–6.

129 Kançal-Ferrari, *Kırım'da Kalan Miras*, 52–53, 57.

130 "Gazi Giray Sultan, son of Mubarek Giray Sultan, son of Selamet Giray Khan ... settled down in glory in Kaçısaray, in the capital of his felicitious rule, on the sultanic throne. He took his place on the cushion of nuredins"; see Hacı Mehmed Senai, *Historia chana*, 92/5 (the first page number refers to the Polish translation of the chronicle and the second refers to its Ottoman Turkish version).

131 Matuz (ed.), "Eine Beschreibung des Khanats," 148; the fact that some *nuraddins* maintained residencies outside the capital can be probably explained by their particular relations with the rulers. Nonetheless the subject merits a study.

132 On this village, see Jankowski, *A Historical-Etymological Dictionary*, 245–248.

133 Murzakevich (ed.), "Spisok s stateinago," 629 and 641.

134 Peysonnel, *Traité sur le commerce*, 2:255; Tott, *Mémoires* (Eng. = 2:146).

135 See, for example, the letters sent by Saadet Giray, the *nuraddin* of Murad Giray, to the Muscovite tsars (RGADA, Fond 123, *Posol'skii prikaz. Krymskie dela*, op. 3, nos. 218, 231, 233, 236, 243), to the Habsburg Emperor (available only in the seventeenth-century translations,

The descriptions of Peysonnel and Tott suggest that the *nuraddin*'s officials, whose titles were modeled on those of the officials of the khan or the *kalga*, did not have any specific responsibilities in times of peace. However, when the *nuraddin* was appointed an army commander, the members of his court accompanied him to perform duties similar to their counterparts in the retinues of the khan or the *kalga*. For instance, during wartime, the *kadı* of the *nuraddin* acted as a judge in the army.[136] The account of the French consul should be compared with the data extracted from the *sicil*s. Unfortunately, the court registers dating to the reign of Murad Giray contain only one entry referring to the judicial power of the *nuraddin*'s judge. This concerns a simple conflict regarding a commercial transaction: a certain Mehmed Ağa from the Çetirlik district accused Ali Hacı Arab, from the Kara Su district, of not handing a female slave over to him. The plaintiff stipulated that he had bought the woman from the defendant two years earlier for sixty-five *altun*s. He added that the case had been resolved by Salih Efendi, the *nuraddin*'s judge, who had ruled in his favor after two witnesses confirmed his version of events. In the *kadıasker* court, Mehmed Ağa asked, one more time, for the defendant to return his money. Ali Hacı Arab confirmed that the case had already been heard by Salih Efendi, yet he claimed that the sentence was legally invalid as it was based solely on the testimony of the plaintiff's witnesses, who were not speaking the truth. Consequently, he asked the *kadıasker* to hear the case again.[137] The entry does not reveal the circumstances of the former court proceeding. Therefore, it is unclear where the *nuraddin*'s judge heard the case. We also do not know why, in the original instance, Mehmed Ağa brought his case to Salih Efendi instead of bringing it to a district judge. There is at least one explanation. If Mehmed Ağa was a member of the *nuraddin*'s retinue, it would be natural for him to bring his case to the judge who also served his patron. Since the entry in question is the only one with information on the judge of the nurradin, we must acknowledge that much remains unclear about this official.

During the reign of Murad Giray, Saadet Giray held the post of *nuraddin*.[138] From a list of gifts delivered by the Russian envoys in 1682, we learn the titles of officials in the retinue of the *nuraddin*; these included his *ağa*,[139] *hazinedar*

HHStA, Türkei I, no. 149, fols. 12–13; no. 150, fol. 80; no. 152, fol. 84r), or to the Danish king (Matuz (ed.), *Krimtatarische Urkunden*, 233–238).

136 Peysonnel, *Traité sur le commerce*, 2:255.

137 ORRNB, Fond 917, *defter* 23b/67b/2.

138 Vasilii Tiapkin and Nikita Zotov describe him as a tall man around thirty years old, who was blind in one eye; the envoys praised his kind and agreeable manners (Murzakevich (ed.), "Spisok s stateinago," 587).

139 RGADA, Fond 123, op 3, *Posol'skii prikaz. Krymskie dela*, no. 72, fol. 566.

(treasurer),[140] *balcı başı*,[141] *çaşnigir* (taster),[142] *hazine yazıcı* (scribe in the treasury),[143] and *kapıcılar kethüdası*.[144] In addition, gifts were sent to eight other members of the *nuraddin*'s court.[145] In the *kadıasker* court register from the same period, we find the *kapı ağası* of the former *nuraddin*, Safa Giray, who was named Aliş Ağa and acted as the vekil of his master.[146]

To conclude, the *nuraddin* did not hold a permanent semi-autonomous position in the khanate, a position that would be comparable to that of the *kalga*. We presume that the *nuraddin*'s influence on state affairs depended on his relations with the khan, who could assign him a part of his domain or allow him to command an army. Therefore, in comparison to the *kalga*, the *nuraddin* had limited opportunities to conduct his own policy or act independently from the khan.

4 The Khan's Council

The composition of the khan's council suggests that in its origin it was the group of the khan's most important vassals (*karaçı beğ*s), in addition to the *kalga* and the *nuraddin* (after the creation of this post), and by the khan's key officials, whose functions were patterned on those of the Ottomans. The council was gathered by the khan or, during the ruler's absence, by his *kaymakam*. Its function was to advise the khan in military and political matters, and act as a court, before which the khan's subjects could seek the ruler's justice.

4.1 *Cases Judged at the Khan's Council*

The idea of a just monarch as a caretaker and protector of the poor predominated in many Muslim societies.[147] According to the Near Eastern concept of sovereignty, the just ruler was supposed to protect his poor subjects against abuse from officials. In medieval Muslim states, the *mazalim* court served this function. This institution allowed wronged subjects to appeal directly to the

140 RGADA, Fond 123, op. 3, *Posol'skii prikaz. Krymskie dela*, no. 72, fol. 566.
141 RGADA, Fond 123, op. 3, *Posol'skii prikaz. Krymskie dela*, no. 72, fol. 565v.
142 Ibid.
143 Ibid.
144 Ibid.
145 RGADA, Fond 123, op. 3, *Posol'skii prikaz. Krymskie dela*, no. 72, fols. 565v, 566.
146 ORRNB, Fond 917, *defter* 23b/25a/2.
147 As Paul Sartori points out in the example of the late eighteenth-century Bukhara khanate, the judicial prerogatives of its ruler were considered to have roots not only in Muslim, but also in the Chingisid tradition, see Paul Sartori, *Vision of Justice: Sharia and Cultural Change in Russian Central Asia* (Leiden and Boston, 2017), 57–58.

ruler and dealt with the petitions of common subjects seeking redress against unjust officials.[148] From the narrative sources and the *sicil*s, we learn that the khan's subjects who felt aggrieved could petition the khan's council directly. Our understanding of the judicial functions of the khan's council, which has not yet been discussed in the literature, might benefit from the ongoing debate on the parallel role of the Ottoman Imperial Council,[149] which was recently summarized by Başak Tuğ, who points out that the sultan's *divan*

> functioned as a parallel but superior judiciary organ that heard petitions, judged some important cases of petitioners in its own court (*divan*), and in other cases sent imperial orders to provincial governors and judges in order to resolve issues there. The judicial functions of the Divan-ı Hümayun were carried out by the military judges of Rumelia and Anatolia. They were responsible for the supervision of the judges in their respective provinces and for hearing cases in the Imperial Council. While adhering to legal procedures similar to those applied in the *shariʿa* courts, the ruler's ratification through the grand vizier was necessary for the implementation of their decisions.[150]

The Imperial Council could order a reinvestigation of a case before the district judge[151] or have a new trial held in a larger neighboring city. Eyal Ginio, for example, describes the case of a Christian, who was first adjudicated in Tatar

148 M. Kurz, "Gracious Sultan, Grateful Subjects: Spreading Ottoman Imperial Ideology throughout the Empire," *Studia Islamica* 107, no. 1 (2012), 96–121.

149 The modern literature on the petitions to the Ottoman Imperial Divan is quite vast. See, for example, H. Inalcık, "Adaletnameler," *Belgeler* 2, nos. 3–4 (1965), 49–145; H.G. Majer (ed.), *Das osmanische "Registerbuch der Beschwerden" (Şikāyet defteri) vom Jahre 1675* (Vienna, 1984); S. Faroqhi, "Political Activity among Ottoman Taxpayers and the Problem of Sultanic Legitimation (1570–1650)," *JESHO* 35, no. 1 (1992), 1–39; Linda T. Darling, *Revenue-Raising and Legitimacy: Tax Collection and Finance Administration in the Ottoman Empire, 1560–1660* (Leiden and Boston, 1996), 248–260; Ergene, *Local Court*, 43–56; M. Ursinus, *Grievance Administration (Şikayet) in an Ottoman Province: The Kaymakam of Rumelia's 'Record Book of Complaints' of 1781–1783* (London and New York, 2005); E. Ginio, "Coping with the State's Agents 'from Below': Petitions, Legal Appeal, and the Sultan's Justice in Ottoman Legal Practice," in *Popular Protest and Political Participation in the Ottoman Empire: Studies in Honor of Suraiya Faroqhi*, ed. E. Gara, M.E. Kabadayi, and C.K. Neumann (Istanbul, 2011), 41–56. Recently, the issue was addressed by Başak Tuğ, see *Politics of Honor*.

150 Tuğ, *Politics of Honor*, 46.

151 R.C. Repp, "Courts of Law, Ottoman," *EI*³. Readjudication of a case is strictly related to the issue of the *kadı*'s error, which has been examined by, among others, Ulrich Rebstock, "A Qāḍī's Errors," *Islamic Law and Society* 6, no. 1 (1999), 1–37.

Pazarı, and whose petition to the sultan's *divan* resulted in a retrial in Edirne.[152] We know about the judicial functions of the Imperial Council from the collection of 530 registers of complaints, records in the *sicil*s of provincial courts, and documents left by councils of the provincial governors.

In contrast to the Ottoman Empire, sources on the judicial functions of the khan's council are very limited. The only two European accounts with detailed descriptions of two cases brought to the khan's *divan* are discussed in detail in the next sections. This serves as a preface to the subsequent analyses of twenty-three cases heard before Murad Giray's council in the years 1678–82 and recorded in the *sicil*s. Hopefully, these two accounts will help us understand the stories concealed under the formal language of the court entries. The first case described by a European author concerned a political crime brought before Mengli II Giray's council. The second one involved another European—a German merchant.

4.1.1 A French Consul in Pursuit of Nogay Rebels

Gilles Veinstein provides a fascinating case study of the trial of two Nogay noblemen at the council of Khan Mengli II Giray. It is based on the letters and reports of Xavier Glavani, the French consul in Bahçesaray from the 1720s to the 1730s. In Eastern Europe, this period was marked by growing tensions over the succession of the aging Polish King Augustus II (d. 1733). Glavani was supposed to uphold the interests of the French candidate to the throne, Stanisław Leszczyński, against the Saxon Prince Frederick Augustus. While the Saxon candidate enjoyed the support of Russia and the Habsburgs, it was opposed in Paris, Istanbul, and Bahçesaray.[153] It comes as no surprise, therefore, that in 1730 Glavani was alerted to the news of two Nogays who were arrested and sent to the capital by the *serasker* of Bucak, Kalem Giray. The prince accused them of instigating other Nogays to raid the territory of the Polish-Lithuanian Commonwealth, which in that period was in chaos. The Nogays confessed that they had acted on behalf of a certain Yusuf Mirza, who had taken refuge at the court of the late Polish king, Augustus II. Glavani considered them spies of Augustus; his suspicions were confirmed by the fervent efforts of the Polish royal envoys to release the two Nogays. Hence, the French consul sought to have the two "spies" punished. He knew that the defendants would be judged before the court at the khan's council, so he went to listen to the proceeding. The khan began the interrogation of the Nogays by asking the older one whether

152 The trial took place in 1761; Ginio, "Coping with the State's Agents," 50–51.

153 Kołodziejczyk, *Crimean Khanate and Poland-Lithuania*, 198.

he confirmed the accusation of the Bucak *serasker*. The defendant answered that he was only a faithful servant of his master, Yusuf Mirza, who had sent him to deliver a few letters to his friends. According to the defendant, this was his reason for traveling to Bucak. The *beğ* of the Şirins commented on the Nogays' testimony, which he seemed to accept. After his statement, the khan ordered that the Nogays be handcuffed and sent to prison. Much to Glavani's disapproval, the first hearing was over. The French consul, who started to worry that the spies might go unpunished, took more decisive actions against them. With the excuse of delivering a medicine, he visited the Crimean vizier and eventually gained his support by arousing the official's anxiety that a potential Nogay rebellion would displease the Ottomans. The Porte might resolve to replace the inefficient khan and his officials, including the vizier. Then, Glavani visited the mufti to obtain a *fetva* condemning the defendants' deeds. Initially, his arguments did not persuade the mufti, who was convinced that no Muslim should be sentenced to death for delivering his master's letters. Finally, Glavani offered a bribe of 44,000 piasters. This was clearly the right strategy, as he left the mufti with the following *fetva*:

> Query: What should be done to a Muslim, who has sworn allegiance to his sovereign and then breaks his oath?
> Answer: He becomes an infidel and deserves death.

Glavani delivered this legal opinion to the vizier. He completed his mission the next morning by visiting the khan's harem and lecturing the breakfasting ruler on what the French kings used to do to traitors.

Shortly thereafter, the khan summoned the council once again and asked the *kadıasker* what should be done with the defendants. The official answered that they should be punished, but not with the death penalty. The vizier opposed the *kadıasker* and stated that the Nogays deserved capital punishment. These opinions were followed by an animated discussion between the members of the council; this ended with the khan's declaration of a sentence. The ruler apparently tried to satisfy both parties. He was well aware that the *beğ* of the Şirins, the *kadıasker*, and their allies sympathized with the defendants, while the vizier and the mufti, acting on behalf of the French consul, asked for capital punishment for the Nogays. The khan then sentenced the older nobleman, who was already advanced in age, to the death penalty and allowed the younger one to live.[154]

---

154 Veinstein, "Les Tatars de Crimée," 34–36.

4.1.2 A Merchant Robbed in the Crimean Khanate

Nicolas Kleemann was a merchant from the Habsburg monarchy who undertook to travel to the Middle East through the Crimea in 1768–70.[155] In April 1769, he was robbed in Kara Su by his Armenian interpreter, Khachatur Kyriagos. Local inhabitants advised him not to waste his time seeking justice before the district court, but to take his claims directly to Bahçesaray. Consequently, Kleemann went to the capital city, where he asked for help from the French consul, Monsieur Jerémie.[156] On 12 April, the latter presented Kleemann to the khan's *kaymakam* who also acted as the Crimean mufti.[157] When the official learned about the merchant's misfortune, he sent janissaries to various Crimean cities, such as Kara Su and Kefe, to search for Khachatur and bring him before the court. In three days (on 15 April), the emissaries returned to Bahçesaray with the Armenian. Kleemann, accompanied by Monsieur Jerémie, immediately arrived at the *kayamakan*'s palace for the court proceeding. The khan's deputy, seated on an elevated sofa and with a staff in his hand, was surrounded by numerous officials. Khachatur was already there. As soon as Kleemann greeted the *kaymakam* in the Turkish style, he and his proxy were allowed to sit. The merchant was the first to testify. Then the *kaymakam* asked Khachatur to answer the accusations. The interpreter, instead of commenting on Kleemann's grievances, talked at length about his work for Kleemann from the time of their departure from Vienna. While he was describing the cruelty of the German merchant, the *kaymakam* ordered him to be quiet. Then he asked Kleemann if he preferred to conclude an amicable settlement with the defendant or if he would rather rely on the court's justice. When the merchant chose the second option, the *kaymakam* warned the accused about the horrible consequences of his crime. Moreover, he advised Khachatur Kyriagos not to deny the accusation any longer and warned that if he did not plead guilty, he would flogged or confess after torture. Out of fear, the Armenian admitted his guilt and promised to return everything that he had stolen from Kleemann. The next day (16 April), Khachatur left Bahçesaray to return to Kara Su. Before his departure, Kleemann obtained a letter with the record of the proceedings from the

155 For the story of Nicolas Kleemann, see also Królikowska-Jedlińska, "Foreigners," 149–150.

156 Monsieur Jerémie was most probably a deputy left by Tott who then accompanied Kırım Giray during his campaign in Moldavia and Bucak; cf. Tott, *Mémoires*, 2:109–110.

157 According to Tott, Kırım Giray left the Crimean Peninsula for the military campaign in Moldavia in January 1769. He was accompanied by the *kalga*, *nuraddin*, vizier, *kadıasker*, and many other officials. Apparently, he left the mufti as his *kaymakam* in Bahçesaray. The khan died in Moldavia in March 1769 and his successor was not sent to the Crimea before April. At the end of April, Kleemann had not yet learnt about the khan's death; see Tott, *Mémoires*, 2:109–110, 139–142, 146; Kleemann, *Voyage de Vienne à Belgrade*, 108–109.

kaymakam for the *kadı* of Kara Su. Once there, Kleemann had to present the document in the local court, because Khachatur Kyriagos appeared to be unwilling to return the stolen goods. When the district *kadı* saw the *kaymakam*'s writing, he helped the German merchant retrieve his belongings.[158]

These two cases and the description by Peysonnel[159] reveal valuable information about the court at the khan's council. First, the ruler, surrounded by the council members, acted as a judge for his subjects from various parts of the khanate. Second, the hearings were open to the public. Third, a case could be initiated by an individual (Kleemann) or by an official (Serasker Kalem Giray). Finally, the procedure utilized in the court at the council was similar in some ways to the dispute resolution processes known from Ottoman sharia courts. These similarities include (1) the order of the depositions (Kleemann, as a plaintiff, made his accusation before Kyriagos, the defendant, was allowed to respond); (2) the *kadı* pushed the disputants toward settlement (Kleemann versus Kyriagos); (3) the judgment was based solely on the litigant's depositions, in which Kyriagos admitted his guilt; and (4) the decision, which took the form of a *fetva*, was taken into consideration by the khan in the trial of Nogays, but was not followed slavishly.[160]

4.1.3 Proceedings at the Khan's Council Registered in the *Sicil*s

How do we distinguish the records of cases heard before the khan's council from those resolved by the *kadıasker* or the Bahçesaray district judge? In just twelve of the twenty-three cases, it is explicitly written that the case was heard by the khan's council (*divan-i 'ala, divan-i hümayun, divan-i padişahi*)[161] or that the members of the council were among the case witnesses (*ve sair ehl-i divan*);[162] the remaining eleven records do not contain explicit references to the *divan*.[163] Yet, the latter entries list, among of the case witnesses, the names and titles of the council members and the khan's highest officials. From the European accounts, we learn about various members of the council who were

158 The merchant included a French translation of this document, which looks like a typical record of court proceeding, Kleemann, *Voyage de Vienne à Belgrade*, 90–107.

159 A general description of the court convened at the khan's council can also be found in Peysonnel's account. Unlike Glavani or Kleemann, he did not mention his personal participation in proceedings. Therefore, his account offers a less detailed picture of this institution; Peysonnel, *Traité sur le commerce*, 2:290–291.

160 Coşgel and Ergene, *Economics of Ottoman Justice*, 136–143, 215–216, 243–245.

161 ORRNB, Fond 917, *defter* 22/78b/1, 23b/6a/2, 23b/121b/3, 23b/123a/5, 23a/142b/7, 23a/148a/3, 23a/173a/4/, 23a/176a/4, 23a/181b/3, 23a/192b/1/.

162 ORRNB, Fond 917, *defter* 23a/179a/1, 23a/181b/3.

163 See translation and transcription of a record like this in appendix II.

involved in the proceedings.[164] Evliya Çelebi also mentions that petitioners could make their claims directly to the khan's council, which was composed of the most important state dignitaries and officials.[165] Given the reference to the khan's *divan* in twelve cases and the similar lists of case witnesses with names of council members, we propose to regard these entries with similar lists of case witnesses as accurate depictions of the proceedings of the court convened at the khan's council. We argue that the presence of the vizier or the *kaymakam*, surrounded by various key and palace officials,[166] indicates that a given case was heard by the khan's council.

The limited number of cases means that we cannot make a reliable statistical analysis. Nevertheless, we examined the residential affiliation and social background of the litigants involved in the cases heard by the khan's council. We know that they comprised a cross-section of the society and came from various parts of the khanate. Nonetheless, we must emphasize that a majority of the litigants inhabited the territories recognized as the domains of the khan and the *kalga*. Even individuals from remote areas such as Tamak or Kara Kurt appeared and sought justice before the khan's council. In just two cases, the parties came from areas that were most probably controlled by the ruling families.[167] We return to these cases later. Typically, the parties came from the same court district. In two cases, the plaintiffs and the defendants were from different administrative units. In two other cases, we do not have data to establish the parties' residential affiliations. Fortunately, we can establish the litigants' social backgrounds from the markers of identity in the records (see figure 2).

It is notable that in the majority of cases, the parties were of different social backgrounds (in twelve of twenty-three cases). By comparison, just 20 percent of such cases were brought to the *kadıasker* court in the same period.

---

164 "Le supreme Tribunal est le Divan ou le grand Conseil du Khan. Le Prince y préside toujours, et les Sultans en charge et autres y assistent, lorsqu'ils se trouvent à Baktchiseraï. Les membres du Divan sont le Kalga-Sultan, le Nouradin-Sultan, l'Or-beï, les Seraskiers du Boudjeak, de Jetsan et de Kouban, le Chirin-Beï, quand il se trouve auprès du Khan, le Mufti, le Visir, le Kazi-Asker, le Khasnadar-Bachi, le Defterdar, l'Achtadji-Bei, le Kilerdji-Bachi, le Divan-Effendi, le Naib ou Lieutenant du Kazi-Asker, le Cheir-Kadissi ou le Juge de la ville, le Koullar Agassi, le Kapidji-Bachi, le Kapidjilar, le Kiaïassi, le Bachbulukbachi; ou Colonel des Gardes, assiste ordinairement au Divan, mais il n'y a point de voix délibérative; il y est debout, armé d'un gros bâton"; Peysonnel, *Traité sur le commerce*, 2:290–291.

165 Abrahamowicz, Dubiński, and Płaskowicka-Rymkiewicz (trans.), *Księga podróży Ewliji Czelebiego*, 277; Evliya Çelebi, *Tam Metin Seyahatnâme*, 349–350.

166 Appendix III contains lists of case witnesses in the cases judged at the khan's council.

167 ORRNB, fond 917, *defter* 23b/6a/2, 23b/92b/2.

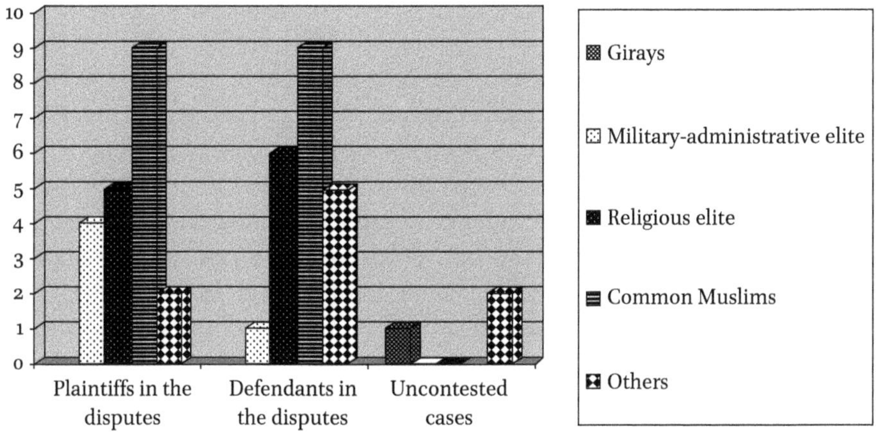

FIGURE 2 Litigants in cases judged at the khan's council

Therefore, it would seem that the court convened at the khan's council offered a good chance for a fair trial in conflicts between members of different social groups.

Not surprisingly, ordinary Muslims brought the majority of cases. Members of this social group were plaintiffs or defendants in equal measure. As we see in Chapter 5, this group appeared with similar frequency (over 40 percent of disputants) in the *kadıasker* court and in the Kara Su court. Village communities, consisting of individuals of various social origins, were parties in four proceedings, in which the charges concerned collective responsibility for murders or assaults committed within the territory of the village in question. It should be noted that members of the military-administrative and religious elites appeared before the council's court more frequently than in other types of judicial courts. The cases brought by these two groups were equal in number to the suits of common Muslims. Charges against members of the religious elite only slightly exceeded those they brought to the court (six to five). Members of the military-administrative elite acted as plaintiffs in four suits, while they faced charges in just one case: the plaintiff was the wife of the khan's provincial official (*emin*) who had died after being wounded by three janissaries. Although the number of cases is too small to allow any sort of generalization, it is worth noting that elite members appeared in the court at the council av frequently as they appeared in the *kadıasker* court (over 35 percent of disputants were from the elite). To compare, the elite constituted only around 10 precent of the disputants in Kara Su.

This brings us to the issue of the types of cases heard by the court at the khan's council. We might ask whether the suits heard by this judicial forum were different in character from those judged by the *kadıasker* and the district *kadı*s. The analysis of types of cases brought to the three types of courts demonstrates a remarkable difference in the proportions of various types of cases. Some matters, like contracts, family disputes, theft, and usurpation cases (i.e., seizure of property) were not brought to the *divan* (the case of Kleemann is an exception). And financial and property disputes were less frequently heard by this organ than by the other courts. Yet, the most striking difference concerns the cases related to murder and assault, which constitute two-thirds of the cases heard by the court of the khan's council (fourteen of twenty-two cases) and fewer than 10 percent of the cases heard by the *kadıasker* or the judge of Kara Su (159 and 20 cases respectively).

We can but wonder why the cases related to murder and assault were over-represented among those heard by the khan's council. When a sentence pronounced by the khan and his council was recorded, it imposed financial obligations on the individuals found guilty, whereas I have not found any record of flogging or capital punishment. This fact seems to suggest that the cases related to murder and assault that were brought to the council were perceived as a specific type of financial disputes. On the other hand, the high number of such cases heard at the khan's council seems to indicate that the plaintiffs and the ruler attached special importance to them. The lack of references to previous proceedings in district courts or in the *kadıasker* court may indicate that individuals brought their cases directly, like Kleemann did, to the khan's council. Then, why did not they trust local judicial courts to establish guilt or innocence? Apparently, it was not because of the judicial knowledge of the local *kadı*s, as equally complex legal cases are known to have been heard by district and *kadıasker* courts.[168] Perhaps the over-representation of the cases related to murder and assault should be explained by other factors. The plaintiffs could decide to move the proceedings if they feared unfavorable local conditions. Rather than losing in a local court, they preferred to bear the costs of a lawsuit in the capital. Still, why did they choose to avoid having a district *kadı* judge their case? Were they afraid that because of his relations with the defendants, he would not judge impartially? Although the possibility of corruption of district *kadı*s is worth examining, it still does not explain the high ratio of one sort of cases, i.e., those related to murder and assault.

Perhaps a comparison with cases recorded in the petitionary registers of the Ottoman Imperial Council might explain the high ratio of criminal cases recorded as adjudicated by the central authority. Başak Tuğ noted that, among the petitions brought to the Imperial Council, routine issues such as debt,

168 ORRNB, Fond 917, *defter* 22/78b/1, 23a/134b/2.

loans, and other small financial disputes comprised a small number compared to the criminal cases recorded. According to Tuğ, the majority of cases concerning less important matters were simply left unregistered. Fariba Zarinebaf, on the other hand, stresses that Muslim and non-Muslim courts usually reported serious crime to the Imperial Council, and prosecuted less important ones in their local communities.[169]

Frequent changes on the Crimean throne created a chance for litigants to revisit the sentences pronounced under previous khans. For example, during the reign of Murad Giray, a certain Mehmed from the district of Dib Tarkhan claimed blood money from a village in the same district, in recompense for the death of his sons. Abdulkerim Monla and Seyyid Sufi, who represented the village in the *kadıasker* court where the lawsuit took place, produced witnesses who stated that the plaintiff withdrew his charges during the proceeding in front of the council of the previous khan, Selim I Giray. According to the latter's sentence, blood money was to be paid by an inhabitant of the village, a man named Ibrahim, son of Akay, who had actually killed the plaintiff's sons.[170] In this case, the defendants were able to produce the witnesses from the former proceeding, so it was impossible to change the previous sentence or reopen the lawsuit. Yet, the very fact that Mehmed tried to change the previous sentence obtained at the court of the *kadıasker* indicates that, in his eyes, the first judicial forum did not have more authority than the *kadıasker* court, especially after the khan who had pronounced the earlier sentence was deposed. He could try again and again in the hope that he might finally obtain a preferable sentence.

• • •

In this Chapter I presented the most important institutions of the khanate, beginning with a description of the khan's household. I paid special attention to the women of the ruling dynasty, and their role in domestic and foreign policy. Materials dating to the period between the early sixteenth and the mid-eighteenth century allow us to observe that while the Giray women began to follow the Muslim custom of seclusion more strictly, they also enjoyed some influence on foreign and domestic policy. I also described the officials and servants who surrounded the members of the ruling dynasty residing in the khan's palace. While some of them were slaves, others were recruited from non-*karaçı* noble families. The latter were appointed to the most important executive

169 Zarinebaf, *Crime and Punishment*, 142.

170 ORRNB, Fond 917, *defter* 23b/52a/6.

offices, those of the *vizier*, the *defterdar* and the *hazinedar*, who are among the members of the khan's council. Aside from the khan and the above-mentioned officials, this institution included the *kalga*, the *nuraddin*, the *karaçı beğ*s, the mufti, and the *kadıasker*. In the next two Sections I discussed the powers and responsibilities of the *kalga* and the *nuraddin*, who were, respectively, first and second heir apparent to the khan. In the final Section I described the khan's council and focused on the judicial prerogatives of this institution as it judged cases at the council. In addition to two European descriptions of such hearings, I analyzed the records of twenty-three such cases that were preserved in the *sicil*s from the reign of Murad Giray. This material indicates that the litigants from various social groups could bring their claims to the council. It also points to differences in the types of cases brought to this forum, as compared to the *kadıasker* court or district court. About two-thirds of the cases brought to the council concerned murder and assault, as opposed to fewer than 10 percent in the other two courts.

CHAPTER 3

The Khan and the Nobles

> In addition to them [the khan, the *kalga*, and the *nuraddin*], the Şirin *beğ*s and the Crimean *mirza*s each had thousands of Tatars at his service in his domain; they [i.e., the Şirin *beğ*s and the Crimean *mirza*s] have the laws, [i.e., the customs and the codes of law].[1]

Over the last twenty years, various scholars have argued that no Chingisid khan could act as a despotic ruler. In 1986, Uli Shamiloglu described the role of four *karaçı beğ*s who took an active part in the government of the post-Chingisid states,[2] while David Sneath, an anthropologist, elaborated on the vital role of the aristocracy in the steppe polities of Inner Asia.[3]

The Crimean Khanate, as a successor of the Islamized Golden Horde, had a complicated political and administrative structure based on a combination of Golden Horde and Islamic traditions. The strong position of nobles in the khanate constitutes a vital part of the heritage of the Great Steppe.

Much remains unknown about the Crimean nobles. While their political role is relatively well documented, basic facts concerning their internal organization remain obscure. In this chapter I endeavor to fill this gap. At the present stage of research, numerous questions concerning the relations between various groups of nobles, the size and location of their estates, as well as their organization and the scope of the khan's power within the borders of these estates, remain

1 "Bunlardan ma'ada Şirin begleri ve Kırım mirzaları vardır ki her birinin tahti hükümetde nice bin Tatar hizmetgüzarları vardır, töreleri ya'ni 'adetleri ve kanunlarıdır"; see Zajączkowski (ed.), *La chronique*, 59.

2 U. Shamiloglu, "Tribal Politics and Social Organization in the Golden Horde," PhD diss. (Columbia University, 1986).

3 The author exposes some misconceptions about the so-called tribal societies of Central Asia, which are usually described in contrast to the agricultural and urban-based societies of Europe. The relative equality of the tribal societies compared to the hierarchy and social stratification of European societies was central in such descriptions. Sneath rejects the view that kinship was a dominant factor in the organization of tribal societies. Numerous twentieth-century studies made it clear that many tribal societies did not, in fact, share a genealogical kinship. Sneath also disagrees with Albert Hourani, who maintained that even if the members of a tribe were not related, they claimed to be by inventing a so-called *fictive kinship*; see D. Sneath, *The Headless State: Aristocratic Orders, Kinship Society, and Misrepresentations of Nomadic Inner Asia* (New York, 2007), 50.

 DOI:10.1163/9789004384323_005

unanswered. The extent of the nobles' economic independence seems to have had a great impact on their relations with the ruler. In the present chapter I describe the internal organization of the Crimean nobles and its possible impact on their relations with the khan. The chapter is divided into three parts. The first contains general remarks on the origins of the Crimean noble families and their position before the reforms of Sahib Giray (prior to 1532). The second depicts the *karaçı* families and describes the rights and duties of their powerful *beğ*s. The *beğ*s, along with their families, are described as clients and coordinators of the khanate's judicial system. The third part focuses on the non-*karaçı* families, and describes their social position as revealed by narrative sources. This section is followed by two micro-studies based on cases involving noblemen. The first study offers some general statistics concerning the types of cases in which the nobles were involved. The second centers on the members of the Yaşlav family in the *kadıasker* court and is based on information largely drawn from the *sicil*s dating back to Murad Giray's reign. Thus, our research covers a limited period. It is clear that only research based on the whole collection of the Crimean court registers can provide satisfactory data on the inner organization of the noble families. Nonetheless, these two micro-studies present a methodological proposal for future research on Crimean history.

1 The Crimean Nobles to 1532

A considerable segment of the Crimean nobility could trace its roots back to the Golden Horde. Uli Shamiloglu demonstrated that until the reign of Sahib Giray the Crimean nobility could be divided into two groups: the *karaçı* families and the non-*karaçı* noble families. The author pointed out that up up to the end of the fifteenth century, in numerous aspects the Crimean *karaçı beğ*s resembled their counterparts in other successor states of Chingis Khan's empire. The *beğ* headed his tribe and administered its estate (*beylik*). He had authority over the tribal hierarchy which was separate from the administration of the khan. In wartime, the *beğ* led his kinsmen and client nobles. The *beğ*s played an important role in Crimean foreign policy, for instance, they confirmed the treaties concluded by the khan. Finally, the *beğ* took part in the general diet (*kurultay*), which elected the ruler. The non-*karaçı* noble families consisted of nobles who were clients of either the *karaçı beğ*s or the ruler. They also took part in the *kurultay* and thus had the right to elect a new khan.

Vladimir Syroechkovskii studied a somewhat later period, namely the reign of Mehmed I Giray (1515–23); he drew his data mainly from Russian and Lithuanian diplomatic sources. Syroechkovskii stated that many types of nobles coexisted in the Crimean Khanate, i.e., the *karaçı beğ*s and their families, the *ulans*, *içki beğ*s, and *mirza*s. Unlike Shamiloglu, he did not restrict his classification to the two groups. At the same time, he made valuable remarks on the hierarchy and position of nobles in the state organization. A part of his study concerning the *karaçı beğ*s provides us with information on their origin and role in the foundation of the khanate. His remarks concerning the internal hierarchy of this group are of particular importance to our study. Syroechkovskii observed that the Şirins, who had the most power, were followed by the Barıns. The Mangıts, who by the seventeenth century became the Şirins' major rivals, were still newcomers during the reign of Mehmed I Giray, whose father, Mengli I Giray, highly respected their head, who settled in the Crimea. The khan granted the Mangıt leader the title of "great prince" (*velikii knaz*), thus recognizing his noble origins (traced back to Edigei) and military power.[4] However, despite their virtues, the Mangıts did not automatically receive *karaçı* status. The Crimean tradition attributed their promotion directly to Khan Sahib Giray.[5] Syroechkovskii also attempted to determine the number of *karaçı beğ*s. He reached two interesting conclusions: first, he observed that at the beginning of the sixteenth century, the Şirins and Barıns had no equals among other *karaçı*s; second, he admitted that, apart from these two families, the composition and size of this group was not clear. Syroechkovskii identified a few possible candidates, e.g., the Seceuts, Kipçaks, and Argıns. Yet, in another place he observed that their status was similar to that of other families, such as the Koirats and Kiyats.[6] He suggested that the most important indicator of *karaçı* status was the permanent place of the family head in the khan's council. Unfortunately, Syroechkovskii's sources did not provide clear criteria on how to distinguish *karaçı beğ*s from other noble members of the council.

Another important issue addressed by Syroechkovskii involves the role of the general diet (*kurultay*). This institution made the choice of a new khan from among the members of the Giray dynasty. The khans also used to call the *kurultay* to obtain its approval of military campaigns. Yet, from the time of Mehmed I Giray, the khans preferred to discuss political matters in a smaller group of councilors consisting of the Giray princes, the *karaçı*s, *ulans*, and a select group of *beğ*s and ulemas. In sum, Syroechkovskii gives us a picture of a state in the process of reshaping its institutions inherited from the Golden Horde. The composition and prerogatives of its most important institutions, like the khan's council, the *kurultay*, and the *karaçı* group, were not yet clearly defined.

---

4 Syroechkovskii, "Mukhammed-Gerai," 34–39.

5 Kazembeg (ed.), [*Seyyid*] *Muhammad Riza*, 93.

6 Syroechkovskii, "Mukhammed-Gerai," 31.

2 The Crimean Nobles in the Years from 1532 to 1774

In his seminal article, Halil Inalcık described Khan Sahib Giray's reforms, which were designed to strengthen his power.[7] The introduction of Ottoman administrative and military solutions, the promotion of the Mangıts to *karaçı* status, and the increase in the number of the khan's noble clients all served this purpose. The khan aimed to use the new groups of influence to balance the power of the old *karaçı* families and the rebellious members of the Giray dynasty. These political moves seemed to be successful during the first part of his reign. Remmal Hoca left a convincing picture of a wise and strong ruler who secured internal peace and led successful military campaigns. At the very peak of his power, Sahib Giray appeared to have the power of life and death over his vassals. For instance, he executed his former ally Baki Beğ, the leader of the Mangıts, when the latter became a threat to his rule.[8] Remmal Hoca made it clear that neither the Ottomans nor the Crimean vassals desired such a powerful khan. When Sahib Giray excused himself from sending auxiliary troops to the sultan's campaign in Persia in 1546, the pashas at the Porte, according to the chronicler, raised an alarm before the sultan:

> Our Lord, thanks to you the khan ascended the throne, you have augmented his treasury and strengthened his army. [But now] he shows disrespect to [You] Our Lord. The proof of it is that he now dares to oppose your orders and to make excuses for not sending auxiliary troops. The moment you pass away he thinks he will gain possession of all the territories [in the Crimea] .... If he unites his forces with the Nogays, no one can be a match for him and resist. Now it is the time to take precautions.[9]

Sahib Giray lost Ottoman support, and a few years later the Sublime Porte sent Devlet Giray, his nephew, to seize the Crimean throne, and Bölük Giray Sultan killed Sahib Giray.[10] He probably had support among the Crimean and Nogay nobles, who were also tired of Sahib Giray's despotic policies. Thus, the khan's effort to subdue the *karaçı* families ended in failure. Below we discuss the names and number of these families, as well as their political rights and internal organization.

---

7 Inalcık, "The Khan and the Tribal Aristocracy."
8 Gökbilgin (ed.), *Tarihi Sahib Giray Han*, 69–70/208–209.
9 Gökbilgin (ed.), *Tarihi Sahib Giray Han*, 114–115/247–248; Inalcık, "The Khan and the Tribal Aristocracy," 464.
10 Gökbilgin (ed.), *Tarihi Sahib Giray Han*, 142.

2.1 *The karaçı Families*

2.1.1 The Names and Number of the *karaçı* Families

Narrative sources provide various names and numbers of the *karaçı* families; these are clearly demonstrated in Table 2, which contains information extracted from various Crimean and European accounts on the subject.

From these accounts, we know that there were between four and six *karaçı* families. The Crimean chroniclers were aware that according to the Chingisid tradition, there should be four *karaçı*s;[11] its increase in the Crimean Khanate was attributed to Sahib Giray. Remmal Hoca stated that he had elevated the Mangıts to the status of *karaçı beğ*s, while Seyyid Mehmed Riza credited him with the promotion of two families: the Mangıts and the Seceuts. This suggests that Khan Sahib Giray tried to alter the Golden Horde institution of four *karaçı beğ*s to suit his needs. It is equally noteworthy that numerous sources, regardless of the time they were written, mention fewer than four dignitaries. This fact might also indicate that the number of *karaçı beğ*s remained flexible.

All the accounts make it clear that the Şirins were the most eminent vassals of the khan. Their leader enjoyed the title of the *head karaçı* (*baş karaçı*). Until the 1570s, the Barıns were second in rank. However, by the mid-seventeenth century they were superseded by the Mangıts. The Argıns and Seceuts were also frequently listed among the *karaçı* families from the mid-sixteenth to the eighteenth century. The sixth family, the Kipçaks, remains a mystery. In the sixteenth century, they were listed among the *karaçı*s. In addition, Seyyid Mehmed Riza, the eighteenth-century chronicler, mentioned them in reference to the sixteenth century. Yet, no source listed them among the *karaçı*s in the seventeenth and eighteenth centuries. Admittedly, the Russian lists of nobility, dating to 1807 and 1839, referred to the Kipçak leaders as "*beğ*s,"[12] a title that suggests that they still enjoyed *karaçı* status. Yet, we cannot ignore the fact that the same sources also listed the Yaşlavs as *beğ*s, and they did not hold *karaçı* status in the Crimean Khanate. It is quite possible that after the sixteenth century the Kipçaks became so weak that they lost their privileged status.

To sum up, our sources provide us with some information about the names and number of the *karaçı beğ*s. Yet, the descriptions differ so much that only the leading role of the Şirins emerges as a constant. In numerous sources we encounter five *karaçı* families, next to the Şirins, these were the Mangıts/Mansurs, Barıns, Argıns, and Seceuts. The divergent descriptions of their number and composition should not be ignored, though the reasons for such

11 Hacı Mehmed Senai, *Historia chana*, 92/7; Abdulgaffar Kyrymi, *Umdet al-akhbar*, 222.

12 Lashkov, "Istoricheskii ocherk," *ITUAK* 22 (1895), 69–70.

TABLE 2 The *karaçı* families.

Author	*Karaçı* families
Remmal Hoca (1530s–1550s)	1) Şirin, Barın, Mangıt, and Kipa 2) Şirin, Barın, Mangıt, Kipçak, and Argın[a]
Marcin Broniewski (1570–1580s)	Şirin, Barın, Mangıt, and Kipçak[b]
Ivan Sudakov (1580s)	Şirin, Seceut, Kipçak[c]
Khachatur (1620s–1650s)	Şirin and Mansur[d]
D'Ascoli (1630s)	Şirin and the *beğ*s of Crimea (Eski Kırım?) and Mangup[e]
Khan Bahadır Giray (1640)	Şirin, Mansur, Argın, Seceut, and Barın[f]
Abdullah, son of Rizvan Paşa (1630s–1640s)	Şirin[g]
Evliya Çelebi (1660s)	Şirin and Mansur as the members of the khan's council[h]
Mehmed Senai (1650s)	Şirin, Mangıt, Seceut, and Argın[i]
Khan Murad Giray (1682)	Five *karaçı beğ*s[j]
ORRNB, Fond 917, *defter* 22, 23a, 23b, 25 (1670–1680s)	Şirin, Mansur, Argın, Barın, and Seceut[k]
Vasilii Mikhailov Tiapkin and Nikita Zotov (1680s)	Şirin[l]
Vasilii Aitemiriev (1690s)	Şirin, Mansur, Argın, Seceut, and others[m]
Mehmed Giray (1700s)	Şirin, Mansur, Seceut[n]
Abdulgaffar el-Kırımi (1750s)	Şirin, Mansur, Barın, Seceut[o]
Said Giray (1750s)	Şirin, Mansur, and Seceut[p]
Charles Peysonnel (1760s)	Şirin, Mansur, Seceut, Argın, Barın[q]
François de Tott (1770s)	Şirin, Mansur, Seceut, Argın, Barın[r]
Nicolas Kleemann (1770s)	Şirin, Barın, Mansur, and Seceut[s]
Seyyid Mehmed Riza (second half of the eighteenth century)	1) Until the reforms of Khan Sahib Giray: Şirin, Barın, Argın, Kipçak 2) After the reforms of Khan Sahib Giray: Şirin, Barın, Argın, Kipçak, Seceut, and Mansur[t]

a Gökbilgin (ed.), *Tarihi Sahib Giray Han*, 113/245; 288.
b Broniewski, *Tartariae Descriptio*, 14.
c Ivan Sudakov clearly distinguished the *beğ* of the Şirins from other *karaçıs*. As the tsar only sent gifts to the first one, he ordered that any demands from the others be rejected. Interestingly,

in the Russian list of Crimean nobles who received gifts from the tsar, the *beğ*s of the Yaşlavs, Kulikovs, and Akchigaevs (?) were recorded just after the *beğ* of the Şirins. Yet, their names were not preceded by the title *karaçı*, in contrast to the names of the *beğ*s of the Şirins, Seceuts (recorded as Chizhiuts), and Kipçaks; cf. Lashkov, "Stateinyi spisok moskovskogo," 50 and 53.

d Schütz (ed.), "Eine armenische Chronik," 173–174.

e d'Ascoli, *Descrittione*, 23.

f The treaty between Bahadır Giray and the Polish-Lithuanian Commonwealth (AGAD, AKW, Dz. tatarski, k. 63, t. 32, no. 495).

g Zajączkowski (ed.), *La chronique*, 59, 89, 93.

h Next to the Şirins and the Mansurs, Evliya also mentioned the *beğ*s of the Seceut, Dair, and Saruhan as commanders who led warriors during military campaigns (Abrahamowicz, Dubiński, and Płaskowicka-Rymkiewicz (trans.), *Księga podróży Ewliji Czelebiego*, 234, 278–279; Evliya Çelebi, *Tam Metin Seyahatnâme*, 311, 351).

i Hacı Mehmed Senai, *Historia chana*, 92/7.

j Murad Giray referred to five *karaçı beğ*s in his letter to the tsars, Ivan and Peter. Unfortunately, he did not mention their family names (Faizkhanov and Vel'aminov-Zernov (eds.), *Materialy dla istorii*, no. 264).

k ORRNB, Fond 917, *defter* 23b/6a/2; ORRNB, Fond 917, *defter* 23a/243a/2; ORRNB, Fond 917, *defter* 25/5b/2; ORRNB, Fond 917, *defter* 25/5b/4.

l Murzakevich (ed.), "Spisok s stateinago," 633.

m Markievich (ed.), "Spisok," *ZOOID* 18 (1895), 31, 65; *ZOOID* 19 (1896), 48, 51.

n Köhbach (ed.), "Der Tarih-i Mehemmed Giray," 146, 157.

o Abdulgaffar Kyrymi, *Umdet al-akhbar*, 222.

p Kellner-Heinkele (ed.), *Aus den Aufzeichnungen*, 109.

q Peysonnel, *Traité sur le commerce*, 2:269–274.

r Tott, *Mémoires* (*Memoirs*, 2:405).

s Kleemann, *Voyage de Vienne à Belgrade*, 209.

t Kazembeg (ed.), [*Seyyid*] *Muhammad Riza*, 93.

an equivocal picture remain obscure. We would argue that—apart from the Şirins—in order to confirm the *karaçı* status of a given family we must examine the sources, both Tatar and foreign, relevant to each khan's reign.

2.1.2 The Internal Organization, Rights, and Duties of the *karaçı* Families

Uli Shamiloglu stated that the elevated position of the *karaçı* families in the early history of the Crimean Khanate was a result of their Chingisid heritage. He listed their numerous privileges, such as their autonomous internal organization, and their right to elect the khan, influence the khanate's foreign policy, and lead their clients during military campaigns. In the present section I examine whether these rights survived Sahib Giray's reforms. And if the status quo was not preserved, what was changed?

Narrative sources suggest that the *beylik*s' autonomy was preserved. The chronicle of Mehmed Senai contains the following statement regarding the enthronement of Islam III Giray in 1644:

> From ancient times and according to Chingisid law, there have been four dignitaries called *karaçı*. Each of these exalted *emir*s holds the rank of the *emir* of *liva*. The first is the *emir* of the *liva* of the Şirins, the second of the Mangıts, the third of the Seceuts, and the fourth of the Argıns. Their family estates (*ocaklık*s) are ruled by the *beğ*s (*begler*), who are neither nominated nor dismissed [by the khans] but perform their duties [from the time of their appointment] to the ends of their lives. All of them, wearing robes of honor, approached the khan, walking on foot, and leading their horses, as is prescribed by law. [Then the ruler] confirmed their [current] ranks. In addition, [in the Crimea] there are plenty of *beğ*s who rule their family estates (*ocaklık*s). According to ancient custom, their ranks were also confirmed [by the khan].[13]

From this passage we learn that the *karaçı* families were headed by *beğ*s whose ranks, which they already held, were confirmed by the khan. Nonetheless, Syroechkovskii suggested that, at least in the early sixteenth century, the ruler could directly interfere in their appointments.[14] While normally the khan simply confirmed the next in line, he could overlook seniority and give the post to his favorite. In the mid-eighteenth century, Peyssonel observed that the khans influenced the appointments of new *beğ*s, but informally and indirectly.[15] In general, the noble families followed the Mongol tradition of succession, i.e., the eldest male member of a family became its head.[16]

A question arises as to how the *beğ* ruled the *beylik* and his family. What were his responsibilities? Could he rely on the help of other officials? If so, how were they recruited and what were their prerogatives? An examination of the main fields of activity of the *beğ*s of the *karaçı* families sheds light on these issues.

Not surprisingly, the *karaçı beğ*s played an important role in politics. Their crucial role in the khan's council was described by Abdulgaffar elKırımi (quoted in Uli Shamiloglu's translation) as follows:

> Let it be known that it is not legal for a glorious order (*emr-i azîm*) to be executed without its first having passed to the able hands of the four principal beys, who are the firm pillars of the organization of the *divan* and other affairs of the Crimean khans, and being voted upon by them

13 Hacı Mehmed Senai, *Historia chana*, 92/7 (my translation).

14 Syroechkovskii, "Mukhammed-Gerai," 35.

15 Peysonnel, *Traité sur le commerce*, 2:251.

16 Tott, *Mémoires* (*Memoirs*, 2:406).

> [i.e., the four beys]. The first of the four pillars, called *karaçıs*, is the Şirin, the second the Mansuroğlu, the third the Barın, and the fourth the Sicivut. When a matter of state comes up … the four *karaçı* beys along with their *mirzas* (and the leaders of others clans as well as the elders of the Crimean Porte) enter into a protocol (*mükaleme*) following consultation. Once the emirs who have a vote [i.e., the *qaraçı* beys] and who govern foreign affairs have affixed [their] seals (*hitam*) to the protocol, it is submitted to the ulema with the question: "Is it in conformity to the canonical law?" If so, it is signed and submitted to His Excellency, the khan of famed noble qualities, to be acted upon as required.[17]

According to the chronicler, the khan could not issue an order without the consent of the *karaçı beğs*. Hence, in this system, the ruler's government should have remained under the control of his vassals. As the khan's council also acted as a judicial court, its members participated in delivering justice. As case witnesses, they could control its proceedings. Glavani suggests that they could also influence the khan's ruling.

The role of the *karaçı beğs* in the *kurultay* also appears to be of great importance. From the accounts of Vasilii Aitemiriev (1696) and François de Tott (1760s), we learn that the *karaçı beğs* had the right to summon the *kurultay*. As both descriptions provide important details on the subject, I quote them *in extenso*. Aitemiriev's report contains the following observations:

> December 8 [1695]: The *karaçı beğs* [that is,] the Şirin and Mansur *beğs*, requested that the *kaymakam* Apkerim Efendi, along with the mufti, the *kadıasker*, and the well-known *mirzas* and *ağas* who lived in Bahçesaray, set out for [a place in] the vicinity of Kara Su.[18] There, they held a council. [When it ended,] on December 16, the *kaymakam* and other officials [who had traveled] from Bahçesaray returned [to the capital].
>
> News spread from this council that it was said that the khan and the Crimean army should return to the Crimea and defend their homes. For the last ten years, the Crimean warriors have helped the Turkish army every year. [The Tatars] not only did not benefit [from these campaigns], but they lost many people and horses. They died, weak, after having lost their horses during such long expeditions. Because of [these campaigns,] all the Tatars are going to perish. Only last summer, when the

17 Shamiloglu, "Tribal Politics," 184–185; Abdulgaffar Kyrymi, *Umdet al-akhbar*, 222.

18 "White Rock" (Ak Kaya), which is situated in the vicinity of Kara Su, was a traditional place for periodic assemblies (*kurultay*) of the Tatar nobility.

> Crimean and Bucak armies were absent from home, the Russian army and the Don and Zaporozhian Cossacks raided the territories of Crimea and Bucak. They ravaged villages and settlements. They wiped out [their inhabitants]. Thus [the council] decided that [the Tatars] should not go to Hungary or distant Wallachia, but should defend the Crimea against the pillaging of the Cossacks. It is written by the unbelievers in the Quran [i.e., the Russian envoy, Vasilii Aitemiriev]:
>
> If someone has a close enemy and instead of fighting that enemy, helps to fight a faraway enemy, it is not right. And after they [i.e., the participants of the council] wrote their decisions, they sent [them] to the khan to Adrianople by a servant of the khan's court, who was named Hacı Receb. And [they notified Khan Selim I Giray] that if he wished to remain their khan he should return to the Crimea immediately. If not, they would find another khan in the Crimea.[19]

In the following century, Tott stated

> The assemblies are never convoked but on the extraordinary occasions, to prevent the Kam [i.e., khan], who has the privilege of calling together the grand vassals, from taking advantage of their absence, to extend his authority beyond the bounds of the feudal system: the Bey of the Chirins constantly represents the Beys; and this Chief of the Tatar nobility, as well as the Sovereign, has his Calga, his Nouradin, his Ministers, and the right of calling together the assembly of the Beys, should this convocation, neglected by the Khan, become necessary to counteract even his designs.[20]

It is not clear who exactly had the right to summon the general diet (*kurultay*). According to Aitemiriev, all the *karaçı beğ*s, exemplified by the Şirin and Mansur *beğ*s, exercised such power. However, Tott stated that next to the khan only the Şirin *beğ* enjoyed this privilege, as the head of Tatar noblemen. His version conforms with the notion that the chief *karaçı beğ* enjoyed a special position. With regard to the circumstances in which the general diet could be summoned, both authors agreed that it served to protect the rights of the nobles against the ruler's authoritarian designs. Thus, the *beğ*s of the *karaçı*

---

19 Vasilii Aitemiriev got this information from his interpreter, who was present with the *kaymakam* just before the departure of Hacı Receb. Aitemiriev claimed that the interpreter had seen the council's letter to the khan; Markievich (ed.), "Spisok s stateinogo," *ZOOID* 19 (1896), 48–49.

20 Tott, *Mémoires* (*Memoirs*, 2:406).

families were supposed to act on behalf of the whole nobility. As Aitemiriev's report suggests, the *beğ*s acted in unison with the chief mufti to secure the support of the highest religious authority. Their decisive, if not openly rebellious, message to the khan was backed by the appropriate religious explanation. Several notes on the assemblies of *beğ*s and *mirza*s can also be found in the chronicle of Abdulgaffar el-Kırımi. Although he did not use the term *kurultay*, he referred to noble meetings that made vital decisions, for instance to send letters to the Ottoman sultan with requests to depose the khans in 1717 and 1724.[21] Xavier Glavani's report confirms that in 1724, the Şirins indeed summoned a few thousand noblemen to Ak Kaya, the customary meeting place of *kurultays*.[22] To sum up, the *beğ*s believed that the khan should govern in a way that respected their ancient rights. As members of the khan's council, they could control the ruler and if the latter made a decision threatening their vital interests, they could exercise their right to summon the general diet and withdraw their allegiance.

The political power of the *beğ*s was not limited to domestic policy, since they influenced the foreign relations of the khanate. The Crimean Tatars concluded numerous treaties with their neighbors; treaties that were confirmed by the Giray dignitaries as well as the *karaçı beğ*s. Foreign courts, which were familiar with the limitations of the khan's power, often requested, in the instructions given to European diplomats dispatched to the Crimea, confirmation of peace by the *karaçı beğ*s. Curiously, it happened that such demands were denied, not only by the khan but by the *karaçı*s as well. For instance, during the negotiations preceding the Bahçesaray Treaty of 1681, the Russian envoys requested that the peace should also be confirmed with the signatures of the *karaçı beğ*s. As the Russian instrument was confirmed only by the tsar, the *karaçı beğ*s argued that their ruler would be treated as less significant if anyone other than Murad Giray confirmed the treaty.[23] This case seems to show that in the second half of the seventeenth century the *karaçı beğ*s no longer regarded their participation in the confirmation of international treaties as an indispensable privilege and indicator of their status.

---

21 Abdulgaffar Kyrymi, *Umdet al-akhbar*, 161, 163–164.

22 Veinstein, "La révolte des mirza," 327–339.

23 "Krymskie chestnye piati rodov: Shirinskie, Suleshevy, Arginskie, Mansurovy, Kulikowy i s nimi bei i karachei i vse blizhnie ludi govorili nam: domogaetes' de vy poslanniki Ts[arsko]go V[elichest]va u nas togo, chego v Krymu ot veka ne povelos,' shtoby my ruki svoi i pechati prikladywat' k gramote Khanova V[elichest]va, ot chego by imelo byt' gosudaru ikh Khanovu V[elichest]vu i Kalge i Nuradynu saltanom chesti ikh velikoe umalenie, i zazor, i sherti ikh i k krepkomu soderzhaniu ne doverstvo"; see Murzakevich (ed.), "Spisok s stateinago," 631–633.

Apart from the confirmation of treaties, the *beğ* of the Şirins exercised the privilege of corresponding with the Ottoman sultan.[24] The *karaçıs* also used to send letters to European courts.[25]

Conducting military campaigns was yet another privilege and responsibility of the ruling *beğ*s. They led their subordinates, i.e., their relatives, clients, and common subjects, during military campaigns. Tatar incursions could be headed by members of the Giray dynasty or by members of the *karaçı* families. Our sources provide divergent data on the strength of the military units commanded by the karaçi families. The numbers concerning the Şirins range from between 5,000 and 30,000, and for other families between 1,000 and 10,000.[26] Unfortunately, the majority of sources only provide general numbers concerning the whole Crimean army. For instance, from a report of a Russian translator, Nikifor Ivanov, we learn that in 1683 Murad Giray left the peninsula for the Vienna campaign with 30,000 Tatars.[27] The ratio between the units directly subordinated to the Girays and those of the *karaçı* families remains unclear. We can only conclude that the *karaçı beğ*s had a considerable military power at their disposal, one that probably even outnumbered the army of the khan and his lesser clients. Yet, we must remember that the ruler headed the units of *sekban*s, patterned on the Ottoman janissaries and equipped with firearms, and this gave him an advantage over the Crimean nobility bearing traditional arms (e.g., swords, daggers).

The war constituted an important part of Tatar life and was a vital source of their income.[28] Participation in military campaigns created opportunities to gain wealth and honor. Yet, war was also a risky business. Aitemiriev's report, quoted above, clearly demonstrates that the *beğ*s were reluctant to take part in unprofitable and dangerous campaigns. The khan's orders to participate in such expeditions frequently caused serious disagreements between him and his vassals. The *beğ*s, as in 1696, believed that in such circumstances they had no duty to follow the ruler's order and even had the right to depose him.

---

24 Bennigsen, et al. (eds.), *Le khanat de Crimée*, 64–71.

25 See, for example, their letter preserved in the Polish archives, AGAD, AKW Dz. tatarski, k. 60; t. 29, no. 32; k. 61, t. 146, no. 290; k. 61, t. 153, no. 297.

26 D. Skorupa, *Stosunki polsko-tatarskie 1595–1623* (Warsaw, 2004), 28; Abrahamowicz, Dubiński, and Płaskowicka-Rymkiewicz (trans.), *Księga podróży Ewliji Czelebiego*, 279; Evliya Çelebi, *Tam Metin Seyahatnâme*, 351–352.

27 RGADA, Fond 123, *Posol'skii prikaz. Krymskie dela*, op. 1, no. 71, fols. 177v–178.

28 In February 1678, Jan Gniński, the Polish envoy to the Sublime Porte, met Murad Giray, who had recently been designated to the Crimean throne. During their meeting, Murad Giray stated, "You know that the Tatars live from booty and that it is easier to enrich ourselves in your territories than in Muscovy"; see Pułaski (ed.), *Źródła do poselstwa*, 77; Inalcık, "The Khan and the Tribal Aristocracy," 460–463.

Finally, the *beğs* were responsible for the administration of the *beyliks*. As stated by Fedor Lashkov, the *beylik* had Golden Horde origins and its function was to serve the interests of a specific family. Therefore, its lands could not be transferred out of the family, but constituted the common property of all the family members. The *beğ* was in charge of its administration and the division of income. The rents and tithes paid by the *beylik*'s inhabitants constituted a source of income for the members of the *karaçı* family. In 1802, the Russian commision gathered information on the number of days of unpaid labor previously provided by the common inhabitants of the *beyliks* to the noble families, but the sides involved provided different answers. While the commoners testified that they helped the nobles whenever they were asked, the *mirzas* specified that this labor amounted to eight to ten days yearly. According to Lashkov, the differences in these answers resulted from the fact that the amount of unpaid labor provided changed over time and differed between various *beyliks*.[29] From a privilege of Mehmed II Giray to the *beğ* of the Argıns, which dates back to 1577, we learn the names of other taxes which constituted an additional source of the *beğ*'s income: *tumanend*, *savga*, *buralka*, *ceraim*, and *koluş-kalanka*. All of these, apart from the *ceraim* ("fines" in Arabic), seem to have Mongol origins.[30] Perhaps we can find analogies between the *beyliks* and the *divani-malikanes* in the early Ottoman Empire, since both were administrated by individuals who acquired them through their hereditary rights, rather than by appointment from the khan. But here the similarities end. The owners of the *divani-malikane*, as described by Nicoara Beldiceanu and Huri İslamoğlu-İnan, were entitled to rent from their land; and this rent was determined not by them, but by Ottoman law. They had no judicial authority over the inhabitants of their lands. As noted, there is not enough evidence to determine whether the *beylik*'s inhabitants paid only the taxes levied by the khan, and whether the *beğ* had judicial authority over this group. Moreover, the owners of the *divani-malikane*, unlike the *beğs* and the members of the ruling families, could sell their revenue shares, divide them among their heirs or convert them into *vakfs*.[31] Perhaps, the *beylik* had more in common with the English institution of entail, which was used to limit succession to the line of the eldest son, since

29 ORRNB, Fond 917, *defter* 38/33a/4 38/33a/2; Lashkov, "Istoricheskii ocherk," *ITUAK* 23 (1895), 96–97.

30 Lashkov, "Istoricheskii ocherk," *ITUAK* 23 (1895), 88; Lashkov, "Sbornik dokumentov," *ITUAK* 23 (1895), 127.

31 N. Beldiceanu, *Le timar dans l'État ottoman (XIVe-XVe siècles)* (Wiesbaden, 1980), 33; H. İslamoğlu-İnan, *State and Peasant in the Ottoman Empire: Agrarian Power Relations and Regional Economic Development in Ottoman Anatolia During the Sixteenth Century* (Leiden and Boston, 1994), 62–70.

both institutions were designed to secure the economic and social position of a noble family by maintaining the unity of the estate.[32]

Numerous officials assisted the *beğ* in performing his administrative functions. As the *beylik* of the Şirins is better described than the others, we use it as an example to discuss the *beylik*'s officials. From the account of Tott quoted above, we know that the *beğ* of the Şirins had at his side a number of dignitaries with titles similar to those of the khan's officials. The French consul listed "his Calga, his Nouradin, his Ministers."[33] Unfortunately, he did not record the titles of the ministers. The court registers from the times of Murad Giray mention only one possible member of the *beğ*'s council: his steward, referred to by the Ottoman title *kethüda*.[34] The *kadıasker sicil* no. 26, which contains the records from the reigns of Hacı II Giray and Selim I Giray (3rd reign) and is chronologically the nearest to Murad Giray's reign, does not shed much more light, as apart from the *beğ*, it only mentions his steward[35] and scribe (*katib*).[36] Thus, we do not know whether the *beğ* had other officials modeled on those known from the khan's court, such as the *defterdar*, *hazinedar*, or *kapıcı başı*.

In domestic affairs, according to Lashkov, the *beğ* relied on elders (*stariki*).[37] As I discuss in detail in the next chapter, little is known about the judicial competences of the elders; just that they were certainly restrained by the judicial prerogatives of the local *kadı* and the khan's council. Still, we must take into consideration that it constituted an alternative forum to which disputes could be addressed for resolution. From Abdulgaffar el-Kırımi's chronicle it is clear that the *mirza*s advised the *beğ* in cases of political conflict.[38]

The *beğ* had subsidiary dignitaries titled "*kalga*" and "*nuraddin*." It is not clear how these ranks were designated.[39] Peyssonel's account offers ambiguous answers. In his description of the Şirin *beylik*, he stated that the oldest male relatives of the *beğ* automatically took these positions. Yet, Syroechkovskii notes that Khan Mengli I Giray and Khan Sahib Giray secured such prominent posts for younger members of the family.[40] Thus, the rule of seniority might have been broken in certain cases, or might have been somewhat flexible.

32 E. Spring, *Law, Land, and Family: Aristocratic Inheritance in England, 1300 to 1800* (Chapel Hill, NC, 1993), 69–71.
33 Tott, *Mémoires* (*Memoirs*, 2:406).
34 ORRNB, Fond 917, *defter* 26/ 19a/1.
35 ORRNB, Fond 917, *defter* 26/8a/4.
36 ORRNB, Fond 917, *defter* 26/58b/4.
37 Lashkov, "Istoricheskii ocherk," *ITUAK* 23 (1895), 79–90.
38 Abdulgaffar Kyrymi, *Umdet al-akhbar*, 187–190.
39 Josef Matuz discovered that the titles of *kalga* and *nuraddin* of the Şirins and the Mangıts were recorded for the first time as late as 1632–33; this suggests that the posts were modeled on those held by the Giray princes; see Matuz, "Qalga," 103.
40 Syroechkovskii, "Mukhammed-Gerai," 35.

The *beğ* seemed to face problems similar to those of the khan, with regard to control over his second and third in command. From Riza's account we learn about the tense relations between the three dignitaries during a family dispute among the Şirins in 1725. In that case, it is noteworthy that the khan's council was perceived as an appropriate institution to resolve their conflict.[41]

A question arises as to what extent we can extrapolate our results concerning the Şirins to other *karaçı* families. We would argue that the administrative competences of the *beğ*s within their *beylik*s were similar. This argument is supported by the example of the Yaşlav family (see below) who were the khan's lesser clients. We would not expect all the *karaçı beğ*s to maintain a similar number of officials, given that the income of the Şirins exceeded those of other *beylik*s.

2.1.3 The *karaçı* Families in the Sharia Courts

In the present section I focus on the members of the *karaçı* families as clients and case witnesses in the sharia courts. This is followed by a short analysis of the cases involving individuals from the Şirin, Argın, and Mangıt judicial districts. Unfortunately, none of the court registers from these *kaza*s has survived to our time. As the *sicil*s from the reign of Murad Giray contain just six entries involving two *karaçı* families (Argın and Seceut), our research is based on very limited data.[42] Thus, our sources offer only vague indications on the boundaries of the khan's legal power and the limits of judicial autonomy enjoyed by the *beğ*s.

Five out of six entries relating to the *karaçı* families concern conflicts about inheritances in the Argın family.[43] Kutlu Şah Mirza, a member of the Argın family from the village of Argın, left property worth 1,886 *guruş*. In September/October 1679, this property was divided between his wife, Alem Sultan; his mother, Mah Sultan; and his two brothers, Bahadır Şah Beğ[44] and Adil Mirza.[45] Each was to receive one-quarter of Kutlu Şah's property, i.e., 471.5 *guruş*. The second entry contains Mah Sultan's confirmation that she received her share of

---

41 Kazembeg (ed.), [*Seyyid*] *Muhammad Riza*, 330–332.

42 Peysonnel stated that the Crimean nobles solved their conflicts only in the *kadıasker* court or in front of the khan's council; cf. Peysonnel, *Traité sur le commerce*, 2:262. The entries recorded in the Kara Su *sicil*s make it clear that in the 1680s, the Crimean *mirza*s used the district court as well.

43 It is noteworthy that even the Şirins brought their disputes concerning the division of inheritance to the *kadıasker* court; cf. Lashkov, "Sbornik dokumentov," *ITUAK* 23 (1895), 118–120; Lashkov, "Istoricheskii ocherk," *ITUAK* 23 (1895), 105–107.

44 Bahadır Şah Beğ, the *beğ* of the Argıns, is also listed among the case witnesses of a hearing that took place at the khan's council; cf. ORRNB, Fond 317, *defter* 23b/113b/7. He is also mentioned in an order of Khan Murad Giray in 1682. The khan secured Bahadır Şah Beğ's share in the gifts brought by Russian envoys; see Lashkov, "Sbornik dokumentov," *ITUAK* 23 (1895), 128.

45 ORRNB, Fond 317, *defter* 23b/43b/1; 23b/44a/1–2, 23b/44b/1.

the inheritance, and the third entry concerns the repayment of debts incurred by Kutlu Şah Mirza. The fourth entry records a dispute between the heirs and the late *mirza*'s slave, in which the latter proved that his master had set him free; thus, he no longer constituted a part of the inheritance. As his statement was confirmed by two witnesses, he was proclaimed free. The four cases above were recorded consecutively, which suggests that they were brought to the court at the same time. The fifth entry was registered one and a half years later, in April 1681. It contains an amicable settlement concluded by the widow and the two brothers of Kutlu Şah Mirza. Alem Sultan, daughter of Can Mehmed Mirza, confirmed that she had received her share of the inheritance of her late husband. Earlier, she had claimed a few properties that she had obtained from her husband during the marriage, properties that were erroneously listed among the inheritance, so her brother-in-law, Bahadır Şah Beğ, concluded an amicable settlement with her and gave her money and slaves in exchange for the real estate given to her by Kutlu Şah Mirza.[46] It was common for Crimean women to prefer money and material objects to land or, as in this case, river mills.

In addition to the cases discussed above involving Bahadır Şah Beğ and his protégé, Abdulşahid Efendi, who was appointed as a *kadı* of the Argın district, the *sicil*s from Kara Su contain just one other case involving members of the *karaçı* families. This concerns a simple purchase of slaves made by the *beğ* of the Seceuts.[47] This record, like those involving the Argıns, concerns exclusively financial matters. It is of interest that in the case regarding the Argın inheritance the conflicts recorded in the *sicil*s only refer to disputes between the family members and "outsiders," i.e., those individuals who were not blood relatives of Kutlu Şah Mirza: his wife[48] and his slave. In these disputes, the Argın family appeared united and was represented by the *beğ*.

Yet another public role performed by the *karaçı beğ*s involved serving as case witnesses in hearings at the khan's council. The question arises, did they take part in the proceedings intentionally, or by chance. Research on members of the Ottoman elite acting as circumstantial witnesses and *şuhudülhal* reveals that they frequently assumed these roles in the court. Here we should reinterate that the case witnesses seemed to serve a variety of functions, such as supervising the *kadı*'s work and confirming the reliability of individuals ap-

46 ORRNB, Fond 317, *defter* 23b/69a/1.

47 ORRNB, Fond 317, *defter* 25b/5b/4.

48 It is worth noting that the mother of Kutlu Şah, in contrast to his wife, was treated as a family member. Presumably, because she had given birth to at least one son, while her daughter-in-law seemed to be childless.

pearing in court.[49] Thus, it comes as no surprise that we encounter members of the elite of the local community. In the case of the khanate, we would expect to find nobles frequently listed among the *şuhudülhal*.

The twenty-three cases judged at the council of Murad Giray that were discussed earlier reveal that the *karaçı beğ*s were only listed among the case witnesses twice. The *beğ* of the Mangıts was present during a case concerning a mosque situated in the Mangıt district. Thus, he attended a dispute among individuals who came from his own *beylik* or its vicinity. The case concerned a quarrel between two ulema families over the right of patronage over the said mosque. Both parties claimed the right to appoint and dismiss its religious officials, i.e., the imam and khatib. The sentence seemed to result in a compromise between the parties' claims. There is no evidence that the *beğ* directly influenced the verdict.[50] Bahadır Şah Beğ, the *beğ* of the Argıns, is the second karaçi listed among the case witnesses. As noted, he had no clear interest in the outcome of the case in which he served as a case witness.[51]

In six other cases brought to the khan's council, the parties involved came from territories situated in the vicinity of at least one *beylik*. However, the respective *karaçı beğ*s were not recorded among the case witnesses. The *beğ*'s absence is especially noteworthy in a case concerning the right of patronage over a mosque situated in the Şirin district.[52] Although the dispute was similar to the case from the Mangıt district described above, unlike the *beğ* of the Mansurs, the head of the Şirin family did not appear as a case witness.

It seems that the *karaçı beğ*s were not obliged to supervise their subjects' proceedings in the khan's council or to support their claims. Apparently, such activity was regarded as exceeding the customary obligations of a patron toward his clients. Nonetheless, the account of Xavier Glavani proves that,[53] if needed, the *beğ*s could influence the proceedings in the khan's council.

Before moving on, it is important to establish whether the inhabitants of the Mangıt, the Argın, and the Şirin districts used the sharia courts. During the reign of Murad Giray, they were involved in fourteen cases registered in the *kadıasker sicil*s and in eight cases recorded in the Kara Su *sicil*s. Inhabitants of the Argın and Şirin *kaza*s appeared with similar frequency (eight and eleven cases respectively), while individuals from the Mangıt *kaza* were involved in only three cases. The litigants had different social backgrounds and the major-

49 See, for example, Canbakal, *Society and Politics*, 123–149; Coşgel and Ergene, *Economics of Ottoman Justice*, 70–75.

50 ORRNB, Fond 917, *defter* 23b/92b/2.

51 ORRNB, Fond 917, *defter* 23a/142b/7.

52 ORRNB, Fond 917, *defter* 23b/92b/2.

53 Veinstein, "Les Tatars de Crimée," 34–36.

ity of claims concerned financial matters. Only six cases were related to other issues: the right of patronage (i.e., the two cases discussed above), assault (two cases), divorce (one case), and the manumission of a slave (one case). In sum, there was nothing uncommon in the way the inhabitants of the *beylik* districts used the courts.

2.2 *Non*-karaçı *Noble Families*

2.2.1 The Social Position of the Non-*karaçı* Noble Families

Numerous sources underline the vital difference between the *karaçı* and non-*karaçı* noble families. The latter group consisted of two types. The first was composed of less eminent families who had settled in the khanate in the time of the Golden Horde. They owned family *beylik*s whose administration was analogous to that of the *karaçı beylik*s and whose inhabitants owed them rent and unpaid labor.[54] These families were clients of the Giray dynasty or the *karaçı beğ*s. The second group was composed of the Girays' former servants, who were granted income, from the khan, derived from the ruler's domain.[55] The khan used to reward his faithful servants by granting them *soyurgal*s. The institution of *soyurgal*, which means "favor" in Mongolian, was rooted in the Mongol-Turkic tradition and also functioned elsewhere in the Middle East.[56] Over the course of time, the meaning of the term evolved from simple monetary grants to a grant of immunity from the interference of government officials in land belonging to the beneficiary or in crown land bestowed on the beneficiary.[57] It is possible that the institution of the Mongol *soyurgal* was gradually replaced in the Crimea by the Ottoman *timar*, or was reshaped to resemble the latter.[58] In 1684/85, Hacı II Giray listed *dirlik sahibi*s among the various types of military units, whereas in Ottoman usage the term *dirlik sahibi* referred to a *timar* holder.[59] Although research on the Crimean *timar* system

---

54 See, for example, a dispute between Şahbaz and Orus, sons of Ahmed Mirza, with the inhabitants of their village situated on the Kaçı River. The judge confirmed that each year the noblemen were entitled to the customary rent, that is, one day of unpaid labor and one cart of firewood (ORRNB, Fond 317, *defter* 22/73b/2).

55 Lashkov, "Istoricheskii ocherk," *ITUAK* 23 (1895), 91–95; Syroechkovskii, "Mukhammed-Gerai," 44–47.

56 K. Paydaş, "Moğol ve Türkİslam Devletlerinde Suyurgal Uygulaması," *Bilig* 39 (2006), 195–218.

57 A.K.S. Lambton, "Soyūrghāl," *EI*[2].

58 Based on Lashkov's research, Alan Fisher states that *timar*s were introduced in the Crimean Khanate as early as 1550; Fisher, *Crimean Tatars*, 23; Lashkov, "Istoricheskii ocherk," *ITUAK* 23 (1895), 92–93.

59 ORRNB, Fond 917, *defter* 25/112b/2.

is beyond the scope of the present study, the issue certainly deserves further investigation.

What were the political rights of the non-*karaçı* noble families? As members of the *kurultay* they formally participated in the election of a new ruler, but their influence on its result was in fact limited. Those among them who held posts in the khan's central administration took part as witnesses in cases judged at the khan's council. Peysonnel even stated that they had the exclusive right to positions in the central offices.[60] Tott mentioned that all the non-*karaçı* noble families, like the *karaçı* families, had permanent representatives in the khan's council, a duty that was usually performed by the head of the Yaşlavs.[61] Considering this, the members of non-*karaçı* noble families could exercise some influence on the khanate's policy, but their real strength derived from their military power. They could influence the broader political situation, especially during military campaigns and internal conflicts, because both the Girays and the *karaçı*s needed their support.

2.2.2 The Non-*karaçı* Nobles as Clients of the Sharia Courts

During the reign of Murad Giray, noblemen appeared in the *kadıasker* court in all types of cases, as plaintiffs and defendants, and as parties in uncontested cases. The number of nobles recorded as litigants in the *sicil*s reached 302, while the total number of litigants was 3,155. It is noteworthy that nobles seem to have appeared less frequently in the district court. Only 5 of 542 litigants recorded in the Kara Su *sicil*s in the same period were nobles.[62] This leads us to wonder about the reasons for such a disproportion between the *kadıasker* court and the district court. Peysonnel stated that the cases between nobles were to be judged by the *kadıasker*, yet the French consul did not provide any further explanation. Hence, the origin and reasons for this rule remain unclear. We might presume that it was a way to emphasize the nobles' high social position. In addition, the khan might have been interested in supervising any conflicts between nobles, as these disputes could threaten internal peace. Peysonnel made no mention of cases between nobles and members of other social groups, but it seems that during Murad Giray's reign the majority of such cases was also resolved by the *kadıasker* and not by district judges. Regardless of whether the nobles were plaintiffs or defendants, such cases were brought to the capital. This suggests that the *kadıasker* court was commonly perceived as a judicial arena suitable to resolve cases that involved the nobles. Yet, the

60 Peysonnel, *Traité sur le commerce*, 264–265.
61 Tott, *Mémoires* (*Memoirs*, 2:405–406).
62 Two belonged to *karaçı* families.

fact that some cases involving noblemen were brought to the Kara Su district court indicates that the nobles were not exempted from the judicial power of a district *kadı*, rather the use of the *kadıasker* court was a matter of social usage.

According to my basic statistical analysis, the nobles constituted 13.3 percent of those initiating cases and 11 percent of second parties in uncontested cases, such as contracts (including amicable settlements), manumissions, legal agencies, and inheritances. Women constituted a considerable group among the court's noble clients. In cases involving nobles, as many as 41 percent of nobles initiating cases and 21 percent of noble second parties were female.

In the recorded court disputes, nobles appeared less frequently and constituted 6.5 percent of plaintiffs and 7.7 percent of defendants. The proportion of noble women involved in such conflicts was significantly lower than their proportion among the litigants in non-disputed cases. In the latter type of cases involving the nobles, only 22 percent of noble plaintiffs and 13 percent of noble defendants were female.

In the next section, in which I focus on the Yaşlav family, I present the typical court roles of the members of the Crimean non-ruling nobility. Yet, since according to our sources the Yaşlavs were not involved in disputes concerning theft, murder or assault, here I discuss, albeit briefly, these types of conflicts with other nobles. The *kadıasker sicil*s from Murad Giray's reign reveal that in two cases, noblemen brought charges of theft and four times of murder or assault.[63] Yet, nobles were accused of assault seven times.[64] For instance, Bay Şah and Azamet Mirza, the sons of Ali Beğ from the Kara Kurt district, were accused by Abdurrahman Çelebi from the Taşlı district and Abdulkadir Monla from the Zuya district of attacking the plaintiffs on a public road. The two ulema stated that the nobles (Bay Şah and Azamet Mirza) had beaten them severely and as a result the ulema were afraid for their lives.[65]

2.2.3 The Yaşlav Family in the *kadıasker* Court

In the present section I describe how the members of the Yaşlav family used the *kadıasker* court. The center of the Yaşlavs' *beylik* was located in a small village registered in the *sicil*s as Yaş Dağı (the Crimean Tatars called it Büyük Yaşlav). It was situated in the vicinity of Bahçesaray. According to Henryk Jankowski, the placename "Yaş Dağı" might have been invented by an Ottomanized clerk

63 ORRNB, Fond 917, 23b/66a/1; 23b/76b/1; 23b/88a/3; 23b/119a/1.

64 ORRNB, Fond 917, *defter* 23b/15a/1; 23b/72b/6; 23a/148a/1; 23a/178a/2; 23a/193b/1; 23a/204b/1; 23a/211a/5.

65 ORRNB, Fond 917, *defter* 23b/77b/6.

who replaced the old Kipchak name with an understandable Turkic form.[66] The Mongol origin of the Yaşlav family name is well established, as their ancestors could be found among the service *beğ*s of Mamai.[67] In the Crimean Khanate they were responsible for diplomatic relations with Russia, charged with preparing embassies to Moscow and organizing visits of Russian envoys in the Crimea.[68] Hence, they attained prominence as a non-*karaçı* noble family whose members were the khan's clients. In the eighteenth century, both Tott and Peysonnel considered them the most important non-*karaçı* noble family and, in the 1790s, Pallas referred to them as the sixth "ancient family" after the Şirins, Barıns, Mansurs, Seceuts, and Argıns.[69]

The Yaşlavs were involved in nine cases registered in the *sicil*s during Murad Giray's reign. The proceedings—either conflicts or the registrations of contracts—were initiated by Yaşlav family members. The Yaşlavs appeared before the *kadıasker* court only in financial matters such as manumission of slaves,[70] corroboration of debt,[71] the registration of contracts, and the resolution of property-related disputes.

The cases concerning land ownership constitute a treasure trove of information on the organization of the *beylik* and relations between the *beğ* and his family. They also provide data on the common inhabitants of the *beylik* and their relations with the Yaşlavs.

Thus, we begin with two fascinating entries related to land ownership. The first one contains an agreement between the *beğ* of the Yaşlavs and nine *mirza*s from the Yaşlav family. It begins with a statement from the *mirza*s, who confirmed that their *beğ*, Devlet Şah, had the right to administer the whole property constituting the *beylik*. The court scribe formulated their statement as follows: "A person, who is the *beğ*, is entitled to administer it [i.e., the *beylik*]."[72] In turn, Devlet Şah agreed that he would give his family members the right of usage of three-quarters of the *beylik*'s land.[73] While he retained control over

66 Jankowski, *A Historical-Etymological Dictionary*, 362–363.

67 For more about the Yaşlavs, see Lashkov, "Istoricheskii ocherk," *ITUAK* 22 (1895), 73.

68 They also performed these duties during Murad Giray's reign. For instance, see the reports on the meeting between Veli Şah Mirza and Petr Khovanskii in Perevoloch in 1681 (RGADA, Fond 123, op. 1, *Posol'skii prikaz. Krymskie dela*, no. 64, fol. 1), or the mission of Ustemir Mirza to Moscow in 1681 (RGADA, Fond 123, *Posol'skii prikaz. Krymskie dela*, op. 1, no. 71, fol. 1.)

69 The seventh and last place on this list was taken by the Dair family; cf. Pallas, *Travels Through the Southern Provinces*, 4:90.

70 ORRNB, Fond 917, *defter* 23b/75a/2; 23b/95b/2; 23a/227a/4.

71 ORRNB, Fond 917, *defter* 23b/72b/1.

72 *Kim beğ olursa onların tassaruflarıdır*; ORRNB, Fond 917, *defter* 23b/19b/1.

73 Ibid.

the whole land, only one-quarter would remain in his direct possession. From the second entry we learn that Devlet Şah died just a few months after the agreement. The plaintiff in the second trial, Veli Şah Mirza, who is described in the sources as an acting *beğ*, reclaimed his right to control the *beylik*'s land. He started by accusing two *mirza*s from his family of illegally using the land and produced witnesses who confirmed that the land in question constituted a part of the *beylik*'s land.[74] Hence, it could not be inherited by the defendants after the death of the former *beğ*. It is noteworthy that both defendants had taken part in the previous agreement concluded with the late Devlet Şah. They probably hoped that the change to the post of the *beğ* would enable them to convert the usufruct of the *beylik*'s land into a full ownership. These two cases reflect a long-lasting conflict between the *beğ* and his family members. It is clear that the *beylik*'s land provided a living for numerous members of the family. While the *beğ*s tried to protect its integrity and secure their control over its distribution, the *mirza*s wanted to siphon off a bit of the family's fortune and gain economic independence. In addition, we should note that the Yaşlavs possessed, or owned, land outside the *beylik*'s territory. In fact, there are a few entries in the *sicil*s depicting them as land owners.[75]

The Yaşlavs also sought justice in their conflicts with inhabitants of Yaş Dağı who were not family members. For instance, Veli Şah Beğ summoned fourteen individuals to pay rent from the land on which they had built their houses. The accused disagreed on the grounds that their houses had been constructed by their ancestors a hundred years earlier. They argued that such a long time secured their right of ownership to the land in question. Hence, they did not regard themselves as the *beğ*'s tenants and believed that they were no longer required to pay him rent. Veli Şah Beğ put forward a counter argument by stating that fourteen years earlier Khan Adil Giray (1666–71), in the presence of Abdulfatah Efendi, the *kadıasker* of the time, had confirmed the Yaşlavs' rights to the land in question. The *beğ*'s statement was confirmed by three witnesses, but he did not produce the certificate (*hüccet*) issued by the *kadıasker* or the khan's *yarlığ*. As I discuss in detail in Chapter 5, the statute of limitations in the khanate was fifteen years. Therefore, if the former khan's alleged confirmation had happened only one year earlier, the court would not have been able to confirm the plaintiff's rights; this fact sheds some doubt about the *beğ*'s credibility. Leaving aside this problem, the case demonstrates that the *beğ* sought justice from the khan in conflicts with his non-noble tenants and the latter were subordinated to the khan's judicial power. This conclusion can be

74 ORRNB, Fond 917, *defter* 23b/86a/6.

75 ORRNB, Fond 917, *defter* 23b/73b/1.

confirmed by other cases brought to the *kadıasker* court by non-noble Muslims as well as non-Muslims from Yaş Dağı.[76] As these cases did not directly involve the Yaşlavs, they did not disclose the character of the litigants' relations with the local noble family. We can only speculate that the litigants were the Yaşlavs' tenants or servants.

Aside from freeborn Muslims and non-Muslims, such as the previously mentioned opponents of Veli Şah Beğ, the Yaşlavs's estates were inhabited by slaves, who could be manumitted and then settled on their patrons' land. For instance, a slave named Esaf concluded a contract with Adil Şah Beğ in which he agreed to take care of the *beğ*'s flock in return for freedom and a certain number of sheep.[77]

To conclude, the Yaşlavs used the courts to resolve disputes within the family as well as those with their tenants. It is noteworthy that the conflicts or contracts involving the Yaşlavs concerned only financial matters. By contrast, common inhabitants of Yaş Dağı resolved all types of cases in the *kadıasker* court.

•••

The nobility of the Crimean Khanate had its roots in the Golden Horde. We could argue that the powerful position of the noblemen contributed to the uniqueness of the khanate's political system. In the present study, we divide the Crimean nobility into two main groups: the *karaçı* and non-*karaçı* families.

Much remains unknown about the pattern of noble landholding. It is clear that the institution of *beylik* constituted the base of the economic and social position of a noble family. However, our sources offer only a few precise indications. The *beylik*s were held by *karaçı* families and by some ancient non-*karaçı* noble families. These two noble groups administered their family estates in similarly: it was forbidden to alienate a part of a *beylik* and the whole land was administered by the *beğ*.

On the basis of the above evidence, we propose that the extent of a *beylik*'s autonomy depended on the status of its owners. The *beylik* of the Şirins, the most powerful *karaçı* family, should be considered the most powerful. Next to the everyday administration of his family estate, the Şirin *beğ* exercised the right to collect taxes and to lead his clients during military campaigns. The career of Abdulgaffar el-Kırımi indicates that the *beğ* could influence the appointment of the *kadı* of the Şirin district that covered the *beylik*'s territory.

76 ORRNB, Fond 917, *defter* 23b/33b/2; 23b/62b/3; 23a/179a/5; 23a/185b/2; 23a/249a/3.
77 ORRNB, Fond 917, *defter* 23b/75a/2.

Still, we would argue that the relevant *kadı*, at least formally, remained an appointee of the khan. In consequence, the ruler's royal monopoly to deliver justice was not officially limited. Yet, we must bear in mind that the inhabitants of the *beylik* addressed the Şirin *beğ* and his council of elders as alternative judicial forums. To be sure, the khan exercised certain judicial control over the *beylik* of the Şirins, whose inhabitants brought their suits to the district court in Kara Su, to the *kadıasker* court, and to the court at the khan's council.

Presumably, the autonomy of other ruling families was similar in terms of collecting taxes and commanding their own military units. By contrast, it seems that the *beylik*s of the Argıns and Seceuts covered considerably smaller territories than those of the Şirins and Mangıts. For instance, the judicial district of Argın likely comprised both the Argıns' and the Seceuts' *beylik*s. In that case, it remains unclear how the two families managed to exercise control over the local judiciary. It is worth noting that the *karaçı* families used the courts to resolve disputes concerning financial matters or to register contracts. Although the very limited number of cases makes it impossible to draw firm conclusions, it seems that, unlike the inhabitants of their *beylik*s, they probably did not bring other types of suits, at least during the reign of Murad Giray.

The non-*karaçı* noble families possessed the *beylik*s and the land granted them by the ruler. We believe that *beylik*s were held only by those families who had settled in the Crimea during the time of the Golden Horde, for example, the Yaşlavs or the Dairs. *Beylik*s remained inalienable and indivisible and were supposed to remain under the family *beğ*'s administration. Nobles who settled later or individuals ennobled by the khan could be granted land properties by the ruler. Such grants could also be bestowed on members of families tracing their origins back to the Golden Horde. Unlike the case of *beylik*s, it was possible to sell such properties or divide them between one's heirs. Members of the non-*karaçı* noble families appeared in the judicial courts as either plaintiffs or defendants in various types of cases. However, it should be noted that the most eminent, i.e., the Yaşlavs, only settled financial suits in the *kadıasker* court. This suggests that the noble elite resolved disputes regarding family matters or those related to murder and assault in a different way, in front of alternative judicial bodies, while the petty nobility used the khan's court, as did other social groups.

The *karaçı* families wielded political power and influence unknown to other members of the nobility. Next to their military power, the *karaçı*s had a great influence over foreign and domestic policy because they had the right to participate in the khan's council. The *beğ* of the Şirins, as the most important of the nobility, could summon the *kurultay* and even turn this institution against the khan. He had also the ear of the Ottoman sultan. Thus, to some extent, he could influence the depositions and nominations of the Crimean rulers.

Members of non-*karaçı* noble families could gain power as retinue members of the Girays. Yet, with the increasing instability and frequent changes on the khan's throne, the job of the highest officials became progressively more risky. This is clearly visible from the example of the khan's viziers, Sefer Gazi Ağa and his son Islam Ağa, whose careers were discussed in Chapter 2. The fate of the latter demonstrates that even a vizier backed by the khan could not diminish the influence of the *karaçı* families.

CHAPTER 4

Provincial *Kadı*s and Their Courts

The Crimean Khanate had two systems of territorial division. First, the land was divided between the khan and his family and clients on one side and the ruling families and their clients on the other. Second, the khans introduced *kaza*s or court districts, which were typical territorial units in a Muslim state. We know from the court registers drawn in the times of Murad Giray the names of the *kaza*s' centers: Ak Mescid, Arabat, Argın, Bahçesaray, Baynaq, Burulça, Congar (Dip and Orta Congar), Çetirlik, Dair, Eski Kırım, Ferahkerman, Gözleve, Kara Kurt, Kara Su, Karavul, Kerç (Dip and Orta Kerç), Kaçı, Küçük Kara Su, Mangıt, Salgır, Samarcik, Saqal, Şeyh Eli, Şirin, Tamak, Tarkhan, and Taşlı.[1] The issue of whether the division into the Giray domain and the nobles' *beylik*s matched the districts' borders merits further study. It is clear that the domains of the khans and the *kalga*s were extensive and were scattered in the territory of multiple *kaza*s. Thus, the lands, which were directly administered by the Girays, as well as those owned by nobles and common subjects, were situated in the same districts. In some cases the *beylik*s were located in the districts named after the *karaçı* family, for example, the *beylik* of the Mangıts was in the *kaza* of Mangıt, while the *beylik* of the Şirins was in the *kaza* of Şirin. At present, we do not know if the *beylik*s of the aristocratic clans were under the authority of the officials of the respective districts or if they constituted semi-autonomous territories within their *kaza*s. Furthermore, what were the limits of the khan's authority in the province? To answer these questions, we examine the competencies of district officials and the possible limitations of their authority, such as the rights of the *karaçı* families.

1 The *Kadı* and Court Personnel

1.1 *The Qualities of a Crimean kadı*

The *kadı*s played a vital role in Islamic societies; indeed their role and conduct was prescribed by the Prophet and his successors. In premodern Islam,

1 The *kaza*s of Boçala, Müfti Arpalık, Nasıv, Yukarı, Aşağı İçki, and Zuja, which are listed in the first Russian register from 1783, are not mentioned in the *sicil*s from the reign of Murad Giray; cf. Lashkov, "Statisticheskaia svedeniia o Kryme," 100–102. This does not necessarily mean that the above-mentioned *kaza*s were established after 1683. It is possible that their inhabitants did not bring their disputes to the *kadı* court or, more likely, we are unable to identify them from among the courts' clients, because their territorial affiliation is not recorded.

 | DOI:10.1163/9789004384323_006

many Muslim jurists and theologians authored texts describing the qualities of a judge and his relations with rulers and with different groups of Muslim society. Each of the four schools of law developed principles of the *kadı*'s conduct. Thus, it comes as no surprise that the literature on this issue is vast. It is beyond the scope of this book to survey studies on the topic. In this section, my purpose is to identify and concisely summarize the most important qualities of a *kadı* according to the Hanafi school.

In the opinion of Muslim authorities, an ideal judge should be a free Muslim who is neither blind, nor deaf or mute. He should have certain moral qualifications and be pious, virtuous, patient, and responsible. Moreover, he should be wise, someone who could use analogy (*kıyas*) and interpret law (exercise *ictihad*) as necessary.[2] Ghulam Murtaza Azad adds that noble origins and wealth were highly desirable for an officeholder because such a person was less likely to accumulate material goods by unlawful means. A judge should refrain from activities that might affect his impartiality, e.g., from trade or even simple purchases (he should ask someone else to perform these tasks for him) as he was obligated to treat all parties equally and hear the cases in the order in which they arrived (i.e., he should not adjudicate the cases of more important members first). He could give priority to some cases, but only in special circumstances, e.g., the complaints of travelers who could not remain long in the country. The *kadı* should refrain from judging the cases of his enemies, and, according to some jurists, of his own family.[3]

It is of interest whether Muslim rulers sought the same virtues in *kadı*s, who were appointed as Muslim judicial authorities. In most Islamic states, *kadı*s performed both judicial and administrative functions. As we see in the following sections, in the Crimean Khanate, in addition to sentencing and acting as public notaries *kadı*s performed various administrative duties. A *kadı* was, in fact, the most important official of the ruler within the court district; he acted as an intermediary between the ruler and the local community. Thus, it is important to examine what kind of work the khan expected from the *kadı*s. Once again, a comparison with the Ottoman Empire may prove helpful. From the reign of Selim I, the sultans promulgated "rescripts of justice" (*adaletname*) to admonish officials to treat common people justly, and not to abuse the subject population. The *kadı*s were threatened with severe consequences if they harmed the poor.[4] In this context, Marlene Kurz suggests that at the time, poverty was understood not merely as an economic condition; "poverty should not

2 Rebstock, "A Qāḍī's Errors," 8–9; M.K. Masud, "Adab al-qāḍī," *EI*³.
3 G.M. Azad, "Conduct and Qualities of a Qadi," *Islamic Studies* 24 (1985), 51–61.
4 Inalcık, "Adaletnameler"; Faroqhi, "Political Activity," 10–12.

be understood as material distress, but rather as being defenseless and therefore dependent on the protection of the sovereign and his deputies."[5]

Numerous orders issued by the khans and written in the *sicil*s seem to have played a role similar to that of the Ottoman *adaletname*. In 1612, Canibeg Giray issued detailed orders instructing judges on how to perform their duties, and how to organize the daily work of the district courts. The khan enumerated types of cases from which the judges could collect strictly defined court fees. He prohibited the *kadı*s from extracting any additional money from the subjects. The khan admonished the *kadı*s to judge the cases themselves, and not leave the task to their *naib*s or other deputies. The *kadı* should be competent enough to enter the information in the *sicil*s, issue sentences, and supervise the work of his subordinates.[6]

We have limited knowledge about the *kadı*s' education, or the extent of their intellectual and professional abilities, as we do not have lists of Crimean *medrese* students or books of biographies of Crimean ulema comparable to those composed in Ottoman lands. The notes of Said Giray on the famous ulema of his time constitute the most important source on the subject. The table below presents data on their education and careers.

In sum, Said Giray provides us with data on the education and careers of forty-four members of the ulema from the Crimea and the Nogay steppes. It is clear that the majority were trained by local teachers, either in the Crimea or in municipal centers of the Black Sea region, such as Akkerman or Bender. The borders between the khanate and the Ottoman Empire were essentially non-existent in matters of education. Students moved easily from the Ottoman parts of the steppe or the peninsula to those areas controlled by the khan. It would seem that studying in the core Ottoman lands was less popular. Only four ulema traveled that far, in their youth, to study. Of the forty-four scholars mentioned by Said Giray, only fifteen were referred to as judges. From among them, only one was known to have been educated in the Ottoman capital.[7] The rest were probably educated in various local schools.[8] Clearly, an education in the Ottoman capital was not required. As noted in the cases of eminent ulema families of Kaçı and Çuyunçu, good family origins may have done more for a young graduate than being educated in an Istanbul *medrese*.

5 Kurz, "Gracious Sultan," 102.
6 ORRNB, fond 917, *defter* 1/71b/1. For transcription and translation of the order, see Appendix I.
7 Kellner-Heinkele (ed.), *Aus den Aufzeichnungen*, 212–246.
8 Cf. O. Aslanapa, "Kırım Türk Eserleri," in *Sanatı, Tarihi, Edebiyatı ve Musikisiyle Kırım*, ed. O. Aslanapa (Ankara, 2003), 11–57.

TABLE 3 The education and careers of Crimean ulema as described by Said Giray. [a]

Name	Education	Career
Kul Mehmed Efendi from the Kaçı family	studied under Huseyin Efendi in Bahçesaray	*kadı* of Kalga Selamet Giray,[b] *kadıasker* and then mufti of Khan Selamet Giray, *kadıasker* of Khan Selim Giray, *kadıasker* and then mufti of Khan Arslan Giray
Feyzullah Efendi, son of Şeyh Efendi	studied under contemporary ulema	*kadı* of Kara Su during Mengli Giray's first reign, *kadı* of Kara Su during Mengli Giray's second reign, his *kadıasker*, then mufti and the head of the *seyyid*s in Kefe
Feyzullah Çelebi Efendi, son of Kul Mehmed Efendi	studied under Osman Efendi and Halil Efendi in Bahçesaray	*kadıasker* of Khan Halim Giray
Mehmed Efendi, son of *naib* Osman Efendi	no data	judicial posts for *serasker*s; twice *kadı* of Bahçesaray
Hamid Efendi, son of Şehbaz Efendi	no data	*divan efendi*
Şeyhi Mehmed Efendi, son of Şerefüddin Efendi	studied under the Crimean ulema	*kadı* of the *kalga* during Halim Giray's reign
Mustafa Efendi, son of Şerefüddin Efendi	no data	*kadı* of Ferahkerman during Halim Giray's reign
Hüşamuddin Efendi, son of Şerefüddin Efendi	no data	*kadı* of the Camboyluk Nogays
Halil Efendi	studied under Latif Efendi in the Khanate	well-known teacher in Bahçesaray
Osman Efendi, from the village Dört Gökgöz	studied in Istanbul	well-known teacher and preacher in Bahçesaray
Çelebi Akay Efendi, son of Karakaş Mehmed Efendi, a teacher in the village of the Salgır noble family	studied under contemporary ulema	well-known teacher in the village of Oyrat

TABLE 3 The education and careers of Crimean ulema as described by Said Giray. (*cont.*)

Name	Education	Career
Mirza Ömer Efendi	studied under contemporary ulema	teacher in the village of Kaya
Ali Efendi	studied under contemporary ulema	teacher in Ak Mescid
Gaffuri Efendi (Abdulgaffar el-Kırımi)	no data	*kadı* of the *beğ* of the Şirins, *divan efendi* for Khan Feth Giray, *kadı* of the *kalga* during the reign of Khan Selamet Giray
Ebussuud Efendi, son of *kadıasker* Mehmed Efendi	studied under Huseyin Efendi	*kadıasker* in the reigns of the khans Mehmed Giray, Selamet Giray, and Arslan Giray
Şeyh Mehmed, son of Hamid Efendi, former head of the Helveti order in Kara Su	studied under Koca Mustafa Paşa Şeyh in Istanbul	*derviş*
Külec Şeyh Mustafa Efendi, son of Veli Efendi	studied under contemporary ulema	head of a tekke in Külec(?)
Kaçı Şeyh Abdulhalim Efendi, son of Abdullah Efendi	studied Quran recitation	head of a tekke in Kaçı
Taşlı Şeyh Mehmed	no data	*şeyh* of the Helveti order in Taşlı
Yağmurci Şeyh Abdullah Efendi, son of Seyyid Ali Efendi	no data	*Derviş*
Sarı Mehmed Efendi	studied Quran recitation	teacher in Ulaklı
Dost Mehmed Efendi from Akkerman	studied in Akkerman, continued in the khanate	*kadı* for the Akkerman *serasker* at the beginning of Halim Giray's reign
Abdullah Efendi, son of Halim Efendi from the Orakoğlu Nogay clan from Akkerman	studied under contemporary ulema	*kadı* for the Bucak *serasker* and then mufti in Bender during Halim Giray's reign

Name	Education	Career
Abdulkerim Efendi	studied under contemporary ulema like Davud Efendi, the mufti of Bender	teacher; *divan efendi* of the Yedisan *serasker*
Kan Mehbet Efendi from the Or Mehmedoğlu Nogay clan from Bucak	studied under contemporary ulema; studied in Istanbul	teacher in various villages in Bucak, then a member of the ulema in Özü
Ali Can Efendi	studied under contemporary ulema in Istanbul	well-known teacher in the judicial district of Ismail
Dagestani Mehmed Efendi from the Kasbulatoğlu clan from Kuban	studied under contemporary ulema in Bucak	imam, *şeyh*, and preacher in Bender
Nuri Efendi	studied under Dagestani Mehmed Efendi in Bucak; studied in Istanbul	teacher and preacher without stable work (was a known opium addict)
Ilyas Efendi from the Citcecioğlu clan from Kuban	studied under contemporary Crimean ulema, for example, under Ebussuud Efendi, mufti of Kefe	led a pious life among his native clan in Kuban, then in Yedisan
Bay Akay Efendi from the Tuvilğa clan from Yedisan	studied under contemporary Crimean ulema	teacher
Ali Efendi from the Nökis clan from Yedisan	studied under contemporary Crimean ulema, for example, under Nurullah Efendi from Bukhara, the head of the Nakşbendi order	became a *derviş* at an advanced age
Hacı Kurman Efendi from Yedisan	studied Quran recitation under contemporary ulema	no data
Kence Efendi from the Nökis clan from Yedisan	studied under contemporary Crimean ulema	*kadı* for Piri Mehmed Ağa, the *kaymakam* of Yedisan
Ali Efendi, from the Pavirdak family of the Ced-i Nokta clan from Yedisan	studied under Şeyh Ahmed Efendi in Bender	teacher in his clan

TABLE 3 The education and careers of Crimean ulema as described by Said Giray. (*cont.*)

Name	Education	Career
Mengli Ali Efendi, from Bakılçak family of the Ced-i Nokta clan from Yedisan	studied under contemporary Crimean ulema	teacher in his clan
Hacı Mehmed Efendi, from the Kökkök clan from Yedisan	studied under contemporary ulema	teacher in his clan, member of the Nakşbendi order
Hacı Bay Efendi, from the Nökis clan from Yedisan	studied under contemporary ulema, for example, under Şeyh Ahmed Efendi in Bender	teacher in his clan
Abbas Kadı, from the Kışlık clan from Yedisan	studied under contemporary Crimean ulema	*kadı* of Yedisan and teacher

a Kellner-Heinkele (ed.), *Aus den Aufzeichnungen*, 212–246.

b This table refers to the reigns of the following khans: Mengli II Giray (first reign: 1724–30; second reign: 1737–40), Kaplan I Giray (third reign: 1730–36), Feth II Giray (1736–37), Selamet II Giray (1740–43), Selim II Giray (1743–48), Arslan Giray (first reign: 1748–56), and Halim Giray (1756–58).

The *sicil*s confirm that there was a school network in the khanate. The schools were founded and supported by members of various social groups. *Medrese*s were usually supported by independent foundations that derived an income from the endowments of individual benefactors. Presumably, as in the Ottoman Empire, the khanate's *medrese*s were more or less hierarchical structures. The prestige of a *medrese* depended on the wealth of its foundation, as this determined teacher salaries and the number of students. The khans' foundations were presumably the most important among them, for example, the well-known Zincirli Medrese founded by Mengli I Giray in Salacık near Bahçesaray. The order of Saadet III Giray preserved in the *sicil*s indicates that the ruler did not limit himself to financial support of education, but was also concerned with its quality. He could influence the teaching program and the appointment of teaching staff.[9] Unfortunately, we have no data concerning

9 See the *yarlığ* of Saadet III Giray dated 15 Rebi I 1136/13 December 1723. The khan appointed Musalli Efendi as a teacher in a *medrese* in Gözleve. The ruler praised him for his knowledge of experimental sciences and mathematics. He hoped that this appointment would help to restore good order to the *medrese* (ORRNB, fond 917, *defter* 51/54b/1). The *sicil*s contain one

the khans' influence on legal studies in the khanate's *medreses*. Presumably, the rulers supported Hanafi scholars, as the Hanafi school was the ruling law school in the khanate. Nonetheless, Evliya Çelebi maintained that the members of the three remaining law schools also participated in the khan's council. He suggests that their members also received the khan's support and that such scholars might also have lectured in the khanate's *medreses*. Taking into consideration the Ottoman influence on the khanate's legal practice, which is discussed in Chapter 5, it is probable that some law students from the khanate were educated in the Ottoman Empire. Ilber Ortaylı and Ismail Akçay name a few ulema with Tatar or Kefe origins who, after studying in Ottoman *medreses*, started careers in the Ottoman world beyond the Crimean Peninsula.[10] However, we have no evidence that education in Ottoman *medreses* facilitated careers within the khanate. We lack information about the ratio between the Tatar ulema trained in the khanate and those educated abroad (in Kefe province or in more remote parts of the Ottoman Empire). More detailed research, based on the Ottoman sources, on the career patterns of the Crimean ulema is clearly needed.

Although we have limited data on the education of the Crimean judges, the *sicil*s offer some indication of its quality in terms of the literary and professional skills students gained. The *sicil*s contain entries written in Ottoman Turkish (rather than Arabic or Persian), in the handwriting of a variety of people; thus it differs orthographically and grammatically. Judicial formulas used in the entries also vary in terms of their sophistication. Although Canibeg Giray ordered that, whenever possible, district judges should record their sentences in their own hand,[11] in fact, numerous entries contain the names of court scribes; these names appear among the case witnesses, indicating that the scribes, rather than the judges, frequently recorded the information in the *sicil*s.[12] In contrast to judges in some Ottoman districts, Crimean judges did not sign their

---

other order concerning the *medreses*; this order was issued by Selim III Giray on Cemazi I 1174/9 December 1760–7 January 1761). The khan forbade the *medrese* students from working as carriers in Bahçesaray. It is not clear whether the khan aimed to force the students to focus on their studies or wanted to protect the professional carriers from competition (ORRNB, fond 917, *defter* 85/37b/1).

10 I. Ortaylı, "Türkiye'de Kırımlı Aydınlar," in *Sanatı, Tarihi, Edebiyatı ve Musikisiyle Kırım*, ed. O. Aslanapa (Ankara, 2003), 58–64, esp. 62–63; I. Akçay, "Kırım'dan Yetişen Türk Alimleri," *Emel* 203 (1994), 11–17.

11 ORRNB, Fond 917, *defter* 1/71b/1.

12 For example, on the first five folios of the *kadıasker sicil*s from the reign of Murad Giray, the writer, Abdulbaki, is listed among the case witnesses in fifteen of fifty-five entries (ORRNB, Fond 917, *defter* 22/70b/1,4; 22/70b/3; 73a/2–4; 22/74a/1,3,5; 22/74b/2; 22/75a/5; 22/75b/1–3, 5).

rulings. Therefore, it is harder to distinguish between a record formulated by a judge and one worded by another member of the court personnel. Presumably, judges, who were better educated than their subordinates, worded their texts in a more sophisticated way. Consequently, we assume that the lower court personnel authored the entries with more misspellings. The various qualities of the entries may also reflect differences in education among the staff of the court. In sum, the entries in the *sicil*s demonstrate that in the district courts well-educated professionals worked next to clerks who formulated the records in a very simple way.

In the aforementioned order issued in 1612, Canibeg Giray reminded the *kadı*s that delivering justice to the poor constituted an essential part of their work. The khan admonished the judges to fulfill their responsibilities personally. If they were to rely on the work of their *naib*s, then they were supposed to supervise them closely. The khan made the *kadı*s fully responsible for any mistake of their subordinates. From this order, we learn that the khan repeated some classical guidelines for a *kadı*, like the necessity that he be uncorruptible, honest, and dedicated to his work. The fact that the khan considered it necessary to remind his officials of such essential aspects of their work suggests that the state of affairs may have been less-than-ideal. Nevertheless, we have not found any complaints about district *kadı*s registered in the *sicil*s dating back to Murad Giray's reign. We have no data about *kadı*s accepting bribes, levying illegal court fees or behaving unjustly in any other way. European accounts, which praised the lawfulness of the Crimean courts, add to the picture of principled local *kadı*s. Nicolas Kleemann's story demonstrates that an individual could win in the khan's court without bribing the judge or his staff. The European descriptions of the honesty of the courts in the khanate differ from western observations about the Ottoman judicial system; for example, that of Hans Ulrich Krafft, who negotiated the price of a favorable sentence with the judge of Tripoli.[13] We have not yet identified sources that prove that the Crimean judges gained from illegal activities. Thus, we cannot categorically exclude the possibility that bribery took place.

Canibeg Giray's order, along with data from the *sicil*s dating to his reign, provide important information on local *kadı*s' absence from their districts. From the lists of case witnesses of the proceedings in the *kadıasker* court, we learn, for example, that both before and after the promulgation of Canibeg Giray's order, a majority of the district *kadı*s spent some time in the capital. They came

13 Ergene, *Local Court*, 115–119.

from neighboring (e.g., Ak Mescit,[14] Burulça,[15] Çuyunçu[16]) districts, as well as more distant regions (e.g., Congar,[17] Eski Kırım,[18] Ferahkerman,[19] Gözleve, Kara Su-Tamak[20]) and appeared in Bahçesaray with varying frequencies, though not more often than four times a year. The *kadıasker* registers from Murad Giray's reign consist of similar data concerning the *kadı*s' visits to Bahçesaray.[21] There is no evidence that the presence of a district judge was required for example, during a proceeding in the capital concerning an individual from his district. Although it is possible to find a few such cases, district judges often acted as case witnesses in proceedings that had no clear connection to their districts. Whether they left their district on official or private matters, they were not afraid to appear in public in the *kadıasker* court, even shortly after the publication of Canibeg Giray's order. It is possible that the Crimean *kadı*s, like the Ottoman *kadı*s, could remained outside their districts,[22] e.g., in the capital, as long as they supervised their *naib*s, who performed the *kadı*s' daily duties. It should also be noted that even the most remote districts in the khanate were just a few days journey from Bahçesaray, which means that *kadı*s could personally assume their responsibilities and still visit the capital frequently.

1.2 *The Duties of a Crimean* kadı

Administering justice constituted an essential part of the duties of the *kadı*s. They were authorized to deal with all the legal issues between the khan's subjects, with some exceptions, which are discussed in the final section of this chapter. First, *kadı*s were supposed to resolve judicial conflicts between individuals. According to classical jurists, as Aida Othman points out, a *kadı* should encourage the parties to settle amicably instead of entering into lawsuits.[23] As I discuss in detail in Chapter 5, researchers such as Işık Tamdoğan and Boğaç Ergene refer to the ability of the *kadı* and other members of the court to act as mediators or legal experts and encourage the parties to conclude settlements

---

14 ORRNB, Fond 917, *defter* 1/34b/3.
15 ORRNB, Fond 917, *defter* 1/15a/2; ORRNB, Fond 917, *defter* 1/91a/5.
16 ORRNB, Fond 917, *defter* 1/18b/2.
17 ORRNB, Fond 917, *defter* 1/8b/3.
18 ORRNB, Fond 917, *defter* 1/11a/3; ORRNB, Fond 917, *defter* 1/88a/4.
19 ORRNB, Fond 917, *defter* 1/11a/3.
20 ORRNB, Fond 917, *defter* 1/3b/4.
21 See Appendix IV.
22 Coşgel and Ergene, *Economics of Ottoman Justice*, 68.
23 A. Othman, "*And Amicable Settlement Is Best*: Sulh and Dispute Resolution in Islamic Law," *Arab Law Quarterly* 21, no. 1 (2007), 63–90.

before trial.[24] If the parties decided to proceed and litigate, the *kadı* was expected to give them a fair trial. The Crimean judge did not seek out cases to try, rather he adjudicated only on those brought to him. The classical Islamic doctrine of evidence emphasizes the strict use of procedure and stresses the importance of oral statements; it leaves little space for other evidence. This importance of oral testimonies in court proceedings is derived from the Quran and Sunna. Scholars of the four Sunni law schools were fully aware that a *kadı* might be unable to distinguish between true and false statements; therefore, in certain circumstances the Hanafi school allowed *kadı*s to use circumstantial evidence in corrolation with other elements (e.g., an expert opinions and their own knowledge) to reach decisions.[25] In the Crimean Khanate, police and detective work could be done by other officials, whose role in the court proceeding is described in the next section. Judges were seldom personally involved in gathering evidence. During Murad Giray's reign, there is only one entry that refers to a *kadı*'s work outside his court. That case concerned the inhabitants of a village in the *kaza* of Arbat. They asked their district judge, Abdulgariz Efendi, to visit the scene of the crime; they then used his testimony in the case with the victim's family who claimed the right to blood money from the village as a whole. The judge confirmed that the victim, who had been wounded twice in the head by an axe, was found not on the village's land but on the grounds of a certain Sefer Ali. After the judge visited the scene of the crime, he ordered that the body be buried,[26] as there was no need of other evidence and further inquiry.

But what happened in the event that a *kadı* failed to discover the truth from the oral testimony and circumstantial evidence? In the Ottoman Empire, according to the law code of Suleyman I, a *kadı* was allowed to take into account information extracted during torture from suspects accused of theft.[27] In case

---

24 Tamdoğan, "Sulh and the 18th Century Ottoman Courts"; B. Ergene, "Why Did Ümmü Gülsüm Go to Court? Ottoman Legal Practice between History and Anthropology," *Islamic Law and Society* 17, no. 2 (2010), 215–244; Coşgel and Ergene, *Economics of Ottoman Justice*, 142.

25 For further details on the Islamic theory of proof and procedure, see B. Johansen, "Signs as Evidence: The Doctrine of Ibn Taymiyya (1263–1328) and Ibn Qayyim al-Jawziyya (d. 1351) on Proof," *Islamic Law and Society* 9 (2002), 168–193; Coşgel and Ergene, *Economics of Ottoman Justice*, 213–251; Ergene, "Evidence in Ottoman Courts"; P. Powers, "Evidence," *EI*[3]. I discuss the evidentiary procedures used in the courts in the khanate in Chapter 5.

26 ORRNB, Fond 917, *defter* 23a/222a/2.

27 U. Heyd, *Studies in Old Ottoman Criminal Law* (Oxford, 1973), 78/116, 80/118 [the first page number refers to the Ottoman text of the law code and the second refers to its English translation]; Peirce, *Morality Tales*, 326–327; Tuğ, *Politics of Honor*, 202. Fariba Zarinebaf notes that *kadı*s in eighteenth-century Istanbul sometimes rejected the use of torture and confession made under duress, see Zarinebaf, *Crime and Punishment*, 161–162.

of the khanate, Nicolas Kleemann's account is unique as it refers to the possibility of using torture to extract a confession from a person accused of theft. As noted, the threat of torture sufficed to make Kyriagos admit his guilt.[28] We lack data on the use of torture in the khanate, therefore, we cannot establish whether its use was subject to similar rules as in the Ottoman Empire.

The registration of so-called uncontested cases constitutes a second important branch of a *kadı*'s duties. The order of Canibeg Giray regulated the court fee (8 *akçe*) for notarizing transactions and for the division of estates among heirs (32 *akçe*). In the Crimean *sicil*s, individuals recorded various types of transactions, such as loans, the transfer of rights to use land, the purchase of real estates and moveable property, or cases concerning private matters, for example, establishing agencies, initiating divorces or determining custody over children.

In addition to their judicial and notarial roles, *kadı*s served as provincial representatives of the khan. As a key provincial-level administrative unit, the court registered and transmitted orders from various dignitaries and officials. The number of orders the ruler and his officials addressed to *kadı*s and recorded in the Crimean *sicil*s, is limited in comparison to the number of analogous orders written in the Ottoman *sicil*s. The Crimean decrees resemble their Ottoman counterparts in content. These documents provide information on the division of responsibilities between the *kadı* and other district officials. They address the issue of the *kadı*'s role in his district as the deputy of the khan and the *kalga* in respect to tax collection and the mobilization of troops. Additionally, they deal with the problem of the *kadı*'s role in economic life and and his judicial control over pious foundations (*vakf*) in his district. Moreover, provincial *kadı*s served as intermediaries between the ruler and the population of the district. They ensured that the orders of the khan and the *kalga* were put into effect in the province.

The *kadı*s also served as links between the khan's central treasury and the districts. They supervised the process of tax collection and made sure that only lawful taxes were levied on the subjects. For instance, we learn that Gazi II Giray forbade the collection of a sheep tax like the Ottoman tax,[29] while Hacı II Giray ordered the *kadı*s of Kara Su and Gözleve to supervise the collection of the cizye tax from Crimean and Ottoman subjects by his appointee Moşe.[30]

---

28 Kleemann, *Voyage de Vienne à Belgrade*, 90–107.

29 See the order of Gazi II Giray dated the first ten days of Rebi I 1019/4–13 June 1609 (ORRNB, fond 917, *defter* 1/12b/1 and 2). For more on this order, see H. Inalcık, "Kırım Hanlığı Sicilleri Bulundu," 175; Lashkov, "Sbornik dokumentov," *ITUAK* 22 (1895), 112–113.

30 See the order of Hacı II Giray dated 16 Rebi II/2 April 1684 (ORRNB, fond 917, *defter* 25/115a/3).

Judges had broad prerogatives to regulate economic life. Numerous orders from Hacı II Giray and his *kalga*, Devlet Giray, demonstrate that district *kadıs* were required to oversee trade conditions within their districts.[31] For instance, when Armenian merchants were accused of unfair trade practices by local tradesmen, we know that a judge had to solve the problem. Judging by an example from Kara Su and Bahçesaray, a district *kadı* or his *naib* also confirmed the list of fixed prices (*narh*).[32] Unfortunately, our source does not disclose whether the judicial officials were actively involved in fixing them.

Kadıs were also responsible for supervising pious foundations (*vakfs*). They controlled the legality of their establishment, the upkeep of *vakf* properties, transactions, and the appointments of trustees.

In contrast to the Ottoman Empire,[33] in the khanate the *kadıs* seem to have played an insignificant role in the mobilization of troops and the requisition of military supplies. Only two documents, one Crimean and one Ottoman, concerned the participation of the *kadıs* in organizing a military campaign. In the first, the *kalga* Devlet Giray asked the *kadı* of Kara Su to prepare accommodation for the *kalga*'s troops.[34] The second document sent by Ibrahim, a *kethüda* of Ottoman janissaries, concerned preparation for a military campaign in Gözleve in 1738.

1.3 *The Crimean* kadı *as the Girays' Employee: Relations with the Rulers*

Isabel Calero Secall states,

31 ORRNB, fond 917, *defter* 25/112b/1; 25/115a/1, 25/115a/2, 25/115a/6.

32 For a list of fixed prices recorded in the Kara Su *sicils* in 1684, see ORRNB, Fond 917, *defter* 25/ 117b/3 and Özdem, *Kırım Karasubazar'da*, 151–157. The list from Bahçesaray (ORRNB, Fond 917, 24/120b/1) was transcribed incorrectly by Fehmi Yılmaz and Ahmed Cihan (Cihan and Yılmaz, "Kırım Kadi Sicilleri," 149). The following is the correct version with a translation: "Oldurki mah-i Rebiü 'l-evvel gurresinden buğdayın beşşeresi seksen akçe olmak üzere dakik batmanı yirmi dört [a crossed word] hubz-i matbuh iki yüz yetmişdir nam narh olundı fi sene el-mezbur." [From the first day of Rebi I [1090/12 April 1679] onwards the list of fixed prices is as follows: *beşşere* of wheat costs eighty *akçes*, *batman* of flour costs twenty-four. A loaf of bread weights 270 [*dirhem*].] According to Fırat Yaşa, in the third quarter of the seventeenth century, one *beşşere* was equal to 112–115 kilograms and one *batman* to 7.7 kilograms, see Yaşa, "Bahçesaray (1650–1675)," 160–161. In the seventeenth-century Ottoman Empire, one *dirhem* was equal to 3.2 grams and one *beşşere* to 112–115 kilograms (H. Inalcık, "Introduction to Ottoman Metrology," in *Studies in Ottoman Social and Economic History*, ed. H. Inalcık (London, 1985), 311–348).

33 D.R. Khoury, "The Ottoman Centre Versus Provincial Power-Holders: An Analysis of the Historiography," in *The Cambridge History of Turkey*, vol. 3: *The Later Ottoman Empire, 1603–1839*, ed. S. Faroqhi (Cambridge, 2006), 150.

34 ORRNB, fond 917, *defter* 25/119a/1.

> when examining the relationship between the rulers and judges in Muslim society, it is important to keep in mind that the distinction between the spiritual and the temporal, the political and the religious has been rejected since the beginning of Islam and that judiciary is above all an institution of a religious character. This tension is not treated in classical Islamic theory, not even as a historical anachronism. The ruler exercises political and legal—but not legislative—powers, although he may participate in the interpretation of the law and is subject to it.[35]

The existence of a general body of law, which came from God, gave the *kadı* a certain independence from the ruler. Ronald Jennings, who studied the position of *kadı*s in the Ottoman Empire, emphasized that the *kadı* should not be perceived as just the sultan's appointee responsible for the implementation of the sharia and *kanun*. Judges were guarantors of the execution of the sharia. For this reason, according to Jennings, he was free from the control of political authorities and had autonomy in his judicial decisions.[36] Nevertheless, we must bear in mind that the administration of justice came under the ruler's control and that the *kadı*s were in fact appointed and dismissed according to the ruler's will. Data preserved in the court registers suggest that their connections and loyalty to the khan and the two other Giray dignitaries seemed to be the main reason behind the appointment. The *kadı*s were dismissed and appointed along with the changes on the Crimean throne, as we can easily observe from the example of the reigns of Murad Giray and his predecessor, Selim I Giray (1st reign), as well as that of his successors, Hacı II Giray and Selim I Giray (2nd reign). During their reigns, vital judicial offices were held by multiple people, indicating frequent turnover in appointments (see table 4).

Such changes in judicial posts might indicate that they were filled at the whim of the new ruler. A judge seems to have faced risks similar to those of the khans, namely of losing his post due to political changes. He also faced unemployment if the khan was not satisfied with his job. The above might suggest that judges were the ruler's appointees in the province, rather than independent administrators of the sharia. The degree of their independence may have been influenced by a variety of factors. Presumably, a *kadı*'s relations with the local community could significantly strengthen or weaken his position versus the ruler. Unfortunately, we lack crucial information about the appointments of

35 I. Calero Secall, "Rulers and Qadis: Their Relationships during the Nasrid Kingdom," *Islamic Law and Society* 7, no. 2 (2002), 235–255.

36 R. Jennings, "Kadi, Court and Legal Procedure in 17th Century Ottoman Kayseri," *Studia Islamica* 48 (1978), 133–172.

the *kadıs*. We do not know whether the khan appointed judges in the districts from which they originated or followed the Ottoman practice of nominating judges who were not residents of their districts. Similiarly, we do not know whether judges who were strangers in their districts brought along their own employees (like *naibs* or *katibs*), or whether they were recruited locally. Most probably, the personnel decisions taken in the capital caused tensions in the khanate's provinces. Yet, it is clear that a judge had to develop and maintain amicable relations with the local community in order to successfully perform his duties in the district. While the Crimean rulers maintained a network of civil and military officials, whose functions is discussed below, rule was based on collective responsibility and local self-government and the various social groups played a crucial role in maintaining law and order in the state. For this reason, a district judge was instrumental in reconciling the ruler's orders with local demands and expectations. It is quite possible that petitions sent to the

TABLE 4 Changes in vital judicial posts in the Crimean Khanate.

Official	**Selim Giray (1st reign 1671–78) last known officeholder 1677–78**	**Murad Giray (r. 1678–83) officeholders**[a]	**Hacı Giray (r. 1683–84) officeholders**	**Selim Giray (2nd reign 1684–91) first known office-holder 1684–85**
kadıasker	Ibrahim[b]	Hasan Efendi	Abdulaziz Efendi[c]	Abdulgaffar Efendi[d]
kadı* of the *kalga	Abdulfatah Efendi[e]	Bekir Efendi	no data	Abdurrahim Efendi[f]
kadı* of the *nuraddin	no data	Salih Efendi	no data	no data
***kadı* of Ak Mescit**	Abdullah Efendi[g]	Abdulveli Efendi, later Abdullah Efendi	no data	Abdulkerim Efendi[h]
***kadı* of Bahçesaray**	Ebussuud Efendi[i]	(1) Musalli Efendi;[j] (2) Abdulfatah Efendi	no data	Abdulkerim Efendi[k]
***kadı* of Ferahkerman**	Mehmed Efendi[l]	Ismail Efendi	unknown, but not Ismail Efendi[m]	Abdulveli Efendi[n]

kadı of Gözleve	Hasan Efendi[o]	Osman Efendi	no data	Mehmed Efendi[p]
kadı of Kara Su	Ahmed Efendi[q]	(1) Mustafa Efendi (2) Ibrahim Efendi	Abdülalim?[r]	Abdulgaffar Efendi[s]

a For their location in the *sicil*s, see Appendix IV.
b ORRNB, Fond 917, *defter* 22/1a/1.
c ORRNB, Fond 917, *defter* 26/1a/1.
d ORRNB, Fond 917, *defter* 26/22a/1.
e ORRNB, Fond 917, *defter* 22/61b/1.
f ORRNB, Fond 917, *defter* 26/44a/6.
g ORRNB, Fond 917, *defter* 22/59b/1.
h ORRNB, Fond 917, *defter* 26/42a/1; 26/73b/1.
i ORRNB, Fond 917, *defter* 24/1a/1.
j ORRNB, Fond 917, *defter* 24/116a/3.
k ORRNB, Fond 917, *defter* 26/65b/1.
l ORRNB, Fond 917, *defter* 22/59b/1.
m In this period, Ismail Efendi was recorded as the former *kadı* of Ferahkerman, cf. ORRNB, Fond 917, *defter* 26/4b/6.
n ORRNB, Fond 917, *defter* 26/41b/1.
o ORRNB, Fond 917, *defter* 22/18b/5.
p ORRNB, Fond 917, *defter* 26/83b/3.
q ORRNB, Fond 917, *defter* 22/58a/1.
r ORRNB, Fond 917, *defter* 25/36a/1.
s ORRNB, Fond 917, *defter* 26/41b/5.

khans or *kalga*s might have been formulated by the Crimean judges and their staff. Numerous orders recorded in the Crimean *sicil*s were, in fact, issued in response to the subjects' petitions.[37] The Crimean courts, like those of the Ottomans, could furnish the local community with clerks capable of formulating such petitions. Hence, we presume that a district judge in the khanate acted as an intermediary between the inhabitants of a province and the ruler.[38]

37 The orders the khan issued in response to petitions from his subjects resemble the practice of Ottoman sultans, who promulgated *adaletname*s to address the complaints of the population. Several studies address the relations between the content of the petitions, *adaletnames*, and the role of the provincial *kadı*s in formulating the petitions; for example, see Faroqhi, "Political Activity"; Ginio, "Coping with the State's Agents."

38 The studies of Faroqhi and Ginio noted above discuss the role of the Ottoman *kadı*s in formulating petitions to the higher authorities. The subject was also noted by Boğaç Ergene. Based on his research on the Çankırı and Kastamonu court registers, he determined

The duties of a judge, as discussed, included a number of non-judicial tasks that ranged from the enforcement of decrees related to market prices to the supervision of the khan's accommodation during military campaigns. We know little about specific tasks assigned to *kadıs* by the khan; and this is unfortunate, as these might reveal personal relations between the ruler and his appointees. Typically, the khan did not entrust his appointees with diplomatic missions, nor did he use their talents in state propaganda. If former or active *kadıs* performed such duties, like Abdulgaffar Efendi, who was sent in a mission to the Sublime Porte, or Mehmed Senai, who was commissioned with writing a panegyric about Islam III Giray's war against Poland-Lithuania, it was because of their other qualities. The judicial post constituted but a step in the career of Abdulgaffar Efendi, who was closely connected to the powerful Şirin clan, and who held various offices in his lifetime. Mehmed Senai was a former secretary (*munşi*) of the khan's council. These extracurricular activities probably made them suitable for the assigned tasks.

1.4 *The Crimean* kadı *as the Girays' Employees: Payment and Career Perspective*

How did the khans reward the loyal *kadıs*? What was the source and amount of their income? Narrative accounts dating to the mid-seventeenth century indicate that district *kadıs* were organized in a hierarchy that consisted of at least two ranks and was reflected in the amounts of their daily allowances. Hence, we know that two groups of district judges received daily allowances of 150 *akçe*[39] and 300 *akçe*[40] respectively. The order of Canibeg Giray fixed the amount of court fees that judges could collect. The question then arises, did these fees constitute part of a *kadı*'s income? We should take into consideration the following possibilities:

(1) the judges were paid directly from the khan's treasury and they returned all court fees they collected to the treasury;
(2) they deducted 150 *akçe* or 300 *akçe* (i.e., their daily allowance) from the court fees they collected and returned the surplus to the treasury;
(3) they were paid directly from the treasury and in addition were entitled to a share of the court fees; or

---

that the *kadıs* played a limited role in drafting petitions related to the misdeeds of local officials (Ergene, *Local Court*, 53).

39 Hacı Mehmed Senai, *Historia chana*, 89.

40 Abrahamowicz, Dubiński, and Płaskowicka-Rymkiewicz (trans.), *Księga podróży Ewliji Czelebiego*, 303; Evliya Çelebi, *Tam Metin Seyahatnâme*, 617. In the Ottoman Empire, judges in ordinary districts received 150 *akçes* while in the *sancak* centers their payment was 300 *akçes* (I. Uzunçarşılı, *Osmanlı Devletinin İlmiye Teşkilatı* (Ankara, 1984), 94–95).

(4) they were not paid directly from the treasury, but retained all the court fees with the exception of the shares of the lower personnel (such as *naib*s or *katib*s).

If the Crimean practice was based on that of the Ottomans, the *kadı* and his staff was paid according to the third or the fourth variant. Interestingly, the amounts of the court fees prescribed in 1612 in the order of Canibeg Giray reveal analogies to those stipulated in the *kanunname* of Sultan Ahmed I, composed in the years 1608–10. Both rulers ordered that the same amount of *akçe*s be paid for two of the four most important court services (see table 5).

TABLE 5 A comparison of court fees in the Crimean Khanate and the Ottoman Empire.

Court service	**Court fees stipulated in Canibeg Giray's order (1612)**	**Court fees stipulated in Ahmed I's *kanunname* (ca. 1608–10)**[a]			
		***kadı's* share (in *akçes*)**	***naib's* share (in *akçes*)**	**katib's share (in *akçes*)**	**total (in *akçes*)**
Recording a case in the sicils (*resm-i sicillat*)	8 *akçes*	5	2	1	8
Issuing a certified copy of an entry (*resm-i süret*)	32 *akçes*	26	4	2	32
Issuing a certificate of manumission (*resmi itakname*)	1 *guruş*[b]	**from well-off individuals**			
		40	6	4	50
		from poor individuals			
		30	6	4	40
Supervising the division of inheritance (*resm-i kısmet*)	2.5% (1 *akçe* for every 40 *akçes*)	1.5%[c]			

a A. Akgündüz (ed.), *Osmanlı Kanunnameleri ve Hukuk Tahlilleri* (Istanbul, 1996), 9:518–519.

b It is not clear whether the document referred to *riyal guruş* or *esedi guruş*. Their exchange rates to the Ottoman *akçe* were not the same. In 1618, the *riyal guruş* was equal to 100 and the *esedi guruş* was equal to approximately 70 Ottoman *akçes*; see Ş. Pamuk, *A Monetary History of the Ottoman Empire* (Cambridge, 2000), 144.

c Ergene, *Local Court*, 77 and 84. Although the official charge should amount to 1.5 percent of the value of the effects, Ottoman courts often requested larger portions. Ergene's detailed analysis demonstrates that in Kastamonu and Çankırı, the court took about 3.5 percent. In seventeenth-century Bursa, the charge amounted to between 5 and 10 percent of the value of the divided inheritance (Abacı, *Bursa Şehri'nde*, 173).

We cannot ignore the fact that the term *akçe* in these documents may refer to two different coins (those minted in the Ottoman Empire and those minted in the Crimean Khanate) bearing the same name but differing in silver content. According to Şevket Pamuk, the exchange rate of one Crimean *akçe* to one Ottoman *akçe* varied considerably, from two to eleven.[41] If the court fees were not expressed in the same type of *akçe*, the income of the judges would have differed considerably. Nonetheless, the above-mentioned similarities lead us to wonder if the Crimean court fees were modeled on the Ottoman system. If so, were the Crimean judges paid in the same way as their Ottoman counterparts? Introducing the Ottoman practice into the khanate would mean that the khan paid daily allowances only to high-ranking judges, while less important ones derived most of their income from court fees. Thus, the references to the Crimean judges' daily allowances amounting to 150 *akçe*s or 300 *akçe*s (Ottoman or Crimean), found in the accounts by Mehmed Senai and Evliya, might refer to the fixed salaries of the higher ranking judges. Still, we must bear in mind that the Crimean practice was similar, but not identical, to the Ottoman one prescribed in the *kanunanme* (e.g., the different charge for the division of inheritance).

The findings of Metin Coşgel and Boğaç Ergene on the income of the Ottoman court personnel suggest that the picture is even more complicated than this. These researchers elaborated on differences between the amounts prescribed in the *kanunname*s for different court services and the actual payments the *kadı*s and his subordinates collected based on the registers of two Anatolian cities. They also emphasize that "we are quite uninformed about how much the court functionaries actually charged."[42] Hence, with regard to the income of judges, we cannot be sure whether the khan followed these Ottoman prescriptions or other prescriptions of an Ottoman practice (as yet unknown) from a neighboring Ottoman province.

Unfortunately, we have no data about the fixed salaries of judges during the rule of Murad Giray. Presumably, their salaries increased along with inflation. The limited data about court fees indicate that in Murad Giray's period they were higher than those fixed in the times of Canibeg Giray. For instance, in 1682, in Kara Su, the payment for registering a case in the *sicil* was between forty-five and sixty-eight *akçes*,[43] though the tax for the division of inheritance remained unchanged, at 2.5 percent of the value of the inheritance.[44]

---

41 Pamuk, *Monetary History*, 106.

42 Coşgel and Ergene, *Economics of Ottoman Justice*, 77–81.

43 ORRNB, Fond 917, *defter* 25/11b/4; 25/34b/2.

44 See, for example, ORRNB, Fond 917, *defter* 25/ 24a/3; 25/25b/2; 25/26a/2; *defter* 23b/15a/3.

Even if the salaries paid by Murad Giray remained at the same level as those described in the narrative sources from the 1650s, the *kadıs* likely enjoyed economic security. For example, during the reign of Murad Giray, the minimum daily allowance for minors or slaves was 2 to 5 *akçes*.[45] Contemporary lists of the fixed prices of basic commodities demonstrate that a *kadı*'s salary was more than sufficient to secure the purchase of everyday articles.[46] Some judges had enough money to invest in businesses, like Musalli Efendi, who invested 100 *altuns* in the purchase of a mill, including the surrounding land and a slave named Rustem, who worked there as a miller.[47]

A judge could crown his career by being appointed to the post of *kadıasker*. According to Peyssonel, this post was financially rewarding.[48] Although we have no data about the exact payment a *kadıasker* received, the *sicils* offer us some information on the wealth of individual *kadıaskers*. For instance, we know that in 1678 Ibrahim Efendi, the *kadıasker* during Selim Giray's first reign, left his heirs movable property and real estate worth 4,880 *guruş*.[49] This leads us to wonder whether such property placed the *kadıasker* among the economic elite of the society. A comparison with the effects of other deceased people, recorded in the *kadıasker sicils* from the same period, demonstrates that Ibrahim Efendi's effects corresponded in value to those left by noblemen[50] or the members of the administrative military elite.[51] While the *kadıasker* was far richer than common individuals, his estate still seems quite modest in comparison to that of a deceased Giray prince, Avs Giray Sultan.[52] The above remarks on the

45 In 1681, daily allowances paid for the maintenance of slaves caught by a *bölük başi* in Bahçesaray amounted to between 2 and 5 *akçes*; ORRNB, Fond 917, *defter* 23a/135b/3.

46 The Kara Su *sicils* contain a list of fixed prices dated May 1684. From this source, we know, for example, the price of 1 *okka* (*vukiye*) of honey from Rumelia (14 *akçe*), 1 *okka* of rice (7 *akçe*), 1 *okka* of chick peas (6 *akçe*), or 1 *okka* of beans (4 *akçe*); see ORRNB, Fond 917, *defter* 25/117b/3. Another entry fixing the weight (370 *dirhem*) and price (1 *akçe*) of a loaf of bread and the price of 1 *okka* of wheat (60–70 *akçes*) is recorded in the Kara Su *sicils* from the same period; see ORRNB, Fond 917, *defter* 25/121b/3.

47 ORRNB, Fond 917, *defter* 23a/228a/1. Fırat Yaşa's findings for the years 1650–75 indicate that while the khans maintained the fixed price for a loaf of bread as 1 *akçe*, they adjusted its weight as market conditions changed. For example, it amounted to 480 *dirhems* in 1665, 140 *dirhems* in 1673, and 180 *dirhems* in 1675; cf. Yaşa, "Bahçesaray (1650–1675)," 142.

48 Peysonnel, *Traité sur le commerce*, 2:262.

49 ORRNB, Fond 917, *defter* 23b/45a/1; ORRNB, Fond 917, *defter* 23b/46b/1; ORRNB, Fond 917, *defter* 23b/47b/6.

50 For example, Kutlu Şah Mirza, a brother of Bahadır Şah Beğ, the chief of the Argın clan, left his heirs possessions worth 1,886 *guruş*; ORRNB, Fond 917, *defter* 23b/67a/1.

51 The estate of Devlet Gazi Ağa, a former *emin*, was valued at 6,000 *guruş*, while *odabaşı* Derviş left property worth 2,430 *guruş*; ORRNB, Fond 917, *defter* 23b/2a/1; 23b/14a/1.

52 The prince left an estate valued at 12,447 *guruş*; ORRNB, Fond 917, *defter* 23b/11a/1.

wealth of the members of the religious elite in the khanate are consistent with some results of the ongoing research on the probate inventories of the Ottoman ulema. The findings of Abraham Marcus on eighteenth-century Aleppo suggest that the majority of the members of the religious elite should be categorized as "middle-class."[53] The research of Boğaç Ergene, one conducted in cooperation with Ali Berker and another study with Atabey Kaygun,[54] indicate that religious leaders should be divided into two groups. While the one group left estates comparable to the estates of common people, the higher echelons of ulema left estates that place them in the upper class. On the wealth of ulema, Phokion Kotzageorgis and Demetrios Papastamatiou point out that the ulema were among the wealthiest inhabitants of eighteenth-century Salonica. They held judicial posts only once in a lifetime, but given their considerable wealth, which allowed them to live without working, they did not need to seek reappointment.[55]

The data from the Crimean *sicil*s and the results from research on the Ottoman ulema indicate that the most prominent members of this group had considerable wealth, while the others enjoyed economic security. We should keep in mind that along with their elevated status, the high-ranking ulema likely also passed this wealth along to the next generations. Thus, family connections contributed to the financial prosperity of the judges. Data on their income in the khanate also indicate that even those who did not benefit from accumulated family wealth enjoyed financial security while performing their duties. However, frequent changes in judicial posts lead us to wonder how stable the income from a judicial career was. How many years during his lifetime could a member of the ulema hold a post? What was the average tenure of someone in this office? How long were the intervals between appointments? We can offer only tentative answers based on the data from the reign of Murad Giray. We would suggest that the relative scarcity of judicial posts was parallel to an overabundance of qualified candidates. In the 1660s, Evliya Çelebi praised the number of Crimean *medrese*s and their scholars and students. We do not have detailed information on the level of education required for judges, nor do we know how many candidates qualified for the job. Nonetheless, Evliya's description suggests that there was considerable competition within the profession. The lists of case witnesses recorded in the *kadıasker sicil*s confirm the Evliya's

53 Marcus, *Middle East on the Eve of Modernity*, 66–67.

54 Ergene and Kaygun, "Spouse Selection," 3–20; B. Ergene and A. Berker, "Wealth and Inequality in 18th-Century Kastamonu: Estimations for the Muslim Majority," *IJMES* 40, no. 1 (2008), 23–46.

55 P. Kotzageorgis and D. Papastamatiou, "Wealth Accumulation in an Urban Context: The Profile of the Muslim Rich of Thessaloniki in the Eighteenth Century on the Basis of Probate Inventories," *Turkish Historical Review* 5 (2014), 165–199, esp. 182–188.

account. They contain the names of numerous ulema, including former judges. Apparently these former judges were without posts. Perhaps they attended proceedings in the main court in the capital while waiting for their next appointments. The fact that Selim I Giray, Murad Giray, and Hacı II Giray easily filled all vital judicial posts with new ulema as soon as they ascended the throne seems to indicate that the number of candidates exceeded the number of available posts. So how did the khan divide the lucrative jobs among the ulema. Did he introduce the practice of limited tenure, as it was known and practiced in the contemporary Ottoman Empire?[56] Data from the reign of Murad Giray offer us ambiguous answers. Of the six most important judicial posts, four remained in the same hands throughout his reign, while two *kadı*s were replaced by other ulema.

The limited number of cases and the lack of data on the circumstances of dismissals prevent us from making generalizations. We must bear in mind that appointments could have been made to satisfy the demands of prominent ulema families or the patrons of individual ulema. Unfortunately, our sources do not provide information on the relationships between the judges and influential groups such as the Giray princes, key officials, or members of *karaçı* families. For this reason, much about the nature of judges' appointments, the length of tenure in office, and dismissals during Murad Giray's reign remains a mystery.

1.5 *Court Personnel and Other Subordinates of the* kadıs

The *kadı* remained the most important official in the court. He had at his disposal deputy judges (*naib*s) and minor officials such as scribes (*katib*s), summons officials (*muhzır*s), and those who divided inheritances (*kassam*s). According to Evliya Çelebi, as many as nine *naib*s worked in a large district such as Kara Su. It is probable that in small court districts *kadı*s remained the only functionaries or low-ranking court employees performed more than one function.

1.5.1 *Naib*s and *katib*s

The order of Canibeg Giray mentioned above requested that *kadı*s supervise the work of the *naib*s. The exact duties of the latter remain unclear; in the

56 Madeline Zilfi maintains that in the seventeenth century the average tenure of a member of the ulema lasted approximately eighteen months in the case of the most important posts, while a district *kadı* could be appointed for two years. In both cases, the tenure could be extended or immediately renewed; see M.C. Zilfi, "The Ottoman Ulema," in *The Cambridge History of Turkey*, vol. 3: *The Later Ottoman Empire, 1603–1839*, ed. S. Faroqhi (Cambridge, 2006), 3:221.

records, the *naib*s are even less visible than the judges. With the exception of Canibeg Giray's order, the *sicil*s offer almost no data on the subject and seldom reveal details on the duties of *naib*s. In the majority of entries, the *naib*s are recorded as case witnesses or as parties and witnesses in private cases. This limited data makes it impossible to establish whether the *naib*s assisted the *kadı*s in the district centers or were delegated to provide judicial service in the more remote settlements of a *kaza*. In this respect, the data in the *sicil*s is ambiguous. Acting as case witnesses in many subsequently recorded cases might indicate that the *naib*s assisted the *kadı*s during their daily work in the courts. On the other hand, the *sicil*s offer some indication that the *naib*s worked outside the district center. For instance, Hani, a woman from the Mangıt district, requested that Rahime, a woman from the sub-district (*nahiye*) of Tamak situated in the *kaza* of Kara Su, pay the debts of her (Rahime's) deceased husband. The plaintiff brought her claim to the court of Kara Su. The defendant's agent responded that the parties had already reached an agreement in front of Abdulhalik Efendi, the *naib* of the district judge (*toprak kadısının naibi*), and that Hani had already obtained her money. The plaintiff then requested to see the *naib*'s ruling. The defendant's agent was unable to provide this; he was given three days to send his servant to bring the document. It is noteworthy that the parties did not ask Abdulhalik Efendi to appear in person in the court nor did they look for the ruling in the *sicil*s. Apparently, this was not recorded in the Kara Su court register. Perhaps, like Mustafa Efendi, the *naib* of Bahçesaray who was responsible for register no. 24,[57] Abdulhalik Efendi recorded the entries related to adjudicated cases in a separate *defter*. Since the conflict regarded a considerable amount of money (150 *altun*s), presumably, the parties would have been willing to spend the few pennies necessary to pay to have their case recorded.[58] All this suggests that the *naib* was out of Kara Su at the time of the proceeding and that his earlier ruling, assuming it was not the defendant's fabrication, took place outside Kara Su, most probably in Tamak, which was a *nahiye* center. Thus, we can assume that in large districts, such as the *kaza* of Kara Su, *naib*s were delegated to sub-districts (*nahiye*s) in order to represent the *kadı* and enforce the law.[59]

The Crimean *kadıasker*s also relied on the help of *naibs*. *Kadıasker* Hasan Efendi, who held this office during Murad Giray's reign, had at least one *naib*

57 ORRNB, Fond 917, *defter* 24/1a/2.

58 In 1612, this fee amounted to 8 *akçe*s, cf. ORRNB, fond 917, 1/71b/1.

59 In the Ottoman Empire, *kadı*s were allowed to send their *naib*s to assume their responsibilities in the district, provided they were honest and qualified. Thus, *kadı*s could remain outside the *kaza*, cf. Ergene and Kaygun, "Spouse Selection," 3–20; Ergene and Berker, "Wealth and Inequality," 68.

named Abdulgaffar Efendi. Several records in the *kadıasker sicil*s and in the *sicil*s of Kara Su contain notes about his work; thus, we know something about his rulings.[60]

Scribes (*katibs*) constituted another group of court officials. They were typically given titles like *efendi* or *çelebi* and hence, we assume that they had some legal and religious education. Their names, frequently recorded under the entries, suggest that in fact they wrote the texts in the *sicil*s. Perhaps they also prepared certified copies of case records and other registered documents. The shifts in calligraphic and narrative style, which are visible between successive entries in one *defter*, indicate that more than one scribe served in one court. On the other hand, the same person could act as *naib* and *katib*, as we know from the example of Abdulbaki Efendi, who performed both functions in Kara Su.[61] His case suggests that *naib*s and *katib*s may have had a similar education and social position.

Our sources reveal only a little about the working conditions of *naib*s and *katib*s. What we know suggests that there were numerous analogies to Ottoman practices. Thus, presumably, like in the Ottoman Empire, their income consisted of a percentage of the fees charged by the court for its service. Although Canibeg Giray's order provides us with information on the rates of these fees in the Crimea, it does not discuss any internal division between the judge and his staff. If the Crimean *naib*s and *katib*s received shares similar in value to their Ottoman counterparts, their income was likely a little higher than the average revenue of common people.[62]

In sum, the posts of *naib* and *katib* can be regarded as reasonably well-paid jobs for Islamic school graduates. They probably constituted the first steps of a young man's judicial career. For the same reason, the number of candidates must have exceeded the number of available posts. Unfortunately, our sources do not reveal more about the pattern of appointments and dismissals of *naib*s and *katib*s. Basing our assumption on similarities between the Crimean judicial administration and the Ottoman system, we would argue that the court personnel were nominated by the judge. Evidence from the reign of Murad Giray indicates that they were appointed and dismissed along with the *kadı*. We know little about the social origins of other lower-level judicial employees. Judging by the titles of their fathers, which were sometimes recorded in the *sicil*s, *katib*s and *naib*s were frequently the sons of educated men.

---

60 ORRNB, Fond 917, *defter* 23a/131a/4.

61 ORRNB, Fond 917, *defter* 25/2b/4.

62 Cf. table 2.2. For the income of the court personnel, see Coşgel and Ergene, *Economics of Ottoman Justice*, 79–81.

1.5.2 Summons Official (*muhzır*)

In the Ottoman Empire, a court also employed a *muhzır*, an officer who summoned people and produced them in court. In the case of the Crimean courts, this official is rarely visible. The entries in the *sicil*s do not mention *muhzır*s at work. In contrast to officials such as the *zabit*, *beytülmal emini*, and their assistants, *muhzır*s are not mentioned as the ones who fetch individuals to the court. However, if they had no problem performing their duties, there would be no need to mention them in court. Their actions would be hidden under laconic expressions frequently used by court writers: "A, son of B, was summoned."[63] The fact that *muhzır*s were recorded among case witnesses also points to this possibility.[64] Unfortunately, there is almost no data concerning the number of *muhzır*s in a court or what they were paid. A unique note concerning their income derives from the already discussed order of Canibeg Giray.[65] The khan stated that no *muhzırıyye* tax should be collected in addition to the court fees.[66] This order implies that the *muhzır* had no share in the court's income and suggests that he was paid in a different manner, for instance, by the judge from his share. The fact that Canibeg Giray forbade the collection of *muhzırıyye* suggests that this charge was levied, though we do not know in what circumstances.

1.5.3 Case Witnesses (*şuhudülhal*)

Court proceedings were observed by so-called case witnesses (*şuhudülhal*). A list of case witnesses followed each entry, with the exception of orders sent to the court by the khan and the *kalga*. The institution of case witnesses also existed in the Ottoman Empire; researchers working on the court registers have discussed their role extensively.[67] This research focused on two issues:

---

63 *A ibn B ihzar olunub*.

64 Ciğdem, "Crimes Threatening Bodily Integrity," 69–70.

65 ORRNB, fond 917, *defter* 38/33a/1.

66 According to Halil Inalcık, the prohibition of collecting the *muhzırıyye* fee only related to the division of inheritances. Following this interpretation, the *muhzırıyye* could be collected as another fee, in addition to the charge for registering a case, issuing certified copies, etc.; cf. Inalcık, "Kirim Hanlığı," 172.

67 The literature providing important data on the institution of case witnesses is vast. See, for example, K. Barkey, "The Use of Court Records in the Construction of Village Networks: A Comparative Perspective," *International Journal of Comparative Sociology* 32, nos. 1–2 (1991), 209; K. Barkey and R. Van Rossem, "Networks of Contention: Villages and Regional Structure in the Seventeenth Century Ottoman Empire," *American Journal of Sociology* 102, no. 5 (1997), 1379; Canbakal, *Society and Politics*, 130–137; Ergene, *Local Court*, 27–29; Coşgel and Ergene, *Economics of Ottoman Justice*, 70–79, 141–142; R. Jennings, "Limitations of the Judicial Powers of the Kadi in 17th Century Ottoman Kayseri," *Studia Islamica* 49 (1979), 151–184; Peirce, *Morality Tales*, 97–98.

First, they studied the role of case witnesses in the legal process. Second, they sought to figure out who could serve as a case witness. Did the social composition of case witnesses differ depending on the type of case? Did they constitute a select group of the society? In relation to the first issue, Ronald Jennings points out in one of his classical studies, based on seventeenth-century Kayseri *sicil*s, that the case witnesses were an important element in the court legal structure. They monitored the work of the judge and his subordinates and attested to the authenticity of the proceedings.[68] This opinion was shared by later scholars. For instance, Leslie Peirce states that "their function was to act as a check on the correctness of legal procedures observed in the case as whole and to serve as repository of communal memory of the incident at issue."[69] The second question concerning the recruitment of case witnesses is more complicated. It is clear that they did not form a well-defined group. Among case witnesses, one finds individuals frequently attending court proceedings as well as people interested in specific cases. Some witnesses seemed to have no obvious connection to the proceedings. Case witnesses originated from different social groups. Scholars vary in their opinions regarding the connection between particular court cases and the selection of witnesses to these cases. Ronald Jennings and Karen Barkey were inclined to see the witnesses as personally uninvolved and neutral to the case.[70] The more recent studies of Boğaç Ergene and Leslie Peirce suggest that in some cases the appearance of certain individuals might not have been pure coincidence.[71] Based on the court records of Çankırı and Kastamonu, Ergene observes that "a well-defined group of people regularly attended the judicial and administrative proceedings as witnesses in the courts."[72] The research of Hülya Canbakal on the city of Ayntab in the second half of the seventeenth century suggests that case witnesses, like witnesses for the plainiffs or defendants, were recruited from "righteous men," who were, for the most part, distinguished with honorific titles. An analysis of 6,432 instances of testimonies involving *şuhudülhal*, witnesses, and informants, led Canbakal to conclude that "in 90% of the instances of testimony (80% without summoners), the witness was someone who served in more than one case,"[73] while "the total number of people in the category of most

68 Jennings, "Limitations of the Judicial Powers," 151–184.

69 Peirce, *Morality Tales*, 97.

70 Jennings, "Kadi, Court and Legal Procedure," 145–146; Barkey, "The Use of Court Records," 209; Barkey and van Rossem, "Networks of Contention," 1379.

71 Peirce, *Morality Tales*, 97.

72 Ergene, *Local Court*, 29; Coşgel and Ergene, *Economics of Ottoman Justice*, 70–79.

73 Canbakal, *Society and Politics*, 134.

recurrent witnesses would be 110."[74] Thus, the researcher suggests that a "pool of witnesses" (*şuhudülhal* and circumstantial) existed in the city of Ayntab. Such individuals were reputable and credible members of the community and their presence supported the credibility of the court.[75]

Similar questions arise with regard to the case witnesses recorded in the Crimean *sicil*s. Perhaps they played roles similar to that of their Ottoman counterparts, i.e., they checked the correctness of legal procedures and confirmed their authenticity. The Crimean case witnesses were all male Muslims, recruited from various social groups. They were usually listed in groups of four to five individuals, but some entries were followed by as many as nine or ten names, while the record on a case judged at the khan's council contains names of twenty case witnesses. It appears that at least two witnesses must be recorded as present during the legal proceeding. When case witnesses constituted a particularly large group, the scribe recorded only a few names, followed with the set formulae: "and the others" (*ve gayruhum*) or "and others from among those present" (*ve gayruhum min el-hazirin*). Case witnesses were frequently recorded in a hierarchical order of their social status, though this was not a formal rule.

Unfortunately, there is no satisfactory answer to the question of whether case witnesses in the khanate represented identifiable interests that related to the state, community or private persons. In a few cases studied here, certain individuals recorded among *şuhudülhal* seem to have monitored particular cases in order to secure the interests of their family or community. This subject, which is strictly related to the issues concerning the court clients, is discussed in chapters 3 and 5. Still, it is not clear how a case witness could manipulate the court. Their actions remain invisible. In the majority of the cases studied there is no evidence that witnesses were personally interested in their outcome. As in seventeenth-century Ayntab studied by Canbakal, a considerable percentage of the Crimean *şuhudülhal* were knowledgable and trustworthy people trained in religious, administrative, and legal matters. Perhaps, prominent people in the khanate took part in legal proceedings to observe the court's services. Like Ronald Jennings suggests, these were people active in business, with a personal interest in "the fair and effective functioning of the court."[76] Acting as a case witness on behalf of the whole community likely gave one prestige.

74 Ibid., 133.
75 Ibid., 123–149, esp. 133–134.
76 Jennings, "Kadi, Court and Legal Procedure," 143.

1.5.4 Law Enforcement Officials

Law enforcement officials called *zabit*s and their assistants, both of whom were recruited from among the janissaries, also reported to the district judge. They were forbidden to act independently in matters concerning judicial proceedings. Devlet Giray, the *kalga* in 1684, severely reprimanded the Kara Su *zabit, bölükbaşi* Cafer, for imprisoning a certain merchant on his own authority, without orders from the *kadı*. Devlet Giray wrote,

> We made you the *zabit*, but this does not mean that you can do whatever comes to your mind. When my order arrives, you are to release the prisoner. Hereafter, do not act according to your own knowledge. Act in the way the former *zabit* worked. Do nothing without the consent of *kadı efendi*.[77]

While it is clear that the *kalga* strongly supported the *kadı*, this order also indicates that members of the military class may have tended to overstep the bounds of their authority and infringe on that of the judges.[78] Other orders (*yarlığ*s) of Kalga Devlet Giray and Khan Hacı Giray, recorded in the court register of Kara Su, confirm that the *zabit* and his assistants were obliged to execute the judge's decisions. Their police work consisted of arresting and bringing to court those suspected of violating "God's claims." For instance, the Kara Su *zabit, bölükbaşı* Cafer, brought a married woman named Saime and Ibrahim, son of Hasan, to the local court. The official had found them together at night in the woman's house while her husband was absent. Saime defended herself by saying that she had found Ibrahim already in her house when she had returned home in the evening. She stated that she had not invited him. For his part, perhaps to avoid a more serious charges of robbery or rape, Ibrahim maintained that he had come at her invitation. He produced witnesses who confirmed his version. Consequently, both defendants were found guilty of having illicit sex and

---

77 See the order of Kalga Devlet Giray dated the last ten days of Cemazi I/6–15 May 1684 (ORRNB, Fond 917, *defter* 25/115a/4).

78 Fariba Zarinebaf describes the responsibilities of "police" officials in the eighteenth century and their relations with the local *kadı*s similarly: "In the Ottoman Empire, policing was formally the function of certain divisions of the janissary corps in Istanbul and other cities and of the cavalry in the countryside. Ideally, there was a division of labor between the kadi, who conducted the trial and issued the sentence, and the police division of the janissary corps, which carried out the arrest and punishment. The police officers were expected to execute the sentences of the judiciary (shari'a courts) and the Imperial Council. However, it is clear from the records that sometimes the various police officers arrested and punished repeat offenders without any trial or authorization from the kadi." (Zarinebaf, *Crime and Punishment*, 134).

the judge sentenced them to a discretionary punishment (*ta'zir ile hükm şod*)[79] instead of the fixed penalties prescribed in the Quran.[80] Muslim jurists accepted flogging as the *ta'zir* punishment for free individuals convicted of engaging in illicit sex.[81]

The story of Innocent Felici shows that those accused of this offense risked imprisonment before the trial. For example, the Dominican missionary was held in custody in the house of an officer of the khan. From Innocent Felici's description of the trial, we know that the judge warned the witnesses that if they unlawfully accused others of having illicit sex (*kazf*), they would also be sentenced to flogging.[82] Presumably, the punishment would be carried out by the *zabit*s. These two cases indicate that in the khanate, as in the Ottoman Empire, the *zabit*s were involved in pursuing, and then executing the judge's sentences , at least in relation to *hadd* crimes.[83]

---

79 ORRNB, Fond 917, *defter* 25/48a/4; it seems that punishments for petty crimes used to be executed immediately after the trial. In the 1790s, Marie Guthrie described earlier Crimean practices: "Justice while in the hands of the Tatars, was of so summary a kind, that little can be said of it. Indeed, when we consider that the whole Code of Laws sacred and profane is contained in the Koran of the Mahomet, it is easy to conceive, that it could not be very complicated. The proper magistrate administered justice on the spot; so that the contending parties were put to no expense to obtain it; nor alternately agitated by hopes and fears. Crimes likewise were immediately and publicly punished. A shopkeeper caught in the act of cheating with sale or short weights was nailed by the ear to his own shop-door, that the whole market might know the knave, and watch him in future; a punishment which set Jews, Armenians, and Greeks, the ordinary offenders in the country (for the Turks and the Tatars are little given to cheating), much on their guard, as they had little chance of escaping the vigilant police. Lesser offences were instantly punished with the bastinado, and greater with the bow-string, if a true believer, for a halter was the portion of an infidel; as they thought their old Scythian weapon dishonored by the neck of a Christian or Jew. All this is now, of course changed, under the Russian dominion; where several courts of justice supply the place of the Cady's market-tribunal." See Guthrie, *A Tour Performed*, 222–223.

80 Rudolph Peters points to the fact that, according to the sharia, only under very special circumstances can individuals accused of illicit sex be punished with the fixed penalties of 100 lashes or death by stoning, see Peters, *Crime and Punishment in Islamic Law*, 60.

81 Ibid., 35. There is no indication that the khans followed the Ottoman practice and collected fines from individuals convicted of sexual crimes. For fines prescribed in the Ottoman *kanuns*, see Heyd, *Studies in Old Ottoman Criminal Law*, 95–97; Zarinebaf, *Crime and Punishment*, 106; Tuğ, *Politics of Honor*, 161–162.

82 The letter of Innocent Felici of Malta to Philippe de Harlay, comte de Césy, the French Ambassador in Istanbul, APF, SOCG, vol. 106, fols. 335r–337v.

83 On the *zabits*' role in apprehending criminals and implementing court sentences in cases involving crimes such as illicit sex (*zina*) and the unlawful accusation of illicit sex in eighteenth-century Anatolia, see Tuğ, *Politics of Honor*; for eighteenth-century Aleppo, see Semerdjian, "*Off the Straight Path.*"

Along with the *beytülmal emini*, the *zabit* and his assistants were responsible for catching runaway slaves. The court records show *zabit*s registering arrested slaves; this was done in order to fix a daily allowance for their maintenance.[84] In Bahçesaray, during Murad Giray's reign, the khan specially appointed an official to be responsible for the custody of fugitive slaves.[85] He was named Halil and referred to in the *sicil*s as a *bölükbaşı*. A record in the *kadıasker* court register states that he requested that a daily allowance (two *akçe*), be set for a fugitive slave of Hungarian origin.[86] The allowance was to be paid back by the owner after the *bölükbaşı* found and returned the man's slave. For instance, a certain Suleyman from the Eski Kırım district reimbursed the court two *akçe* for each day that his runaway slave, Kutlu Bay, had spent in custody in Bahçesaray. At the same time, we know that *bölükbaşı* Halil kept this slave for four months.[87] If a former owner did not come to collect his slave, the latter was sold at auction in order to reimburse the court for his or her maintenance. The said *bölükbaşı* Halil kept a female slave in custody for five months and seventeen days, spending three *akçe* per day for her maintenance. When no one came to reclaim her, she was sold at auction for forty-three *altuns*. The cost of her maintenance as well as the court charges were paid from this sum.[88]

Sometimes the *zabit* and his assistants supervised the measuring and pricing of goods in the market, based on the khan's orders.[89]

When security and the law were violated, other officials could step in and fulfill the tasks primarily attributed to *zabits*. For instance, Ali Çelebi, a scribe of the *beytülmal emini*, accused a cotton processor Aslan of wounding his work mate. The official met Aslan and his suffering companion near the intersection of the roads to Bahçesaray and Kara Su and brought them both to the court. The defendant stated that his friend had wounded himself by accident while they were having a good time together. The injured processor confirmed this story, stating, "It happened after we got drunk. Because of that I wounded

84 ORRNB, Fond 917, *defter* 23b/116a/9.
85 ORRNB, Fond 917, *defter* 23a/140b/3.
86 ORRNB, Fond 917, *defter* 23a/135a/4.
87 ORRNB, Fond 917, *defter* 23a/135a/5.
88 The entry is followed by a detailed account: the total worth of the allowance = 501 *akçes*, the fee collected by a broker (*delal*) = 30 *akçes*, the cost of the certified copy = 40 *akçes*, the registration of the amount of the allowance = 8 *akçes*, the charge from runaway slave (?) = 40 *akçes*, the announcer's fee (*ücret-i muhbir*) = 15 *akçes*; for a total of 634 *akçes*; ORRNB, Fond 917, *defter* 23a/140b/3. The 'announcer' (*muhbir*) was someone who spread information about something, perhaps in this case, he spread information about the auctions.
89 ORRNB, Fond 917, *defter* 25/115a/1; 25/117a/7; 87/45a/1.

myself."[90] The scribe was satisfied with the explanation and withdrew his charges (*ta'arruzdan men' olunub*). The official probably intervened promptly because the assault took place near a public road.

Other district officials, such as the *beytülmal emini*, the head billeting officer (*konakçı başi*), and the *pencik emini* were supervised by the judge as well. The responsibilities of the *beytülmal emini* covered various matters related to financial administration and security. He was charged with the collection of certain taxes. Mehmed Ağa, the *beytülmal emini* of Kara Su in the years 1683–84, collected *haraç* from twelve winehouse owners. The tax amounted to one *altun* for grape mush (*üzümi haraç*) and two *altun*s for grapes brought to market in barrels (*fıçılari haraç*).[91] Presumably, the *beytülmal emini* also supervised the prices, weights, and measures of taxed goods.

The *beytülmal emini* was also responsible for the management of property left by those who died or were permanently absent without heirs. For example, Naste, a woman from the Tarkanlar neighborhood (*mahalle*) of Kara Su, died without an heir. Her properties (worth 1360 *akçe*) were sold after her death. After paying the court costs (forty-five *akçe* for registering the case in the *sicil* and fifteen *akçe*s for the auction), the rest of the money, i.e., 1,300 *akçe*, was handed over to the aforementioned *beytülmal emini*, Mehmed Ağa.[92]

The *beytülmal emini* was given the job of capturing runaway slaves and holding them in custody. Mehmed, an assistant of the *beytülmal emini* and also the warden of the prison in Kara Su, caught a male slave named Gözme[93] who confirmed that he had run away from a certain Bölük Sufi. The court assigned a daily allowance for the fugitive and handed him over to Mehmed.[94]

The case of Imam Salih Çelebi reveals that the duties of the *beytülmal emini* included looking after lost property. The imam found a crippled ox by the road. He handed it over to Islam Atalık, an assistant of the *beytülmal emini* Mehmed Ağa, on 2 October 1683.[95] Two days later when, apparently, the owner of the ox had not appeared, the Kara Su court allowed him to sell the animal for 300 *akçe*. The *betülmal emini* was entrusted with the money that remained after the court fees (23 *akçe*) and the costs of keeping the ox (24 *akçe*) were paid.[96]

---

90 *Sarhoşlık ile mustanlık sebebiyle kendim kendim cerh eyledim* (ORRNB, Fond 917, *defter* 25/31a/3).

91 ORRNB, Fond 917, *defter* 25/18a/2; also see the orders of Islam III Giray, where *beytülmal emini* is listed among the tax collectors and the order of Kalga Devlet Giray, which forbids the *beytülmal emini* from collecting taxes from the Jewish subjects of Veli Şah Beğ, cf. ORRNB, Fond 917, *defter* 2/55a/1; 25/114b/1.

92 ORRNB, Fond 917, *defter* 25/11b/4.

93 *Emin hüddamından Mehmed tomrukçı nam kimesne* (ORRNB, Fond 917, *defter* 25/101b/1).

94 ORRNB, Fond 917, *defter* 25/ 119b/1.

95 ORRNB, Fond 917, *defter* 25/ 119b/6.

96 ORRNB, Fond 917, *defter* 25/ 119b/7.

1.5.5 Billeting Officers (*konakçı*)

Head billeting officers (*konakçı başıs*) and billeting officers (*konakçıs*) were commissioned to secure law and order when Crimean dignitaries and troops were quartered in local towns. From the Kara Su *sicil*s dated 1698 we know that Kalga Devlet Giray appointed the *konakçı başı* of the town to protect its inhabitants. An official named Huseyn Beşe was ordered to ensure that no subject (*reaya*) should be deprived of his home, but, the townspeople should provide lodgings for traveling noblemen (Tatar, Nogay or Circassian), officials, *sekban*s, or the khan's guests.[97] The extant order seems to be analogous with two similar orders regulating the billeting policy, sent to the Kara Su judges by Hacı II Giray in 1684[98] and Kalga Şahin Giray in 1744/45.[99] In contrast to Devlet Giray's order, the last two do not specify that the *konakçı başıs* are responsible for implementing the orders; we do not know whether the orders from 1684 and 1744/45 were also executed by *konakçı başıs* or if the judges entrusted the task to other officials. Similar regulations in all the three orders suggest that the task was given to the *konakçı başıs*.

While the *kalga* appointed Huseyn Beşe as *konakçı başı*, the inhabitants of Kara Su had the right to choose their own local billeting officer (*konakçı*). This conclusion is based on an entry recorded in the Kara Su *sicil*s in 1684. The inhabitants of the town (*Kara Su reayası*) registered their choice of the billeting officer, a recent convert to Islam (*muhtedi*)[100] named Sefer and they agreed to pay him 4 *akçe* daily to perform this function.[101] In the *sicil*s we studied, the *konakçıs* only appear in relation to private cases or their witnesses,[102] hence several aspects concerning their work, such as the scope of their duties or their official subordination, remain unclear. Presumably, they reported to the *konakçı başı* or directly to the *kadı*.

1.5.6 *Pencik emini*

The *pencik emini* was an official responsible for collecting a tax called *pencik*, which was imposed on the sale of slaves. Evidence from the Kara Su *sicil*s

---

97 ORRNB, Fond 917, *defter* 33/67a/1.

98 In the order to the judge of Kara Su dated May 1684, Hacı II Giray replied to a petition sent by local non-Muslims concerning the right for soldiers to billet in their houses. Thereafter, the conditions that were set for billeting were supposed to be fair and just. The khan also addressed the problem of individuals who were not permitted to settle in the city. The *zabit* had to present these individuals to the judge (ORRNB, Fond 917, *defter* 25/115b/2).

99 Replying to a petition of the inhabitants of Kara Su, the *kalga* regulated who could obtain lodgings in the city. The document is dated 1157/ 1744–45 (ORRNB, Fond 917, *defter* 65/34b/1).

100 A *muhtedi* means a convert to Islam.

101 ORRNB, Fond 917, *defter* 25/118a/4.

102 ORRNB, Fond 917, *defter* 25/1a/3; *defter* 23a/195a/5.

suggests that the *pencik emini* did not work alone, but was assisted by *delal*s, that is, lower ranked fiscal officers who were supposed to supervise commercial transactions and who acted as middlemen. For instance, we learn that a *pencik emini* named Yusuf Çelebi repeatedly sent a *delal* to a grocer named Mehmed, son of Allahverdi, who failed to pay the *pencik* tax for a slave who had been sold. Because Mehmed consistently refused to pay, Yusuf Çelebi decided to intervene in person. The debtor refused once again, insisting that the slave was not his property. When this argument did not convince the official, Mehmed slandered him and eventually wounded his head with a pipe stem. When he was brought to the court, the grocer pleaded guilty and was sentenced to be flogged.[103]

2 The Limitations of the Judicial Power of the *kadı* and His Subordinates

In the previous section the discussion left off at the duties and prerogatives of the *kadı* and his subordinates. The *kadı* was described as the most important deputy of the ruler in the district. In this section, I turn to the limitation of the *kadı*'s judicial power by examining who could limit his authority and how this could be done? Could the judge summon anyone to his court? If not, what types of matters or kinds of persons were beyond his judicial power? Finally, was the verdict of a district judge final or was it possible to reopen a case in another venue.

None of these questions is new; the limitations of the *kadı*'s judicial power have been studied by numerous scholars working on the history of various Islamic states. Here we limit ourselves to mentioning the main findings related to the Ottoman Empire. First, scholars emphasize that the subject is not yet clearly understood. Second, they generally acknowledge the limitations of the *kadı*'s power in relation to the *askeri*. Third, they emphasize that the range of a *kadı*'s judicial power differed from one province to another and evolved throughout the early modern period. Some studies, for example, the monograph of Haim Gerber on seventeenth-century Bursa, support the notion that judges enjoyed judicial monopoly with regard to taxpaying subjects in the district.[104] This idea was questioned by Michael Ursinus, who pointed to the judicial prerogatives of provincial councils (*divan*s) and the imperial council

103 ORRNB, Fond 917, *defter* 25/82b/3.
104 H. Gerber, *State, Society, and Law in Islam: Ottoman Law in Comparative Perspective* (New York, 1994).

(*divan-i hümayün*).[105] Recently, Başak Tuğ added to our understanding on the role of this institution in relation to the prosecution of crimes involving illicit sex in eighteenth-century Anatolia.[106] The studies of numerous scholars such as Suraya Faroqhi (on the late sixteenth- to mid seventeenth-century Anatolia),[107] Rossitsa Gradeva (on the city of Sofia and its surroundings in the seventeenth century),[108] Abraham Marcus (on eighteenth-century Aleppo),[109] and Eyal Ginio (on eighteenth-century Salonica)[110] add to the image that district judges were being steadily deprived, over time, of their judicial monopoly. These discussions of the procedures of judicial review in the Ottoman Empire challenge the idea that the *kadı*'s decision was, in practice, final.[111]

In this section, I focus on officials and institutions in the khanate that might have been potential competitors of the *kadı* within the province administration. These include the market inspector (*muhtesib*), the local commander (*serdar*), and the head of the *seyyid*s (*nakıbüleşrafs*), the mufti, autonomous jurisdictions of non-Muslims; and finally, the *beğ*s of the *karaçı* families, and the khan's council.

2.1 *Market Inspector* (muhtesib)

In her comprehensive study on *muhtesib*s in Mamluk Egypt, Kristen Stilt points out that the *muhtesib*'s duty to maintain law and order in markets and public places required combining two sources of law: Islamic law and the orders of the rulers. The author emphasizes the vital role of the *muhtesib*, next to the judge and the mufti, in the administration of justice.[112] Although no one has yet researched the role of the *muhtesib* in the Ottoman Empire, his responsibilities seem limited in comparison with that of previous periods.[113] The Ottoman *muhtesib* was particularly active in inspecting weights and measures, as

105 Ursinus, *Grievance Administration.*

106 Tuğ, *Politics of Honor.*

107 Faroqhi, "Political Activity."

108 R. Gradeva, "On Judicial Hierarchy in the Ottoman Empire: The Case of Sofia, Seventeenth–Beginning of Eighteenth Century," in *Dispensing Justice in Islam: Qadis and Their Judgements*, ed. M.K. Masud, R. Peters, and D.S. Powers (Leiden and Boston, 2006), 296–298.

109 Marcus, *Middle East on the Eve of Modernity.*

110 E. Ginio, "Patronage, Intervention and Violence in the Legal Process in Eighteenth-Century Salonica and Its Province," in *Law, Customs, and Statute in the Muslim World. Studies in Honor of Aharon Layish*, ed. R. Shaham (Leiden and Boston, 2007), 111–130; Ginio, "Coping with the State's Agents."

111 For the survey of literature on the judicial review in Islamic law, and especially on Ottoman legal practice, see Tuğ, *Politics of Honor*, 191–205.

112 K. Stilt, *Islamic Law in Action: Authority, Discretion, and Everyday Experiences in Mamluk Egypt* (Oxford, 2011).

113 See Stilt, *Islamic Law in Action*; Gerber, *State, Society, and Law*, 69–84.

well as prices and the quality of goods. He dealt with minor offenses that did not merit the *kadı*'s attention, though more complicated cases were brought to the court. The *muhtesib*'s field of work was of particular significance to the highest state dignitaries. As Suraiya Faroqhi remarks, at least in the capital "the quality and quantity of goods available was of direct relevance to the political fortunes of rulers and viziers. This explains why fairly mundane problems involving Istanbul craftsmen were often discussed in the afternoon meetings of the grand vizier and his advisers."[114] The grand vizier regularly inspected the markets of Istanbul in person, accompanied by higher officials and the capital's *muhtesib*.[115] Nonetheless, even given the attention the Porte paid to their job, the *muhtesib*s' was not independent from local *kadı*s.[116]

In the case of the khanate, Crimean dignitaries also attached special importance to the availability and quality of staples. The *sicil*s of Kara Su dating to the reign of Hacı II Giray contain a list of fixed prices as well as regulations concerning the weight and price of bread and grain. Although it is not explicitly stated in the sources, this suggests that enforcing such regulations constituted the main responsibility of local *muhtesib*s. Unfortunately, we do not have any information on the process of fixing prices. Therefore, we do not know whether the Crimean elite was involved, as in the Ottoman Empire.[117] The office of the *muhtesib*, which has Islamic origins, seems to have been introduced in the khanate according to the Ottoman pattern. Numerous extant *yarlığ*s of various khans mention the appointment of market inspectors. The documents demonstrate that these officials were well paid; for instance, in 1674 one was granted a daily allowance of 150 *akçes*.[118] In the *sicil*s from the reign of Murad Giray, active as well as former *muhtesib*s are registered as case witnesses or litigants only. Unfortunately, they were not depicted performing their official

114 S. Faroqhi, "Guildsmen and Handicraft Producers," in *The Cambridge History of Turkey*, vol. 3: *The Later Ottoman Empire, 1603–1839* (Cambridge, 2006), 3:345.

115 Heyd, *Studies in Old Ottoman Criminal Law*, 231–232.

116 In his study of seventeenth-century Bursa, Haim Gerber considered the *muhtesib* "the kadi's only legal contender for carrying out adjudication," yet Gerber failed to produce convincing evidence about the *kadı*'s independent judicial power; cf. Gerber, *State, Society, and Law*, 69.

117 Canbakal, *Society and Politics*, 165.

118 See the order of Selim I Giray, announcing the appointment of a certain Bekir as *muhtesib* with a daily allowance of 150 *akçes*. Bekir was supposed to start performing his duties in June 1674. Similarly, in 1706, Gazi III Giray appointed a certain Kantemir as *muhtesib*, with an allowance of 160 *akçes* (ORRNB, Fond 917, *defter* 40, 39a/1), while Selim III Giray offered this job to Ömer in 1764 and 1765 (ORRNB, Fond 917, *defter* 85/92b/3; 85/93a/1), and in the following years to Abbas and Ismaıl (ORRNB, Fond 917, *defter* 85/93b/1; 87/45a/1). The *sicils* also contain the order of Khan Maksud Giray appointing a certain Ali Ağa to this office in June 1767 (ORRNB, Fond 917, *defter* 89/48a/3).

duties. Thus, we do not have a description of the activity of the Crimean *muhtesib*, orthe types of offenses that fell within their authority, or the types of offenses that they brought to the court. In addition, we do not know to what extent these officials were subordinated to the district judge, and we do not have evidence on the legal doctrines these officials enforced. This limited knowledge prevents us from determining the differences in competencies and the daily work of Crimean and Ottoman market inspectors. If we assume that their duties and rights were similar in the two states, the prerogatives of a *muhtesib* did not constitute competition to the authority of a district judge.

2.2 *Local Military Commander* (serdar) *and Other Military Officials*

The local military commander may also have competed with the *kadı* for judicial monopoly. The question of the former's judicial power and his role in executing the *kadı*'s sentences brings us to the complex and much debated issue of administrative justice (*siyasa shar'iyya*).

Frank E. Vogel defined *siyasa shar'iyya* as "governance in accordance with the sharia." He states that it is "a Sunnī constitutional and legal doctrine emerging in late mediaeval times and calling for harmonisation between the law and procedures of Islamic jurisprudence (*fiḳh*) and the practical demands of governance (*siyāsa*)."[119] As Sadıq Riza points out

> an earlier generation of Western scholars characterized the distinction between jurisprudential doctrine and executive practice as a fundamental fault line in Islamic law, an irreconcilable schism between theory and practice. In this view, many practices of criminal-law enforcement by Muslim political authorities constituted departures from the *sharia*, indeed contraventions of it, creating a running contradiction between theory and practice. More recent analysis, however, locates criminal practice by executive authorities soundly within classical doctrines that permit rulers to consider the real-world exigencies of governance in implementing God's law, particularly the doctrine of "governance in accordance with the *sharia*"(*siyasa shar'iyya*), which cedes daily governance to political authorities *as a matter of* the *sharia.*[120]

In her recent discussion of *siyasa shar'iyya* in the Ottoman Empire, Başak Tuğ, following other new studies on Ottoman law, also challenges the idea of "dual

119 F.E. Vogel, "Siyāsa," *EI*², 9:694.

120 S. Riza, "Islam's Fourth Amendment: Search and Seizure in Islamic Doctrine and Muslim Practice," *Georgetown Journal of International Law* 40, no. 3 (2009), 714–715.

system" that divides the law on 'religious' and 'political,' sharia and *kanun*, *fiqh* and *siyasa*. Instead, she proposes to elaborate on "the praxis in which religious doctrine interplays, negotiates, and comes to terms with the sovereign's discretion in various historical contexts." She adds that, "in Ottoman history, as in other historical and regional contexts, the term of this relationship was not fixed; rather it took on multiple forms according to the social-political configuration of power relations between different groups in different periods."[121]

The last remark adds to our understanding of relations between a *kadı* and a local military commander in the khanate. As we see above, our data on the subject, which is limited to three orders from two rulers, demonstrate that the each khan defined the jurisdiction of the khans' military commanders versus that of judges differently.

Among the orders issued by the Crimean khans, three documents directly address the problem of the division of judicial prerogatives between judges and military commanders. Curiously, the khans resolved it in different ways. The first order was issued by Murad Giray. He nominated Mehmed, the head swordsman (*matrakçı başı*) in Bahçesaray, as the *zabit* in the military corps. The khan ordered that members of the standing army who were accused of breaking the law be handed over to Mehmed for judgment. Thus, members of the military corps were exempt from the *kadı*'s jurisdiction. In light of Murad Giray's order, the *kadı*'s judicial power did not extend to standing regiments.[122] A few years later, Hacı II Giray had a different definition of the judicial prerogatives of military officials. In two orders concerning the standing troops in Kara Su, he stated that their members should be judged before the district court. The local commander was merely required to execute the *kadı*'s sentences pertaining to the members of standing regiments and *timar* holders.[123] A comparison of these orders, issued by two khans for two towns, does not enable us to draw general conclusions about power relations between the military and judicial branches of provincial administration. Yet, it demonstrates that the *kadı*'s jurisdiction over members of the military class was not, by any means, clear. Unfortunately, the *sicil*s do not reveal how other Crimean rulers dealt with this issue. Moreover, Murad Giray's order is recorded at the end of the last *defter* composed during his reign, hence we cannot study how it was put into practice, nor can we determine which option prevailed throughout the history of the khanate.

---

121 Tuğ, *Politics of Honor*, 39.

122 ORRNB, fond 917, *defter* 23a/211b/1.

123 ORRNB, Fond 917, *defter* 25/114b/1, 25/118b/3.

Why did Murad Giray and Hacı Giray handle this problem differently? We would argue that the decision in this matter reflected the ruler's conception of state administration. By exempting the military class from the *kadı*'s authority, the khan created a group of people deprived of the right to trial in a sharia court. Thus, he formed a class of people directly and exclusively subject to his judgment, perhaps modeled on the Ottoman *askeri*. In contrast, common people faced the khan's punishment only after a trial in the sharia court. Presumably, Crimean rulers wanted to maintain a balance of power between the judiciary and military authority. Consequently, they were likely to strengthen the official who, at the moment, appeared less powerful. Their decisions might also have reflected their current relations with the two groups of state employees. If so, Murad Giray demonstrated his distrust toward judicial clerks, while Hacı II Giray preferred not to rely on the loyalty of his standing army.

2.3 *Marshal of the Descendants of the Prophet* (nakıbüleşraf)

Seyyids, the descendants of the Prophet, enjoyed respect and privileges in numerous Islamic states. Damir Iskhakov's study on *seyyid*s in the hereditary states of the Golden Horde confirms their high social position.[124] In the Ottoman Empire, they were included in the *askeri* class. Thus, they were part of the ruling elite who were exempted from paying taxes, as opposed to the tax-paying commoners. The *seyyid*s formed their own organization headed by an official called *nakıbüleşraf*.[125] He or his local deputies were in charge of confirming the *seyyid* status of individuals and monitoring the *seyyid*s' good conduct. In court, the *seyyid*s were recognized with the honorary status of righteous (*'udul*) witnesses if they participated in judicial proceedings. Therefore, they were valued as potential witnesses and enjoyed advantages if they were a party in legal conflicts, since their oral testimony played a crucial role in the sharia courts. The words of a reliable and respectful individual were regarded as more convincing than the testimony of an ordinary person.[126] The studies of Stefka Parveva on Bulgaria and the work of other scholars with regard to Arab lands also point to an improvement in the "'status, solidarity and economic conditions' of the *sadat*/*ashraf* starting in the seventeenth century."[127] The research of Hülya Canbakal on the *seyyid*s confirms that, in seventeenth-century Ayntab, their prestige translated into economic and political power. Canbakal

124 D. Iskhakov, "Seidy v pozdnezolotoordynskikh tatarskikh gosudarstvakh," *Tatarica* 1 (1997–98), 63–78; Syroechkovskii, "Mukhammed-Gerai," 40.

125 This title means, literally, the "leader of nobles."

126 R. Kılıç, *Osmanlı'da Seyyidler ve Şerifler* (Istanbul, 2005).

127 H. Canbakal, "On the Nobility of Provincial Notables," in *Provincial Elite in the Ottoman Empire*, ed. A. Anastasopoulos (Rethymno, 2006), 40.

draws attention to a phenomenon in this period, namely, an unnatural increase in *seyyid* titles by people who were not descendants of Muḥammad. She indicates that "seyyidization was the channel of mobility preferred and controlled by the local elite, particularly as it crystallized in the 18th century."[128] Thus, Canbakal links the increasing number of claims to the *seyyid* title to the changing composition of the *askeri* class and the problem of center-periphery relations in the Ottoman Empire.[129]

Although our sources do not provide an abundance of data on the *seyyids*, they confirm that this group enjoyed certain privileges in the khanate. The *kadı*'s judicial power was slightly limited in relation to the marshal of the *seyyids* (*nakıbüleşraf*). This conclusion arises from an order by Kalga Devlet Giray sent to the district judge of Kara Su in February/March 1684. The *kalga* reminded the *kadı* that Seyyid Muharrem Efendi, the head of the *seyyids* in the khanate, appointed Seyyid Emir Abbas as his deputy in Kara Su. The *kadı* was instructed that if it was necessary to arrest a *seyyid*, male or female, he or she should be taken into the custody of Seyyid Emir Abbas rather than to prison by the *kadı*'s subordinates.[130]

This order shows that the *seyyids* were not exempted from the *kadı*'s jurisdiction. Perhaps the *kadı* judged the *seyyids* separately, while they were in the custody of the *nakıbüleşraf*. We also know from the *sicils* that *seyyids* often appeared as plaintiffs and litigants in a variety of types of cases. Their leaders could even be summoned to the court in relation to internal matters, such as the issue of someone refusing to recognize their *seyyid* status. For instance, Mustafa Çelebi, an immigrant to the khanate from the Anatolian *sancak* of Tire,[131] complained that the local *seyyids* refused to recognize his status and so he brought a complaint against the aforementioned local *seyyid* leader, Seyyid Emir Abbas, in the court of the Kara Su district. The plaintiff produced witnesses from his home *sancak*, who confirmed that his father and grandfather were *seyyids*.[132] Thus, in disputes concerning *seyyid* status, the *seyyids*' own authorities constituted the first instance. Only after they issued their verdict, could an individual appeal to the *kadı*. In contrast to Canbakal's studies of Ayntab, in the khanate there is no evidence of an increase in claims to the *seyyid* title. In fact, we know of only one claim made by an Ottoman *seyyid* during the reign of

128 Canbakal, *Society and Politics*, 88.
129 Ibid., 61–67, 77–83, 88.
130 ORRNB, Fond 917, *defter* 25/114a/2.
131 Tire is a town located between Izmir and Aydın.
132 ORRNB, Fond 917, *defter* 25/48b/2; Özdem, *Kırım Karasubazar'da*, 23.

Murad Giray. Perhaps, in the khanate the noble status inherited through blood or acquired in the khan's service secured more prestige than the *seyyid* title.[133]

2.4 *The Mufti*

In the Ottoman Empire, the *kadı* played a key role in the daytoday application of the law, while the mufti remained the central figure in its development and judicial consultations. In her book on the work of the court of Ayntab in 1540–41, Leslie Peirce states that

> muftis were unlike judges in two respects. First, while a judge's ruling (*hükm*) was binding, a mufti issued a "nonbinding advisory opinion to an individual questioner." In other words, muftis might differ in their answer to a query. Secondly, while judges were officially appointed to their office, muftis might or might not hold official appointments, and in fact the majority most probably did not.[134]

A slightly different picture of Ottoman muftis emerges from the recent study of Guy Burak, which is devoted to the development of the state school of Islamic law in the mid sixteenth-century Ottoman empire. Burak believes that this important change has roots in both Mongol dynastic law and the Islamic legal tradition. Officially appointed muftis played a crucial role in the development of the state school. Burak suggests that the network of officially appointed muftis, with the *şeyhülislam* or chief mufti as the head of the hierarchy, existed in the Ottoman Empire alongside unofficial legal experts. He states that in the most important *medreses* (those built by members of the royal household in major cities across the empire) the teachers served as the local muftis. In smaller urban centers, there were also jurists who held a state appointment to serve as mufti.[135] Burak points out that the "chief muftīs increasingly underscored the binding and enforceable nature of their legal opinions, insisting that all members of the Ottoman learned hierarchy, muftīs and judges alike, were to follow their rulings." He emphasizes that legal opinions issued by officially appointed muftis in the province "were respected as binding and enforceable."[136] Yavuz Aykan challenged Burak's idea that the Ottoman learned hierarchy, holding

133 This is not to say that the *seyyids* lacked power and wealth. For example, an order of Khan Adil Giray dated 1669 depicts one as the warden of the guilds, cf. ORRNB, Fond 917, *defter* 14/76b/4.

134 Peirce, *Morality Tales*, 115.

135 G. Burak, *The Second Formation of Islamic Law: The Hanafi School in the Early Modern Ottoman Empire* (Cambridge, 2015), 39–41.

136 Burak, *Second Formation*, 42.

the vital posts of muftis and teachers in the *medrese*s, generated what he calls a "canon consciousness." The latter points out that this assertation was made without thoroughful research based on the *sicil*s. Aykan claims that the content of the court registers of Diyarbakir provides data on the judicial authority of the muftis who never held posts in the Ottoman learned hierarchy.[137] That is, while the Ottoman Empire had networks of muftis who were controlled by the central authorities, these jurists had no monopoly on issuing legal opinions that carried weight in court. Here, it should be stressed that according to the research of Ergene and Coşgel for eighteenth-century Kastamony and Çankırı, *fetva*s could and in many cases did influence the outcomes of trials, but this did not constitute the basis for judgments.[138] Legal practice suggests that in contrast to Burak's proposal, the decisions of the muftis should not be treated as "binding and enforceable."

In relation to the Crimean Khanate, it is clear that it had its own network of muftis, with the chief mufti at the top of the hierarchy. As in the Ottoman Empire,[139] he held an official post and issued legal opinions at the request of the *kadı* or in the case of conflicts. He was also a member of the khan's council. The *sicil*s from Murad Giray's reign contain just one case that involved the legal opinion of a chief mufti; this was issued in a financial dispute. Kadı Feyzullah Efendi, whose claims were backed by the mufti, won in this conflict.[140] In another record, a certain Mufti Abubekir Efendi, who must have held the post of judge, appears. In this case we find specific information on a special document stating the facts of the case (*hüccet*), according to Abubekir Efendi. With regard to the discussion on the binding or non-binding character of the *fetva*, it is of of note that in both cases, the parties used a *fetva* and a certificate by witnesses to support their claims. Thus, in this unique case the *fetva* did not serve as a basis for the judgment.

The narrative sources, e.g., the accounts of Glavani and Aitemiriev, demonstrate that the *fetva*s of the chief mufti constituted an important argument in political conflicts. The very limited data we have suggest that his legal opinions were treated with respect and constituted an important argument in judicial and political conflicts. Yet, we do not have sufficient information to establish whether *fetva*s in the Crimea were binding.[141]

---

137 Y. Aykan, "The Second Formation of Islamic Law: The Hanafi School in the Early Modern Ottoman Empire (Book Review)," *IJMES* 48 (2016), 793–795.

138 Coşgel and Ergene, *Economics of Ottoman Justice*, 243–245.

139 H. Necâti Demirtaş's comprehensive study on Ottoman muftis includes a detailed description of their role in the local judicial system and many of their *fetva*s; see H.N. Demirtaş, *Açıklamalı Osmanlı Fetvâları*, vols. 1–2 (Istanbul, 2011–12).

140 ORRNB, Fond 917, 23a/229b/2.

141 ORRNB, Fond 917, *defter* 22/78b/1.

Neither the *sicil*s nor the narrative accounts provide us with data on the local muftis in the khanate. Presumably, their provincial organization might have been patterned on the Ottoman practice. If so, we might apply the results of Colin Imber's research on the Ottoman Empire to what we know of the khanate. He states that "every city had a learned man willing to exercise this function, particularly among the professors (*mudarris*) at the religious colleges (*madrasa*), but they do not, in the provinces, appear to have had official status."[142]

2.5 *Non-Muslim Jurisdictions*

While the study of non-Muslims in the Ottoman Empire constitutes an important field of research, its counterpart in the khanate is still in its infancy. We know little about the number, customs, and social and judicial organization of the numerous and diverse non-Muslim communities in the Crimea. The question of whether the so-called *millet* system utilized by the Ottomans had an analogy in the khanate remains open,[143] but it is beyond the scope of this study to address this problem. In the present section I only aim to offer a glimpse of the non-Muslims jurisdictions. This discussion does not describe the laws and legal procedures used by numerous religious communities and is limited to preliminary considerations concerning the extent of their judicial autonomy. I focus on their relations with the *kadı* as the khan's judicial deputy, as the question about the extent to which non-Muslims were exempted from his judicial power is central for our study.

The story of a certain non-Muslim murderer, which appears in the account of Baron de Tott, sheds light on this issue. The French consul in Bahçesaray in the years from 1767 to 1769 described the judicial procedure of the slave of a Jew who was accused of murdering his owner:

> The slave of a Jew has murdered his master in his vineyard; the complaint is made by the nearest relations. The murderer is apprehended, and, previous to his trial, some zealous Mahometans prevail on him to become a Turk, in hopes of obtaining for him a pardon. The conversion of the criminal was opposed to the sentence of death pronounced by the Kam:[144] it is proper to observe, that by the Tatar law the criminal must perish by the

142 Imber, *Ebu's-su'ud*, 7.

143 For the state of research and a bibliography on non-Muslims and the *millet* system in the Ottoman Empire, see Minna Rozen, "The Ottoman Jews," in *The Cambridge History of Turkey*, vol. 3: *The Later Ottoman Empire, 1603–1839* (Cambridge, 2006), 3:256–271; and B. Masters, "Christians in a Changing World," in *The Cambridge History of Turkey*, vol. 3: *The Later Ottoman Empire, 1603–1839* (Cambridge, 2006), 3:272–279.

144 That is, the accused slave hoped that his conversion would mitigate the punishment.

> hand of the injured person, or by his heirs. It was objected then, but in vain, that a Turk could not be delivered up to the Jews. "I would deliver up my brother to them" replied the Kam, "if he was guilty; I leave Providence to reward his conversion, if it be sincere, it is my duty to do justice." The intrigues of the devoted Mussulmen succeeded, however, in deferring the execution [382] until the Friday afternoon, in order to render the law favorable to the proselyte, which obliged the injured party to execute the sentence in four and twenty hours, and the law compelling the Jews to shut themselves up for their sabbath at the sunset. The murderer, however, loaded with chains, was conducted to the butt appropriated to this sort of execution; but a new obstacle presented itself. The Jews must not shed blood; a public cryer is sent through the town to offer a considerable sum to any Jew who will lend his hand, and it was amongst the most wretched of all people that this research was fruitless. This new incident was reported to the tribunal of the Kam, and the bigots expected to derive great advantage from it, but they were deceived in their expectations. Maksoud-Gueray permitted the Jews to execute the criminal according to the law of the old Testament, and the scene terminated by stoning him to death.[145]

This fascinating story of a murderer from among the Jewish community reveals the complexity of our subject. This case study, provided by the French consul, shows us how a non-Muslim was adjudicated by the khan, and indicates that the claim was investigated at the khan's council. Tott notes that the suspect was apprehended, perhaps by the *zabit*. Yet, he did not offer any information on the circumstances of the imprisonment of a slave. According to Muslim law, a homicide is a private action prosecuted by the victim's next of kin. In this case, Tott notes the role of the next of kin solely in the execution of the sentence. Clearly, they wanted capital punishment for the slave, and according to Muslim law, the victim's next of kin had the right to demand this retaliation. Tott suggests that the type of capital punishment that was implemented originated from Jewish law, which indeed recognized stoning as a method of execution.[146] Thus, the judicial procedures of non-Muslims appear to have combined the elements of the law of their community with that of Islamic law.

The account of Tott also brings up the topic of non-Muslims converting to Islam as a strategy to avoid or diminish the punishment. Notwithstanding the slave's conversion and contrary to the expectations of Muslim subjects, Khan

145 Tott, *Mémoires* (*Memoirs*, 2:381–382).

146 M. May, "Jewish Criminal Law and Legal Procedure," *Journal of Criminal Law and Criminology* 31, no. 4 (1940), 438–447.

Maksud Giray maintained his decision, and secured the right of the next of kin of the Jewish man to execute the convicted murderer according to Jewish law. Thus, in the case described by Tott, the conversion did not improve the slave's difficult situation. From the research Marc Baer conducted on the court registers of seventeenth-century Istanbul, we learn about a case in which conversion to Islam allowed a Christian to change the type of death penalty from stoning to the less painful execution by sword.[147]

The slave described above was adjudicated by the khan, thus, the story does not reveal anything about the composition and procedures of non-Muslim judicial bodies. Presumably, as in the Ottoman Empire, these judicial bodies consisted of religious and civil leaders from each community who performed their judicial duty with the ruler's permission, and as his deputies. To be sure, the judicial organs of non-Muslim communities did not enjoy legal authority over the members of these communities. From the *sicil*s we learn that non-Muslims (*zimmi*s) used the sharia courts in a variety of cases, including family matters, even though these matters were certainly regulated by Jewish, Karaite, Orthodox, and Armenian religious laws. We encounter non-Muslims as both plaintiffs and defendants in these cases. Conflicts between members of one religious minority were also brought to the *kadı*s' courts in the Ottoman Empire.[148]

At the present stage of research of the khanate, we can only speculate on the ratio between non-Muslim cases investigated outside the *kadı*s' courts and those brought to the courts. In regard to the latter group, a basic statistical analysis of the contents of the *sicil*s from the reign of Murad Giray provides us with some data concerning the frequency and types of cases involving non-Muslims.

As we see in figure 3, non-Muslims indeed used *kadıasker* courts and even more frequently brought their cases to the *kadı*'s court in Kara Su. It is worth asking whether the ratio of non-Muslims visible in the Islamic courts reflects

147 M. Baer, "Islamic Conversion Narratives of Women: Social Change and Gendered Religious Hierarchy in Early Modern Ottoman Istanbul," *Gender and History* 16 (2004), 435–436; Zarinebaf, *Crime and Punishment*, 106.

148 Numerous scholars have studied the litigation of non-Muslims in sharia courts. See, for example, R. Gradeva, "Orthodox Christians in the Kadi Courts: The Practice of Sofia Sheriat Court, Seventeenth Century," *Islamic Law and Society* 4, no. 1 (1997), 37–69; E. Ginio, "Jews and European Subjects in Eighteenth-Century Salonica: The Ottoman Perspective," *Jewish History* 28 (2014), 289–312; A. Fotić, "Non-Ottoman Documents in the Kadis Courts (Mōloviya Medieval Charters): Examples from the Archives of Hilander Monastery (15th–18th C.)," in *Frontiers of Ottoman Studies: State, Province and the West*, ed. C. Imber, K. Kiyotaki, and R. Murphey (New York, 2005), 2:63–73. Fotić's chapter also discusses the use of non-Ottoman documents in dispute resolution practices in Ottoman courts of law.

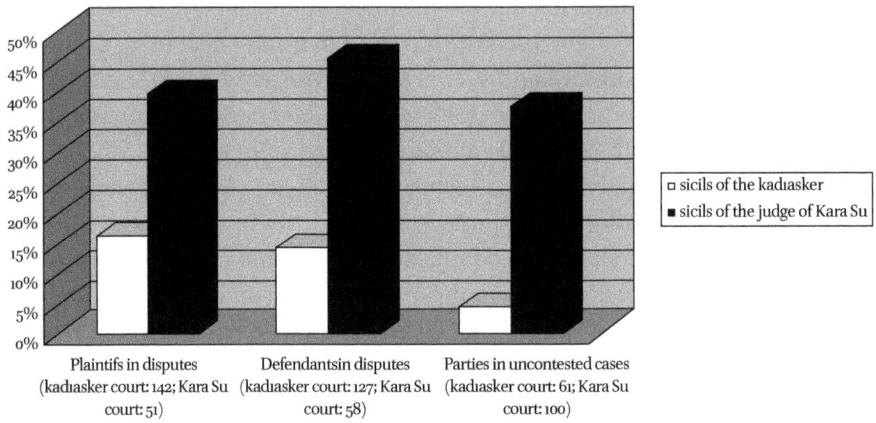

FIGURE 3 Non-Muslims brought before the *kadıasker* court (1678–82) and the Kara Su district court (1683–84).

the ratio of non-Muslims in the khanate society. The answer to this question is vital to determine whether *zimmis* used Islamic courts in a way similar to that of the Muslims, or whether the majority of non-Muslims avoided it and preferred to settle their disputes before the judicial organs of their communities. Unfortunately, we can only speculate on the size of the non-Muslim Crimean population in the 1680s. We know only two administrative sources that shed some light on the subject.[149] The first is an entry in the Kara Su *sicils* concerning a special tax collected for the purchase of guns. This entry tells us that local Greeks and Armenians paid 40 *altuns* while nine Muslim neighborhoods together collected the same amount of money.[150] It is possible that non-Muslims were charged a higher rate per person than the Muslims, and if this is indeed the case, there were more Muslims than non-Muslims in Kara Su, though the number of the latter seems to have been considerable. The question whether non-Muslims amounted to 35 to 40 percent of the population, in accordance with the percentage of non-Muslims in the district court remains open. The second source is a *defter* from the Ottoman province of Kefe, dated 1682; it

149 The first statistical data about the khanate's non-Muslim population appeared as late as 1778. From that year, we have two registers containing lists of houses that Greek and Armenian immigrants to Russia left in the Crimea. As these sources are silent about the rest of population (Muslims, Karaites, and Jews), we cannot establish the ratio between Muslims and non-Muslims. Nevertheless, the *defters* are evidence that numerous *zimmis* lived in various towns and villages of the khanate until 1778. Fehmi Yılmaz prepared a detailed analysis of these registers (see his article, Yılmaz, "On Sekizinci").

150 ORRNB, Fond 917, *defter* 25/119b/4.

provides us with some indication of the size of the non-Muslim population. In the Mangub *kaza*, non-Muslims constituted approximately 20 percent of real estate owners.[151] While we cannot simply extrapolate data from Ottoman territories and apply it to the khanate; nonetheless, we know from the Kefe *defter* that the territory situated just beyond the Ottoman border, which offered similar living conditions, was inhabited by a considerable group of non-Muslims.

To return to the number of non-Muslims using the Islamic courts in the khanate, we know that the case of Kara Su might indicate that the ratio of non-Muslim court clients might parallel to the ratio of non-Muslims in the society. Our results, which are based on data extracted from the *kadıasker* court, demonstrate that non-Muslims used this legal venue less frequently than the Kara Su court, as they acted as plaintiffs in 16.5 percent of disputes and as defendants in 14 percent. The most striking difference between the usage of the Islamic court and that of the non-Muslim court by non-Muslims concerns contracts. In contrast to the Kara Su court, non-Muslims seem to have been reluctant to register them in the *kadıasker* court (4.6 percent). A similar phenomenon was observed by Ergene and Coşgel for Kastamonu in the late seventeenth and eighteenth centuries. Non-Muslims rarely brought their legal matters to these courts, which might indicate that they preferred alternative mechanisms of resolving disputes.[152]

In sum, there is no evidence that there were limitations on the judicial power of the *kadı*s in respect to non-Muslims. Their appearance in sharia courts suggests that the legal organs of the minorities did not exercise a judicial monopoly over their co-believers, nor did non-Muslims avoid Islamic courts. Both examples we have indicate that non-Muslims used the judicial courts with considerable frequency, a fact that might reflect their substantial number in the state. Still, when we recall the story recounted by Tott, we are reminded that in certain circumstances, non-Muslims could apply their proper laws and the interaction between these laws and the justice administered by the *kadı* remained an open question.

2.6 Karaçı *Families*

The issue of the judicial autonomy of the *karaçı* families remains unclear. Was the khan's judicial authority limited to the territories of their *beylik*s? According to Alan Fisher, the situation was clear, as "the bey controlled the activities

151 NBKM, Or. Dept., Fond D737, 24–68; for the proportion of Muslims and non-Muslims in the city of Mangub in the first half of the sixteenth century, see Öztürk, *Osmanlı Hakimiyetinde Kefe*, 236–237.

152 Coşgel and Ergene, *Economics of Ottoman Justice*, 119–121.

and selection of the kadis in their own beyliks."[153] Since Fisher bases his opinion on the study of Fedor Lashkov, it is useful to quote a relevant passage from the latter:

> Jurisdiction and judicial proceedings within his *beylik*'s borders constituted the duties of the *beğ*. The judicial court and process were certainly controlled by the *beğ*, as is clear from the *yarlığ*s by which the khans confirmed the *beğ*s. Such *yarlığ*s usually contained the following formula: "[let the *beğ*] rule and govern the *beylik* it the same way as [his] fathers and grandfathers have done."[154] Consequently, they [i.e., the *beğ*s] were to rule [their *beylik*s] as in earlier times, when delivering justice constituted the most important responsibility of the authorities. In addition, we learn from the accounts of contemporary witnesses that the *beğ*s of the Şirins and Barıns had their own *kadıasker*s, who were responsible for administering justice.[155] The others [i.e., other *beğ*s], even if they did not have their own judges, were nonetheless obliged to perform judicial duties using the court of elders (*sud starikov*), the institution which enjoys judicial power up to date [the end of the nineteenth century]. Unfortunately, given our limited data, we are unable to determine the precise boundaries of the *beğ*s' judicial power. Undoubtedly, the independence of the *beğ*s' jurisdiction was restricted by the sharia court, which was competent to solve disputes concerning religious practice. Moreover, important criminal cases should have been brought to the khan's council, which acted as the supreme court of the khanate. Finally, we observe that the Yashlavski *beğ*s settled their disputes concerning land ownership in front of the khan's *kadıasker* court. Nonetheless, it seems that they chose to obey its authority because they lived in the vicinity of Bahçesaray. In sum, the inhabitants [of the *beylik*s' territories] were subordinated to the judicial and administrative authority of their *beğ*.[156]

Lashkov does not explicitly state that the *beğ*s selected or controlled the *kadı*s. He points out that the leaders of the *karaçı* families exercised judicial power over their subjects or shared this prerogative with the elders. He suggests that the *beğ*s of the Şirins and Barıns could have delegated their judicial power

---

153 Fisher, *Crimean Tatars*, 23.

154 Here Lashkov cites his study, "Arkhivnyia dannyia o beilikakh v Krymskom khanstve," *Arkheologicheskii S'ezd: Trudy* 6, no. 4 (1889), 103.

155 Here Lashkov cites J.E. Thunmann, *Description de la Crimée* (Strasburg, 1786), 30.

156 My translation; Lashkov, "Istoricheskii ocherk," *ITUAK*, 23 (1895), 87.

to their *kadıaskers*. Yet, his source concerning this point seems unreliable.[157] Each *karaçı beğ* also headed a council of elders, which presumably consisted of the most eminent members of the family and clients. These councils also had some judicial prerogatives. Lashkov explicitly states that *kadıs* must have restricted the judicial power of the *beğs*, yet he does not explain how the judicial power within a *beylik* was divided between the *beğ*, his *kadıasker*, and the council of elders on one side, and the relevant *kadı* on the other.

Lashkov makes a point of juxtaposing the Golden Horde institutions with those of Ottoman-Islamic origin. As noted in Chapter 3, the internal organization of the *karaçı* families and the foundation of the majority of *beyliks* date to the times of the Golden Horde. Therefore, their organization preceded the rise of the Crimean Khanate. Hence, we should examine whether the khans were able to subordinate these territories and their inhabitants to the authority of the khanate's administration patterned on the Islamic-Ottoman practice. The position of nobles and the institution of *beylik* are discussed in detail elsewhere; in this section we limit ourselves to addressing the following four issues that strictly relate to the *kadı*'s jurisdiction over the beylik: (1) Did every *beylik* constitute a separate judicial district; (2) Who appointed the *kadı* in a district that comprised a *beylik* of a *karaçı* family; (3) What were the responsibilities and influence of the *kadıs* and what were the limits of their judicial power in their districts; and (4) How did the *beylik*'s inhabitants use the sharia courts.

157 Lashkov based his statement about the *kadıaskers* of the Şirins and Barıns in the following passage from Johann Erich Thunmann's description of the Crimea: "Les Kyrym-Beghjleri sont princes dans leurs hordes, c'est le plus ancient de Mourses qui dans chaque horde est élevé à la dignité de Kyrim-beghi, et confirmé par le Khan. Célui des Chirines réside à Eski Krim: il y a une nombreuse cour, un Kalgasoultane qui est un prince du sang, un Kaïmakam, un Moufti Noureddine, un Kadieleskjer. Celui des Bahrines a aussi son Kaïmakam, son Nouraddine, et son Kadieleskjer; mais les deux autres n'ont que leurs Nouraddines. On peut les comparer aux Pairs de certains royaumes; ils balancent le pouvoir du Khane, ils sons les défenseurs de la liberté du peuple, de même que des loix, en un mot les co-régens du Khane; ils l'elisent, le confirment, et pevent aussi déposer"; see Thunmann, *Description*, 30. It is noteworthy that Thunmann (1746–78), a Swedish theologian and historian who was a professor at the University of Halle from 1772, likely never visited the khanate. His work seems to be a compilation of several well-known descriptions, such as that of Tott, Peysonnel, or Kleemann (cf. Jobst, *Die Perle des Imperiums*, 92–93). The passage concerning the *karaçı* families contains a few easily recognizable mistakes. He states, for example, that the *kalga* of the Şirins bore the title of "sultan," while in fact this title was reserved for the Giray princes. The rank of *nuraddin*, in combination with that of mufti, also makes no sense. These drawbacks indicate that Thunmann had a limited knowledge of the inner workings of the khanate. For this reason, he might have inadvertently suggested that the *beğs* held councils modeled on that of the khan. Thus, his statement is not entirely reliable.

With regard to the first issue, the whole territory of the khanate was divided into *kaza*s. These covered not only the Girays' domains, but also the territories of the *beylik*s. It is evident that some of these territories were situated in districts that bore the names of the relevant *karaçı* families; for instance, the Argıns possessed land in the Argın *kaza*, the Mangıts in the Mangıt *kaza*, and the Şirins in the Şirin *kaza*. It is worth mentioning that not all families who had *karaçı* status gave their names to separate *kaza*s; for instance, there were no Barın or Seceut *kaza*s. The Barıns possessed lands between Kara Su and Eski Kırım.[158] The Seceuts also possessed lands in the vicinity of Kara Su.[159] Hence, the administrative division of the khanate did not necessarily coincide with the borders of the *beylik*s of the ruling families. These facts indicate that the khanate's provincial structure did not automatically parallel the division of land from the times of the Golden Horde.

This brings us to the question of the extent to which the provincial structure, which included three judicial districts named after three *karaçı* families, revealed pre-khanate conditions. In the case of the Şirin *kaza*, there are some indications that it contained only the Şirins' land. From the *sicil*s we learn that this district was also referred to by two alternative terms: *kaza* or *liva* ("province"; lit., "standard"). For example, on two neighboring folios of a court register, the district *kadı*, Abdullah Efendi, is referred to as *el-kadı bi-kaza-i Şirin* ("the judge of the Şirin *kaza*") and then as *el-kadı bi-liva-i Şirin* ("the judge of the Şirin province").[160] Interestingly, in the *sicil*s from the reign of Murad Giray, the term *liva* referred exclusively to the Şirins' land. This term was also used analogously by the Crimean chroniclers.[161] For instance, Mehmed Senai recalls that when Sefer Gazi Ağa fell out of favor with the khan, he took refuge in the "liva of the Şirins."[162] In the eighteenth century, Abdulgaffar el-Kırımi revealed that he was a judge in the Şirin *liva*.[163] More generally, the term *liva* referred to lands and subjects of the *karaçı beğ*s. Such a meaning can be found in the chronicle of Mehmed Senai, who states that every *karaçı beğ* headed the *liva* of his family.[164] While the sources offer some indications that the Şirin *kaza* covered only the territory of the Şirins' *beylik*, the argument is not conclusive.

158 Lashkov, "Istoricheskii ocherk," *ITUAK* 23 (1895), 80.
159 Ibid., 82.
160 These entries were recorded in 1684, during the second reign of Selim I Giray; ORRNB, Fond 917, *defter* 26/7a/3; *defter* 26/8a/2.
161 The term *liva* was used exclusively to describe the estates of the *karaçı* families, while the term *ocak* referred to a *beylik* of any noble family.
162 Hacı Mehmed Senai, *Historia chana*, 95/10–11.
163 "Ol vakitde liva-i Şirin'de hakimü 'şşer'i idim"; see Abdulgaffar Kyrymi, *Umdet al-akhbar*, 188.
164 Hacı Mehmed Senai, *Historia chana*, 92/7.

By contrast, the Şirins owned various pieces of land in other judicial districts. It is unclear whether these lands were also parts of the Şirins' *beylik* or were privately owned by individual family members.

We must bear in mind that the Şirins were the most important vassals of the khan. Therefore, we should be very cautious in extrapolating information about them and applying it to other *karaçı* families. Clearly, not every *beylik* formed a separate *kaza*; for instance, the *beylik*s of the Seceuts and Barıns were probably situated, at least in part, in the Kara Su judicial district. Unfortunately, there we do not have sufficient data to determine whether the *beylik* of the Mangıts covered the whole territory of the relevant *kaza*.

Who nominated the *kadı* in a district which comprised a *beylik* of a *karaçı* family? The order of Canibeg Giray from 1612 suggests that the district judges were generally appointed by the khan.[165] The order did not concern Şirin, Mangıt, and Argın *kaza*s in particular, perhaps because the khan only named the *kadı*s of major towns, while rural districts, such as the above mentioned "*beylik kaza*s," were probably hidden under the formula "and others."

The khan's monopoly in appointing district judges is questioned in two narrative sources. We begin with a remark made by Said Giray, who extensively described the Crimean ulema of his time in the mid eighteenth century. He presented their careers, and focused on the role of the khan's favor in their appointments to various judicial posts, including those of the *kadı* of the *kalga* or the *kadı*s of the *serasker*s appointed to command the Nogays.[166] In reference to Abdulgaffar el-Kırımi, Said Giray only described him as a "*kadı* by Cantimur Beğ,"[167] the *beğ* of the Şirins, while the khan's role in the *kadı*'s appointment was not mentioned at all. We must recall that, in his chronicle Abdulgaffar presented himself as a judge in the Şirins' *liva*, hence both sources were certainly referring to the same office. The wording used by Said Giray suggests that the post was controlled by the Şirins' *beğ*. It is likely that the *beğ* only entrusted such important functions to his client. Unfortunately, Said Giray did not provide a conclusive argument. Peysonnel is the second author who described the *kadı*s as appointees of the *beğ*s. He states, "In the districts subordinated to them, all noblemen of the five great families have the right to appoint the *kadı*s or judges, who receive provisions from the *kadıasker*."[168]

165 See the text of the order in Appendix 1.

166 Kellner-Heinkele (ed.), *Aus den Aufzeichnungen*, 212–246.

167 "Gaffuri Efendi ... Cantimur Beğe kadi olub"; for the facsimile of the relevant passage, see Kellner-Heinkele (ed.), *Aus den Aufzeichnungen*, 317.

168 "Tout les Gentilshommes des cinq grandes maisons ont la nomination des Kadis ou Juges de tous les Kadiliks de leur dépendence, moyennant les provisions du Kazi-Asker," Peysonnel, *Traité sur le commerce*, 2:282.

Finally, there are some indications in the *sicil*s that the *karaçı beğ*s influenced the staffing of the judicial posts. To illustrate this, we invoke the story of the relations linking Bahadır Şah Beğ, the *beğ* of the Argıns, and his protégé, Abdulşahid Efendi, as revealed in the *sicil*s from the reign of Murad Giray. We first encounter them in April 1681, when Abdulşahid Efendi, with the title *naib* of Kara Su, acted as a legal agent of the *beğ*. Two months later, Abdulşahid Efendi[169] seems to have accompanied Bahadır Şah Beğ on a meeting of the khan's council, as both were registered among the case witnesses in a case judged at the council.[170] Although the entry concerns the inhabitants of Kara Su and Tamak districts, there is no clear connection between the adjudicated case and the *beğ* or the *naib*. It is hard to establish whether the *beğ* and the *naib* traveled to Bahçesaray to take part in the proceeding, which concerned their neighbors or whether they were there for other reasons. Almost two years later (1683), we again encounter both of them in the court of Kara Su. This time, Bahadır Şah Beğ appointed Abdulşahid Efendi as his legal agent. In the same year, the Kara Su registers refer to Abdulşahid Efendi as the *kadı* of the Argın district. Apparently, he was promoted, thanks to his close relations with the local *karaçı beğ*. This story suggests that the *karaçı* families influenced the appointments of the *kadı*s in "their" districts.

On the basis of the evidence above, we suggest that a kind of compromise existed in regard to the appointment of *kadı*s in the judicial districts covering the *beylik*s. It seems unlikely that the khan entirely gave up his monopoly over the formal appointments of all those administering justice in his state. Yet, it would be equally surprising if the *beğ*s had accepted that the *kadı*s, who were appointed by the khan, perform all the typical judicial and non-judicial tasks in their *beylik*s. Therefore, we assume that the candidates for *kadı*s might have been chosen by the local *karaçı beğ*s and then confirmed by the khan (or the *kadıasker* of the khan, from whom they received their provisions). Thus, the *kadı*s were, at least formally, the appointees of the khan. The scope of their non-judicial duties in the beyliks' territory is less clear. Perhaps their authority was limited with respect to the *beğ*s' own officials.

What was the judicial power of a *kadı* in respect to the *beylik* and its inhabitants? It seems unlikely that they exercised authority similar to that of their counterparts in the Girays' domains. Their functions were probably limited by the *beğ*s and the councils of elders. Unfortunately, we know almost nothing about the daily practices of the *kadı*s in question, since they are barely visible

169 In this entry, the *naib* of Kara Su is referred to as "Abdulşah." Presumably, it is the name "Abdulşahid" written incorrectly; ORRNB, Fond 917, *defter* 23a/142b/7.

170 See ORRNB, Fond 917, *defter* 25/3b/5; 23b/69a/1; 25/25a/4; 23a/142b/7.

in the *sicil*s. The registers I examined do not reveal a single entry about the personnel of the *kadı*'s court. Nonetheless, this observation is equally true in relation to the majority of rural districts, including those situated in the Girays' domains. It seems unlikely that rural *kadı*s had at their disposal numerous officials known from the registers to work in Bahçesaray or Kara Su. We can only wonder whether the *kadı*s turned to the *beğ* or to the khan in case they needed assistance in executing their orders. Unfortunately, we lack sufficient data to describe his place in the power relations between the khan and the *karaçı beğ*s.

As discussed in Chapter 3, only one issue concerning the *beylik*s of the ruling families seems certain; namely, that the *beylik*s' inhabitants used the sharia courts. They appeared in a variety of cases, both as plaintiffs and defendants in front of the Kara Su court as well as the *kadıasker* court.

2.7 *Cases Judged at the Khan's Council*

As the cases brought to the khan's council have been extensively described above, here we can limit ourselves to a few brief remarks. Apparently this council was the only institution that we know with certainty challenged the *kadı*'s judicial monopoly. Once there, individuals from all strata of khanate society could directly address the ruler (or his representative, be it the *kaymakam* or the vizier). Thus, an aggravated person could circumvent the district court. The council became a legal arena, where the ruler could be directly engaged in administering justice to his subjects. As the case of Nicolas Kleemann illustrates, a case brought to the council was automatically exempted from the authority of the relevant local *kadı*. The latter's function in such a case was limited to enforcing the khan's (or the *kaymakam*'s) sentence.

•••

This chapter concerns the district *kadı*s, who were the most important provincial officials and whose roles combined judicial and administrative functions. An important part of the section concerned descriptions of their education, career perspectives, and income. Unfortunately, based on the available sources, we cannot establish the models of education and career of the Crimean *kadı*s. The *sicil*s from the reign of Murad Giray reveal a great deal in regard to their judicial and administrative duties; for example, it is clear that the *kadı*s supervised the day-to-day work of the court personnel, which included officials such as *naib*s, *katib*s, *zabit*s, *muhzır*s, and the *beytülmal emini*. The judge likely relied on them while also performing his administrative duties, which ranged from enforcing decrees on market prices to supervising tax collection. The final section concerns the limitations of the judicial power of the *kadı* and his personnel. As stated, the network of sharia courts covered the whole territory of the Crimean Khanate. Yet, it is not entirely clear whether the judge of each district was appointed and dismissed by the khan. Our doubts concern the judicial districts covering the domain of the *kalga* and the *beylik*s of the ruling families. We suggest that a kind of compromise might have existed in these areas. The judges might have been formally appointed by the khan. Yet, the choice of particular candidates may have been made by the *kalga* and the *beğ*s of the ruling families. Moreover, it appears that the power of judge was limited by the prerogatives of the khan's other appointees (e.g., local commanders) and institutions (the khan's council) and by the privileges of certain communities, for instance, noblemen.

CHAPTER 5

Law and Its Practice in the Khanate's Sharia Courts

Beginning with the *kadıs* and their courts, in the present chapter, I describe the day-to-day practice of the sharia courts by analyzing clients according to social, religious, gender, and residential characteristics. I also explore the ratio between various types of cases recorded in the *sicils*. I briefly discuss evidentiary standards (the testimony of witnesses and oaths) and the tools of litigation (*fetvas* and written documents) used in trials. It is my hope that the analysis of these issues will bring us closer to understanding whether any correlation existed between the litigants, the evidentiary tools they used, and the outcomes of disputes in which they were involved. Research on the patterns of behavior of various groups of individuals may reveal who was able to secure a favorable verdict in the court, and in what circumstances, and whether a common subject could win a case against someone from the elite. By analyzing the social background, residential affiliation, and gender of individuals appearing before the *kadı*, we can determine the territorial, political, and social limitations of the judicial authority of the khan's appointees.

I begin with general information on the law as it was applied in the courts in the khanate, then proceed to an examination of the court records. I am particularly interested in the elements that differed from the sharia, since these may indicate how the Crimean judiciary supplemented or modified the sharia, and whether they invoked Mongol customs or applied Ottoman solutions.

1 The Law Applied in the Crimean Courts

Previous chapters provided glimpses on the law applied in the Crimean judicial courts. As discussed in Chapter 2, the order of Canibeg Giray issued in 1612 clearly depicts the khan as a just ruler who would not hesitate to punish *kadıs* who disregarded the principles of justice. In this order, the khan proudly styled himself as a Muslim ruler, whose principal duty was to exercise power to safeguard and protect the population from oppression, especially that committed by government agents. According to the Hanafis, the official school of law in the Crimean Khanate, issues related to public order, such as tax collection and prosecution of *hadd* crimes, were entrusted to the government. Responsibility went with special power, as the Hanafi jurists accepted for the executive authority to dispense with impractical evidentiary procedures prescribed in the

 | DOI:10.1163/9789004384323_007

Quran, and instead prosecute crimes based on somewhat looser rules and apply discretionary punishment (*ta'zir*). When even the latter tools did not meet the practical demands of governance, a new doctrine of administrative justice (*siyasa shar'iyya*) emerged in the medieval Sunni states.[1] *Siyasa shar'iyya* extended the discretionary powers of the executive authorities, and in order to secure justice, it armed them with a wider range of tools than those provided by discretionary punishment.[2] The definition of justice, as Linda Darling points out, was strictly related to a concept of ideal relations linking the subjects and the ruler, relations that guaranteed a harmonious, prosperous, and secure state.[3] This goal sanctified the use of *siyasa shar'iyya*, which regulated matters of public order such as taxation and criminal law above all others. Thus, as Timothy J. Fitzgerald stressed, late medieval Muslim jurists defined *siyasa shar'iyya* as an idealized harmony, because "sharia and the state—the repository and executor of *siyasa*—in fact depended on each other."[4]

As an Islamic ruler, the Crimean khan supported the sharia courts in his domain and expanded his *siyasa*-based sphere of action: he heard the grievances of his subjects in the court at the council, and supported his *zabit*s, who executed punishments—those prescribed in the Quran and discretionary ones.

Legal practice in the khanate resembled that of the Ottomans in many aspects. In the earlier chapters we elaborated on a few of these similarities, e.g., the court at the khan's council could be compared to the judicial functions of the imperial divan, some of the Crimean orders were comparable to the Ottoman *adaletname*s, and *kadı*s of both states prescribed discretionary punishments which were executed by officials acting on behalf of the ruler. Having said this, we move to the topic strictly related to *siyasa*, namely to the Ottoman *kanunname*. As the vast literature on the *kanun* has been surveyed by Başak Tuğ, here we limit ourselves to quote two of her vital conclusions. First, that the Ottoman *kanun* should be conceptualized as

> part of political struggles between different authorities of juridical and legislative powers in the Ottoman polity. Rather than conceptualizing the

1 Vogel, "Siyāsa." For Abbasid times, see, for example, Roger M. Savory (ed.), *Introduction to Islamic Civilization* (Cambridge, 2000), 58; for the Mamluk state, see Stilt, *Islamic Law in Action*; for the Ottoman Empire, see Imber, *Ebu's-su'ud*, 24–95.

2 Tuğ, *Politics of Honor*, 35; B. Ergene, "On Ottoman Justice: Interpretations in Conflict (1600–1800)," *Islamic Law and Society* 8, no. 1 (2001), 61–62.

3 L. Darling, "Circle of Justice," *Encyclopaedia of Islam, Three*, ed. K. Fleet, G. Krämer, D. Matringe, J. Nawas, E. Rowson (Brill online, 2017).

4 T.J. Fitzgerald, "Murder in Aleppo: Ottoman Conquest and the Struggle for Justice in the Early Sixteenth Century," *Journal of Islamic Studies* 27, no. 2 (2016), 196. Note that Fitzgerald defines the term *siyasa* to refer to 'statecraft.'

> "religious" as fixed and the "political" as a changing system, one should look at the praxis in which religious doctrine interplays, negotiates, and comes to terms with the sovereign's discretion in various historical contexts. In that sense, as a historical example of such an interaction, the Ottoman *kanun* has both commonalities with and differences from the earlier and later empires in Islamic geographies. In other words, one should concentrate on the historical applications of Islamic law in order to identify how politics has shaped the relationship between the ruler and jurists as sources of legal authority. In Ottoman history, as in other historical and regional contexts, the terms of this relationship was not fixed; rather it took on multiple forms according to the socio-political configuration of power relations between different groups in different periods.[5]

Second, Tuğ states that the *kanun* should no longer be perceived as "secular" as opposed to the "religious" sharia. In fact, she emphasizes that the law books "revealed a high level of accommodation of local practices, imperial customs, and Hanafi legal principles of the *miri* land regime."[6]

In the next section, I investigate what legal solutions, in addition to the sharia, shaped law in the khanate. Although there are no codified law books for the khanate, the preserved orders, cases recorded in the *sicil*s, and narrative sources indicate that the khan, like the Ottoman sultan, regulated various areas of the lives of his subjects by evoking either Golden Horde customs or Ottoman legal practice.

1.1 *Golden Horde Customs and Ottoman Legal Practice as Sources of Law*

1.1.1 Golden Horde Influences on State Administration

Since the institutions rooted in the Golden Horde tradition have been described in detail in previous chapters, in the present section I offer only a brief description. According to the customs of the Great Steppe, the khan embodied supreme power; his very title referred to his supreme authority. The Crimean-Tatar tradition provided some rules concerning succession. First, as the khanate was a continuation of the Chingisid Empire, the khan had to be a male member of the Giray dynasty, which traced its origins to Chingis Khan. Second, it was expected that the eldest male from this line would ascend to the throne. Yet, the new khan was supposed to be selected by the *kurultay*. This grouping of Crimean nobles was dominated by the *karaçı beğ*s, the most powerful of the khan's vassals. Their diverse political goals and the personal ambitions of various members

5 Tuğ, *Politics of Honor*, 37–38.
6 Ibid., 47–48.

of the Giray dynasty were of utmost importance in the process of selecting a new khan. Thus, in practice, any member of the Giray dynasty could come to power as the candidate of a successful faction. After the Ottoman conquest of the southern part of the Crimean Peninsula, the sultans began to play an important role in the designation of the new khans. It should come as no surprise that rival groups sought the Sublime Porte's support to turn the scales in their favor. Consequently, conflicts allowed the Sublime Porte to intervene more and more frequently in Crimean succession disputes. The rival groups and the Ottomans evoked the rule of agnatic seniority only when it favored their candidates, who recruited from among the members of the Giray dynasty. Up until the very end of the khanate in 1783, it was clearly understood that only the descendants of Chingis Khan could claim the heritage of the Golden Horde.

The crucial political institution and dignitaries of the khanate, such as the *kurultay*, *karaçı beğ*s, the first and second deputy of the khan, were of Mongol origin. Although much remains unknown about the *kurultay*, it is clear that in the Crimean Khanate it was a consultative institution that brought together the Tatar nobles. It had its roots in the Mongol custom of gathering for military purposes. It could be summoned by the khan or the most powerful *karaçı beğ*. In the case of a conflict, the khan and the *karaçı beğ*s would seek support from the remaining members of the *kurultay*. If the rebelling nobles were successful, they would start a 'lawful rebellion' designed to change the khan's policy or even to replace him with a new ruler. The elevated position of the heads of the most powerful noble families (*karaçı beğ*s) constituted a part of the Chingisid heritage as well. The noble families who settled in the Crimea during the times of the Golden Horde had semi-autonomous family estates (*beylik*s), which constituted the basis of their economic, military, and social position. Finally, the posts of the first (*kalga*) and the second deputy of the khan (*nuraddin*) had their roots in the Golden Horde tradition. These positions did not exist when the Crimean Khanate was founded, but were created later to serve the political goals of particular rulers. The post of *kalga* dates to the reign of Mengli I Giray (1478–1515),[7] while the post of *nuraddin* was created by Mehmed II Giray in 1579.[8] Both posts were secured for the members of the Giray dynasty. A prince appointed to the office of *kalga* was assigned part of the khanate's territory with the capital of Ak Mescid (Simferopol). Within his domain, he enjoyed certain autonomy, as he controlled it through his own officials, whose titles and functions were modeled on those of the khan (which are described below). Unfortunately, our sources offer ambiguous data on whether the *nuraddin* had

7 Matuz, "Qalga," 101–129.
8 Ürekli, *Kırım Hanlığının*, 74–77.

a domain of his own. Although this dignitary undoubtedly modeled his court on that of the khan, we cannot be certain that any well-defined territory was permanently assigned to him.[9] Finally, it is worth noting that the *karaçı beğ*s, the *kalga*, and the *nuraddin* influenced foreign and domestic policy, as they had the right to participate in the khan's council.

1.1.2 The Ottoman Influence

As emphasized earlier, numerous administrative institutions of the khanate were modeled on the Ottoman system. The reshaping of the administration was an ongoing process from the first half of the sixteenth century and was related to the reforms of Khan Sahib Giray (1532–51), who reshaped the Crimean ruler's position on the Ottoman model in order to strengthen his own power. From this period onward the Ottoman solutions were implemented more and more frequently to organize the khan's household and shape and rename a majority of the central and provincial offices. For example, many officials during the reign of Murad Giray (1678–83) bore titles known from the Ottoman court, such as vizier, mufti, *kadıasker, defterdar, kethuda, katib* of the council, *kapıcı başı, mirahor*, or *silahdar*.[10] They had duties similar to those of their Ottoman counterparts. The Ottoman influence was also visible in the provincial administration. The Crimean Khanate had two systems of territorial division. First, the land was divided between the khan, his family and clients on one side and the great vassal families and their clients on the other. Second, the khans introduced court districts (*kaza*s), which were typical territorial units in a Muslim state. Judges performed both judicial and administrative functions. In the Crimean Khanate, as in the Ottoman Empire, in addition to passing sentences and acting as public notaries, judges performed various administrative duties. In a court district, the *kadı* was, in fact, the most important official of the ruler. The Ottoman influence on the khanate is also visible in the structure of the provincial court; in both states the *kadı* had at his disposal minor officials such as deputy judges (*naib*s), scribes (*katib*s), summons officials (*muhzır*s), and those who divided inheritances (*kassams*). Having said this, we cannot ignore the existence of semi-autonomous *beylik*s of the powerful aristocratic families. As noted in Chapter 3, these aristocratic families could influence the appointment of their local *kadı*, and seemed to enjoy a certain judicial autonomy. Thus, the privileges of the *karaçı*s limited the extent of the judicial and administrative power of the *kadı*s.

9 Kançal-Ferrari, *Kırım'da Kalan Miras*, 52–53, 57.

10 On the officials during the reign of Murad Giray, see ORRNB, Fond 917, *defter* 22/78b/1; 23b/6a/2; 23b/245a/1; 23b/121b/3.

1.1.3 Taxes

Tax law is an important branch of public law. Since no tax register from the Crimean Khanate has survived to our times, research on local taxes constitutes a great challenge. Our data on the subject is limited to the taxes mentioned in the khan's orders and income entries recorded in the Crimean *sicil*s. The taxes levied in the khanate seem to combine Islamic, Mongol Golden Horde, and Ottoman systems. For this reason, we divide Crimean taxes according to their origin into three groups: (1) Islamic canonical taxes, (2) Mongol Golden Horde taxes, and (3) taxes which were not canonical, did not have Mongol or Golden Horde origins, and presumably had their roots in Ottoman practice.

The Islamic canonical taxes reflect the fundamental division of individuals into Muslims and non-Muslims. It consisted of taxes such as the following.

(1) A tithe (*ʿöşr*) on all agricultural products. There is no data as to how the Crimean khans proved their rights to collect this tax. Perhaps they borrowed the Ottoman reasoning, which was fully expressed by the chief mufti, Ebussuud. His theory concerned "tribute" land, i.e., land conquered as a result of *jihad* and not divided among Muslim soldiers at the time of the conquest. The ownership of this land was thus reserved for the common treasury of the Muslims, which remained at the disposal of the Muslim ruler. The ruler could lend the fields to his subjects, but in exchange they were obliged to pay to the treasury a proportional tribute (*haraçi mukaseme*) in the form of a tithe (*ʿöşr*). In the Ottoman Empire, the tithe paid by peasants often formed a source of income assigned to various types of beneficiaries, for example, the *timar* holders.[11] Based on the khan's orders and the cases recorded in the *sicil*s, we know that the tithe was collected by the khan, the *kalga*, and the *karaçı* and non-*karaçı* noble families. The rights of the Crimean ruler and his first deputy can be comprehended in accordance with this theory. Analogously, the ruler granted the right to collect taxes, including a portion of the agricultural products from a given land, to non-*karaçı* nobles, as can be seen in the extant orders issued by the khans. The khans also confirmed that the *karaçı beğ*s had the right to collect various taxes, though admittedly the tithe was not listed explicitly. Nonetheless, the extant orders contain vague expressions such as "the customary usage of fields along with winter and summer pastures," which might also allude to the collection of tithe.[12]

11 Imber, *Ebu's-suʿud*, 125; S. Faroqhi, "Crisis and Change, 1599–1699," in *An Economic and Social History of the Ottoman Empire*, vol. 2: *1600–1914*, ed. H. İnalcık and D. Quater (Cambridge, 2000), 2:531–538.

12 Lashkov, "Sbornik dokumentov," *ITUAK* 23 (1895), 123–128.

(2) The poll tax (*cizye*) was a canonical tax unrelated to land, payable by adult non-Muslim males. The Hanafis calculated the individual amount on the level of the income of a taxpayer. According to Islamic law, the *cizye* was collected on behalf of the ruler, who spent the income on his army. Thus, in the khanate, the poll tax also went to the khan's treasury.[13]

(3) The fifth (*hums*) was a tax on the spoils of war. The ruler was entitled to one-fifth of all spoils taken in *jihad*. The Crimean chronicles make it clear that the khan received a share of the spoils of war.[14] Yet, it seems that the Islamic fifth was replaced by the Mongol *savga*, which amounted to 10 percent. This is discussed in the next section.

(4) The alms (*zakat*) tax, i.e., the voluntary offering from all Muslims, which was to be spent on the poor. A letter of Devlet I Giray to Ebussuud, invoked by Colin Imber, proves that the khan deliberated on the matter of how this tax should be collected in the khanate.[15] The Crimean ruler asked the famous mufti whether he should pay *zakat* on the wealth in his own treasury. This fact suggests that in the 1570s there were no developed procedures on the collection of *zakat* in the khanate. Perhaps the tax had been introduced recently or was about to be introduced. As there are no other sources on the subject, it remains unclear whether the *zakat* was collected in the Crimean Khanate at all, or whether the khans followed the Ottoman practice in this matter. According to Colin Imber, *zakat* "never existed as a reality."[16] Nonetheless, as Imber emphasizes, charitable trusts and individuals, including members of the ruling dynasty, supported the poor and followed the Quranic recommendation to share their wealth with needy members of society.

Mongol tax regulations have been examined by a considerable number of scholars, among them we can mention the classical studies of Herbert F. Schurmann,[17] I.P. Petrushevskii,[18] John M. Smith,[19] and Ann K.S. Lambton.[20] These researchers endeavored to understand the nature of over forty Mongol

13 See the *yarliğ* of Hacı II Giray dated 16 Rebi II 1095/2 April 1684 (ORRNB, fond 917, *defter* 25/115a/4).
14 Abdulgaffar Kyrymi, *Umdet al-akhbar*, 181–182; Hacı Mehmed Senai, *Historia chana*, 111/30; Kazembeg (ed.), [*Seyyid*] *Muhammad Riza*, 167.
15 Imber, *Ebu's-su'ud*, 82.
16 Ibid., 139.
17 H.F. Schurmann, "Mongolian Tributary Practices of the 13th Century," HJAS 19 (1956), 304–389.
18 I. Petrushevsky, "The Socio-Economic Condition of Iran under the Il-Khans," in *The Cambridge History of Iran*, ed. J.A. Boyle (Cambridge, 1968), 5:494–524.
19 J.M. Smith, "Mongol and Nomadic Taxation," HJAS 30 (1970), 46–87.
20 A.K.S. Lambton, "Mongol Fiscal Administration in Persia," *Studia Islamica* 64 (1986), 79–99.

taxes present in the Chingisid Empire and its successor states. Many researchers agree that, in general, Mongol taxes can be divided into two groups: the permanent tribute and the extraordinary levies paid occasionally to the ruler. In addition, many scholars have noted that the numerous tax-related terms does not necessarily imply that such a wide range of taxes was actually collected; rather it is testimony that different terms applied may have applied, in different times and places, to the same or similar taxes. Unfortunately, most of these terms were recorded in non-Mongolian sources and in non-Mongol languages (e.g., Persian, Russian, Turkic or Chinese), and the translations left them subject to distortion and further contributed to the present difficulty of their interpretation. Some scholars even questioned whether taxes were regularly collected from the post-Chingisid states and whether the Mongols developed their own tax system. David Morgan doubts whether "what the Mongols did in this sphere [i.e., taxes] be dignified with the name of 'system.'"[21] Ann Lambton points out that even the most typically "Mongol" taxes, such as *qubchur*, *qalan*, and *tamga*, "meant different things at different times and in different places."[22] These theories suggest that the name of a tax did not suffice to determine the type of obligation it imposed. In the case of the Crimean Khanate, a number of taxes and duties referred to with Mongol terms or described as "ancient" or "Chingisid"[23] have survived to our times, but we rarely know their precise meaning and function. These taxes are listed below.

(1) *Tamga*,[24] *tumanend*, *savga*, *buralka*, *koluş-kalanka*.[25] Such taxes are mentioned in nineteenth-century Russian translations of the khans' orders, which date to the fifteenth and sixteenth centuries. Of these, only the *savga* and *tamga* are mentioned in the extant sources from the second half of the sixteenth century and in the later period. It is not clear whether they were still levied in the seventeenth and eighteenth centuries. Unfortunately, for the reasons discussed above, the nature of these taxes remains vague.[26] Yet, documentary

21 D. Morgan, *The Mongols* (Oxford, Malden, and Carlton, 2007), 87.

22 Lambton, "Mongol Fiscal Administration," 84.

23 In the sources, these taxes are referred to as following the "Chingisid law" (*kanun-i cingiziyye*) or being in accordance with the "ancient law" (*kanun-i kadim*).

24 V. Smirnov, "Tatarsko-khanskie iarlyki iz kollektsii Tavricheskoi Uchenoi Arkhivnoi Kommissii," *ITUAK* 54 (1918), 13; *tamga* was a tax on commercial goods.

25 Lashkov, "Istoricheskii ocherk," *ITUAK* 23 (1895), 88; Lashkov, "Sbornik dokumentov," *ITUAK* 23 (1895), 127.

26 The term *tumanend* might refer to *tuman*, a Mongol military unit. The *buralka* is a mystery. The term *koluş-kalanka* is a generic binom that refers to an unidentified tax. According to Shamil Muhamedyarov and István Vásáry, the term *koluş* derives from the verb *kol-*, which means "to ask for, to pray." The scholars found it in the binom *qoluš-qoltka* in an early sixteenth-century *yarlığ* of Sahib Giray, the khan of Kazan. They argue that its

and narrative sources provide some data on the *savga*. It was a tithe collected by a ruler from the booty taken by the Mongols.[27] In the Crimean Khanate, it seems to have been associated with the Islamic fifth (*hums* or *pencik*).[28] The khan's share was indeed limited to one-tenth, but chroniclers justified his right by referring to both the Mongol custom and Islamic law.[29] Thus, the collection of *savga* is an interesting example of a tax prescribed by both the Mongol and Islamic laws. It is noteworthy that the khan settled for a lower rate, i.e., 10 percent instead of collecting 20 percent.

(2) The *şişlik* was a Mongol tax on sheep, apparently lower than its Ottoman counterpart named *adet-i agnam*. In 1609 Khan Ghazi II Giray issued an order in reply to a petition presented by his subjects who asked the khan to follow the Mongol tradition rather than introduce the Ottoman practice. The order prohibited the collection of a sheep tax other than *şişlik*.[30]

Finally, our sources provide data on taxes levied in the khanate that seem to have no clear Islamic or Mongol roots. Taxes for the maintenance of musketeers (*tüfenkçi*) constitute a good example. According to Crimean chroniclers, the tax was introduced by Gazi II Giray (1588–96, 1597–1608), and was paid in sheep to be delivered to the khan's kitchen.[31] Crimean *sicil*s from the Kara Su district contain an entry (dated 1683) concerning the collection of a tax for the purchase of guns.[32] Each neighborhood (*mahalle*) within the town constituted a tax unit. The neighborhoods were charged different rates, which might

---

"Russian contemporary translation must have been *zapros* or *zaprosy*. These terms must have denoted several sorts of compulsory bounty given to the khan, the landlord, etc. on certain occasions"; see S. Muhamedyarov and I. Vásary, "Two Kazan Tatar Edicts: Ibrahim's and Sahib Girey's Yarliks," in *Between the Danube and the Caucasus*, ed. G. Kara (Budapest, 1987), 196–197. The term *kalanka* seems to refer to the Mongol tax called *qalan*. Scholars differ as to the precise meaning of *qalan*. According to John M. Smith, it was a catch-all term for pre-Mongol taxes; see "Mongol and Nomadic Taxation," 59, 83. Ann Lambton, who discusses various uses of this term in Persia, proposes that the *qalan* probably meant a kind of labor service; see Lambton, "Mongol Fiscal Administration," 94. David Morgan agrees, in some respects, with Lambton; he states that although the *qalan* tax remains obscure, it referred to some kind of labor service rather than a pre-Mongol tax; see Morgan, *Mongols*, 89. Given our poor understanding of the terms *koluş* and *qalan*, it is hard to determine what type of obligation a tax referred to by *koluş-kalanka* might be.

27 Abdulgaffar Kyrymi, *Umdet al-akhbar*, 181–182.

28 On the collection of *pencik* in the Ottoman Empire, see Imber, *Ebu's-su'ud*, 86–87.

29 Abdulgaffar Kyrymi, *Umdet al-akhbar*, 181–182; Hacı Mehmed Senai, *Historia chana*, 111/30; Kazembeg (ed.), *[Seyyid] Muhammad Riza*, 167.

30 Cf. Inalcık, "Kirim Hanlığı," 175.

31 Kazembeg (ed.), *[Seyyid] Muhammad Riza*, 110; Halim Giray, *Gülbünü Hânâni* (ed. Günay, Başer, and Günaydın), 47.

32 ORRNB, Fond 917, *defter* 25/119b/4.

reflect their inhabitants' ability to pay. It remains unclear whether the tax was levied regularly or was an extraordinary tax to finance the Vienna campaign.

Extraordinary taxes for military campaigns should be included with this group as well. Before his departure to "punish" the Circassian *beğ*s in 1707–08, Khan Kaplan I Giray ordered a population census in the khanate. His order stipulated that one man from every household should take part in the campaign. Country households in which there was no man, and town dwellers, who were apparently not valued as soldiers, were obliged to pay a cash equivalent for the maintenance of the khan's regular troops (this was referred to as *kapıkulu* and *sekbans*).[33] We may assume that such taxes were levied more often during preparations for military campaigns.

There is also evidence of a cask fee on wine consumption (*fıçılar-ı haraç*),[34] which seems to resemble a tax on wine consumption that was levied in the Ottoman Empire and termed *resm-i fuçi*.

We must emphasize that three of five of the taxes mentioned above were levied to support military units such as *sekban*s, which were patterned on the Ottoman janissaries. Other sources confirm that the Crimean *sekban*s were supported by the Ottomans, who paid a stipend to the khan for this purpose. Therefore, the taxes mentioned above might have been an additional source of financing. They resemble the Ottoman extraordinary war-time tax called *avarız*. The latter became a permanent tax in the seventeenth-century Ottoman Empire. Initially, it was collected in kind, and then gradually, it started to be paid in cash. In the Crimean Khanate in the second half of the sixteenth century, Gazi II Giray also taxed his subjects in kind for military purposes. For example, he ordered the delivery of flocks of sheep for the maintenance of his *sekban*s.

The two taxes mentioned above, the tax for the purchase of guns, which was imposed on Kara Su inhabitants in 1682, and the war-time tax ordered by Khan Kaplan I Giray, were already paid in cash. The individual rate of the former tax presumably reflected the unequal incomes of the taxpayers, as the tax load was distributed among taxable units comprising unequal numbers of individuals. The same rule applied to the Ottoman tax units termed *avarızhane*, whose size also reflected the unequal incomes of subjects obliged to pay the *avarız* tax. The only notable difference between these taxes was that the Ottomans

---

33 "ahali-i Kırım'ı tahrir ve hane başına bir adam çıkmak ve adamı olmayanlardan ve şehirlerden kapıkulu ve sekban akçesi olmak üzere çokluk kiseler"; Abdulgaffar Kyrymi, *Umdet al-akhbar*, 164. This extraordinary tax was also mentioned by Seyyid Mehmed Riza, see Kazembeg (ed.), [*Seyyid*] *Muhammad Riza*, 312.

34 ORRNB, Fond 917, *defter* 25/18a/2.

introduced a new tax unit specifically for this tax collection while the khan used the already existing institution of the neighborhood (*mahalle*) as a tax unit. In sum, it is highly probable that the Ottoman *avarız* constituted a model for the taxes the khan imposed for military purposes. Yet, we must note that rulers of other post-Chingisid states also levied extraordinary taxes to support their armies. Thus, Crimean extraordinary taxes might have been collected in accordance with both the Ottoman and the Mongol traditions.

This brings us to our next area of interest: the specific taxes on products and economic activities, of which the cask fee on wine consumption is an example. The fact that it was imposed in the khanate has two vital implications. First, it might suggest a direct Ottoman influence on the tax policy in the khanate. As noted above, a very similar tax was levied in the Ottoman Empire. Second, it indicates that the khanate, like the Sublime Porte, introduced non-canonical taxes on specific economic and social activities. A question arises about whether the khan might have collected other taxes that were typical in the Ottoman Empire, such as the bride tax, the Christmas tax or the tax on pigs. In Lashkov's work on the privileges granted to the khan's clients, he referred to several taxes, such as the bride tax levied on non-Muslims, the fee on pasturage or the fee on crimes, which might have been similar to Ottoman taxes.[35] Unfortunately, our knowledge of these specific fees is based on fragmentary sources. We cannot exclude the possibility that the specified taxes levied in the khanate had both Ottoman and Mongol origins and we cannot ignore the fact that the Mongols also imposed taxes on various economic activities (e.g., the *tamga* that was levied in the fifteenth-century khanate).[36]

Although research on the tax system of the Crimean Khanate is still in its infancy, our preliminary remarks offer some indication about the origins and development of the Crimean tax system, which seems to have combined Islamic prescriptions with Mongol and Ottoman ones. Nonetheless, it remains unclear how exactly these three different systems coexisted. Perhaps the Mongol or Ottoman practices were applied to the areas in which Islam offered few applicable solutions. There are some indications that, over time, Ottoman solutions replaced Mongol practices in the tax system of the khanate. Extant sources note fewer taxes with Mongol names in the seventeenth and eighteenth centuries than in the sixteenth century. Moreover, they inform us, with rising frequency, about taxes that seem to have been modeled on Ottoman taxes. Finally, the sources refer to at least one attempt to replace a Mongol tax with an Ottoman tax (e.g., the tax on sheep, discussed above). It is worth noting

35 Lashkov, "Istoricheskii ocherk," *ITUAK* 23 (1895), 88–89.

36 See V. Smirnov, "Tatarsko-khanskie iarlyki", 13.

that in that particular case, the taxpayers managed to successfully prevent a tax reform that would have increased their obligations. An equally interesting example of the *savga* demonstrates that the Crimean Tatars were well aware of certain similarities between the Islamic and Mongol taxes. In such cases, the khan did not impose a double tax but remained satisfied with one. In the case of the *savga*, the ruler seems to have contented himself with a less profitable version.

1.1.4 Private and Criminal[37] Law

The data preserved in the court registers indicate that Crimean Muslims followed the Hanafi school of law in private matters. This Islamic law school also prevailed in the Ottoman Empire and in the Golden Horde.[38] According to Evliya Çelebi, the other three schools enjoyed the khan's protection as well. The famous traveler specified that muftis of all four schools were the members of the khan's council.[39] However, it remains unclear how the khan's courts administered justice to followers of non-Hanafi schools. The entries in the *sicil*s dating back to Murad Giray's reign do not mention the application of legal solutions typical for non-Hanafi schools. Still, this does not mean that the khan's judges did not rule on cases involving non-Hanafi individuals. As emphasized elsewhere, court verdicts were not a part of the formal registration of a case. Thus, only a limited number of recorded entries conclude with the judges' sentences. Therefore, it is difficult to establish whether non-Hanafi legal rulings were used in Crimean practice, as in most cases verdicts are concealed under vague, standard formulae.

In two areas related to private matters there are some indications that Ottoman legal solutions were integrated into Crimean law. Classical Islamic law did not mention a statute of limitation for private law, let alone determine its duration in various types of cases; in fact, the issue of whether an offense could be prosecuted indefinitely remains largely unresolved in classical Islamic law. The Hanafis defined the statute of limitation only in cases concerning the violation of God's claims. In 1550, the Ottoman sultan solved the problem by issuing an imperial decree, in which he forbade *kadı*s from hearing cases if more than fifteen years had elapsed after the crime.[40] For example, the suits concerning

37 According to classical textbooks, criminal law is divided into two groups: offenses against people, and acts that endanger public order (i.e., violations of God's claims and state security).

38 DeWeese, *Islamization*, 132.

39 Abrahamowicz, Dubiński, and Płaskowicka-Rymkiewicz (trans.), *Księga podróży Ewliji Czelebiego*, 277; Evliya Çelebi, *Tam Metin Seyahatnâme*, 349.

40 Peters, *Crime and Punishment in Islamic Law*, 11.

the ownership of a private piece of land could not be heard after fifteen years.[41] The fifteen-year statute of limitation was applied in the Crimean Khanate,[42] which suggests that the idea might have come to the khanate from the Ottoman Empire.

Law in the khanate also seems to have adopted some Ottoman solutions in regard to pious foundations. In classical Islamic law there was no unanimity as to what kinds of property could be legally endowed as pious foundations. The Hanafis alone offered three opinions on the subject. The dispute focused on the possibility of converting movable property into trusts. In the sixteenth century, after decades of judicial arguments, the Ottomans finally defined what could be lawfully donated to a pious foundation. For practical reasons, the sultans permitted pious foundations to accept a wide range of objects, including animals and cash, whose donation had been banned previously.[43] The same practical approach characterized that of the Crimean judges. Among the entries recorded during Murad Giray's reign, we encounter the conversion of various kinds of movable property into pious foundations.[44]

With regard to criminal matters, we must emphasize that in Crimean courts, the principle of private prosecution was applied in cases of criminal offenses against people, such as homicide or bodily harm. Our research on the Crimean *sicil*s suggests that the plaintiffs in these types of cases sought retaliation or financial compensation, in accordance with Islamic law. We found no explicit confirmation that the *kadı* inflicted any type of *ta'zir* punishment based on *siyasa*, as happened in the Ottoman Empire, where the *kanun* allowed the application of modified penalties on individuals found guilty of a variety of offenses. In the khanate, in cases related to assault, we find a formula stating that the ruling was issued according to what is required (*mucebiyle hükm şod*), which may indicate the discretionary punishment accepted by classical jurists. For example, this sentence concludes the case brought to the Kara Su court by Karıt, daughter of Aktay, against her husband Mustafa, son of Receb. The woman stated that the accused beat her and broke her ribs. When her husband denied these allegations, the plaintiff presented four witnesses (three men and a woman), who confirmed her version of events.[45] The same formula appears

41 Ergene, *Local Court*, 147.

42 See references to the statute of limitation in two cases recorded in the *sicils* during the reign of Murad Giray: ORRNB Fond 917, *defter* 23a/150b/1; 23a/171b/2.

43 Imber, *Ebu's-su'ud*, 142–146.

44 For instance, a woman named Rahime donated nine *altuns* for the benefit of the pious foundation of the Great Mosque in Bahçesaray; ORRNB, Fond 917, *defter* 23b/83b/7.

45 ORRNB, Fond 917, *defter* 25/3a/4 or, for the court of *kadıasker*, 23b/30a/1. Zeynep Özdem also notes this formula in a case related to assault, see Özdem, *Kırım Karasubazar'da*, 25.

in a case involving both assault and sexual violence. Two women from Kara Su, Zafiye and Ak Bikçe, accused three men of entering their home against their will in order to conduct "mischief and shameless acts" (*fesad ve şena'at itmek murad eylediler*).[46] When two witnesses of the plaintiff corroborated the allegation, the *kadı* issued the ruling that 'what is required should be done.' In rare cases, we find a record of a dispute related to criminal matters that concludes with the formula discussed, followed by this short sentence (i.e., 'what is required should be done'). We find this pair of entries, for instance, in the Kara Su records. In one case, Bektaş, son of Mehmed, from Sudak, received five *akçe*s to pay for wound dressing and as an allowance for five days (i.e., five *akçe*s daily) from Göktaş Seyyid Gazi. The latter was found guilty of wounding Bektaş in the head; this was recorded in the first of two entries. The entry, which concerns the compensation for wound dressing and the allowance for Bektaş concludes with the formula that this was the discretionary punishment (*ta'zir şod*).[47]

As there is no law book for the khanate, it remains unclear what the formula *mucebiyle hükm şod* or *ta'zir ile hükm şod* means exactly. As noted in the case of Saime and Ibrahim, illicit sex, which was a *hadd* crime, attracted the attention of the *zabit*s, who brought the accused man to the court. In this case, the *kadı* applied less strict evidentiary procedures (i.e., less strict than that required by classical Islamic law) and imposed the discretionary punishment, most probably in the form of flogging.[48] Innocent Felici[49] and Kleemann[50] also noted cases of individuals that were convicted of this type of penalty in the khanate.

2 Litigants of the Sharia Courts: A Basic Statistical Analysis

Taking the above analysis of Crimean law in private and criminal matters as the point of departure, I move on to discuss the types of cases brought to the court as well as the social background, gender, and residential affiliation of the parties involved. I also analyze the dispute resolution practice. The objective of this section is to understand who sought justice in the khanate and what

---

The record of the case of Karıt does not reveal what outcome she expected. It is of interest to note that she did not initiate divorce (*tefrik*), which she would likely have obtained from the *kadı*. Svetlana Ivanova describes the case of an abused woman who demanded and was granted a divorce in the sharia court of Silistra in 1792 (Ivanova, "Divorce," 112–118).

46 ORRNB, Fond 917, *defter* 25/13b/5.

47 ORRNB, Fond 917, *defter* 25/14a/6–7.

48 ORRNB, Fond 917, *defter* 25/48a/4.

49 The letter of Innocent Felici of Malta to Philippe de Harlay, comte de Césy, the French Ambassador in Istanbul, APF, SOCG, vol. 106, fols. 335r–337v.

50 Kleemann, *Voyage de Vienne à Belgrade*, 90–107.

actions increased the plaintiff's chance of success in court. Hopefully, this analysis will bring us closer to understanding whether the court was inclined to support specific groups or whether it was a fair judicial forum.

2.1 *Types of Cases*

For the analyses presented in this study, we divided the recorded cases into two main groups: disputes and uncontested cases. The first group is comprised of cases related to money and property disputes, including conflicts over manumission between slaves and owners/owner's heirs and disputes concerning homicide, bodily harm, and other offenses like usurpation. We identified 971 such entries (of 2,273) in the *kadıasker* register and 134 (of 253) in the Kara Su register. The second group includes financial contracts (sales, debts, other agreements involving property ownership, the division of inheritances), representations, family matters (guardianships, allowances), manumissions and others similar cases concerning charitable endowments, salaries, or grants bestowed on individuals by members of the royal family. The number of contracts recorded in the *kadıasker* register amounts to 1,302 (of 2,273), and in the Kara Su register to 119 (of 253).

Before moving on to a detailed analysis of the types of cases I analyze, a caveat is in order regarding the classification of amicable settlements (*sulh*). In her study on *sulh* in Islamic law, Aida Othman emphasizes that, with certain reservations, 'fair' amicable settlements were encouraged by jurists as dispute resolution practices.[51] Many jurists, she notes, expressed the opinion that it was "preferable to reconcile and settle disputes through *sulh* to maintain the ties of family, brotherhood, and community" than to undergo a trial. Thus, it should come as no surprise that parties were inclined to avoid court trials and seek compromises instead, as this is a common characteristic of Islamic courts at various times and places.[52]

Işık Tamdoğan points out that settlements were "a cherished religious and moral value in Ottoman legal culture."[53] Research on the Ottoman *sicil*s led her to conclude that the parties were given the option of reaching settlements out of court and bringing them to the *kadı* for registration or they could start litigation in court and agree to a compromise during the trial. In the case of a settlement, the *kadı* played the role of notary or mediator,[54] but he did not

---

51 Othman, "*And Amicable Settlement Is Best*," 64–90, esp. 69–73.

52 L. Rosen, *The Anthropology of Justice: Law as Culture in Islamic Society* (Cambridge, 1989), 26–66; Ergene, *Local Court*, 189–207.

53 Tamdoğan, "Sulh and the 18th Century Ottoman Courts," 64.

54 Tamdoğan's description of two ways of concluding an amicable settlement, i.e., outside the court and in the court, constitutes a novelty in the research of Ottoman law (Tamdoğan, "Sulh and the 18th Century Ottoman Courts"). The earlier literature describes

give a ruling.[55] Thus, settlements could be included in the contracts. Yet, bearing in mind that settlements were a form of dispute resolution, we propose to include them in the category of disputes. According to the data preserved in the *kadıasker* register, 117 cases (of 971 disputes) were resolved by amicable settlements, while in Kara Su, we encountered this form of dispute resolution 22 times (of 134 diputes).

The *kadıasker* court and the district court in Kara Su dealt mainly with financial cases, both contracts and disputes. Divisions and registrations of inheritances constituted the third largest group of entries recorded in the *sicil*s. Other types of cases, such as those related to family matters, murder and assault, manumissions, and cases concerning pious endowments were less frequent than those related to money and inheritance disputes. In contrast to Ottoman practice, documents issued by the central or provincial administration were rarely recorded in the *sicil*s. A detailed breakdown of various types of cases is presented in the chart below. The bar chart presents the percentage of a particular type of case from the total number of entries in the *kadıasker* court (2,273 entries) and the Kara Su court (253 entries), while the key provides the number of the particular types of cases in the *kadıasker* court (KC) and the Kara Su court (KSC).

Note that in the Crimean Khanate, theft (*sarika*) and usurpation (*gasp*), which constitute common crimes in many societies, were rarely reported to judges. Their share in the overall number of cases constitutes only 2 percent and in both courts they are grouped among the 'others.' Researchers studying the Ottoman *sicil*s have also stressed the under-representation of criminal disputes.[56] It is certainly true that theft was defined very narrowly in classical

---

sulh as a compromise reached outside the court, see, for example, Jennings, "Kadi, Court and Legal Procedure," 148; Gradeva, "Orthodox Christians," 52–59; Peirce, *Morality Tales*, 120, 186. For further discussion on the need for a new approach to an accurate definition of *sulh* see, for example, Ergene, "Why Did Ümmü Gülsüm Go to Court?"

55 In the Crimean courts, settlements were often registered after the dispute concerning the same matter. For example, Şahin from Gözleve accused a *bölükbaşı* Kutlu Gazi from Bahçesaray in the *kadıasker* court and stated that the latter owed him twelve *esedi guruş* and 60 *akçes*. The accused *zabıta* stated that he had repaid the whole debt and he produced witnesses who confirmed his version of events. In the next entry, we encounter the same parties concluding an amicable settlement. This time, Şahin from Gözleve claimed that *bölükbaşı* Kutlu Gazi should return goods worth forty *altun*s to him. The accused man stated that he did not have in his possession a single piece of property belonging to the plaintiff. Yet, he agreed to pay him sixteen *altun*s on the condition that Şahin give up any further claims (ORRNB, Fond 917, *defter* 22/72b/5 and 6).

56 For instance, Boğaç Ergene's research on Kastamonu demonstrates that the proportion of cases related to theft in the local *sicils* do not exceed 4 percent in ten of the twelve judicial records he studied; Ergene, *Local Court*, 59.

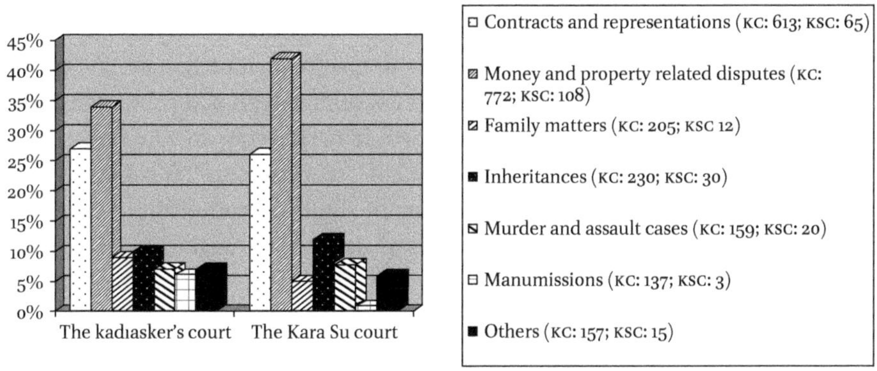

FIGURE 4 Types of cases registered in the Crimean courts.

Islamic law. As one of the violations of God's claims, two eyewitnesses were required for a person to be condemned for theft. Rudolph Peters states that the following conditions as stipulated in classical law must be met for an act to be considered theft: "surreptitiously taking away of (movable) property with a certain minimum value (*nisab*), which is not partially owned by the perpetrator, not entrusted to him, from a place which is locked or under guard."[57]

Other restrictions were added by the four Islamic schools. Jurists agreed that a person must be able to legally own the goods liable to be stolen. For example, a Muslim cannot legally own a swine, therefore, if it were stolen, its Muslim owner would not be able to sue the thief. Moreover, Hanafis defined the minimum value of stolen objects as 29.7 grams of silver. Their definition of theft did not comprise the removal of perishable goods like food. Finally, they regulated procedures for cases of theft. If a defendant returned stolen objects before the sentence, the charges would be dismissed. If a defendant was found guilty, a plaintiff could either demand that the stolen objects be returned or apply for the fixed penalty to be imposed. In cases of theft this meant the amputation of the right hand. It was very difficult to successfully condemn and convict someone of theft. This may be the reason Crimean litigants very rarely brought this matter to the court. However, in classical law, usurpation was more broadly defined and was not limited by the above mentioned restrictions. In cases of usurpation, the original owner could demand the return of goods or their equivalent, if they had been damaged. In the Ottoman Empire, administrative justice (*siyasa shar'iyya*) was applied in cases of usurpation.[58]

57 Peters, *Crime and Punishment in Islamic Law*, 56.
58 Imber, *Ebu's-su'ud*, 222–228; Heyd, *Studies in Old Ottoman Criminal Law*, 118–119.

The story of Nicolas Kleemann indicates that elements of the *siyasa shar'iyya* were also applied in cases involving theft in the Crimean Khanate. From our investigation into the case of the German merchant who was robbed, we can conclude that the Crimean judges did not rely exclusively on standard classical proofs, i.e., confession or the accounts of eyewitnesses.[59] It seems, therefore, that state officials supported victims of theft in their efforts to recover their property.[60] Nonetheless, allegations of usurpation were rarely recorded in Crimean *sicil*s.

2.2 *The Social Background of Litigants*

The courts comprised a cross section of Crimean society. As indicated in the introduction, the court records do not include precise data on the social status of the litigants. Yet, in these entries we find important descriptions of the individuals that appeared before the *kadı*. First, in order to understand their social status we must reconstruct how the Tatars categorized their society and understand the meaning of various terms used to describe a litigant or a case witness. Second, we must comprehend how the judicial formulae reflected the social structure.

It seems that local clerks used Ottoman formulae supplemented by terms typical of Tatar society. Generally, court entries provide important descriptors that indicate religion, social status, and residential affiliation. The social background of the litigants is described by their father's name and title (if applicable). In the case of women, we are often provided with their marital status and data about their husbands. It is usually clear whether the litigants were Muslims or non-Muslims, as different formulae were used to describe members of these groups. Non-Muslims were usually labeled according to their religion, confession, ethnic background, and residential affiliation, e.g., Yahudi (Rabbanite or Karaite Jew) or Armeni (Armenian), but for non-Muslims, it is rarely possible to recognize their social status or occupation, such as *papas* (priest), *bakkal* (grocer), *and tüccar* (merchant).

Fortunately, the social status of Muslims is more clearly described in the court entries; titles are the main indicators. While some titles unquestionably refer to a certain social status, others are more difficult to classify. As noted

59 Kleemann, *Voyage de Vienne à Belgrade*, 90–109.

60 For example, Nuraç, son of Şah Huseyn, from the district of Dib Kerç, successfully took his slave back from Abdulvahab, son of Huseyn, from Bahçesaray. The plaintiff stated that the defendant owned his slave, who had been missing for ten years. In order to defend himself, Huseyn stated that he had bought the slave legally. Yet, the judge ordered him to return the slave to the plaintiff as soon as the latter procured witnesses, who confirmed his claim; ORRNB, Fond 917, *defter* 23b/38a/2.

in the introduction, we propose to divide Crimean Muslims into five social groups, whose members used the titles listed below:

(1) members of the Giray dynasty (khan, sultan, *hani*);
(2) nobles (*beğ, mirza, emeldeş, ulan*);
(3) members of the administrative and military elite (*ağa, beşe*);
(4) members of the religious elite (*çelebi, efendi, hoca, şeyh, dede, seyyid*); and
(5) common people (who had no title other than the honorific *hacı/hacıye* for men/women who had performed the pilgrimage to Mecca).[61]

Some drawbacks of the above classification should be noted. First, in a small number of cases the distinction between nobles and members of administrative, military, and religious elite remains not altogether clear, as there was overlap in categories. This results from the fact that Crimean nobles often pursued careers in state and religious administration. In these cases, we labeled individuals according to their profession rather than status.

Second, it is not altogether clear how to identify the social status of women. In this study, women were classified according to the status of their husbands, when this status was recorded. When this information was lacking, they were included in their father's social group. Such a solution has certain drawbacks: while it was rare for a Muslim woman to marry a man of inferior social status, a Muslim man could marry beneath himself, even a slave. Presumably, a woman's family status prior to her marriage might have influenced the manner in which she exercised her rights in the law court. As the present study does not focus on gender, we decided to treat all wives of elite members equally, whatever their origins. However, there is one exception to this rule: female members of the Giray family were classified as members of the ruling dynasty.

The idea of including women in different social groups of Muslims is by no means a unique solution applied by researchers working on the *sicil*s. For example, in their recent work on the court registers of Kastamonu, Bogaç Ergene and Metin Coşgel classify women as one separate group, while they divide men into three title-based categories (religious-judicial titleholders, military-administrative titleholders, and men without titles).[62] From another study by Ergene, also based on the registers of Kastamonu (co-authored with Ali Berker), we learn that the female community of the city was not homogenous; it included a small group of wealthy women who held the title of *hatun*, a clear

61 Coşgel and Ergene note that individuals who held the title of *hacı/hacıye*, were well-off and stood a better chance in court against common Muslims without titles (Coşgel and Ergene, *Economics of Ottoman Justice*, 55, 296–303).

62 Coşgel and Ergene, *Economics of Ottoman Justice*, 52–57.

indication of their elevated social status.[63] The research of Phokion Kotzageorgis and Demetrios Papastamatiou on eighteenth-century Salonika also lists a few women among the richest inhabitants of the city.[64] During their research on the *askeri* in Damascus in the early eighteenth century, Colette Establet and Jean-Paul Pascual discovered that estates left by widows of the members of the administative-military elite were registered in the probate inventories of the *askeri*.[65] The presence of these inventories of women's estates indicates that the women were included, at least to some extent, in the socio-legal group of their late husbands. Presumably, the behavior of these women in court was more comparable to that of other local notables than it was to common people. Thus, in relation to categorizing women, I maintain my decision to use the titles of women's male next of kin, or in rare occasions, their own status, in order to include them in the title-based categories described above.

Third, this classification ignores economic differences between members of the same group. A few recent studies, such as the works of Ergene and Berker, Atabey Kaygun[66] and Coşgel on eighteenth-century Kastamonu, and Establet and Pascual on the *askeri* in Damascus in the early eighteenth century,[67] clearly demonstrate that the division of the Muslim male community into three categories based solely on titles (religious-judicial titleholders, military-administrative titleholders, and men without titles) does not reflect the differences in wealth and other professional distinctions within these groups. The abovementioned authors apply a more nuanced model of social segmentation, one that would reflect differences in wealth and occupation. Their research based on probate inventories proves that the title-based groups differed in terms of accumulated wealth. In the case of Kastamonu, the results are very promising; they show differences in court usage by members of subsects within the same main category, e.g., elite with religious titles and non-elites with religious titles. In the present study, however, I use the simple title-based division of Muslim individuals and disregard economic or professional differences between the members of the same category because of the lack of literature on differences in wealth in the khanate. Clearly, this vital issue merits a separate study.

The division of society into Muslims and non-Muslims has its roots in Islamic law. It is perhaps appropriate to question the validity of classifying Crimean society using different criteria. An important characteristic of the Ottoman

---

63 Ergene and Berker, "Wealth and Inequality," 23–46, esp. 34.

64 Kotzageorgis and Papastamatiou, "Wealth Accumulation," 165–199.

65 C. Establet and J-P. Pascual, *La gent d'État dans la société ottomane damascéne. Les 'asker à la fin du XVII*[e] *siécle* (Damascus, 2011), 31–32.

66 Ergene and Kaygun, "Spouse Selection," 3–20.

67 Establet and Pascual, *La gent d'État*, 32–38.

Empire was its division into taxpaying subjects (*reaya*) and the military class (*askeri*) who received salaries from the state treasury; this division was rooted in the Ottoman *kanun*s. Members of the military class were subject to a separate jurisdiction. Instead of being adjudicated by regular sharia courts, they came before judicial forums appointed by the sultan. Did such distinctions between taxpaying and tax-exempt subjects exist in the Crimean Khanate? Our sources offer an ambiguous answer. On the one hand, the khans' orders suggest such a division: they adopt common Ottoman terms such as *reaya* in reference to taxpayers, and *askeri* in reference to the military class (the term *kul* is alternatively used in reference to the khan's courtiers and soldiers, albeit not for the khan's judicial and religious officials).[68] The former category, *reaya*, included Muslim and non-Muslim subjects, and the latter encompassed the military and administrative elite. In addition, the rulers seemed to favor a separate jurisdiction for members of the army.[69]

On the other hand, there were substantial differences between the composition of the Ottoman elites and that of the Crimean elites. The Crimean nobility could not be classified along Ottoman lines, which divided subjects into taxpaying commoners and tax-exempt elite. Though it is true that the Crimean elite were exempt from paying taxes to the treasury. For example, some nobles served as the khan's officials and the ruler had the right of life and death over them; therefore, they were treated as members of the military class. Other nobles, especially members and clients of the *karaçı* families, did not have careers in the khan's service. They derived their income from family estates called *beylik*s and from the spoils of military campaigns; thus, these nobles were not paid directly by the khan. The extent of their judicial subordination to the ruler remains unclear and requires further specific research. It is doubtful whether they can be included in the *askeri* class in the Ottoman understanding of the term. Given these examples, it is not altogether clear whether Crimean society can be described as divided between the taxpaying and the tax-exempt elite. Presumably, such a distinction existed in the territories of the Girays. Yet, it is unclear whether such a division can be accurately used for inhabitants of the estates of the *karaçı* families.

The following figures present information on the social background of the clients of the *kadıasker* court and the Kara Su court during Murad Giray's reign. In terms of disputes, the total number of plaintiffs registered in the *kadıasker* court is 876 individuals, and 894 defendants. In the same court, 1,385 individuals were parties in uncontested cases. In the Kara Su court register,

---

68 ORRNB, fond 917, *defter* 9/1b/2, 17/24b/1, 25/113a/5, 51/53a/1.

69 ORRNB, fond 917, *defter* 23/216b/1, 25/118b/3.

we encounter 144 plaintiffs and 130 defendants in the disputes, while 266 individuals are mentioned as parties in financial contracts, representations in contracts, manumissions, and in inheritance records.

These tables demonstrate the court usage of various social groups. In the *kadıasker* court, common Muslim and non-Muslim subjects constituted around 60 percent of litigants in cases involving disputes and other types of cases. Members of the elite groups of the society: the Girays, nobles, and members of the military-administrative and religious elites, were involved in about 35 percent of all cases. Pious foundations represented by their agents also acted as parties in disputes and contracts. Village or neighborhood communities constituted parties in cases involving the interests of all their members. In two types of cases they acted as one party: in cases concerning murder committed in their territories and in disputes concerning common land. In contrast to the Ottoman Empire, there are no indications in the *sicil*s I examined that the khan's subjects acted "en masse" in other matters, for example, to dismiss a corrupt official.[70] In sum, cases involving institutions or organizations were seldom recorded in the *sicil*s.

Finally, slaves and former slaves constituted yet another group of litigants. Usually, they appeared in two types of entries: as parties in disputes or contracts involving their manumission and in various cases as representatives of their owners. A case involving a slave, Avs, son of Abdullah, constitutes a good example. He was brought to the *kadıasker* court by Hacı Suleyman, the *kethüda* of Gazikerman. The latter stated that three months earlier Avs had arrived

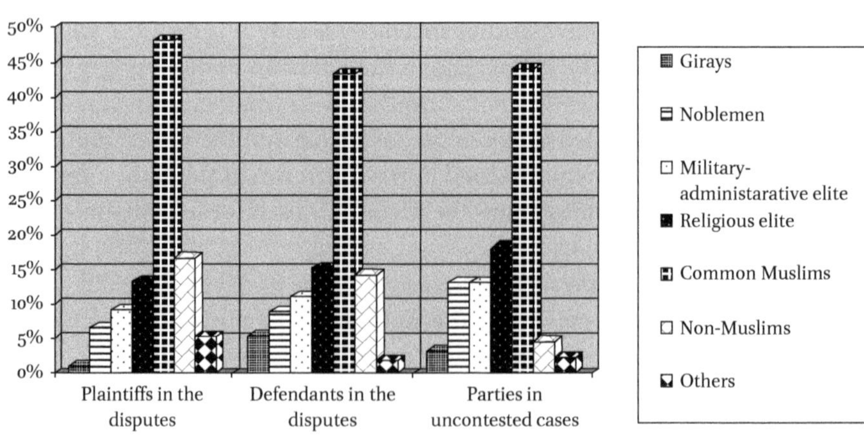

FIGURE 5 The social background of litigants in the *kadıasker* court.

70 Ergene, *Local Court*, 151–153.

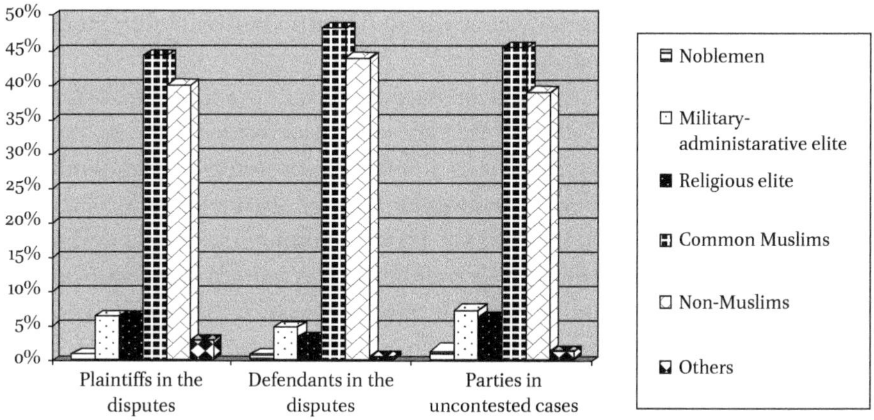

FIGURE 6 The social background of litigants in the district court in Kara Su.

from Gözleve with his master, Iş Mirza, and was going to Gazikerman.[71] After their arrival, the slave converted to Islam and was set free by his master. Just a few days later, Avs was caught on his way to the "abode of war" (*dar-i harb*; presumably this refers to the Polish-Lithuanian Commonwealth or Muscovy). As soon as he was brought back to Gazikerman, he was sold to Hacı Suleyman. Avs questioned the legality of this contract of sale. When he was interrogated in the *kadıasker* court, he stated that Iş Mirza had set him free and produced a document affirming his words. The *kadıasker* court, therefore, confirmed his status as a freeman.[72]

There is a notable difference regarding the "average" social background of litigants appearing in the *kadıasker* court and those appearing in the district court of Kara Su. In the latter, common Muslims and non-Muslims were involved in as many as 80 to 90 percent of cases, while elite members used the district court considerably less frequently (for around 10 percent of cases). It is worth asking why was there such a difference in the extent to which these social groups used the courts. Does this fact reflect the different social structure of the inhabitants of the capital city and the province or does it reflect the way in which the courts were perceived and used by their clients? The difference might have been caused by both reasons, or a combination of the two. Interestingly, in both types of courts, common subjects constituted the majority of litigants while the number of elites remained more limited. This result agrees

71 Gazikerman was an Ottoman (previously Crimean) fortress on the right bank of the Dnieper River. Gazikerman and Şahkerman, a fortress on the opposite bank of the river, guarded the passage to the Black Sea and prevented Cossack raids of Muslim territories.

72 ORRNB, Fond 917, *defter* 23a/ 204b/5.

with our general presumptions concerning the ratio between elite members and commoners in Crimean society.

The differences between the social backgrounds of the individuals appearing in the two courts may suggest that these judicial forums were used differently. Tables 2 and 3 indicate that elite members appeared more frequently before the *kadıasker* than they did before the Kara Su district judge. We propose two possible explanations for this fact. First, the number of elite members in the capital arguably exceeded their number in the more remote parts of the khanate. Second, elite members might have preferred to bring their cases to the *kadıasker*, who had more prestige than a district *kadı*, in order to stress their elevated social status. As noted in Chapter 3, the most striking difference in the composition of the litigants of the two courts concerns the nobles. In the *kadıasker* court they constituted 6.6 percent of plaintiffs and 8.9 percent of defendants in disputes, and 13.0 percent of parties involved in uncontested cases. The proportion of nobles involved in proceedings in the Kara Su district court never exceeded 2.0 percent—this is indeed a striking contrast. These statistics may indicate that the Tatar nobility perceived the *kadıasker* court as a more suitable judicial forum than an ordinary district court. It is also worth noting that in the *kadıasker* court, the number of defendants of noble origin exceeded the number of noble plaintiffs. Although usually the plaintiffs and defendants belonged to the same social group,[73] in the case of nobles, more than one-third of their opponents were of non-noble origin. This fact may suggest that the adversaries of nobles from other social groups sought justice from the *kadıasker* rather than from a district judge. The reasons for which cases were brought to the *kadıasker* court should be further studied.

2.3 *The Gender of Court Litigants*

In the last forty years, historians have turned their attention to women in the Ottoman world. Since the 1970s, numerous studies have covered the role of women in the economic and social life of the Ottoman Empire. The local *sicils* seemed to provide especially fascinating data. This type of source depicted Muslim and non-Muslim women selling, buying, and owning properties, engaging in business, divorcing their husbands, fighting for custody over children, claiming daily allowances from their husbands and legal agents who managed their properties, or bringing suits in all types of judicial disputes. Women in the Ottoman Empire took active roles in numerous areas of day-to-day life. Thus, it became clear that Ottoman women should no longer be perceived as

73 Less than 20 percent of the cases recorded in the *kadıasker sicils* during Murad Giray's reign involved parties of different social origins.

submissive individuals totally controlled by husbands or male relatives. This is not to say that Ottoman women used courts in the same way men did or that they stood a similar chance of success or failure as men. Scholars rightly argue that women appeared in all types of cases, but still less frequently than men; the causes for this constitute a topic of ongoing debate. In the case of contracts, the explanation could be twofold. First, probate inventories indicate that women's estates were, on average, smaller than the estates of men.[74] Thus, women were less likely to become involved in any type of contract related to property transfers. And the women who did enter into contracts were likely to be more reluctant than men to seek solutions in court, knowing there would be fees involved. Second, fewer women than men were involved in any sort of commercial activity and this must have translated into the number of contracts they entered into.[75]

In the case of disputes, one should take into account the social stigma attached to participating in trials, and this might have been a reason women would have avoided courts.[76] Leslie Peirce suggests another explanation; she states that women "experienced greater difficulty in addressing the law, which was less favorable to females than to males in a number of ways."[77] The various limitations they faced in Ottoman society is clear from their rights and role in the court, as defined by custom and law. For example, women could not act as case witnesses, let alone as members of a court's personnel. They enjoyed the same rights as men, but their testimonies carried one-half of the weight of a man's testimony in the court. Litigants who wanted women to testify in their cases had to bring two other people to give testimony in addition to a female witness. At least one of them had to be a man, as it was not acceptable in an Islamic court for testimony to be given only by women, with the exception of areas involving the inspection of sexual parts of a woman's body.[78] Moreover, Hanafis placed further limitations on the types of disputes in which women's testimony was valid. In cases of murder, they could only act as legal witnesses in a few well-defined circumstances, for instance, when a woman's body was found in a women's bathhouse.[79] For these reasons, female legal witnesses were rarely listed in the entries recorded in the Ottoman *sicil*s.

74 Canbakal, *Society and Politics*, 92–93; Coşgel and Ergene, *Economics of Ottoman Justice*, 56–57.

75 Jennings, "Women in the Early 17th-Century"; Gerber, "Social and Economic Position."

76 Coşgel and Ergene, *Economics of Ottoman Justice*, 196.

77 Peirce, *Morality Tales*, 176.

78 R. Shaham, *The Expert Witness in Islamic Courts: Medicine and Crafts in the Service of Law* (Chicago and London, 2010), 83–98.

79 Ciğdem, "Judicial Registers," 7–8.

This fact, as Leslie Peirce notes in reference to the sixteenth-century court of Ayntab, made it difficult for "women to call on other women to support their cases in court."[80] The recent research of Metin Coşgel and Boğaç Ergene calls attention to the fact that women were in general less likely to a win a private case against men. Yet, it should be emphasized that women's success rates depended on the social status of their opponents. While they had little chance of success against men with religious titles, they did relatively well against men without any titles. In criminal matters, the average woman's success rate was relatively higher when her opponent was a man without a title or a man with a military title than it was against a member of the religious elite.[81] These results, combined with the social stigma and difficulties in addressing the law, might indicate that, in general, entering into a lawsuit entailed a greater risk for women than it did for men.

In terms of their participation in courts, the situation of Muslim and non-Muslim women in the Crimean Khanate seems to resemble that of Ottoman women. Judging by the content of the *sicil*s, Crimean women played active roles in various areas of daily life of the khanate. As in the Ottoman Empire, the claims of Crimean women concerned all types of matters, such as those related to physical violence or matters related to property[82] and family issues.[83]

Figures 7 and 8 show the proportion of women among the litigants of the *kadıasker* court and the district court in Kara Su.

The statistical analysis shows that, as in the Ottoman Empire, women did bring disputes to the court, though they did it considerably less frequently than men did. Women were more often involved in uncontested cases than in disputes. It is noteworthy that the proportion of women among the litigants in

---

80 Peirce, *Morality Tales*, 176.

81 Coşgel and Ergene, *Economics of Ottoman Justice*, 272–279.

82 For instance, Arife, through her proxy Huseyn, son of Kaplan, bought a house and a plot of land near the river of Salgır; ORRNB, Fond 917, *defter* 23b/22a/3. Another case depicts a widow, Rahime, bringing charges against her mother-in-law, Fatma; ORRNB, Fond 917, *defter* 23b/24a/1.

83 For instance, a Muslim woman named Nesli requested a divorce from her husband, Arslan Halife. She stated that before their marriage, Arslan had made an oath that if he took another wife or made his slave his concubine, he would give Nesli a divorce (*khul*); ORRNB, Fond 917, *defter* 22/75a/2. Generally, this kind of divorce meant a financial loss for the woman. Some Muslim women succeeded in persuading their husbands to pledge to give them a more favorable type of divorce (i.e., *talaq*) that secured her right to her dowry and maintenance during the waiting period (during which time, she was not supposed to marry another man, as she might be pregnant, and her former husband was to provide maintenance during this period). In the Kara Su district court, a Muslim woman named Zeyneb convinced her husband to make an oath that if he ever got drunk again, he would give her a divorce (*talaq*); ORRNB, Fond 917, *defter* 25/40b/3–4.

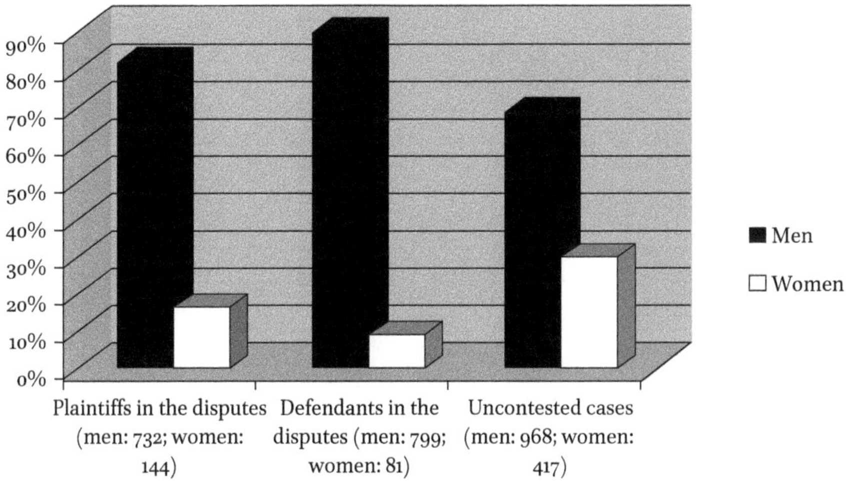

FIGURE 7 The gender of litigants in the *kadıasker* court.

the courts in the khanate is similar to their proportion among the litigants in the Ottoman courts.[84]

Below, I present three cases showing women as a plaintiff, a defendant, and as a legal witness.

> Case 1: Sexual slur
> The case is as follows:
> In the noble court, Nesli Hatun, daughter of Ilkas (?), from the village of Karanki,[85] accused Seyyid Din Mehmed, from the same village, who had been summoned and was present:
> "The noted Seyyid slandered me by calling me without [my having committed] a sin a lover (*muhibbe*). It is my wish that the litigation should be decided."
>
> Because the aforementioned Seyyid answered by denying the allegations, the aforementioned Nesli produced disinterested witnesses from among the upright Muslims: Islam, son of Abdullah; Hatice, daughter of Rizvan; and Sefer Bike, daughter of Abdullah. They were present in the court to give [their] testimony:

84 Cf. the results obtained by Boğaç Ergene for Çankırı (18 percent of plaintiffs, 14 percent of defendants) and Kastamonu (27 percent of plaintiffs, 17 percent of defendants), or by Ronald Jennings for Kayseri (17 percent of all types of litigants); see Ergene, *Local Court,* 66; Jennings, "Women in the Early 17th-Century," 115.

85 The identification of the village remains unclear. Henryk Jankowski notes two villages bearing this name. Both were situated in the vicinity of Ferahkerman (Jankowski, *A Historical-Etymological Dictionary*, 830–831).

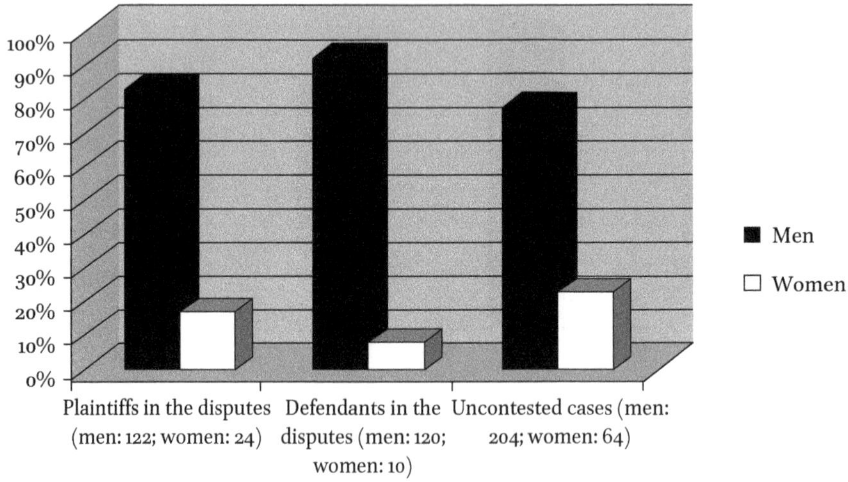

FIGURE 8 The gender of litigants in the district court in Kara Su.

> "We testify as witnesses that the aforementioned Seyyid insulted the aforementioned Nesli by calling her a lover."
> Their testimony was accepted.
> What happened has been recorded along with the required sentence (*mucebiyle hükm birle kayd şod*).
> Case witnesses: Seyyid Osman Efendi, [son of] Mehmed Can Efendi; Abdullah Efendi, [son of] Hacı Murad; the well-known Şahbaz Efendi; Yusuf, who was present; Hurrazad, who was present; Gazanfar, who was present; Kadı Musalli Efendi, and the others.[86]

The case consists of an accusation of slander brought by Nesli Hatun. Her title suggests that she was a respected, honorable woman.[87] She accused Seyyid of insulting her by calling her a 'lover.' His accusation implied that she was having illicit sex. If his accusation were true and proven, she would have been sentenced to flogging. Although very little is known about the Tatar perception of female honor, it is likely that, as in other Islamic states,[88] such a slander would jeopardize her honor. The loss of a woman's honor would have numerous negative implications, such as her social ostracisim (and possibly that of

86 ORRNB, Fond 917, *defter* 23b/28a/1.
87 Ergene and Berker, "Wealth and Inequality," 34.
88 About female virtue in the Ottoman Empire, see M.C. Zilfi, "Women and Society in the Tulip Era," in *Women, the Family, and Divorce Laws in Islamic History*, ed. A. Sonbol (Syracuse, NY, 1996), 290–303.

her family) or disqualification from acting as a witness in the court. Thus, it is not surprising that Nesli Hatun brought charges against Seyyid. When he denied her accusation, she managed to produce witnesses who confirmed her version. As noted, women rarely served as legal witnesses. Therefore, it is interesting that Nesli Hatun brought two women to corroborate her statement. The fact that the plaintiff brought female witnesses from Karanki to the capital is noteworthy. Perhaps the two women, next to Islam (son of Abdullah), were the only available witnesses to the incident. Nesli Hatun might also have chosen these two respectable women to suggest that she shared their status.

Unfortunately, there is no verdict recorded in this entry. Therefore, it remains unclear whether Seyyid was punished for this slander, and if so, what kind of punishment might have been administered. A sexual slur might have been interpreted as a false accusation of illicit sex (*kazf*), which, in accordance with the Quran, was punishable by eighty lashes. The Ottoman courts, as Başak Tuğ notes, very rarely applied the fixed penalty for slander. Usually, those convicted incurred discretionary punishments.[89] As discussed earlier in this chapter, the formula *mucebiyle hükm birle kayd şod* might also suggest that a discretionary punishment was meted out.

Case 2: Assault in self-defense

The case is as follows:

> Selamet, son of Salih, from the village of Yukarı Eğirmen[90] [situated] in the judicial district of Kara Kurt appointed Sufi, son of Ali Halife, as his agent. It was witnessed by the honorable chief gatekeeper (*kapıcı başı*), Murad Gazi Ağa, and the gatekeeper (*bevvab*), Ahmed, son of Abdulvali. [As] Selamet was injured on the right side of his nape, he asked his agent to bring the following accusation against Musa Sufi, son of Hacı Receb, and his wife Rakiye, daughter of Mavlud Ali, from the same village, who were [also] present [in the court]:
>
> "The aforementioned Musa Sufi and his wife Rakiye stabbed my principal on the right side of his nape with a large knife. It resulted in a serious injury. My principal is still lying sick in bed. My wish is that the aforementioned individuals should be heard and the litigation should be decided."
>
> At this moment, the aforementioned Musa Sufi and his wife, the aforementioned Rakiye, were questioned. The aforementioned Musa Sufi denied the charges. The aforementioned Rakiye stated,

89 Tuğ, *Politics of Honor*, 216.

90 Jankowski, *A Historical-Etymological Dictionary*, 581.

> "[Selamet, son of Salih] wanted to commit an act of adultery with me without my consent. In these circumstances, I injured him with a knife." What happened has been recorded upon demand. Written in the third ten days (20–30) Cemazi II, in the year 1091 [19 June–27 July 1680].
> Case witnesses: Ahmed Efendi, [son of] Abdulcemil Efendi; Khatib Suleyman Efendi; Abdullah Efendi, [son of] Hacı Murad; the well-known Şahbaz Efendi; Şahzad; Hurrazad, who was present; Abdulaziz, [son of] Avs, and the others [who were] present.[91]

In the opinion of Muslim jurists, in a case concerning assault, the victim himself/herself was expected to bring a suit in the court, in person or through his/her agent. Therefore, it is not surprising that Selamet brought the matter to the *kadıasker* court. Because he had been wounded, he was represented by his agent, who explained his accusation, namely, that a married couple had injured him with a knife. As entries rarely provide detailed descriptions of the circumstances of related incidents, the short statement of the agent comes as no surprise. The answer of the defendants is equally laconic. Nonetheless, it explains their motive. The wife acknowledged that she had injured the plaintiff, but she justified herself by making a counter-accusation. She stated that she had stabbed Selamet in self-defense, because he wanted to have illicit sex with her. In such a situation, her behavior would be justified.

The entry does not explain where the reported incident took place (in the woman's house or in some other place). It is unusual that neither the plaintiff nor the defendant provided this information, which would help to establish the circumstances of the crime. It is not even clear if it took place in the Kara Kurt district or in the capital. The fact that the legal agency of Sufi, son of Ali Halife, was attested by the khan's courtiers might indicate that the assault happened in Bahçesaray. It hardly seems probable that the ruler's chief gatekeeper (*kapıcı başı*), accompanied by his fellow courtier (*bevvab*), would be present in Kara Kurt in time to confirm the statement of the injured man, giving his power of attorney. The involvement of the courtiers in the case is a mystery. The presence of such important officials, who rarely assumed the role of witnesses in cases of establishing agency for common Muslims, might indicate that Selamet was a client or relative of one of them.

As the entry does not include a verdict, we can only speculate as to the outcome of the dispute. It is noteworthy that the woman did not produce any evidence on which to base her counter-claim, nor did she promise to bring such evidence in the future. As Coşgel and Ergene state "if the defendant 'rebuts' the

91 ORRNB, Fond 917, *defter* 23b/14a/5.

plaintiff's allegation, the burden of proof shifts to the defendant, assuming the plaintiff denies the defendant's rebuttal."[92] Given this evidentiary procedure, we would expect to find information in the record about evidence supporting the defendants' claim. Yet, the married couple remained silent.

If the accused individuals had denied the accusation instead of making a counter-accusation, the plaintiff would assume the burden of proof. We have no way of knowing if Selamet was prepared to produce evidence supporting his version of events. Perhaps, the very fact that Musa Sufi and Rakiye made a counter-claim indicates that they were afraid he could prove his allegation. A question arises, what could they achieve with the rebuttal? Why did the woman risk an accusation of *kazf*?

The study of Boğaç Ergene on Ummü Gulsüm, an Ottoman woman who accused a man of sexual abuse, and who could not prove her allegation, may shed some light on Rakiye's motives. In search of possible explanations of Ummü Gulsüm's behavior (and that of other women in similar circumstances), Ergene proposes that she came to the court to conclude an amicable settlement. Most probably, Ummü Gulsüm was aware of the fact that she could not secure a favorable sentence in a formal hearing without proof. Yet, she could reasonably expect the *kadı* to pressure her offender to accept a settlement (*sulh*). Moreover, she might have believed that the accused man would want to avoid an embarrassing trial, and for this reason would also agree to conduct an amicable settlement.[93] In the case of Rakiye, we have no way of knowing her exact motives. In the short term, by presenting a counter-claim, she and her husband did not have to pay compensation to Selamet. Perhaps, as in case of Ummü Gulsüm, Rakiye hoped for an agreeable settlement. In her situation this might include a withdrawal of the charges against her and her husband and the payment of a handsome compensation.

> Case 3: Women as legal witnesses
> The case is as follows:
> A person named Piri, son of Ömer, from Gözleve, in the presence of Timur Gazi Mirza, son of Arslan Beğ, from the village of Balta Çoğrak,[94] stated in words and expressed his thoughts in the court:
> "The aforementioned Timur Gazi Mirza is a descendant of Zorum(?) Ağa. The latter had a brother, Mevlud Ağa, who had a daughter, Nesli Bike,

92 Coşgel and Ergene, *Economics of Ottoman Justice*, 219.

93 Ergene, "Why Did Ümmü Gülsüm Go to Court?"

94 Balta Çoğrak was a village situated in the judicial district of Bahçesaray; Jankowski, *A Historical-Etymological Dictionary*, 276.

> with my paternal aunt. The aforementioned [paternal aunt] Fatma and my father Ömer were full brother and sister. Their father was [named] Hacı Dursun and their mother was [named] Emine. Although we do not come from the same womb, we remain relatives."
> After an interrogation, Timur Gazi Mirza acknowledged their kinship.
> Although the kinship was not denied, Abdullah, son of Ömer Seyyid; Aliş Mullah, son of Mehmed Çelebi; Akay Çelebi, son of Yusuf Halife; and after them Salihe, daughter of Musli; and Farihzat, daughter of Abdullah, who were [all] upright Muslims, confirmed the testimony of the plaintiff. Their testimony, which was found in accordance with the conditions of acceptance, was accepted. The kinship of Piri was confirmed and was recorded as required by him.
> Case witnesses: Müezzin Şahzad; Çor Akay from the village of Köküş; Bayram Ali, son of Abdullah; the well-known Mehmed Çelebi; the well-known *katib* Abdulbaki, and the others present.[95]

This is an interesting case for two reasons. First, cases concerning confirmation of kinship were rarely recorded in Crimean *sicil*s. Second, the entry reveals an uncommon judicial procedure. As the claim of the plaintiff was acknowledged by the defendant, the latter was not obliged to procure evidence. Nonetheless, the legal witnesses testified to confirm the already well-known facts. Moreover, the number of legal witnesses far exceeded the necessary two. Three men and two women came to the court to confirm the kinship of Piri and his noble relative. It is noteworthy that in a family-related case both men and women were asked to bear testimony. This leads us to wonder what their relations with the parties were. The titles of the male witnesses or their fathers, such as mullah, *seyyid*, *halife*, and *çelebi* indicate that they enjoyed a high social status. More specifically, they seem to have been members of the religious elite. Their testimony would thus be treated with respect in any type of case. It remains unclear whether they were personally related to the litigants. On their part, the female witnesses lacked any honorific titles, which suggests that they were common Muslim women. Presumably, they were not chosen to give evidence because of their elevated social status. Perhaps they were considered reliable witnesses because of their close relations with the litigants: they might have been their neighbors or even relatives. Their professions might have been another aspect of their credibility as legal witnesses: if they worked as domestic servants or local midwives, they would be considered well-informed persons.

95 ORRNB, Fond 917, *defter* 22/75a/1.

In sum, the entries registered in the Crimean *sicil*s demonstrate that the social position of Crimean women was defined by Islamic rules. Therefore, they enjoyed the rights of and faced the limitations common to women living in a Muslim state. In all types of cases, their limited interactions with the courts compared to those of men suggest that they were reluctant to seek assistance from the *kadı*. Most probably, they faced difficulties in the courts similar to those encountered by Ottoman women. The question, to what extent local customs influenced the scope of freedom of Crimean women, remains unanswered. The *sicil*s do not offer any data about local non-Muslim customs on the day-to-day life of local women.

2.4 *The Residential Affiliations of Litigants*

One's residential affiliation is another important detail in the descriptions of litigants found in the court entries. These descriptions usually include the name of village or neighborhood (for city dwellers) in which an individual resided, followed by the name of a judicial district. Numerous entries, however, lack any reference to or affiliation with a district. In such cases, the locations of many small villages remain obscure. We can identify three principal reasons for our current geographical challenges. First, the inhabitants of the Crimea engaged in multiple migrations after the Russian annexation of the Crimea in 1783, and this resulted in major changes in the patterns of their settlements. Second, the majority of the Tatar habitation names were replaced with the Russian names. Third, only a very limited number of pre-Russian sources contain data on Crimean geography and toponyms. Therefore, we must rely on the earliest Russian register of Crimean settlements, which dates to 1783–84. Although this seems to reflect the khanate's administrative structure from the second half of the eighteenth century, it reveals certain differences when compared with data from earlier periods. Henryk Jankowski notes differences in the names of some judicial districts between the time of the Russian register and the seventeenth-century Crimean *sicil*s.[96] For these reasons, we must concede that the exact location of numerous villages remains unclear.

In the present section we discuss whether the residential affiliation of litigants influenced their choice of a given type of court. Figures 9 and 10 contain a statistical analysis of the home districts of the clients of the two courts.

The clients of both judicial courts (3,041 individuals recorded in the *kadıasker* register and 542 in the Kara Su register) can be divided into four main groups: (1) individuals residing in the district that housed the judicial

96 Jankowski, *A Historical-Etymological Dictionary*, 9.

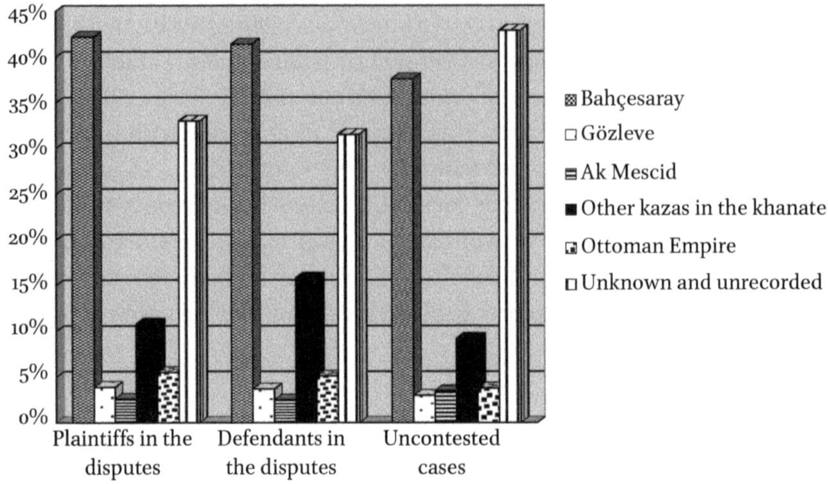

FIGURE 9 The residential affiliations of litigants in the *kadıasker* court.

court, (2) individuals whose residential affiliation was not recorded, (3) inhabitants from other parts of the khanate, and (4) those from the Ottoman Empire and other foreign countries.

Representatives of the first two groups constituted the overwhelming majority (70–80 percent). It is not surprising that among the litigants whose residential affiliation was recorded, local inhabitants outnumber individuals from far-away districts. Presumably, the inhabitants of a given district used their local court more frequently than other judicial fora. One of the serious drawbacks of our analysis is that it was impossible to establish the residential affiliation of about 30 to 40 percent of the litigants. In the majority of entries, this was caused by a lack of data. It is worth asking why Crimean court scribes did not record this information, which was highly recommended by Islamic handbooks of formularies.[97] Their nonchalance in observing chancellery norms is understandable for two types of individuals. First, court scribes very seldom recorded the residential affiliation of high officials, powerful nobles, and members of the ruling dynasty. The court's personnel only needed their name and title to identify them. Second, court scribes dispensed with the residential affiliation in cases concerning simple daily matters, such as debts or purchases of small value. Numerous entries of this kind contain no data about the residential affiliation of the parties involved. Presumably, such daily matters were brought to the court by local inhabitants rather than by individuals from other districts. Thus, we would argue that the majority of cases in which we lack

97 Wakin, *Function of Documents*, 1–35.

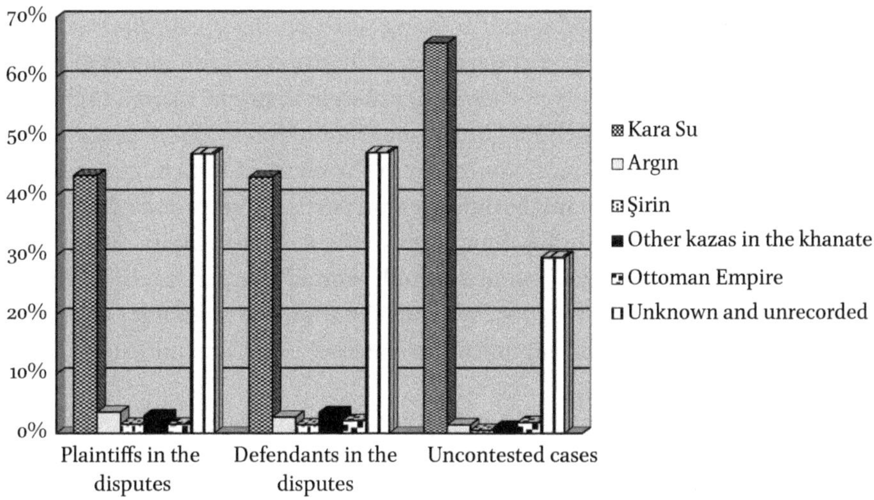

FIGURE 10 The residential affiliations of litigants in the district court in Kara Su.

information on residential affiliation concerns the local inhabitants. Unfortunately, I cannot offer a conclusive argument to support this thesis.

The third group consisted of individuals from Crimean districts other than the one that housed the court. The analysis demonstrates that the court of the *kadıasker* wielded influence over a territory larger than a district court such as the one in Kara Su. According to our results, individuals from the whole khanate brought their suits to the *kadıasker* court.[98] Nonetheless, the number of individuals from districts other than Bahçesaray was limited. Not surprisingly, larger numbers of people came from districts containing populous cities, such as Ak Mescid, Kara Su, and Gözleve. Yet, no single provincial district was represented by more than 4 percent of all the litigants. These results suggest that the khan's subjects from the provinces were reluctant to apply to the *kadıasker* court in the capital. But inhabitants of the Bahçesaray district used the *kadıasker* court frequently. Apparently, they were not formally obliged to first seek justice from their district judge, nor were they intimidated by the *kadıasker*'s authority. These facts indicate that the costs of travel and maintenance in the capital were probably the real obstacle that prevented the khan's subjects from bringing their suits to the *kadıasker* court.

98 The *kadıasker* court registers from the reign of Murad Giray contain cases involving inhabitants of the following Crimean districts: Ak Mescid, Arabat, Argın, Aşağa İçki, Bahçesaray, Baynak, Burulça, Çetirlik, Çongar, Çuyunçu, Dair, Eski Kırım, Ferahkerman, Gözleve, Kaçı, Kara Kurt, Kara Su (Küçük Kara Su, Kara Su-Tamak), Karavul, Kerç, Mangıt, Salgır, Sokal, Şeyh Eli, Şirin, Tamak, (Dib) Tarkhan, Taşlı, and Zuya.

We have already discussed social reasons, such as the corruption of local judges. It seems that such considerations as corruption were deemed to be important in cases involving parties from different districts. Interestingly, the proportion of cases in which litigants came from different districts is considerably higher in the *kadıasker* court than in the court of Kara Su (20 percent versus 1 percent). This fact might indicate that parties from various districts of the khanate preferred to bring their cases to the *kadıasker* court rather than choose a district court that would suit only one of the parties. In addition, such decisions might have taken into consideration the suitability of Bahçesaray and the fact that the capital was a meeting point for individuals from various parts of the state.

The data extracted from the Kara Su judicial records suggest that this court was used almost exclusively by local people. Individuals residing elsewhere, even in neighboring districts like Şirin or Argın, very seldom came to this court as plaintiffs or defendants . These facts indicate that the khan's subjects generally applied to their local court or to the court in the capital.

The khan's courts were also used by foreigners. Most of these came from the Ottoman territories. Many of the Ottomans using the khan's courts resided in the Mangub judicial district of Kefe province. It is noteworthy that individuals from this area appeared in the *kadıasker* court as frequently as the inhabitants of the most populous districts of the khanate. The Ottoman subjects from Mangub were involved in eighty-eight cases recorded in the *kadıasker*'s *sicil*s during Murad Giray's reign. In seventy-six of them, both parties came from Kefe province, mainly from the *kaza* of Mangub. Only twelve cases consisted of contracts or disputes between the subjects of the sultan and of the khan. As no judicial records from Kefe province have survived to our time, we do not have much information about the day-to-day practice of the local courts. The functioning of these courts and the relations between their personnel and local inhabitants remain a mystery. The data extracted from the Crimean *sicil*s suggest that many Ottoman subjects preferred to apply to the khan's judges rather than to Ottoman courts.

Proximity and the availability of the *kadıasker* court must have been important reasons for choosing the khan's court. The Mangub judicial district bordered on that of Bahçesaray. Therefore, the khan's courts in the capital might have been the closest Islamic courts for Ottoman subjects residing near the border with the khanate. There are some indications that there were no significant differences between the law applied in Bahçesaray and that of Kefe province, especially in regard to day-to-day matters. For instance, in one case a litigant appeared before the *kadıasker* court and successfully presented documents issued by the Mangub judiciary as evidence confirming his version of events.[99] Evidently, Ottoman subjects felt that they were judged according to the same norms in the khanate; therefore, it was natural for them to go to Bahçesaray to register claims in such simple matters as the following.

> The case is as follows:
> Sefer, from the village of Ulu Salası,[100] declared in the presence of Mustafa, from the village of Biğa Salası:[101]
> "The aforementioned Mustafa owes me eleven *altun*s. My wish is that the aforementioned person should be heard and the litigation should be decided."
> After interrogation he [i.e., Mustafa] denied the allegation.
> Gazi Halife *el-Kıpti*,[102] an upright Muslim, testified and his testimony was accepted. Then, it was agreed [that the court should] wait for the testimony of a second witness.
> What happened was recorded upon request.
> Case witnesses: Şahbaz Efendi; the gatekeeper Hasan; Hurrazad, who was present; Sefer Gazi, who was present; the well-known *katib* Abdulbaki Efendi; and the others present.[103]

Ottoman subjects appealed to the courts in the khanate when they had a suit against subjects of the khan. Perhaps a plaintiff from the Mangub *kaza*

99 See the title deed issued by the *naib* of Mangub, which was presented in a case concerning the inheritance of land in the *kaza* of Mangub; ORRNB, Fond 917, *defter* 23b/21b/5.

100 The place name is composed of two words. The first is the Turkish adjective *ulu*, which means 'great.' With regard to the second word, Henryk Jankowski translates the topographical term *sala* as 'village.' Hence, the meaning of this place name is 'great village.' Ulu Sala was listed in the district of Mangub in the Russian register from the year 1783 (for further information, see Jankowski, *A Historical-Etymological Dictionary*, 1111–1112). The village of Koca Salası, which name also means "great village," is listed in the Mangub *kaza* in the *defter* of Kefe from the year 1094/1682–83 (NBKM, Or. Dept., Fond D737, fol. 25). Presumably both names refer to the same village.

101 The village was listed in the Russian register from the year 1783 in the district of Mangub (for further information, see Jankowski, *A Historical-Etymological Dictionary*, 313–318). The village of Biga Salası is also listed in the judicial district of Mangub in the *defter* of Kefe from the year 1682 (NBKM, Or. Dept., Fond D737, p. 27).

102 The term *kıpti* denotes both a Copt and a Gypsy. Given that numerous Gypsies (Roma) inhabited the Balkans and Eastern Europe, presumably, Gazi Halife was a Gypsy rather than a Copt. It is noteworthy that he was described as a 'just' (*'udul*) witness, whose testimony was accepted in the sharia court. For more on the complex status of the Gypsies in the Ottoman Empire, see E. Ginio, "Neither Muslims nor Zimmis: The Gypsies (Roma) in the Ottoman State," *Romani Studies—5th Series* 14, no. 2 (2004), 117–144.

103 ORRNB, Fond 917, *defter* 23b/7b/3.

presumed that it was easier to summon the defendant to a Crimean court that to an Ottoman venue. In such a case, a judicial sentence passed down by a Crimean judge might be more effective than a sentence issued by an Ottoman authority. Such considerations might have motivated the plaintiff in the case quoted below.

> This case is as follows:
> Fatma Hatun, daughter of Kıtas, from the village of Gavur[104] in the judicial district of Mangub, declared, in the presence of prominent Sefer Şah, son of Cihan Şah, from the village of Markat(?) in the judicial district of Şeyh Eli:
> "The aforementioned Sefer Şah stabbed my husband Can Arslan,[105] son of Can Gazi, with a knife for no reason and killed him. As the noted Sefer Şah is willing to pay [me] compensation, we have reached a mutual agreement. He should pay [me] seventy *altun*s. Since the agreement was concluded, I have received [only a part] of this sum. The rest of it (sixty-five *altun*s) should be paid in ten days. Then I will abandon all my actions against him and release him from all previous obligations. Even if other actions were brought [against him], they should not be accepted [by the court]."
> The aforementioned Sefer Şah confirmed the recorded statement of the aforementioned Fatma.
> The mutual agreement that was concluded was recorded upon request.
> Written in the third week of Sefer, in the year 1092 [12 March–20 March 1681].
> Case witnesses: the pride of the ulema and the former *kadı* [of the district of] Şirin, Abdulhalim Efendi; Mehmed Şah, [son of] Hami Efendi; Abdulaziz Efendi, [son of] Abdulgani Çelebi; Mehmed Çelebi, [son of] Huseyn; Bekir Efendi, [son of] Şaban; Ahmed Efendi, [son of] Abdulcemil;

---

104 The *defter* of Kefe province (1094/1682–83) lists a village of Gavur in the judicial district of Mangub (NBKM, Or. Dept., D737, fol. 36; see also Jankowski, *A Historical-Etymological Dictionary*, 478–479).

105 Since the judicial entry does not list any other relatives of Arslan, Fatma Hatun might have been the only person entitled to blood money after his tragic death. In the *defter* of Kefe, composed only one year later, she is not registered among the landowners from the village of Gavur. This fact suggests that either Fatma's husband had not owned any land there or she sold it soon after his death; cf. NBKM, Or. Dept., Fond D737, fol. 36. In cases involving land in the Mangub *kaza*, it is possible to identify landowners mentioned in the *sicil*s from among those also listed in the Kefe *defter*, see, for example, a case concerning Abbas, Sefer, Koçkar, and another Sefer from the village of Karlu (ORRNB, Fond 917, 22/19a/3; NBKM, Or. Dept., Fond D737, fol. 26).

> Abdulbaki Efendi; a former *katib*, Abdulhalim Efendi; Azamet Mirza, [son of] Mustafa Mirza; Adil Şah, [son of] Mehmed Mirza; the well-known *katib* Şahbaz Efendi; the well-known Hurrazad Atalık; Kaplan, who was present, and the others.[106]

In this case, the high prestige of the *kadıasker* must have played a role in the choice of a legal venue. As there were no significant differences between the law applied in Bahçesaray and in the province of Kefe (see our arguments above), the Ottoman subjects stood a good chance of having a fair trial in Bahçesaray, according to the norms that were familiar to them. Although our knowledge of the education of the Crimean judiciary is limited, it seems likely that the Crimean *kadıasker*s were better educated than provincial judges of the Mangub district. Therefore, Ottoman subjects living near Bahçesaray might have preferred to apply to the more learned Crimean *kadıasker* than to their local judge.

Finally, the *kadıasker* court constituted an alternative judicial forum. The institution of appeal from a lower court to a higher one was not accepted in classical Islamic jurisprudence. In theory, a sentence properly passed down by a Muslim judge was conclusive and a case that was resolved *lege artis* (following legal procedures and in accordance with the law) was settled once and for all. If someone wanted an issue to be ruled on by a judge of higher rank, he or she had to bring his/her case directly to his court or ask the local judge to send it there before the trial. In practice, litigants who were dissatisfied with the outcome of the proceedings took the same disputes to different courts, even multiple times.[107] The *kadıasker* court in Bahçesaray, therefore, likely offered inhabitants of the *kaza* of Mangub another opportunity to obtain favorable judicial sentences. We have found no indication that the court of *kadıasker* acted as an appellate court.[108]

Another group of entries consists of cases concerning real estate owned by the khan's subjects and located in the Ottoman Empire. In the *defter* of Kefe province dated 1682–83, it is possible to identify land owned by the Girays and the high officials in the Mangub *kaza*. Thus, we know about seventeen properties belonging to seven Giray princes and real estate of the khan's viziers, Mirahor Bekir Mirza, Hazinedar Sadık Ağa, Tat ağası Evliya Çelebi, and Yalı

106 ORRNB, Fond 917, *defter* 23b/104b/6.

107 Ergene, *Local Court*, 107.

108 The problem of judicial retrials and appeals in Ottoman legal practice is a topic of ongoing debate. For summaries, see Gradeva, "On Judicial Hierarchy," 271–274; Tuğ, *Politics of Honor*, 195–200.

ağası Ahmed Ağa.[109] For instance, a Crimean prince Canibeg Giray established through his agent, Inkermanlı Hacı Mustafa, son of Mehmed, a pious foundation consisting of a mill and a garden in the village of Tüli in the judicial district of Mangub.[110] The income derived from this property was earmarked for fifteen ulema (assigned a daily stipend of 2 or 3 *akçe*s), to pray and recite the Quran.[111] Common subjects of the khan also owned properties on both sides of the Tatar-Ottoman border. For instance, Ali, son of Hasan, from the judicial district of Bahçesaray, claimed that Nasif, son of Abdullah, from the village of Tüli in the judicial district of Mangub, constituted a part of the property bequeathed to him by his late father.[112]

All these cases are evidence of the fact that the inhabitants of the Mangub *kaza* and other neighboring Ottoman lands frequently appealed to the khan's courts to solve their disputes and record their contracts. It is significant that the sentences and documents issued by the judges were honored and considered legally valid in the Ottoman Empire, and vice versa. These facts further confirm that similar legal prescriptions were applied on both sides of the Tatar-Crimean border.

2.5 *Winning a Trial*

How did litigants win their trials? What kind of evidence was most convincing? What type of strategy secured favorable outcomes of disputes? Litigants in Crimean courts must have asked these and similar questions. The tables below present the bases of decisions in litigation: acknowledgment of guilt (e.g., the testimonies and oaths of witnesses) and adjudicative tools (representation, *hüccet*s, *yarlığ*s, *fetva*s, expert opinions, information gathered by the court

---

109 NBKM, Or. Dept., Fond D737, fols. 24–68.

110 The *defter* of Kefe province contains information on a garden of 40 *dönüm*s owned by Canibeg Giray in Tüli (NBKM, Or. Dept., Fond D737, fol. 52). Among the properties listed in the village, there is no pious foundation (*vaqf*), although we encounter them in other locations. Canibek's foundation of a *vakf* was registered in the *sicil*s in February 1679 (at the end of the month of Zilhicce 1089, see ORRNB, Fond 917, *defter* 23b/8a/5; 23b/8b/3). Based on the present state of research on the Kefe *defter*, we have no way of knowing what caused such a discrepancy between the tax register and the court register. The notes in the Kefe *defter* indicate that the surveyors visited the villages and collected data in situ (see, for example, fol. 27). Thus, they would have learned about *vakf*s, even those recently established. Perhaps the surveyors did not pay much attention to the Girays' properties, which, judging by estates owned in Rumelia by other family members, might have been exempted from all taxes. On the Girays' estates in Rumelia, see H. Kırımlı, *Geray Hanedanı Mensuplarının Rumeli'ne İskanı*, paper presented at International Congress of Ottoman Social and Economic History (Sofia, 2017); Williams, *The Crimean Tatars*, 206.

111 ORRNB, Fond 917, *defter* 23b/8b/1.

112 ORRNB, Fond 917, *defter* 23b/22a/4.

officials) in Crimean courts during the reign of Murad Giray.[113] In total, there are 1,017 references to the various tools of litigation that litigants used in the *kadıasker* court (KC) and 150 in the Kara Su court (KSC).

In the Crimean khanate a substantial number of cases ended with one of the parties confessing their guilt (KC: 259 of 854, KSC: 45 of 112). Of the identified bases of decisions in litigation in the two courts, 25 percent were decided based on confessions.

Since Islamic law gives a clear preference to oral testimony, it is not surprising that more than one-third of litigants in the *kadıasker* court and over one-half of litigants in the Kara Su court either produced witnesses to support their claims (26 percent in the *kadıasker* court and 27 percent in the district court of Kara Su) or took oaths themselves (KC: 8 percent, KSC: 25 percent). While the ratio of witness testimonies is similar in both courts, we can observe a striking difference in the way these oaths were used. As Coşgel and Ergene rightly point out in reference to the Ottoman Empire "an oath is proposed by the party who assumes the proof responsibility in litigation, but fails to provide evidence."[114] Thus, a high ratio of oaths in evidentiary processes in the district court may indicate that many of the litigants came to court ill-prepared for trial, without witnesses to support their claims. The relatively low ratio of oaths among in the *kadıasker* court suggests that people who chose to take part in litigation in this forum had better access to evidentiary procedures other than oaths. Most probably, the higher ratio of elite members among the litigants in the *kadıasker* court in comparison to their proportion in Kara Su court (35 percent vs. 10 percent) might partially explain this difference. The research of Coşgel and Ergene suggests that elite members could substantiate their claims in court more effectively than other litigants. The practice in Kastamonu suggests that they rarely took oaths. Women and men without titles, on the other hand, more often substantiated their claims using this evidentiary procedure.[115]

Islamic jurisprudence regulated who could effectively bear testimony in court. In short, witnesses were supposed to be upright, free Muslims. In contrast to men, women faced certain limitations as witnesses.[116] In the Ottoman Empire, as Coşgel and Ergene emphasize by drawing on popular legal texts and jurisprudential commentaries, "there are also specific standards based on

113 The bases of decisions and their division into types, such as the acknowledgment of guilt, the use of evidentiary tools, and the use of adjudicative tools is modeled on a comprehensive discussion by Metin Coşgel and Boğaç Ergene (Coşgel and Ergene, *Economics of Ottoman Justice*, 224–251).

114 Coşgel and Ergene, *Economics of Ottoman Justice*, 239.

115 Ibid., 242, 272, 282–288.

116 Peirce, *Morality Tales*, 176, 191.

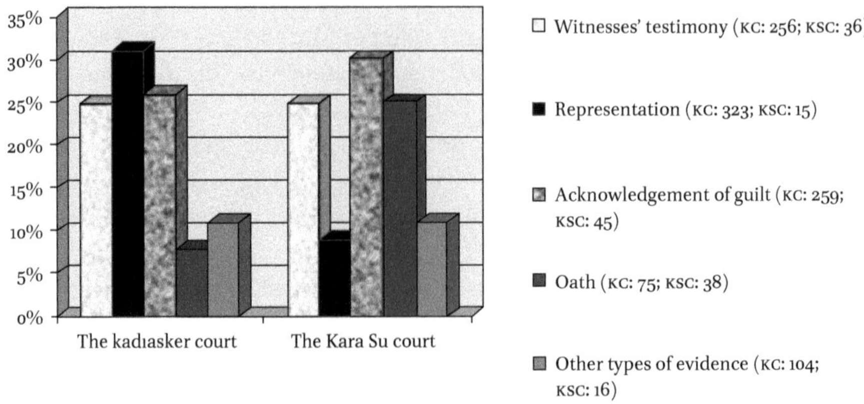

FIGURE 11 The ratio of bases of decisions in Crimean courts.

the relationship between litigants and witnesses,"[117] These rules required the rejection of testimony by individuals who were closely related, by family or professional ties, with the litigants.[118] Unfortunately, we cannot know whether the legal texts used in the Ottoman Empire influenced judicial procedures in the khanate to the same extent.

The high value placed on oral testimony is clearly visible in cases that depened on references to previous proceedings. Many litigants limited themselves to producing oral witness testimonies to affirm that earlier rulings or settlements relevant in the current litigation took place.[119] The parties, who presented the certificates (*hüccet*) or title deeds (*mülkname*), still produced witnesses to confirm what happened during the previous proceedings. For instance, in the trial against the inhabitants of the village of Necsan, Subhan Gazi Ağa presented not only the certificate confirming his right to the disputed piece of land, but he also brought ten witnesses. He found his opponents were well-prepared for the trial. First, they made a counter-claim challenging the legality of his certificate. As soon as the burden of proof was on their side, they produced the title deed and testimony of numerous witnesses (three recorded by name, the rest as "the many others"). These actions convinced Subhan Gazi Ağa to admit that he made a mistake. The entry ends with a description of the notary's actions conducted by the court; that is, the title deed presented by the

117 Coşgel and Ergene, *Economics of Ottoman Justice*, 226.
118 Ibid., 226–227.
119 See, for example, a case recorded in the *kadıasker* court involving inhabitants of the Kaçı district. The plaintiff brought to Bahçesaray two witnesses who confirmed that the parties had already concluded an amicable settlement before the local judge; ORRNB, Fond 917, *defter* 23b/67b/2.

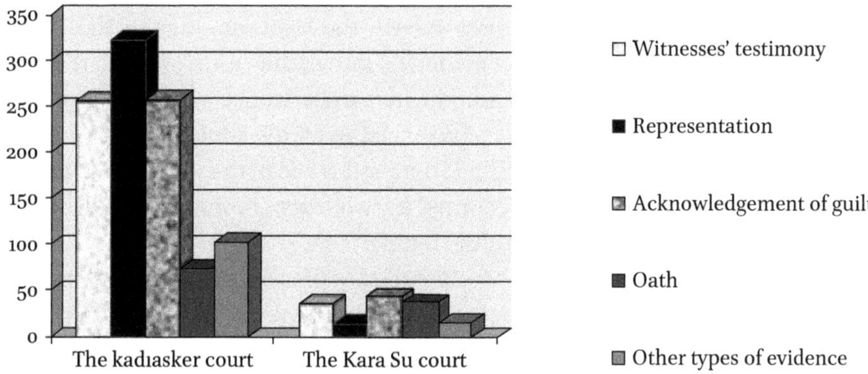

FIGURE 12 The frequency of various bases of decisions in Crimean courts.

inhabitants was registered, and they obtained a sealed confirmation of the current proceeding in order to prevent further disputes.[120] With respect to the records of court proceedings, the practice in Crimean courts seems to resemble the documents written in court in Kastamonu, according to the research conducted by Coşgel and Ergene. Their findings indicate that with the exception of copies of imperial registers, the written court records did not constitute the sole basis of adjudication, but required support from witness testimony.[121] Yet, we believe that the case discussed above concerning land in Necsan, and other cases recorded in the Crimean *sicil*s, are evidence of the high value litigants attached to court records by, and the important role of this evidence in the proceedings.[122]

Next to the certificates and title deeds issued by courts in the khanate and in the Ottoman Empire, Crimean litigants invoked two other types of written documents: the *yarliğ*s of the Crimean khans and *kalga*s, and the legal opinions (*fetva*s) of Crimean muftis. The validity of the first type of documents was not questioned in the courts during the reign of Murad Giray. It seems that producing this type of evidence successfully confirmed the claims of their owners.[123]

Moving on to the much discussed issue of the role played by *fetva*s in litigation, an issue that was mentioned in Chapter 4, again, judges were not obliged to issue sentences according to the legal opinions of the mufti. Moreover, *fetva*s were not considered legitimate forms of evidence in Muslim classical law. The

120 ORRNB, Fond 917, *defter* 22/78b/1.

121 Coşgel and Ergene, *Economics of Ottoman Justice*, 237.

122 For more on the use of written documents in Ottoman courts, see Peirce, *Morality Tales*, 279–285.

123 ORRNB, Fond 917, *defter* 22/102a/6; 23a/223b/2.

Crimean practice followed this rule; indeed, the legal opinions of the mufti were not used as a unique mode of evidence, rather, they were presented along with other types of evidence and adjudicative tools. Nonetheless, the fact that the litigants supported the validity of their claims by referring to legal opinions of a mufti indicates that the latter had some influence in the outcome of a proceeding. Moreover, the verdicts recorded in two cases involving the use of the mufti's legal opinion do agree with the latter's view.[124]

Following Coşgel and Ergene, we included representation (*vekalet*) in the category of adjudicative tools. Their analysis on the *vekil*s and the individuals who sought the assistance of *vekil*s in Kastamonu reveals that women were considerably more likely than men to engage representatives. Among male litigants, those with titles were most frequently represented in court by a *vekil*. The research of Coşgel and Ergene calls attention to the fact that individuals preferred to appoint titled individuals and male members of prominent families as *vekil*s. According to Coşgel and Ergene, this finding suggests that litigants chose representatives from the higher echelons of society, because the elevated status of individuals directly translated into a greater chance of success in the court processes.[125] With regard to gender and the social status of *vekil*s and their principals, our observations of the Crimean Khanate are generally consistent with those based on the Kastamonu records. More women than men brought representatives to the courts (in the *kadıasker* court: 124 to 74; in the Kara Su court the difference is very small: 8 to 7), while more men than women acted as *vekil*s in litigation (in the *kadıasker* court: 121 to 3; in the Kara Su court: 14 to 1). Among male litigants seeking assistance from a *vekil* we encounter members of the highest echelons of the society, e.g., the Girays or the *karaçı beğ*s.[126] Like Ottoman litigants, Crimean men and women often entrusted their disputes to individuals of elevated status, which suggests that they believed it could increase their chance of winning a trial.

With regard to the number of representatives in litigations, Coşgel and Ergene noted that *vekil*s were not particularly common, as about 12 percent of litigants acted through *vekil*s. The proportion in the khanate are visibly different than Anatolia, as they amount to 5 percent for Kara Su (15 of 276 litigants) and 18 percent in the *kadıasker* court (323 of 1,770). We can only speculate about why parties involved in disputes in district courts (relatively) seldom entrusted *vekil*s to deal with their cases, while litigants in the *kadıasker* court opted for this solution more often. We can identify two possible explanations. First, the

124 See, for example, ORRNB, Fond 917, *defter* 22/78b/1.

125 Coşgel and Ergene, *Economics of Ottoman Justice*, 246–251.

126 ORRNB, Fond 917, 23a/142b/7, *defter* 25/5b/4.

kadıasker court had a significantly higher ratio of non-local clients than the Kara Su court. It seems likely that individuals from outside the capital would appoint an agent, to enable them to stay home rather than travel to Bahçesaray. Second, the differences in social characteristics of the clients of the two courts might also have contributed to the fact that representatives were more popular in the *kadıasker* court than in Kara Su court.

In the Crimean *sicil*s, we very seldom encountered some types of adjudicative tools. For example, only one entry recorded during the reign of Murad Giray mentions the use of an expert opinion (*ehl-i hibret*).[127] As Ron Shaham states, it is unclear who was supposed to summon experts to an Islamic court. In what circumstances was an expert provided by a *kadı*, and when could litigants hire an expert? Moreover, it is not clear whether experts were regarded as advisers to *kadı*s or special witnesses for litigants. According to classical law, *kadı*s were supposed to consult experts in matters beyond common legal knowledge. At the same time, the law did not forbid private persons from summoning experts. Litigants in various Muslim states won their cases when experts presented options substantiating their claims as just.[128] The single entry in the Crimean *sicil*s in which an expert opinion appears, concerns a woman who demanded an increase in her allowance (*nafaka*). The entry is formulated in such a way that it is impossible to establish whether it was the plaintiff or the judge who summoned an expert to the court. The woman complained that her allowance, which had been fixed by her husband two years earlier, did not cover her needs. As her husband was a soldier in one of the Crimean fortresses on the northern border (Şahkerman), he did not increase the amount himself. The statement recorded in the entry is followed by the expert, who acknowledged that her claim was justified, as the stipend was too small. As a consequence, the judge ordered that it be increased. Clearly, the woman benefited from the opinion of the expert. Therefore, it would not be surprising for her to have brought him to the court. Nonetheless, it is possible that he was summoned by the *kadı*, who needed advice on socio-economic matters.

Information and objects gathered at crime scenes, so called circumstantial evidence, were rarely mentioned in the Crimean *sicil*s. There is only one case that refers to a *kadı*'s inspection of the murder scene.[129] In another, there are some indications that a *kadı* visited the place where a crime had been committed.[130] As I emphasize elsewhere, the use of circumstantial evidence as

127 ORRNB, Fond 917, *defter* 23b/57a/1; unfortunately, their numbers and names are not recorded.

128 Shaham, *Expert Witness in Islamic Courts*, 58–59, 76–77.

129 ORRNB, Fond 917, *defter* 23a/221a/2.

130 ORRNB, Fond 917, *defter* 23b/78a/1.

expressed in an expert's opinions or gathered during the inspection of a murder scene led to the mitigation of an otherwise formalistic classical procedure. We can conclude from the examination of the court registers that circumstantial evidence was rarely used in the khanate.

• • •

To conclude, the khanate's political institutions were rooted in Islamic, Golden Horde, and Ottoman traditions. Similarly, the khanate's tax system exemplifies how prescriptions of various origins could coexist in one state. Sometimes it is unclear why a specific rule from one origin was applied in a particular matter. Conflicts concerning certain taxes indicate that the khans had to take into account the interest of their subjects and could not necessarily introduce new measures at will. The case concerning the sheep tax demonstrates that Crimean subjects could successfully prevent their ruler from changing the law to their detriment.

In private matters, Hanafi doctrine was followed. The dominance of the Hanafi school was rooted in the heritage of the Golden Horde and further strengthened by the influence of the Ottomans. There are some indications that in two areas related to private matters Ottoman legal solutions were integrated into Crimean law. In criminal matters heard in Crimean courts, the principle of private prosecution was applied in cases such as homicide or bodily harm. Our research on the Crimean *sicil*s suggests that plaintiffs in these types of cases sought retaliation or financial compensation in accordance with Islamic law. Data from the *sicil*s suggests that the *kadı* sentenced those convicted of homicide, assault, and sexual offenses to discretionary punishment (*ta'zir*), which was accepted in classical jurisprudence. We found no information on discretionary punishment involving the payment of fines to the treasury, as in the Ottoman practice.

The basic statistical analysis I utilized provides data on the social origins of the parties in uncontested cases and the litigants in disputes, their gender, and residential affiliation. The analysis reveals differences in the way the two types of courts were used by individuals with different social characteristics. One of the most important results may be the disparity between the ratio of elite members appearing before the *kadıasker* court and the Kara Su court. The data presented suggest that while they constituted over 30 percent of the clients in the first type of court, in the Kara Su court, their ratio did not exceed 10 percent. These dissimilarities point to differences in prestige and the workings of these types of courts. In terms of the strategies applied during the proceedings, the litigants of both courts preferred oral testimony to written documentation.

The ratio of oaths (8 percent in the *kadıasker* court to 24 percent in the Kara Su court) in the two courts differed significantly, which might suggest that the social structure of the litigants who appeared in the courts translated into their ability to secure witness testimony. With regard to the bases of decisions in litigation, the Crimean practice seems to have been in accordance with the classical doctrine on the subject. Although the narrative sources mention the possibility of using torture to extract confessions in the case of theft, we have not yet identified any case that confirms this allegation. It is worth mentioning that, in general, litigants could (and did) produce evidence to support their claims. One seldom encounters cases in which the parties could not substantiate their allegations and still decided to bring them to court (8 percent in the *kadıasker* court and 3 percent in the district court of Kara Su). Here again, we refer to Ergene, who examined certain unsubstantiated claims brought to court as a way to seek a *kadı*'s help in mediation. Given this theory, the difference in the number of unsubstantiated claims between the *kadıasker* court and the Kara Su court would indicate that more individuals sought the assistance of the *kadıasker* judge. This may be related to the higher prestige associated with judges appointed to this post.

Conclusion: A Fragile Balance

In the chapters above, we have described the fragile balance of power between the main Crimean institutions and the various social groups. The way in which power was legally founded was also of great interest to this study. The concluding chapter seems to be the right place to address the utility of the results presented and suggest further avenues of research. The aim of this study was twofold. First, to provide a general description of the core institutions of the Crimean Khanate with special attention to the reign of Murad Giray. My analysis of divergent types of narrative, diplomatic, and judicial sources dating to the period 1532–1774 served this purpose. Yet, it is clear that only carefully searching for information in the whole collection of the Crimean *sicil*s will provide a database sufficient to conduct more nuanced research on the core institutions of the khanate. We certainly need more case studies focused on relations between the members of the Crimean elite, to understand their family connections, career patterns, wealth, and the extent of their dependency on the ruler. Research on these issues would add to our knowledge of the evolution of the most important political institutionsin the period between the reforms of Sahib Giray and the Russian annexation of the khanate.

Second, the study aimed to describe the law and the workings of the sharia courts during the reign of Murad Giray (1678–83). Through an in-depth analysis of the court registers of this period, I was led to a deeper understanding of the judicial prerogatives of the khan and his appointees, as well as limitations of their power. These issues are closely related to questions on the relations between the ruler and the members of his council (such as the *kalga*, the *nuraddin*, the *karaçı beğ*s, the vizier, the *defterdar*, the mufti, and the *kadıasker*). The limited number of entries concerning these most important officeholders leaves us unable to provide clear answers in reference to their usage of the sharia court and the limitations of the khan's authority in the territories of the *kalga*'s domain and the *beylik*s of the *karaçı* families. We hope that future research conducted on the other Crimean court registers will provide enough material to verify our hypotheses concerning, among others: (1) the limits of the *kalga*'s authority in his domain, (2) the judicial role of the khan's council, (3) the role of the muftis in the Crimean judicial system, (4) the judicial and administrative duties of the *kadı*s in the districts including a *karaçı beylik*, (5) the usage of the sharia courts by the inhabitants of a *karaçı beylik*, (6) the usage of the court of the district *kadı* or the *kadıasker* court by the members of the *karaçı* families, and (7) the reasons behind the various ways the two types of courts were used by elite members of society.

 | DOI:10.1163/9789004384323_008

It is clear that there is still much to learn about the political system and practice of law in the khanate and it is safe to say that a better understanding of these issues will follow from further research on the Crimean *sicil*s. The study of the court records in the khanate would definitely benefit from the application of a more subtle quantitative approach modeled on the methodology designed by Çoşgul and Ergene for research on legal practices in Kastamonu. Yet, we argue that the present study provides a general description of the vital political and judicial institutions of the khanate and offers a detailed portrait of these during the reign of Murad Giray. The previous chapters juxtaposed the solutions applied in the Crimean political and judicial institutions with those of the Ottoman Empire and the Golden Horde. In this section, however, I aim to understand whether relations between powerholders such as the ruler, his council, the nobility, and the diet in the khanate and in the European states are comparable. If 'Europe' had existed as a unifying notion in the early modern period, would the Crimean Khanate have had a place in it?

Presumably, the religious differences would have prevailed and the khanate, as an Islamic state, would have fallen beyond this notion. The majority of contemporary research also does not consider the Crimean Khanate among the early modern European states. Moreover, most textbooks do not consider the khanate a state with its own original political system. When it is mentioned, the khanate is treated as a semi-nomadic, watered-down version of the Golden Horde, or yet another vassal state of the Ottoman Empire.[1] In the present study, I demonstrate that the khanate's political system was a combination of well organized and well developed institutions that were rooted in different traditions (Mongol, Islamic, and Ottoman). Therefore, power in the khanate was divided in an uncommon way. Nonetheless, as Alan Fisher states, the khanate "met all of the prerequisites for early modern statehood."[2] Now,we can inquire as to whether its political system had features in common with those in Europe. If so, to which of the European political systems could it be compared?

We would suggest that the Crimean Khanate resembles, to some extent, the system of the limited monarchy. We cannot ignore the similarities between the political institutions in the Crimean Khanate and some of the limited monarchies that existed in Europe. Here we would focus on the institutions of the monarch, the state council, and the diet.

---

1 N. Davies, *Europe: A History* (Oxford, 1996), 105–106; T. Munck, *Europa XVII wieku (1598–1700). Państwo, konflikty i porządek społeczny* (Warsaw, 1998), 263; A. Podraza (ed.), *Wielka historia świata*, vol. 7—*Świat w XVII wieku* (Cracow and Warsaw, 2005), 7:523.

2 Fisher, *Crimean Tatars*, 17.

In theory, the khan was an elected monarch chosen by an elite group from his state, who assembled in the form of a diet (*kurultay*). The same can be said about the elections of the rulers of the Polish-Lithuanian Commonwealth or the Holy Roman Empire. As in the Holy Roman Empire (de facto since the fifteenth century, with the sole interruption in 1740 when a non-Habsburg candidate was elected), the Crimean khan could only be elected from among the members of the ruling dynasty. Outwardly, the khan enjoyed remarkable military and political power. His domain, which covered an extended part of the khanate, provided him with economic and military resources greater than those of the most powerful of the *karaçı beğ*s. As in numerous European countries, the khan administered his state through a council, which consisted of the most important dignitaries and officials who had military, administrative, and judicial functions. Most were his appointees, whom he could promote, punish or even execute at will. Despite some risks, service in the khan's household offered tempting rewards in the form of official posts, economic security, and ennoblement. Nonetheless, the khan could not appoint every member of his council. In accordance with his ancient privileges, he was obliged to accept the *karaçı beğ*s chosen by the aristocratic clans as his advisers. The latter's power derived from semi-autonomous *beylik*s, which secured their financial independence and provided them with military power. Therefore, the khan's policy was closely monitored by his most powerful vassals. Moreover, it seems to have been limited not only by the Quran, but also by vaguely defined customary laws called "ancient laws" or "Chingisid laws." These guaranteed the rights of both the nobility and the commoners (e.g., restrictions on the introduction of new taxes).

In addition to his council, the khan could approach and consult with members of the *kurultay* about his decisions and seek their support for his policies. Yet, we must bear in mind that the diet could also be summoned by the *karaçı beğ*s, if they found that the khan's policies threatened their rights and the vital interests of their clans and clients. Although much remains unknown about the *kurultay*, it is clear that in the Crimean Khanate it was a consultative institution of the Tatar nobles with roots in the Mongol custom of gathering for military purposes. In the case of a conflict, the khan and the *karaçı beğ*s would seek support from the remaining members of the *kurultay*. If members of the *karaçı* families were successful, they could start a "legal rebellion" designed to change the khan's policies or even replace him with a new ruler. Similar mechanisms of legal resistance by the political elite against an unjust ruler existed in various limited European monarchies, for example, in England, in the Holy Roman Empire or in the Polish-Lithuanian Commonwealth.

It would be an oversimplification to consider the khanate's internal policy a fragile equilibrium between just two parties, i.e., those of the khan and the aristocracy. Such a theory overlooks the fact that the Ottomans seemed to have a vested interest in maintaining the balance of power between the two groups in the khanate. From the second half of the fifteenth century, these rival factions saw in the Ottoman presence an opportunity to turn the scales in their favor. They used to seek the Sublime Porte's support in their mutual conflicts. Although we have much to learn about Crimean-Ottoman relations, there was a certain constancy in the Ottoman policy toward the Crimean Tatars. The Sublime Porte needed the khan to be powerful enough to lead the Tatar nobility as auxiliary troops in Ottoman campaigns. Therefore, the khan received military and financial support,[3] which strengthened his position vis-à-vis his vassals and constituted a vital part of the khan's income. In the eighteenth century, with the decrease of income derived from the slave trade, its importance grew. Since the khan was not supposed to become independent from the Ottomans, the sultan's support was not sufficient to allow the Crimean ruler to establish a permanent hegemony over his vassals. The sultan also carefully listened to the complaints of the latter concerning the khan. In addition, the Ottomans could not antagonize the *karaçı* families, as they and their clients constituted a vital part of the Crimean army.

Undoubtedly, the extent of Ottoman influence over the khanate changed over time, particularly during the early modern period. In the mid-sixteenth century, Khan Sahib Giray was accused of seeking to challenge Ottoman power, a realistic enough threat to hasten his fall. In the 1620s, Mehmed III Giray seized the Crimean throne without Ottoman consent and managed to keep it for four years. Yet, at the end of the seventeenth century the khans no longer dared to oppose the Ottoman sultans. As noted, Murad Giray accepted the unjust Ottoman decision of his deposition after the second siege of Vienna. In 1702, Devlet II Giray, yet another outstanding Crimean ruler, abdicated despite the strong support of his vassals.[4] Where, or when, did the turning point in the Ottoman-Crimean relations take place. It would seem to be located in the second half of the seventeenth century, and related to the changes in the balance of power in Central Europe and the Black Sea region. It is worth emphasizing that between the mid sixteenth and the end of the seventeenth century, the theater of Tatar-Ottoman-Russian war shifted from the Volga to the Dniepr and even beyond. This fact must have significantly influenced Ottoman-Tatar relations. In 1569, the Tatars succeeded in foiling the Ottoman project

3 Fisher, *Between Russians*, 19–34; M. Ivanics, "Entstehung und Quellenwert der Krimtatarischen *Tiyiş* Defters," *Acta Orientalia Academiae Scientiarium Hungaricae* 47, nos. 1–2 (1994), 115–122.

4 Abdulgaffar Kyrymi, *Umdet al-akhbar*, 158.

of recapturing Astrakhan from Muscovite hands. Apparently, the Ottoman presence on the northern shore of the Caspian Sea threatened Tatar claims to its Chingisid heritage.[5] Two years later, the Tatars proved powerful enough to burn the suburbs of Moscow. Yet, by the 1670s they dared not oppose the new northern policy of the Ottomans. A report by a Polish emissary, Stanisław Karwowski, which dates from this period, points to this conclusion. At the end of 1671, he was secretly received by Selim I Giray, Murad Giray's predecessor on the Crimean throne; he found the ruler already gathering his troops in a military camp near Bahçesaray for the war against the Polish-Lithuanian Commonwealth. The khan offered the emissary the following apology for the unusual circumstances in which their meeting took place: "Do not mind that I receive you in this way but I must keep our meeting secret from the [Ottoman] *kapıcı başı*. After all, the Turks have already branded you [the Poles] as an enemy in all their lands."[6] When Karwowski stated that the Polish-Lithuanian Commonwealth trusted in their mutual friendship as stipulated in the Polish-Tatar treaty, Selim I Giray answered,

> With all my soul I regret the loss of your friendship, because the former king showed me a lot of kindness. I know all your dignitaries very well, especially the Marshall [i.e., Jan Sobieski] with whom I spent such a long time during the war in Ukraine. But what shall I do? It is not my will, but the will of my Lord, the Caesar, with whose grace I ascended this throne of mine. And I will tell you something in secret, but do not repeat it. If I saw you as strong as before, I would support you and I would say: "Hold on [my] Caesar, the Poles are not guilty, they are our friends, who stand by us whether in good or in bad." The whole Crimea could repeat these words, because many of their rights are also violated by the Porte. But when I see you so impoverished, weak and friendless, what shall I do? I will ruin myself, while I will not save you .... For a long time the Porte prepared itself against you, but either we advised against [the war with you] or we frightened them [by telling them how] powerful and rich you are. But now when they have had a closer look at you, they disdain you and say that within a year they will take your land as far as Warsaw or Cracow. Please understand, therefore, that I will neither send my envoy with you

5 Smirnov, *Krymskoe khanstvo*, 325.

6 Kluczycki, Franciszek (ed.), *Acta Historica res gestas Poloniae illustratia*, vol. 2, *Pisma do wieku i spraw Jana Sobieskiego*, vol. 1, Part I (Cracow, 1880), 1:748.

> to the king nor will I dismiss you without conferring with the [Ottoman] *kapıcı başı*. Otherwise I will be suspected.[7]

In view of this story, it seems that somewhere during the last quarter of the seventeenth century, Crimean inner relations ceased to play the important role it had played up to that moment in the policy of the greater Black Sea region. The khan and the aristocracy had become too weak to successfully influence, let alone oppose, the new northern policy of the Ottoman Empire, although the Tatars must have realized that the Ottoman conquest of the southern province of Poland-Lithuania would deprive them of an important source of slaves and spoils.[8] When, in the eighteenth century, the theater of war gradually came closer to the northern borders of the Ottoman Empire, the Crimea became just one of many border provinces, threatened with secession or foreign conquest, an event that ensued a century later.

7 Kluczycki (ed.), *Acta Historica*, 1:748–749.
8 Kołodziejczyk, *Crimean Khanate and Poland-Lithuania*, 187.

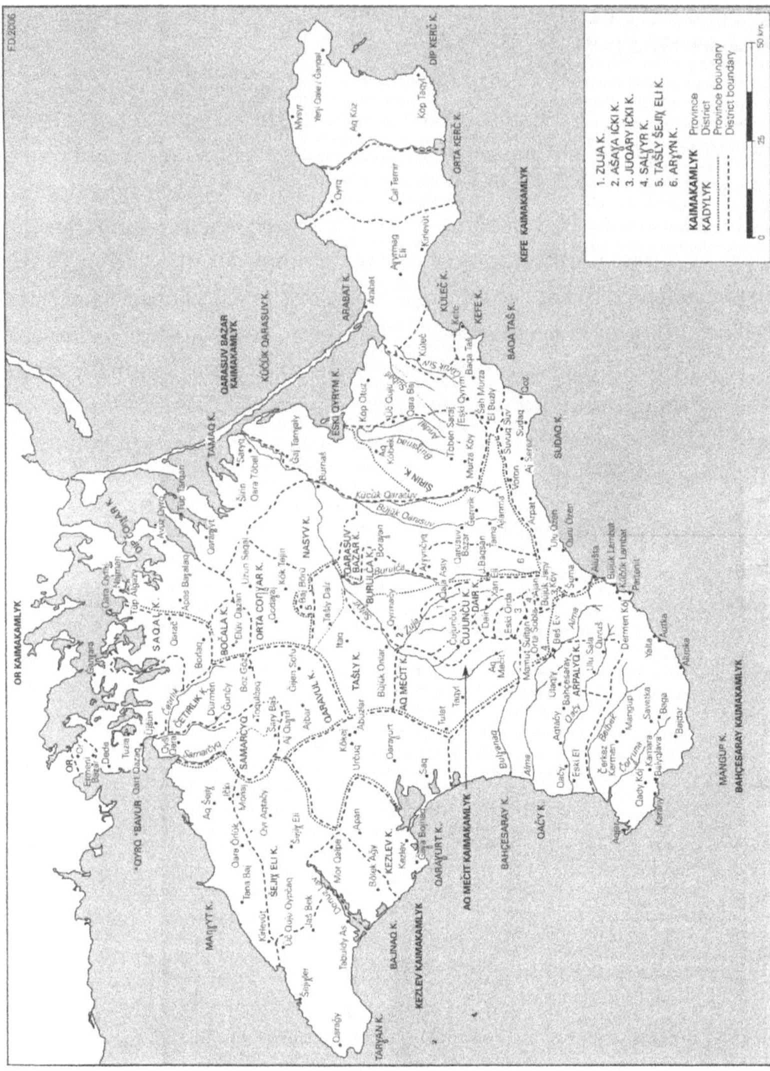

FIGURE 13 *Map of the Crimea at the end of Tatar Khanate.* (First published in Henryk Jankowski, "A Historical-Etymological Dictionary of Pre-Russian Habitation Names of the Crimea", Brill: Leiden-Boston, 2006)

Appendices

APPENDIX I

Transliteration, Translation, and Facsimile of the Order Issued by Khan Canibeg Giray

(ORRNB, fond 917, defter 1/71b/1)[1]

1 Transliteration

Canibeg Giray Han sözüm

Kıdvetü'l-kuzât ve'l-hükkâm umdetü vülâtu'l-islâm bi'l-fil Gözleve Efendisi ve Kara Su

Efendisi ve Ferahkirman Kadısı ve Kırım Efendisi ve sâ'ir kuzâta ba-sehmi i'lâm yarlığı şerif oldur ki

Kazalarınuzda kendinüz olmayup sicil ve hüccetde ve resm-i kısmette hadd-i mahdûddan ziyâde te'addî üzere hareket idenleri istihdâm ve nâ'ib eylediklerinüz mesmû'ı şerifimiz olup buyurdum ki minba'd nefs-i kazanuzda bizzât kendinüz mesâlih-i muslimîne mukayyed olup kendinüz olmadıkça ehl-i ilim ve sâhib-i hilm ve kutub-i sicillât ve kısmet husûslarına rusûh üzere olanları istihdâm idesiz ve ziyâde tenbih idüp sicille sekiz akçe ve sûretine otuz iki akçe ve kısmeti mevârisin kırkta birden, bir akçe ziyâde almayup muhzıriyye dahi bile hesab oluna bundan yafte akçesi diye almayalar ve itak nâmeye bir gurûşdan ziyâde almayalar vechi meşrûh üzere nâ'iblerinüze muhkem tenbîh ü te'kîd idesiz ve kendinüz dahi taht-ı kazanuzda olan fukarâ ile minvâl-i meşrûh üzere mu'âmele idesiz ve rüsûm u avâyidde te'addî eylemeyesin şöyle ki zikr olunandan ziyâde fevkal'âde ve rusûmdan ve avâyidden tama'-ı hâmdan düşüp te'addî olmaya sebebi azlinüz bilüp ana göre icrâ-yı şer'-i şerifde mücid ü sa'y olasız ve nâ'ibinüz itdükleri mahzâ kendinüze âyid olup kendilerinüz mu'ahhiz olursuz nâ'ib-i bahâne olmak ihtimali yoktur minvâli mezbûrdan nâ'ibin te'addîsi dahi muceb-i azldir şöyle bilesiz bu makûle kimesneleri istihdâm itmeyesiz kazanuza kendinüz mukayyed olasız ve mevhubâtdan ve hükm olunandan mutlakâ resm deyü almayasız ve nâ'iblerinüze tenbîh idüp imdî aldırmayasız hemân sicil akçesi sûret olursa sûreti sicilleotuz ikidir bundan ziyâde alınmaya ve vasiyyet ve vâkıf ve bedel akçelerinden dahi resm ü sicill diye bir habbe almayasız ve aldırmayasız ve nâ'iblerinüze iden sebebi azl bilesiz ona göre mukayyed olasız şöyle bilesiz deyü yarlığı şerif verildi tahriren fi evâhir Safer'ül-muzaffer sene 1021.

1 For the transliteration of the order, see Inalcık, "Kirim Hanlığı," 171.

 | DOI:10.1163/9789004384323_009

2 Translation

Canibeg Giray Khan: my word

To the exemplary judges, pillars of religion, the present judges of Gözleve, Kara Su, Ferahkerman, and [Eski] Kırım, and to all other judges, the message of the noble *yarlığ* is that:

Since in the court districts under your control your *naib*s abused [their] authority by collecting fees for recording cases in the *sicil*s, issuing certified copies of entries, and supervising the divisions of inheritances higher than the prescribed amounts, I order you to personally serve the Muslims by registering the documents. Should you be absent, ensure that your subordinates are men of wisdom, masters of decision, and writers of registers, who would not collect more than the prescribed fees, which amount to eight *akçe*s for recording cases in the *sicil*s, thirty-two *akçe*s for issuing certified copies of entries and one akçe for every forty *akçe*sof inheritance. It is forbidden to collect more as *muhzırıyye* and *yafta akçesi*. No one should take more than one *guruş* for issuing a letter of manumission. Repeat this order to your *naib*s. Moreover, when you are in your districts, you should treat the poor according to the above-mentioned rules. You must not harm them. Do not act [based] upon despicable greed and do not collect from them more than the prescribed amount. Be aware that you will be dismissed for infringement of these rules. Work earnestly and diligently practicing the law of Islam. The work of your *naib*s is your responsibility. Your presence should guarantee that the *naib*s will commit no errors. Keep in mind that you will be dismissed for the mistakes of your *naib*s. Thus, do not employ such [mean] individuals and work in your districts in person. Do not collect higher fees than the prescribed amount, and do not allow or order your *naib*s to do so. Should you record an entry in the *sicil*s and immediately after you issue its certified copy, collect no more than the fee for issuing a certified copy, which amounts to thirty-two *akçe*s. Do not take or order to take the least bit of money for registering the inheritance, *vaqf* and *bedel*. Should your *naib*s do so, they are to be dismissed. Perform your duties following these rules.

The noble *yarlığ* was issued in the third ten days of the month of Sefer the Victorous of the year 1021 (23 April 1 May 1612).

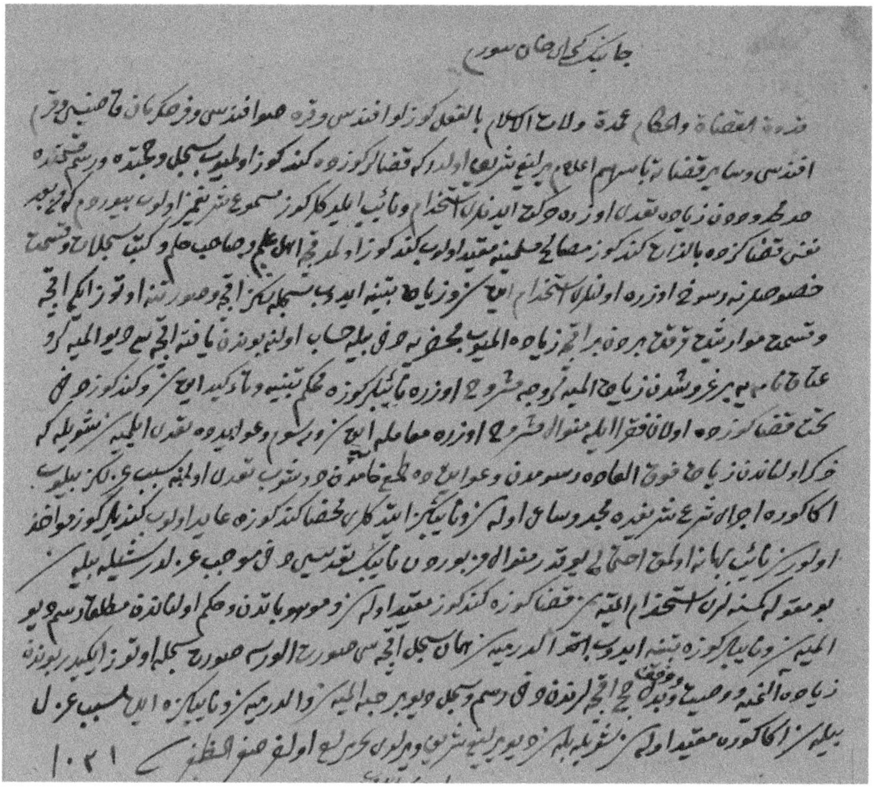

Facsimile 1

APPENDIX II

Transliteration, Translation, and Facsimile of a Case Brought to the Council of Murad Giray

(ORRNB, Fond 917, defter 22/78b/1)

1 Transliteration

Oldur ki karye-i Ulan Eli ahâlisinden Subhân Gazi Ağa el-ma'rûf dîvân-ı 'âlî'l-ezâl mahfûfen bi'l-me'âlî derûnında 'akd-i meclis-i şer' olındukdan sonra karye-i Necsan ahâlîsinden 'Abdişah Efendi muvâcehesinde takrir-i kelam idüp:

Selim Giray Han Çerkes seferine giderken ahâlî-i Necsan ile[1] kadı'asker İbrahim Efendi huzûrında vakı' olınup nehr-i Burulça'nın taraf-ı garbında olup kıbleten Vasilka deresi ve şarkan karye-i Necsan dibinde nehr-i Burulça'ya ve şimalen Kuş Taş ve Taş Kargana ve garben Ulan Eli'nin dağa gider tarikine müntehî işbu hudûd ile mahdûde olan dağ u 'arz olan elinde Subhân Gazi Ağa'nın mülkidür deyü tayi'an ikrâr idüp ve inkâr idenlerün ikrârda isbât idüp buna binâ'en İbrahim Efendi hükm eylemişidi deyü hüccet-i ibrâz eyleyüp kırâ'at olundıkta fi'l-hakîka 'Abdişah Efendi ve andan mâ'ada dokuz nefer kimesnenin kimisi meclis-şer'îde ikrâr idüp ve kiminin ikrârı sebt bulunup su'âl olundıkta 'Abdişah Efendi cevâbında: 'arz tenâzü'l-fîhâ ve dağ-ı mahdûde-i merkûme Burulça başında da'vâda gelindükde üzerine varılmayup Kara Su kurbında Ak Kıyat'dan Subhân Gazi Ağa el-mezbûr mezbûrları sorup götürüp da'vâ itdükde Necsan'da yerleri olmayanların ba'zısı ikrâr ider ve yerleri olanların ba'zısının ikrârına Subhân Gazi Ağa cümle oluşda kendiyle şerîk kimesnelerinden iki şâhid götürüp hükm itdürüb karye-i mezbûrile kışlasalup, evlerimiz dibinden sınur kesüp mer'a ve merta' ve muhattabımız olan yerden ihtitâb u ihtişâş ve irtibâ'dan men' idüp, iki yüz seneden berü mer'a ve merta'mız oldığına selâtin-i sâbıka ve hevâkin-i sâbıkadan kabalemiz var iken mezbûr ağa zülm ü te'addî ve cevr ü cefâya tesaddî itdüğinin şeyhü'l-islâm muftî Ebubekir Efendi hazretlerin üzerine muvellâ götürüp mürâfa'a olundığımızda mezkûrun on adamdan gayri, Necsan ahâlîsinden nisâdan on sekiz nefer ve ricâlden altmış iki nefer meclis-i şer' hâzırûn olup: arz-ı merkûme-i mahdûda mülkümüzdür deyü mülknâmeyi ibrâz eyleyüp mazmûn-i mülknâmede arz-ı mahdûde-i merkûme Necsan

1 The following two words are crossed out.

 DOI:10.1163/9789004384323_010

mer'âsı olmak üzere oldığından mâ'ada 'udûlünden Mehmed Efendi ibn Kâbil Efendi ve Hacı Geldi ibn el-Hac Husrev ve Bayram 'Ali mu'ezzin, bunlardan mâ'ada cem-i kesîr ve cem'i gazîr şehâdet itdüklerinden bize hükm etmişdür deyü hatem-i meymenet-i hitâm ile mühr-i hüccet ibrâz eyleyüp def'-i mutesaddî olup girân olundukta mazmûn-i hüccetle silsile-i kelâm minvâl-i muharrer üzere ihtitâm u[2] ... takrîrde bu vech-i üzere nizâm bulmağın ve minvâl-i meşrûh üzere da'vâ ve hükme Subhân Gazi Ağa el-mezbûr kendi nefer-i mukırr u müte'arrif olmağla Ebubekir Efendi'nin hüccet-i hakkıyyeti zâhire ve sahih olunduğından hükmi imzâ ve inkâz ve karye-i merkûme-i Necsan ahâlîsinin mu'arraza men' olundığı me'a't-taleb ketb ü kaydşod. Cerî zâlik ve hurrire fi âhirü'r-rebi'ayn sene 1089.

Şuhûdu'l-hâl: fahru'l-akran-i hazret-i Han, Mehmed Ağa ibn 'Ali Ağa; Kaya Beğ; Şeyh 'Ali Beğ; Dedeş Ağa, ibn Maliş Ağa; Zal Ağa el-ma'rûf; Kaplan Mirza ibn 'Inâyet Giray Mirza; Kutlu Şah Ağa defterdar; Sâdık Ağa hazinedar; Mustafa Efendi kâtib-i divân; Sultan 'Ali Mirza [ibn] Şeyh 'Ali Beğ; 'Adil Ulan [ibn] Sefer Şah Ulan; Mehmed Efendi el-kâdî-i Kara Su; 'Abdulcemil Efendi el-kâdî bi Bağçesarây el-mahrûse; Musalli Efendi [ibn] 'Abdülhalim Ağa; 'Abdulgaffar Efendi [ibn] el-Hac Mehmed Efendi; Huseyin Efendi el-ma'rûf; kapıcı başı Murâd Gâzi Ağa; Timur Şah Çelebi 'an Salacık; 'Abdul'aziz kethüdâ-i bevvabân; 'Abdulhalim Efendi tâbi'-i 'Adil Giray Han ve cem-i gazîr ve cem'i kesîr mi'n huzzâr-ı meclis.

2 Translation

It happened that Subhan Gazi Ağa, from the inhabitants of the village of Ulan Eli, when the noble sharia court convened at the great council, made an official statement and voluntarily confessed in the presence of Abdişah Efendi:

"On his way to a Circassian campaign, Khan Selim Giray, in the presence of inhabitants of the village of Necsan and the *kadıasker*, Ibrahim Efendi, stated that the mountains and fields bordered to the south by the valley of Vasilka, which is on the western shore of Burulça River, [bordered] in the east by the lowest part of the village of Necsan, [which is] situated on the aforementioned river, in the north by Kuş Taş and Taş Kargan and in the west by the road to Eli'nin Dağı, belong to Subhan Gazi Ağa."

He confirmed that he knows that others have denied it. Regarding this fact, he presented a document (*hüccet*) issued by Ibrahim Efendi. Abdişah Efendi,

2 The following word is illegible.

together with nine other individuals, truthfully confessed in the noble sharia court and their confession was registered. During the interrogation, Abdişah Efendi answered,

"We did not participate in the hearing concerning the above-mentioned land on the Burulça River. The aforementioned Subhan Gazi Ağa, who came from the [clan] of Ak Kiyat from the vicinity of Kara Su, brought individuals who had no land in the village of Necsan [in order] to confess. He also brought two witnesses who have land there and who were shareholders of his property and from whom he obtained the document (*hüccet*). He used the village for winter pasture, he restricted us to our houses and did not allow us to use many pastures, to put our cattle there and to collect firewood. As we have the title deeds (*mülkname*) confirming that these pastures were granted to us by the previous sultans and rulers two hundred years ago, the said *ağa* opresses us, violates our rights, and dares to act unjustly and cruelly. Thus, we, inhabitants of the village of Necsan, i.e., next to the aforementioned ten individuals, eighteen women and sixty-two men, have brought our case to Mufti Abubekir Efendi and we plead before the sharia court: 'The land, within the limits described above, is our property,' and we have presented the title deeds (*mülkname*). Although it includes the pastures in the village of Necsan within the described boundaries, from among the just witnesses Mehmed Efendi, son of Kabil Efendi and Hacı Geldi Hacı, son of Hacı Husrev, and Müezzin Bayram 'Ali, and many others have testified. Thus, we received a sentence." Afterwards, the handwritten document ending with a mighty seal and containing the statement described above was presented. The aforementioned Subhan Gazi Ağa came to confess a fault and explained himself. The legally valid document issued by Abubekir Efendi was registered, the sentence was signed and saved in order to prevent disputes involving the inhabitants of the village of Necsan. Everything was written upon [their] request. It happened and was written during the month of Rebi II of the year 1089 (23 May–20 June 1678).

Case witnesses: the khan's vizier, Mustafa Ağa, son of Ali Ağa; Kaya Beğ; Şeyh Ali Beğ; Dedeş Ağa, son of Maliş Ağa; Zal Ağa; Kaplan Mirza, son of Inayet Giray Mirza; the *defterdar* Kutlu Şah Mirza; the *hazinedar* Sadık Ağa; *katib* of the khan's council Mustafa Efendi; Sultan Ali Mirza, son of Şeyh Ali Beğ; Adil Ulan, son of Sefer Şah Ulan; *kadı* of the Kara Su district, Mehmed Efendi; *kadı* of the Bahçesaray district, Abdulcemil Efendi; Musalli Efendi, son of Abdulhalim Ağa; Abdulgaffar Efendi, son of Hacı Mehmed Efendi; Huseyn Efendi; *kapıcı başı*, Murad Gazi Ağa; Timur Şah Çelebi from the village of Salacık; *kethüda* of the gate keepers, Abdul'aziz; servant of Khan Adil Giray, Abdulhalim Efendi, and all the individuals present in the court.

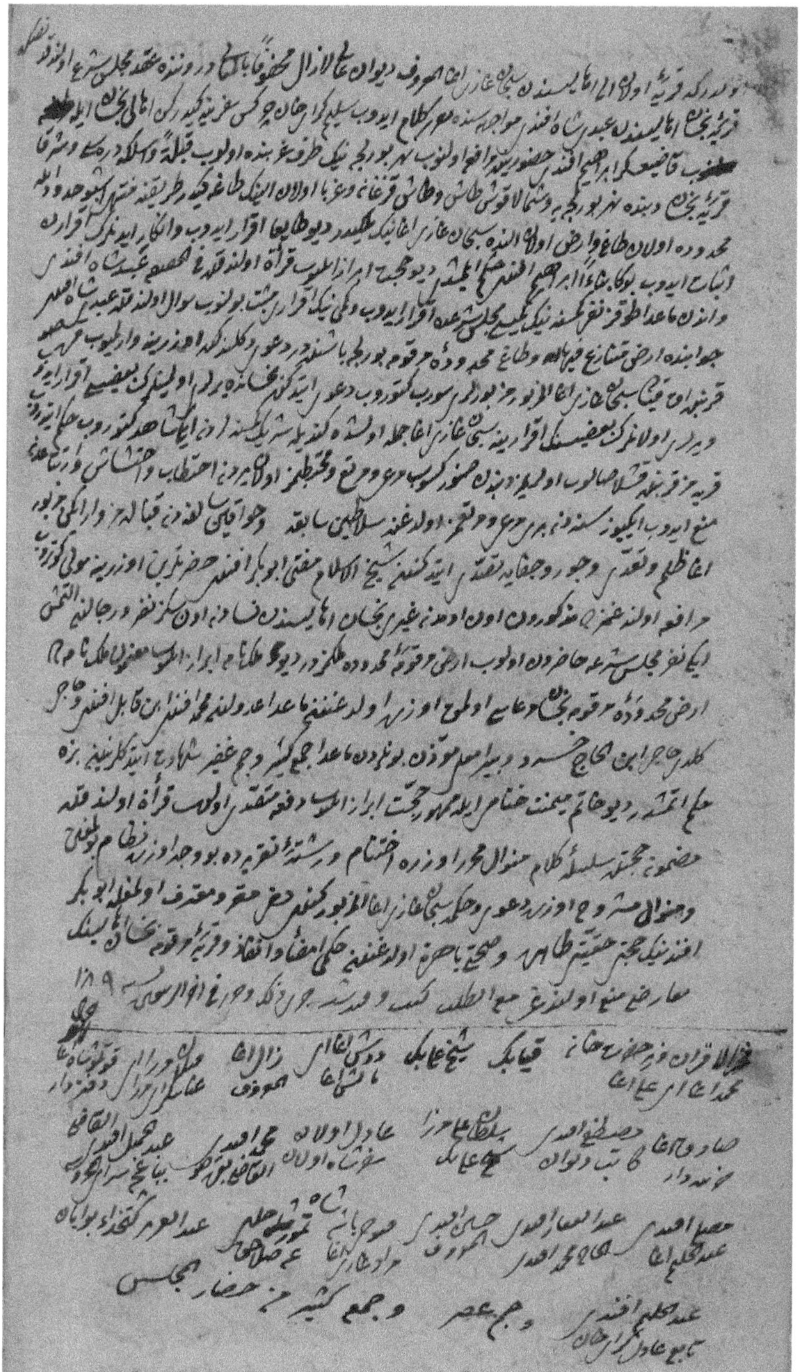

Facsimile 11

APPENDIX III

Summaries of the Cases Judged at the Khan's Council (1678–82)

Page no. and date	Parties in the case	
	Plaintiff	Defendant
22/78b/1 [23 May–20 June 1678]	Subhan Gazi Ağa from the village of Ulan Eli [Gözleve district]	Abdişah Efendi from the village of Necsan on the Burulça River [Ak Mescid, Kara Su or Dair district], and nine other inhabitants of the same village.

 | DOI:10.1163/9789004384323_011

Summary	Case witnesses
Financial case The data concerning the litigants is followed by the plaintiff's allegation. He stated that when the Crimean Tatars went on a Circassian campaign, Khan Selim I Giray (in the presence of *kadıasker* Ibrahim Efendi) granted him a piece of land within the described boundaries. The title deed was recorded by the *kadıasker* and confirmed by the defendant, Abdişah Efendi himself, as well as nine other witnesses. The defendant disagreed with the plaintiff. He stated that the witnesses of Subhan Gazi Ağa were not inhabitants of the village of Necsan and that the local inhabitants had enjoyed various rights and profited from the land (e.g., to pasture cattle) for two hundred years. These privileges were granted to them by the former Crimean khans. The inhabitants of the village, seventy-two men and eighteen women, set their claims before Mufti Abubekir Efendi, who issued a *hüccet*. They provided the mufti with a title deed and the testimonies of numerous witnesses confirming their claim to that piece of land. The court, acting in accordance with the decision of the mufti, forbade anyone to question the rights of the inhabitants to that piece of land.	1. Vizier Mustafa Ağa, son of Ali Ağa 2. Kaya Beğ 3. Şeyh Ali Beğ 4. Dedeş Ağa, son of Maliş Ağa 5. Zal Ağa 6. Kaplan Mirza, son of Inayet Giray Mirza 7. Kutlu Şah Mirza, *defterdar* 8. Sadık Ağa, *hazinedar* 9. Mustafa Efendi, *katib* of the khan's council 10. Sultan Ali Mirza, son of Şeyh Ali Beğ 11. Adil Ulan, son of Sefer Şah Ulan 12. Mehmed Efendi, *kadı* of the Kara Su district 13. Abdulcemil Efendi, *kadı* of the Bahçesaray district 14. Musalli Efendi, son of Abdulhalim Ağa 15. Abdulgaffar Efendi, son of Hacı Mehmed Efendi 16. Huseyn Efendi 17. Murad Gazi Ağa, *kapıcı başı* 18. Timur Şah Çelebi from the village of Salacık 19. Abdulkerim, *kethüda* of the *kapıcı başı* 20. Abdulhalim Efendi "and the others."

Page no. and date	Parties in the case	
	Plaintiff	Defendant
23b/6a/2 [undated]	Abdulhac Çelebi and Asad Çelebi, the sons of Ömer Efendi along with other inhabitants of the village of Kürlevüt; Abdulcemil Çelebi, son of Dost Mehmed Çelebi from the same village [Mangıt district]	Abdurrahman Çelebi, son of Tohta Gazi Şeyh and Iş Akay, son of Cem Ali from the same village [Mangıt district]
23b/92b/2 [26 September 1680]	Incikök [?], son of Dost Ağa from the village of Seyyid Eli in the Şirin district by his *vekil* Abdulgaffar, son of Karmış	Halil Dede, son of İş Mullah Sufi, from the same village

Summary	Case witnesses
Law of patronage The plaintiffs stated that the famous mosque of Abd Efendi had been founded by their ancestor Allahkul Hacı. Then, their father Ömer Efendi financed the renovation and expansion of the building. Their family had always held the right to nominate and depose the imams and *khatib*s of the mosque. Fifteen years earlier the defendants made a claim that their ancestor Huseyn Hacı had also been a founder of the mosque and, as such, should also have the right to nominate and depose officials of the mosque. The defendants said that during the previous fifteen years they had not been able to exercise their right to nominate and depose officials of the mosque. The witnesses stated that the defendants' request should be denied. Thus, it was stated that only Allahkul Hacı and Ömer Efendi should be considered the legal founders of the mosque.	1. Müderris Şakir Efendi 2. Mufti Abubekir Efendi 3. Timur Gazi Beğ, *mirahor* 4. Kutlu Şah Ağa, *defterdar* 5. Mustafa Efendi, *katib*[a] of the khan's council 6. Abdullah Çelebi, son of Abdul [?] Çelebi 7. Abdurrahman Çelebi, son of Musa Efendi 8. *emir* of Ferahkerman, the beg of the Mansurs 9. Sadık Ağa, *hazinedar* 10. Vizier Ahmed Ağa "and the others."
Law of patronage Incikök contested Halil Dede's claim that the latter had built a mosque in their village entirely by himself. Incikök stated that he had given Halil 500 *akçe*s for this purpose. Halil disagreed with this version of events. Yet, witnesses stated that Incikök indeed contributed financially to the founding of the mosque. The court, therefore, confirmed his rights to the building.	1. Mufti Abubekir Efendi 2. Aliş Ağa from Teberti 3. Abdulgaffar Efendi, *kadı* of Bahçesaray 4. Ahmed, son of Abdulcemil Efendi 5. Vizier Ahmed Ağa 6. Bekir Mirza Ağa [son of] Suleyman Ağa, *mirahor* 7. Kutlu Şah Ağa, *defterdar* 8. Mustafa, *katib* of the khan's council 9. Hazır Efendi, *müderris* "and witnesses present at the council"

Page no. and date	Parties in the case: Plaintiff	Parties in the case: Defendant
23b/121b/3 [undated]	Seven underage children represented by their tutor Abdulgani Efendi from the village of Toğa Taş [Kara Su-Tamak district]	Two slaves [residental affiliation unregistered]
23b/123a/5 [19 May–28 May 1681]	Mehmed Gazi's wives, underage sons and daughters, and one of his sons who was of age, were not present in court. They were represented by their agent Arslan, son of Gazanfer Sufi from the village of Baygeldi [Kara Kurt district]	Kaplan, son of Allahverdi Sufi [Kara Kurt district]
23a/125a/1 [undated]	Wife of Emin Mehmed [Kara Su district]	Three Janisaries: Babadağlı Çubar Mehmed, Veli Mehmed, and Sarı Mehmed [Kara Su district]

Summary	Case witnesses
Murder and assault case The plaintiffs accused two slaves (*kazak*) of killing their testator Abdulrahman with an axe. The slaves pleaded guilty.	1. Mufti Abubekir Efendi 2. Hazır Efendi, *müderris* 3. Ahmed Efendi, former *kadı* of Gözleve 4. Huseyn Efendi, *kadı* of Bahçesaray 5. Mullah Seyyid Gazi from Kaçı district 6. Saadet Giray Sultan, *nuraddin* 7. Vizier Ahmed Ağa 8. Murad Gazi Ulan, *kapıcı başı* 9. Sadık Ağa, *hazinedar* 10. Mustafa Efendi, *katib* of the khan's council
Murder and assault case The plaintiffs stated that the defendant stabbed Kutlu Şah to death with a knife. The defendant pleaded guilty. The witnesses confirmed the circumstances of the crime as described by the plaintiffs, and the accused was sentenced to pay blood money.	1. Vizier Ahmed Ağa 2. Sadık Ağa, *hazinedar* 3. Mustafa Efendi, *katib* of the khan's council 4. Timur Gazi Beğ, former *mirahor* 5. Mustafa Ağa, former *emir* of Ferahkerman 6. Mustafa Ağa, *kilerci başı* 7. Abdulfatah from Bahçesaray, *atalık* 8. Ahmed Ağa, former *balcı başı*
Murder and assault case The woman confirms that before his death, her late husband Emin Mehmed accused the defendants of wounding him with a knife on the right side of his body above the breast. The event took place in the vicinity of the coffee shop (*kahvehane*) of Mehmed Şah Mirza in Kara Su. The woman appointed Receb Kethüda, who was the *kethüda* of the gatekeepers of the *kalga*, as her agent. The agent demanded that the accused pay blood money to the widow. He brought four witnesses, who confirmed the plaintiff's version of events.	1. Vizier Ahmed Ağa 2. Şeyh Ali Beğ, [son of] Bahadır Şah Beğ 3. Arslan Şah Mirza, son of Inayet Şah Mirza 4. Kaplan Mirza 5. Mustafa Efendi, *katib* of the khan's council 6. Dedeş Ağa 7. Abdurrahman Çelebi, *katib* "and the others."

Page no. and date	Parties in the case: Plaintiff	Parties in the case: Defendant
23a/129b/5 [18 June–16 July 1681]	Mehmed Beşe, son of Karınsız Hacı [Kaçı district]	Yahi Mullah, son of Islam Sufi from a wife of Şeyh Mehmed Efendi [from a village in the Kaçı district]
23a/132b/7 [undated]	Ivan, a slave of Ruthenian origin [residential affiliation unregistered]	Zaynulabdin Çelebi, son of Hacı Kadır Ağa
23a/133b/3 [5–14 September 1681]	Devin Gazi on behalf of Adil and Mustafa, sons of the late Meydan Ali Mirza, son of Can Ahmed Mirza [Salgır district]	

Summary	Case witnesses
Murder and assault case The plaintiff stated that the body of his father was found on land owned by the defendant in the district of Ismail. The case was adjudicated and Yahi Mullah was sentenced to pay blood money. He had already delivered a part of it, and was supposed to pay the rest. The defendant disagreed and stated that he had already paid the whole sum. He procured witnesses who confirmed his statement. The court accepted their testimony and announced that Mullah was not guilty.	1. Vizier Ahmed Ağa 2. Mustafa Ağa, former çaşnigir *başı* 3. Şah Timur Çelebi, son of Timur Gazi 4. Naib Ali Can Çelebi, son of Sefer Gazi 5. Mehmed Hacı Efendi, son of Hacı İsa 6. Hacı Abdurrahman Çelebi, son of Haşim Efendi
Manumission Ivan requested that the defendant set him free on the basis that the latter had promised to do so five years ago. The defendant disagreed, but the testimony of two witnesses confirmed the plaintiff's version of events.	1. Huseyn Efendi, *kadı* 2. Abdulbaki Efendi, son of Seyyid Efendi 3. Ömer Efendi, son of Abdulfattah Efendi 4. Dost Mehmed Efendi, son of Abdulfattah Efendi 5. Şahbaz Efendi, *katib* 6. Vizier Ahmed Ağa 7. Bahadır Ağa 8. Kutlu Şah Ağa, *defterdar* 9. Sadık Ağa, *hazinedar* 10. Bekir Mirza Ağa, *mirahor* 11. Evliya Ağa
Inheritance and financial case In order to settle all matters related to the inheritance left by Meydan Ali Mirza, Devin Gazi stated that the late *mirza* had given ninety *altuns* to Mehmed Mirza, son of Nur Ahmed Mirza. The latter confirmed this statement.	1. Vizier Ahmed Ağa 2. Bahadır Ağa, retired from the office of vizier 3. Hüsam Giray Sultan, son of Murad Giray Khan 4. Derviş Ağa 5. İsmail Efendi, retired [*kadı*] from the district of Ferahkerman 6. Ahmed, son of Abdulcemil

Page no. and date	Parties in the case: Plaintiff	Defendant
23a/133b/4 [13 September 1681]	Hasan from Eski Kırım and his wife, his children, and other relatives [Eski Kırım district]	Abdulbaki, son of Mehmed from Eski Kırım [Eski Kırım district]
23a/134b/4 [undated]	Mehmed Çelebi, son of Mustafa Çelebi [Mangub district]	Abdulgariz Çelebi, son of Zulfikar [Mangub district]
23a/134b/2 [11–20 March 1681]	Relatives of Ibrahim, son of Ismail [Eski Kırım district]	Emine Sultan and Zeynep Sultan, daughters of Ali [Eski Kırım district]

Summary	Case witnesses
Murder and assault case The plaintiffs stated that their relative Emine, daughter of Hasan, was found dead on land owned by Abdulbaki, son of Mehmed. The accused denied the allegation, but witnesses testified that Abdulbaki had already acknowledged this fact.	1. Vizier Ahmed Ağa 2. Dedeş Ağa 3. Abdullah Efendi, son of Huseyn Ali Efendi 4. Ahmed, son of Abdulcemil 5. Abdulgaffar Çelebi, son of Abdullah Çelebi 6. *katib ağa*, Mehmed Can Efendi "and the others."
Murder and assault case The plaintiff accused the defendant of shooting and killing with a bow his former slave who had already been manumitted. The accused disagreed, but the plaintiff produced witnesses who confirmed his accusation. The parties concluded an amicable settlement, according to which the killer was supposed to pay 300 *esedi guruş*.	1. Vizier Ahmed Ağa 2. Kutlu Giray Beğ 3. Kaplan Mirza 4. Ahmed Efendi 5. Mehmed Şah Mirza 6. Tohtamiş Mirza 7. Hacı Giray Mirza 8. Reis Beğ 9. Abdullah Kethüda "and the others."
Murder and assault case The plaintiffs demanded blood money from Emine Sultan on the grounds that she had killed Ibrahim, their nexttokin. The woman responded that it was her sister Zeyneb Sultan who had killed the man. Zeyneb Sultan acknowledged this fact. She explained that she had done this because Ibrahim raped her in her own house. The witnesses confirmed the circumstances of Ibrahim's death and Zeyneb Sultan was found not guilty of manslaughter.	1. Mufti Abubekir Efendi 2. Vizier Ahmed Ağa 3. Sadık Ağa, *hazinedar* 4. Kutlu Şah Ağa, *defterdar* 5. Bekir Mirza Ağa, *mirahor*

Page no. and date	Parties in the case	
	Plaintiff	Defendant
23a/142b/7 [17 June 1681]	Ak Mehmed, son of Can Mullah; Abdulkerim, son of Rahmet; Hacı Geldi, son of Devlet Gazi from the village of Sadakçı [Kara Su-Tamak district]	Şeyh Ali Beğ [residential affiliation unregistered]
23a/146a/2 [26 July–5 August 1681]	Sefer Odabaşı from Gözleve [Gözleve district]	Abdurrahman, son of Mevlud from the village of Karalar [Gözleve district]
23a/147b/1 [24 August 1681]	Mehmed Çelebi, son of Mustafa Çelebi [Mangub district]	Inhabitants of three villages: Hacı Köy, Evel Şeyh, and Öteş Eli[b] [Bahçesaray district]

Summary	Case witnesses
Financial case The plaintiffs stated that the former rulers had granted their ancestors the right of ownership (*mülk*) over a plot of land. Thus, the defendant owned no title to this land. Şeyh Ali Beğ disagreed and stated he had the right to the land, as confirmed by the khan's order. At the request of the plaintiffs, the defendant's version was confirmed by the testimonies of his witnesses.	1. Sadık Ağa, *hazinedar* 2. Mustafa Efendi, *katib* of the khan's council 3. Murad Gazi Ağa, *kapıcı başı* 4. Bahadır Şah Beğ, *beğ* of the Argıns 5. Abdşah Efendi, *naib* of the Kara Su district 6. Musalli Efendi, *kadı* of Bahçesaray "and the others."
Murder and assault case Sefer Odabaşı demanded blood money and an allowance in amount of 15 *esedi guruş* from Abdurrahman, whose horse trod on his left hand. Since the defendant pleaded guilty, the party concluded an amicable settlement.	1. Vizier Ahmed Ağa 2. Aliş, vizier of the *kalga* (*ağa-i sultan*) 3. Ahmed Efendi, former *kadı* of Gözleve 4. Kaplan Mirza 5. Abdullah Kethüda 6. Abdullah, *katib* 7. Murtaza Mirza, son of Ahmed Ağa "and the others"
Murder and assault case Mehmed Çelebi withdrew all claims previously lodged against the inhabitants of the three villages, where the body of his late father's slave had been found. Before his death, the latter [Mustafa Çelebi] testified that the slave had been killed by certain Abdulaziz, son of Zulfikar Efendi.	1. Haşamatallah [?] Efendi, son of Abdulbaki 2. Hacı Abdurrahman Çelebi, son of Hasim 3. Ali, son of Mehmed 4. Ömer, son of Hürrem 5. Vizier Ahmed Ağa 6. Sadık Ağa, *hazinedar* 7. Mustafa Efendi, *katib* of the khan's council 8. Murad Gazi Ağa "and the others."

Page no. and date	Parties in the case	
	Plaintiff	Defendant
23a/148a/3 [undated]	Murad Giray Khan [residential affiliation unregistered]	
23a/165a/3 and 4 [15–24 September 1680]	Seyyid and Receb, sons of Kasim Sufi; Ayinşah, daughter of Kasım Sufi; Emine, daughter of Sefer Ali from the village of Divan Köy [Çorgun district]	Veli Şah, son of Abdullah from the same village [Çorgun district]
23a/173a/4 [21–30 March 1681]	The inhabitants of the village of Baş Oyrat [Orta Congar district]	Nesli [?] Beğ, daughter of Dede Beğ and wife of Can Akay, Ak Mehmed and Kutlu Can, son and daughter of Can Akay. All three of were represented by Ömer Abd.

Summary	Case witnesses
Manumission The khan stated that from this day onward Dilaver, who became a Muslim, would have the same rights as other Muslims. He obtained a manumission letter confirming his status of a freeman.	1. Vizier Ahmed Ağa 2. Sadık Ağa, *hazinedar* 3. Mustafa Efendi, *katib* of the khan's council 4. Mufti Hasan Efendi 5. Ahmed Efendi, [former *kadı* of] Gözleve 6. Fatah, *atalık* 7. Musalli Efendi, *kadı* of Bahçesaray "and the others."
Murder and assault case **The first entry as heard in the *kadıasker* court** The plaintiffs accused Veli Şah of wounding and killing Şah Gazi Veli. They produced witnesses who confirmed their claim. **The second entry as heard at the khan's council** The plaintiffs waived their claim to blood money from the inhabitants of the village of Divan Köy.	**The case witnesses of the second entry:** 1. Akay Efendi, son of Yusuf, "*halife* of Gözleve" 2. Vizier Ahmed Ağa 3. Mufti Abubekir Efendi 4. Beğ Mirza Ağa, son of Suleyman Ağa 5. Mustafa Efendi, *katib* of the khan's council 6. Arslan Efendi, *kadı* 7. Ahmed Efendi, son of Abdulhalim [?] Efendi "and the others."
Murder and assault case The inhabitants stated that Can Akay, while he was already been in poor health, was attacked by his cattle and died. As soon as they [the villagers] found out about his death, they went to see the body. They saw neither a wound nor a killer. Thus, they ask the widow and the late Can Akay's children to refrain from claiming anything from the village. The relatives of Can Akay agreed to this request.	1. Vizier Ahmed Ağa 2. Sadık Ağa, *hazinedar* 3. Mufti Hasan Efendi 4. Dedeş Ağa 5. Abdulcemil Efendi, former *kadı* of Bahçesaray "and the others."

Page no. and date	Parties in the case	
	Plaintiff	Defendant
23a/176a/4 [undated]	Tonya [?], daughter of Ötemiş and widow of Bay Timur, son of Can Timur and three minors. All were represented by Veliallah Halife, son of Cantay Sufi [Dib Kerç district]	Kantemir, son of Sartay[?] [Dib Kerç district]
23a/179a/1 and 2 [24 April 1682]	Halil Çelebi, father of the late Ibrahim [Ak Mescid district]	Hasan, son of Osman Beşe and Abbas, son of Halil [Ak Mescid district]

Summary	Case witnesses
Murder and assault case **The first entry as heard at the khan's council** The widow accused Kantemir of killing her husband with a knife. The defendant pleaded guilty. **The second entry as heard in the *kadıasker* court** The agent of the widow and three minors concluded an amicable settlement with the killer, who agreed to pay blood money (thirty *altuns*).	**The case witnesses of the first entry:** 1. Vizier Ahmed Ağa 2. Sadık Ağa, *hazinedar* 3. Veli Şah Beğ 4. Adil Beğ 5. Musalli Efendi 6. Abdulcemil Efendi 7. Mehmed Can Efendi 8. Evliya Ağa 9. Abdurrahman Efendi, son of Abdullah Çelebi "and the others."
Murder and assault case **The first entry as heard at the khan's council** The plaintiff stated that his son Ibrahim was wounded by Hasan, son of Osman Beşe, and Abbas, son of Halil, in the neighborhood of Great Mosque in Ak Mescid. The victim was taken back home, where he died three days later. The plaintiff withdrew all his claims against the inhabitants of the above-mentioned neighborhood. He demanded blood money from Hasan, son of Osman Beşe and Abbas, son of Halil. **The second entry as heard in the *kadıasker* court** The father of the victim demanded blood money from the defendants, who denied the accusation. The plaintiff produced witnesses, who testified that the defendants wounded the victim with a sword.	**The case witnesses of the first entry:** 1. Sadık Ağa, *hazinedar* 2. Mufti Hasan Efendi 3. Dedeş Ağa 4. Bekir Mirza Ağa, *mirahor* 5. Veliş Ağa 6. Evliya Ağa, *Tat ağası* 7. Mehmed Efendi, *imam* of the khan 8. Ahmed Efendi, *müderris* 9. İbrahim Mirza 10. Bali Mirza 11. Murtaza Mirza 12. Abrurrahman Çelebi, *katib* of the *hazinedar* 13. Abdurrahman Ağa, son of Timur Beğ Ağa 14. Katib Efendizade Ali Can Çelebi 15. Ahmed Mirza "and the other members of the khan's council."

Page no. and date	Parties in the case	
	Plaintiff	Defendant
23a/181b/1 and 3 [28 April–7 May 1682]	The following relatives of the late Devin, son of Otarcı, from the village of Taş Oba [Arbat district]: [1] his father, Otarcı, son of Çapar[?]; [2] his underage daughter Nesli[?] Bike; and [3] his wife, Canbike, daughter of Bayram Ali.	The inhabitants of the village of Taş Oba [Arbat district]
23a/192b/1 [6 July–4 August 1682]	Bayram, son of Hacı Cem Ali [Bahçesaray district]	The concubine of Cem Ali and his former female slave Gülsinah, represented by Göki Efendi [Bahçesaray district]

Summary	Case witnesses
Murder and assault case **The first entry as heard in the *kadıasker* court** Relatives of the late Devin demanded blood money from two inhabitants of the village Taş Oba, i.e., from Çapar[?], son of İş Gazi, and Ötemiş, son of İş Akay. The plaintiffs withdrew their claims against other inhabitants of the village of Taş Oba, who were also present in the court. **The second entry as heard at the khan's council** The plaintiffs accused the above-mentioned Çapar[?] and Ötemiş of hitting their relative Devin with a stake and killing him. The defendants denied the accusation and the plaintiffs produced witnesses to confirm their version.	**The case witnesses of the second entry:** 1. Vizier Ahmed Ağa 2. Sadık Ağa, *hazinedar* 3. Abdulcemil, *kadı* of Bahçesaray "and the other members of the khan's council."
Financial case Bayram stated that he has the right to receive his share of inheritance, as it was defined in the last will of his late father, which was written down in front of a judge. Yet, Göki Efendi, the agent of Gülsinah, stated that late Cem Ali decided that the concubine should be manumitted after his death. Thus, she was no longer a part of the deceased's property. Witnesses confirmed this statement.	1. Vizier Ahmed Ağa 2. Sadık Ağa, *hazinedar* 3. Mufti Huseyn Efendi, son of Şeyh Cafar Efendi 4. Kadı Abdulcemil Efendi, son of Şeyh Musalli Efendi 5. Dedeş Ağa, son of Abu ... Ağa 6. Mustafa Ağa, former *beğ* of Ferahkerman 7. Ahmed Efendi, former *kadı* of Gözleve 8. Veli Şah Beğ, son of Mehmed Şah Beğ 9. Abdulcemil Efendi, son of Mehmed Efendi 10. Evliya Ağa, *Tat ağası* 11. Hacı Ramazan Ağa 12. Mehmed Can Efendi, *katib* of the council 13. Ahmed, son of Müfti Abdulhamil, *katib* "and the others."

Page no. and date	Parties in the case: Plaintiff	Parties in the case: Defendant
23a/237a/2 [undated]	Individuals of various social backgrounds from the village of Saray located on the Salgır River and the village of Din Mehmed [Ak Mescid district]	

a The Persian word *debir*, which means writer, is used.

b The three villages, which were situated in close vicinity, may have shared common land (Jankowski, *A Historical-Etymological Dictionary*, 474, 540–541, 777–778, map no. F5).

Summary	Case witnesses
Foundation The individuals stated that they bequeathed the tithe of revenue from a plot of land to the imam of the mosque founded by Khan Adil Giray, who granted this land to their community. They presented the khan's order (*ferman*) confirming their rights to the land.	1. Vizier Ahmed Ağa 2. Şeyh Ali Beğ, the *beğ* of the Barıns 3. Bahadır Şah Beğ, the *beğ* of the Argıns 4. Sadık Ağa, *hazinedar* 5. Mustafa Efendi, *katib* of the khan's council 6. Murad Gazi Ağa, *kapıcı başı* 7. Musalli Efendi, *kadı* of Bahçesaray 8. Dedeş Ağa, son of Muaş: Ağa [?] 9. Hacı [?], former *kilerci başı*

List of the Officials Recorded in the Crimean *Sicil*s during the Reign of Murad Giray

1 List of the Officials Recorded in the *kadıasker*'s *sicil*s during the Reign of Murad Giray[1]

Location	Office	Name of the official	His role in the law court	Location in the court register
Ak Mescid	former *kadı*	Abdullah Efendi	case witness	23a/165b/2
	kadı	Abdulaziz Efendi	case witness	23a/175a/3
	kadı	Abdulveli	case witness	23b/96a/2
	kadı	Musalli Efendi, son of Selih Ağa	party in the case	23a/222a/1
	kadı	Şahbaz Efendí	case witness	23a/133b/2
	kadı of the *kalga*	Bekir Efendi	case witness	23b/118a/4–7
	vizier (*ağa*) of the *kalga*	Aliş Ağa	case witness	23a/146a/2
Bahçesaray	*beytülmal emini*	unregistered	performing his duty	23b/743/2
	bölükbaşı	Arslan	case witness	23b/80b/4
	bölükbaşı	Ahmed	testator	23b/113a/12
	bölükbaşı	Halil	on duty	23a/135b/3
	bölükbaşı	Sakir	case witness	23b/40a/4
	çaşnigir başı	Mustafa	legal agent	23a/187b/5
	çaşnigir başı	Mustafa Ağa	case witness	23a/217b/3
	defterdar	Kutlu Şah Ağa	case witness	23b/92b/2
	delal	Yusuf	party in the case	23b/110a/6
	divan katibi	Mustafa Efendi	party in the case	23a/136a/2
	former *kadıasker*	Mustafa Efendi	performing his judicial duty	23b/68a/4

1 Appendix III contains the names of the khan's officials appearing as case witnesses in proceedings brought to the khan's council.

 | DOI:10.1163/9789004384323_012

Location	Office	Name of the official	His role in the law court	Location in the court register
	former *nuraddin*	Safa Giray	party in the case	23b/93b/2
	former *tuz emini*	Mehmed	case witness	23b/90b/6
	hazinedar	Sadık Ağa	party in the case	23a/174a/2
	kadı	Musalli Efendi	performing his judicial duty	24/116a/3
	kadı	Abdulfatah	performing his judicial duty	23a/135b/3
	kadı	Abdulhamil Efendi	case witness	22/25b/5
	former *kadıasker*	Abubekir	party in the case	23a/148a/1
	kadıasker	Hasan Efendi	party in the case	23b/120a/5
	katib of the khan's council	Mustafa	case witness	23b/92b/2
	kapıcı başı	Murad Gazi Ağa	case witness	23a/147b/1
	kilerci başı	Mustafa Ağa	case witness	23a/123a/5
	kethüda of the gatekeepers	Abdulkerim	case witness	22/78b/1
	mirahor	Bekir Mirza Ağa	case witness	23b/92b/2
	silahdar	Mehmed Ağa, son of Abdullah	case witness	23a/179a/4
unregistered [Bahçesaray?]	*konakçı*	Mustafa, son of Oman	performing his duty	23a/190a/5
	former *mirahor*	Timur Gazi Beg	party in the case	23b/85a/1
	naib	Can Ahmed	case witness	23b/90b/1
Çetirlik	*kadı*	Hacı Efendi	case witness	23a/214a/5
Ferahkerman	*kadı*	Abdurrazak	case witness	23a/214a/5
	kadı	Mehmed, son of Hacı Ahmed	case witness	23a/136a/2
	kadı	Feyzullah Efendi	case witness	23b/124b/4–5
	former *kadı*	Ismail Efendi	case witness	23b/133b/3

Location	Office	Name of the official	His role in the law court	Location in the court register
Gözleve	former *emin*	Abdullah Hacı	party in the case	23b/23b/5
	former *emin*	Mustafa Ağa	party in the case	23b/15a/4–5
	former *kadı*	Ahmed Efendi	case witness	23a/136a/2
	kadı	Osman Efendi	case witness	23a/184b/2
	naib	Suleyman Efendi	case witness	23b/15a/6
Kara Su	*kadı*	Ibrahim Efendi	case witness	23a/183b/2
	kadı	Mustafa Efendi	case witness	23a/130a/6
	naib	Abdurrahman	case witness	23b/91b/3
Küçük Kara Su	*kadı*	Ahmed Efendi	case witness	23a/199a/1
Salgır	*kadı*	Abdurrahman Efendi	case witness	23a/179b/2
Şahkerman	*bölükbaşı*	Huseyn	party in the case	23a/222b/7
Şirin	*kadı*	Ali Efendi	case witness	23b/69a/1
	kadı	Abdullah Efendi	case witness	23a/160a/4
Tarkhan	*kadı*	Hatay Efendi	case witness	22/25a/2
unregistered	*balcı başı*	Ahmed Ağa	case witness	23a/175b/3
	kadı of the *nuraddin*	Salih Efendi	performing his judicial duty	23b/67b/2
	kapı agası (chief gatekeeper) of the former *nuraddin* Safa Giray Sultan	Aliş Ağa	legal agent	23b/25a/2
	Tat ağası	Evliya Ağa, son of Hacı Abdulveli	party in the case	23a/196b/1
	vizier	Ahmed Ağa	party in the case	23a/202b/3
	former vizier	Bahadır Ağa	case witness	23a/133b/3
	yalı ağası	Muzaffer Ağa	case witness	23a/189a/3

2 List of the Officials Recorded in the *sicil*s of the District Court of Kara Su during the Reign of Murad Giray

Location	Office	Name of the official	His role in the court	Location in the court register
Argın	*kadı*	Abdulşahid Efendi	case witness	25/3b/11
Kara Su	*bölükbaşı*	Baki Can	case witness	25/8b/2
	beytülmal emini	Mehmed Ağa	on duty	25/11b/4
	emin of the *kalga*'s janissaries	Unregistered	legal agent	25/25a/3
Kara Su	*kadı*	Ibrahim	on duty	25/1a/1
	katib of the *beytülmal emini*	Abdulbaki	on duty	25/31a/3
	former *beytülmal emini*	Mehmed Çelebi Beşe	case witness	25/7b/1
Unregistered	*naib* of the *kadıasker*	Abdulgaffar Efendi	circumstantial witness	25/14b/1
	kethüda of the *kalga*	unregistered	case witness	25/10a/4
	katib of the *kalga*'s *kethüda*	Ali Çelebi	case witness	25/25a/3

Selected Bibliography

Archival Sources

Archivio Storico di Propaganda Fide [Propaganda Fide Historical Archives in Rome; APF]

Acta Sacrae Congregationis (ACTA)

vol. 82, fols. 503–504v

vol. 89, fols. 39r–40r

Fondo Lettere e decreti della Sacra Congregazione e biglietti di Mons. Segretario (Fondo Lettere)

vol. 17, fol. 91r–v

Scritture referite nei Congressi (SC), Bessarabia, Crimea, Moscovia (1679–1856)

fols. 12–14, 16, 20–21

Scritture originali referite nelle Congregatione (SOCG)

vol. 73, fols. 269r–270v

vol. 104, fol. 255v

vol. 106, fols. 334–337v

vol. 123, fol. 1r

vol. 135, fols. 480–486r

vol. 147, fols. 272r–275r

vol. 209, fols. 528r–530r, 496r

vol. 210, fols. 502r–505r

Archiwum Główne Akt Dawnych [Main Archives of Early Acts in Warsaw; AGAD]

Archiwum Koronne Warszawskie [Crown Archives of Warsaw; AKW]

Dz. tatarski, k. 65, t. 68, no. 644

Dz. tatarski, k. 61, t. 57, no. 199

Dz. tatarski, k. 61, t. 82, no. 224

Dz. tatarski, k. 61, t. 102, no. 244

Dz. tatarski, k. 61, t. 111, no. 253

Dz. tatarski, k. 61, t. 113, no. 255

Dz. tatarski, k. 61, t. 140, no. 283

Dz. tatarski, k. 63, t. 32, no. 495

Haus-, Hof- und Staatsarchiv in Vienna [HHStA]

Türkei I, Turcica 150 (1680, Jänner–Juni), fols. 75–78

Türkei I, no. 149, fols. 12–13, 20–21, 81; no. 150, fol. 84r

Oriental'ski Otdel Narodnoi Biblioteki Imieni Sv. Sv. Kirilla i Mefodiia [Oriental Department of Bulgarian National Library 'St. St. Cyril and Methodius; NBKM, Or. Dept.]

Fond D737
Fond 310A, arkh. ed. 252, no. 2
Österreichische Nationalbibliothek [Austrian National Library; ÖNB]
H.O.86
Rossiiskii Gosudarstvennyi Arkhiv Drevnykh Aktov [Russian State Archive of Early Acts in Moscow; RGADA]
Fond 123, *Posol'skii prikaz. Krymskie dela*, op. 1, no. 64, fol. 1 *passim*
op. 1, nos. 67, fols. 24–94
op. 1, nos. 68, fols. 37–38
op. 1, nos. 71, fols. 1–104
op. 1, nos. 72, fols. 1–562
op. 3, nos. 212, 218, 231, 233, 236
op. 4, no. 72
Rossiiskaia Natsional'naia Biblioteka in St. Petersburg [Russian National Library in St. Petersburg, Oriental Manuscript Division of the Russian National Library (Otdel Rukopisev Rossiiskoi Natsionalnoi Biblioteki; ORRNB)]
Fond 917, *defters* nos. 1–121

Primary Sources

Abacı, N. (ed.). *The Ottoman Judges and Their Registers: The Bursa Court Registers B-90/295 (Dated AH 1081/AD 1670–1671)*, parts 1–2. Cambridge, MA, 2007.

Abdülgaffar el-Kırımi. *Ümdetü't-tavarih*. Edited by N. Asim Bey Istanbul, 1343/1927.

Abdulgaffar, Kyrymi. *Umdet al-akhbar*. Edited by D.D. Paşaoğlu. Kazan, 2014.

Abrahamowicz, Zygmunt, A. Dubiński, and S. Płaskowicka-Rymkiewicz (trans.). *Księga podróży Ewliji Czelebiego (Wybór)*. Warsaw, 1969.

Abrahamowicz, Zygmunt. (ed.). *Kara Mustafa pod Wiedniem. Źródła muzułmańskie do dziejów wyprawy wiedeńskiej 1683 roku*. Cracow, 1973.

Akgündüz, A. (ed.). *Osmanlı Kanunnameleri ve Hukuk Tahlilleri*, vols. 8–9. Istanbul, 1996.

Âkif Aydın, M. (ed.). *İstanbul Kadı Sicilleri*, vols. 1–40. Istanbul, 2008–12.

Arberry, A.J. (trans.). *The Koran*. New York, 1955.

Bennigsen, A., et al. (eds.). *Le khanat de Crimée dans les Archives du Musée du Palais de Topkapı*. Paris, 1978.

Bent, J.T. (ed.). *Early Voyages and Travels in the Levant*. New York, 1943.

Biarslanov, M. (trans.). "Vypisi iz kadiaskerskago sakka (knigi) 1017–1022 g. khidzhry (1608/9–1613 g. khr. liet.) khraniashchagosia v arkhive Tavricheskago gubemskago pravleniia." *ITUAK* 8 (1889): 41–51; 9 (1890): 68–70; 10 (1890): 74–78.

Broniewski, M. "Opisanie Kryma." *ZOOID* 6 (1867): 333–365.

Broniewski, M. *Tartariae Descriptio*. Cologne, 1595.

Broniewski, M. *Tartariae Descriptio. Opis Tatarii*. Translated by E. Śnieżewska. Edited by M. Mączyńska. Łódź 2011.

Busbeque, O.G. *The Turkish Letters of Ogier Ghiselin de Busbecq*. Oxford, 1927.

Cleaves, F.W. (ed. and trans.). *The Secret History of the Mongols*. Cambridge, MA, 1982.

Craven, E. *A Journey Through the Crimea to Constantinople*. Dublin, 1786 (reprint: New York, 1970).

Dağlı, Y. and S.A. Kahraman (eds.). *Evliya Çelebi Seyahatnamesi*, 10 vols. Istanbul, 2008.

da Lucca, G. "Opisaniie perekopskikh i nogaiskikh tatar, cherkesov, mingrelov i gruzin Zhana da-Liuka." Edited by P. Yurchenko. *ZOOID* 11 (1879): 473–493.

d'Ascoli, E.D. [correctly P.]. *Descrittione del mare Negro et della Tartaria*. Edited by N. Dashkevich. In *Chtenia v Istoricheskom Obshchestve Nestora Letopisca*, vol. 5, pp. 1–46. Kiev, 1891.

Evliya Çelebi. *The Intimate Life of an Ottoman Statesman: Melek Ahmed Pasha (1588–1622) as Portrayed in Evliya Çelebi's Book of Travels*, translated by R. Dankoff. Albany, 1991.

Evliya Çelebi. *Tam Metin Seyahatnâme*, vol. 7. Edited by Mümin Çevik. Istanbul, 1985.

Faizkhanov, H. and V. Vel'aminov-Zernov (eds.), *Materiały dla istorii krymskogo khanstva izvlechenyia po rasporazheniu Imperatorskoi Akademii Nauk, iz Moskovkogo Glavnago Arkhiva Ministerstva Inostrannykh del*. St. Petersburg, 1864.

Gökbilgin, Özalp (ed.). *Tarihi Sahib Giray Han*. Ankara, 1973.

Guthrie, M. *A Tour Performed in the Years 1795–6 through the Taurida, or Crimea, the Ancient Kingdom of Bosporus, the Once-Powerful Republic of Tauric Cherson, and All the Other Countries on the North Shore of the Euzine, Ceded to Russia by the Peace of Kainardgi and Jassy by Mrs Maria Guthrie, formerly acting Directress of the Imperial Convent for the Education of the Female Nobility of Russia; Described in a Series of Letters to Her Husband, the Editor, Matthew Guthrie, M.D.* London, 1802.

Hacı Mehmed Senai z Krymu. *Historia chana Islama Gireja III*. Edited by Z. Abrahamowicz. Warsaw, 1971.

Halim Giray. *Gülbünü Hânân (Kırım Hanları Tarihi)*. Edited by B. Günay, A. Başer, and A. Günaydın. Istanbul, 2013.

Halim Giray. *Gülbünü Hanan yahud Kırım Tarihi.* Edited by A. Ilmi. Istanbul, 1870.

Halim Giray. *Gülbünü Hanan yahud Kırım Tarihi / Rozovyi kust khanov ili istoriia Kryma*. Edited by A. Ilmi. Simferopol, 2004.

Holderness, M. *Notes Relating to the Manners and Customs of the Grim Tatars Written During a Four Years Residence among that People*. London, 1821.

Kalachov, N. (ed.). "Desiat otkrytkov razhnoobraznogo istoricheskogo soderzhaniia (iz sochinieniia) Mikhalona Litvina 'O pravakh tatar, litovcev i moskvitian.'" In *Arkhiv istoriko-iuridicheskikh svedenij otnosiavshikh do Rossii*, edited by S.D. Shestov, 2–77. Moscow, 1854.

Kazembeg, Mirza (ed.). [*Seyyid*] *Muhammad Riza, Essebüsseyyar ili sem' planet soderzhavshchii istoriu krymskikh khanov ot Mengli Girej Khana pierwogo do Mengli Girej Khana vtorogo t. e. s 871/1466 po 1150/1737*. Kazan, 1832.

Kazimirski, W. (ed.). *Documents sur les rapports diplomatiques de l'ancienne Russie avec les puissances étrangères et notamment la Crimée*. Petersburg, 1884–98.

Kefeli Ibrahim Efendi. *Tevarihi Tatar Han ve Dagistan Moskov ve Deşti Kıpçak Ülkelerinindir*. Edited by Ibrahim Otar. Istanbul, 2005.

Kefeli Ibrahim Efendi. *Tevarihi Tatar Han ve Dagistān, Moskov ve Deşti Kıpçak Ülkelerinindir*. Edited by Seyyid Ahmed Kırımlı. Pazarcık, 1933.

Kellner-Heinkele, B. (ed.). Aus den Aufzeichnungen des Sa'id Giray Sultan. Eine zeitgenössische Quelle zur Geschichte des Chanats der Krim um die Mitte des 18. Jahrhunderts. Freiburg im Breisgau, 1975.

Kleemann, N. *Voyage de Vienne à Belgrade et à Kilianova, Dans le pays des Tartares Budziacs et Nogais dans la Crimée, et Kaffa à Constantinople; que travers de la mer Noire; avec le retour à Vienne; par Trieste. Fait dans les années 1768, 1769 et 1770, par Nicolas-Ernest Kleemann. On y a joint description des choses les plus remarquables concernant la Crimée*. Neuchatel, 1780.

Kluczycki, F. (ed.). *Acta Historica res gestas Poloniae illustrantia*, vol. 2, *Pisma do wieku i spraw Jana Sobieskiego*, vol. 1, part I. Cracow, 1880.

Köhbach, M. (ed.). "Der Tarih-i Mehemmed Giray – Eine Osmanische Quelle zur Belagerung Wiens durch die Türken im Jahre 1683." *Zeszyty Naukowe Uniwersytetu Jagiellońskiego. Prace Historyczne* 75 (1983): 137–164.

Kołodziejczyk, D. (ed.). *The Ottoman Survey Register of Podolia (ca. 1681) Defter-i Mufassal-i Eyalet-i Kamaniçe*, vol. 1. Cambridge, MA, 2004.

Kreutel, R. (ed.). "Osmanische Berichte über Kara Mustafa's Feldzug gegen Wien, Walter Sturminger zum 70. Geburstag." *Die Welt des Islams* 12 (1969–70): 196–227.

Lashkov, F. (ed.). *Pamiatniki diplomaticheskikh snoshenii Krymskago khanstva s Moskovskim gosudarstvom v XVI i XVII v.v., khraniashchiesia v Moskovskom Glavnom Arkhive Ministerstva Inostrannykh Diel*. Simferopol, 1891a.

Lashkov, F. (ed.). "Sbornik dokumentov po istorii krymsko-tatarskogo zemlevladeniia." Part 1, *ITUAK* 22 (1895): 82–115; part 2, *ITUAK* 23 (1895): 118–129; part 3, *ITUAK* 24 (1896): 72–137; part 4, *ITUAK* 25 (1896): 89–158; part 5, *ITUAK* 26 (1897): 24–154.

Lashkov, F. (ed.). "Stateinyi spisok moskovskogo poslannika v Krym Ivana Sudakova v 1587–1588 godu." *ITUAK* 14 (1891b): 43–80.

Litwin, Michalon (Mykolas Lietuvis). *O pravakh tatar, litovcev i moskvitian*. Translated by V. Matuzova. Edited by A. Khoroshkevich. Moscow, 1994.

Markievich, A.I. (ed.). "Spisok s stateinogo spiska podiachago Vasilia Aitemirieva, posyl'annogo v Krym s predl'ozheniiem mirnykh dogovorov. (7200/1692–7203/1695)." Part 1, *ZOOID* 18 (1895): 1–47; part 2, *ZOOID* 19 (1896): 1–58.

Matuz, Joseph (ed.). "Eine Beschreibung des Khanats der Krim aus dem Jahre 1669." *Acta Orientalia (Havniae)* 28 (1964): 129–151.

Matuz, Joseph. (ed.). *Krimtatarische Urkunden im Reichsarchiv zu Kopenhagen*. Freiburg, 1976.

Menger, S.I. (ed.). *Tarihi Sahib Giray Han*. Istanbul, 2000.

Mundt, T. *Krim-Girai, Khan of the Crimea*. London, 1856.

Murzakevich, N. (ed.). "Spisok s stateinago spiska velikago gosudaria ego tsarskago velichestva poslannikov: stolnika i polkovnika inamestnika pereiaslavskogo Vasilia Mikhailova syna Tiapkina, diaka Nikity Zotova." *ZOOID* 2 (1850): 558–658.

Pallas, P.S. *Travels Through the Southern Provinces of the Russian Empire, Performed in the Years 1793 and 1794 by P.S. Pallas, Councillor of State to the Emperor of All the Russia*, etc. 4 vols. London, 1803.

Petis de la Croix, François. *The History of Genghizcan the Great*. London, 1722.

Peysonnel, C. *Strictures and Remarks on the Memoires of Baron de Tott*. London, 1786.

Peysonnel, C. *Traité sur le commerce de la mer noire. Par M. De Peyssonel, ancien Consul General de France à Smirne, Associé des Académies de Marseille, de Lyon et Dijon; Membre Honoraire de celle des Antiquités de Cassel, et Correspondant de l'Academie Royale des Inscriptions et Belles-Letteres de Paris*. 2 vols. Paris, 1787.

Piaseczyński, Ł. "Trzy poselstwa Ławryna Piaseczyńskiego do Kazi Gereja chana perekopskich Tatarów." Edited by K. Puławski. *Przewodnik Naukowy i Literacki* 39 (1911): 135–145, 244–256, 358–366; 467–472, 553–566, 645–660, 756–768, 845–864, 945–960.

Polnoe sobranie zakonov rossiiskoi imperii, vol. 2. St. Petersburg, 1830.

Pułaski, F. (ed.). *Źródła do poselstwa Jana Gnińskiego wojewody chełmińskiego do Turcyi w latach 1677–1678*. Warsaw, 1907.

Pułaski, K. (ed.). "Machmet – Girej chan Tatarów perekopskich i stosunki jego z Polską (1515–1523)." In *Szkice i poszukiwania historyczne*, series 2. St. Petersburg, 1898.

Sak, I. (ed.). *47 Numeralı Konya Şeri'ye Sicili (1128–1129/ 1716–1717). Transkrypsiyon ve Dizin*. Konya, 2006.

Schulhoff, I. *Megilat Oven*. Edited and translated by P. Agostino. Rome, 1982.

Schütz, E. (ed.). "Eine armenische Chronik von Kaffa aus der ersten Hälfte des 17. Jahrhunderts." *Acta Orientalia Academiae Scientiarum Hungaricae* 29, no. 2 (1975): 133–186.

Sergeyev, A.A. (ed.). "Posolstvo Ambrosiia Lodyzhenskago i podiachago Petra Danilova v Krym v 1613 godu (k 300-letnemu iubileiu Tsarstvuiushchago Doma Romanovykh." *ITUAK* 50 (1913): 7–56.

Sicill-i Osmani. Edited by Nuri Akbayar. Transcribed from the Ottoman by Seyit Ali Kahraman. 6 vols. Istanbul, 1996.

Soysal, A.Z. (ed.). *Z dziejów narodów Kaukazu, Nadczarnomorza, Krymu, Moskwy i Polski*. Warsaw, 1935.

Święcicka, E. "The Diplomatic Letters by Crimean Keräy Ladies to the Swedish Royal House." *Rocznik Orientalistyczny* 55 (2002): 57–90.

Thunmann, J.E. *Description de la Crimée*. Strasburg, 1786.

Tott, F. *Mémoires sur les Turcs et les Tatares*, 2 vols. Amsterdam, 1784 (English = *Memoirs of the Baron de Tott on the Turks and the Tatars*. London, 1785; Polish = *Opisy Turków i Tatarów*. Warsaw, 1791).

Yediyıldız, M.A., S. Maydaer, and İ. Oruçoğlu (eds.). *A153 Nolu Bursa Şeri'ye Sicili*. Bursa, 2010.

Zajączkowski, A. (ed.). *La chronique des steppes kipchak: Tevārīh-i Dešt-i Qipčak du XVIIe siècle*. Warsaw, 1966.

Secondary Sources

Abacı, N. *Bursa Şehri'nde Osmanlı Hukuku'nun Uygulanması (17. Yüzyıl)*. Ankara, 2001.

Abrahamowicz, Zygmunt. "Comments on Three Letters by Khan Islam Gerey III to the Porte (1651)." *HUS* 14, no. 1 (1990): 139–143.

Abrahamowicz, Zygmunt. "Tło polityczne i ekonomiczne wyprawy wiedeńskiej Kary Mustafy." *Kwartalnik Historyczny* 90 (1983): 21–54.

Aigle, D. "Le grand *jasaq* de Gengis-khan, l'empire, la culture mongole et la shari'a." *JESHO* 47 (2004): 31–79.

Akçay, I. "Kırım'dan Yetişen Türk Alimleri." *Emel* 203 (1994): 11–17.

Akdağ, M. *Türk Halkının Dirlik ve Düzenlik Kavgası: Celali İsyanları*. Ankara, 1975.

Akgündüz, A. *Şer'iye Sicilleri*. 2 vols. Istanbul, 1988.

Albrecht, S. "Die 'Tartariae Descriptio' des Martinus Broniovius. Enstehung und Wirkung eines Gesandtenberichts aud dem Krimkhanate." In *The Crimean Khanate Between East and West (15th–18th Century)*, edited by D. Klein, 149–168. Weisbaden, 2012.

Ali, Syed Ameer. *Personal Law of the Mahommedans: Mahommedan Law Compiled from Authorities in the Original Arabic*. Vol. 2, *Containing the Law Relating to Succession and Status*. Calcutta and Simla, 1929.

Amitai, R. *The Mongols in the Islamic Lands: Studies in the History of the Ilkhanate*. Aldershot and Burlington, 2007.

Aslanapa, O. "Kırım Türk Eserleri." In *Sanatı, Tarihi, Edebiyatı ve Musikisiyle Kırım*, edited by O. Aslanapa, 11–57. Ankara, 2003.

Ayalon, D. "The Great Yasa of Chingiz Khan: A Reexamination." *Studia Islamica* 33 (1971): 97–140; 34 (1971): 151–180; 36 (1972): 112–158; 38 (1973): 107–156.

Aykan, Y. "The Second Formation of Islamic Law: The Hanafi School in the Early Modern Ottoman Empire (Book Review)." *IJMES* 48 (2016): 793–795.

Azad, G.M. "Conduct and Qualities of a Qadi." *Islamic Studies* 24 (1985): 51–61.

Baer, M. "Islamic Conversion Narratives of Women: Social Change and Gendered Religious Hierarchy in Early Modern Ottoman Istanbul." *Gender and History* 16 (2004): 425–458.

Babinger, F. *Die Geschichte der Osmanem und ihre Werke*. Leipzig, 1927.

Baranowski, B. *Chłop polski w walce z Tatarami*. Warsaw, 1952.

Baranowski, B. "Dzieje jasyru na Gródku Karaimskim." *Myśl Karaimska. Rocznik Naukowo-Społeczny. Seria Nowa* 24 (1946–47): 40–52.

Baranowski, B. "Geneza sojuszu kozacko-tatarskiego z 1648 r." *Przegląd Historyczny* 38 (1948a): 278–287.

Baranowski, B. *"Polska a Tatarszczyzna w latach 1624–1629."* Lodz, 1948b.

Baranowski, B. *Stosunki polsko-tatarskie w latach 1632–1648*. Łódź, 1949.

Barkey, K. "The Use of Court Records in the Construction of Village Networks: A Comparative Perspective." *International Journal of Comparative Sociology* 32, nos. 1–2 (1991): 196–216.

Barkey, K. and R. Van Rossem. "Networks of Contention: Villages and Regional Structure in the Seventeenth Century Ottoman Empire." *American Journal of Sociology* 102, no. 5 (1997): 1345–82.

Beldiceanu, N. *Le timar dans l'État ottoman (XIVe-XVe siècles)*. Wiesbaden, 1980.

Bennigsen, A. and C. Lemercier-Quelquelay. "La Moscovie, L'Empire Ottoman et la Crise Successoriale de 1577–1588 dans le Khanat de Crimée. La Tradition Nomade Contre le Modèle des Monarchies Sédentaires." *CMRS* 14 (1973): 453–487.

Berezhkov, M. "Nur-Sultan, tsaritsa krymskaia. Istoriko-biograficheskii ocherk." *ITUAK* 27 (1897): 1–17.

Berindei, M. and G. Veinstein. "La presence Ottomane au sud de la Crimée et en mer d'Azov dans la premiére moitié du XVIe siècle." *CMRS* 20 (1978): 399–465.

Blaškovič, J. "Ziemie lenne (hass) namiestnika Nowych Zamków w latach 1664–1685." *Rocznik Orientalistyczny* 45 (1977): 83–92.

Boyle, J.A. (ed.). The Cambridge History of Iran. Vol. 5: The Saljuq and Mongol Periods. Cambridge, 1968.

Broadbridge, A. *Kingship and Ideology in the Islamic and Mongol Worlds*. Cambridge, 2008.

Burak, G. *The Second Formation of Islamic Law: The Hanafi School in the Early Modern Ottoman Empire*. Cambridge, 2015.

Bursalı, Mehmed. *Osmanlı Zamanında Yetişen Kırım Müellifleri*. Ankara, 1990.

Calero Secall, I. "Rulers and Qadis: Their Relationships during the Nasrid Kingdom." *Islamic Law and Society* 7, no. 2 (2002): 235–255.

Canbakal, H. "On the Nobility of Provincial Notables." In *Provincial Elite in the Ottoman Empire*, edited by A. Anastasopoulos, 39–50. Rethymno, 2006a.

Canbakal, H. *Society and Politics in an Ottoman Town: Ayntab in the 17th century*. Leiden and Boston, 2006b.

Chodynicki, K. "Marcin Broniewski." *Polski Słownik Bibliograficzny* 2:461–462. Warsaw, 1925.

Çiçek, K. "*Zimmis* (non-Muslims) of Cyprus in the Sharia Court: 1110/39 A.H./ 1698–1726 A.D." PhD thesis, University of Birmingham, 1992.

Ciğdem, R. "Crimes Threatening Bodily Integrity (Assault and Battery): A Legal Analysis of Four Cases from the Judicial Registers of the Bakchisaray/Crimea Law Court." *Ankara Üniversitesi Hukuk Fakültesi Dergisi* 54, no. 1 (2005a): 61–71.

Ciğdem, R. "The Judicial Registers of the Bakchisaray/Crimea Law Court. A Study of Murder Crimes." *Hamdard Islamicus* 28, no. 4 (2005b): 41–53.

Ciğdem, R. "Khul or Dissolution of Marriage by a Woman: A Historical Background and Two Cases from the Bakchisaray/Crimea Court." *Dokuz Eylül Üniversitesi İlahiyat Fakültesi Dergisi* 21 (2005c): 95–115.

Cihan, Ahmed and Fehmi Yılmaz. "Kırım Kadi Sicilleri." *Islam Araştırmaları Dergisi* 11 (2004): 131–176.

Coşgel, M. and B. Ergene. *The Economics of Ottoman Justice: Settlement and Trial in the Sharia Courts*. Cambridge 2016.

Dankoff, R. *An Ottoman Mentality: The World of Evliya Çelebi*. Leiden and Boston, 2004.

Darling, Linda "Circle of Justice." *Encyclopaedia of Islam, THREE*, edited by. K. Fleet, G. Krämer, D. Matringe, J. Nawas, E. Rowson. Brill Online, 2017.

Darling, Linda T. *Revenue-Raising and Legitimacy: Tax Collection and Finance Administration in the Ottoman Empire, 1560–1660*. Leiden and Boston, 1996.

Davies, B. *Warfare, State ad Society on the Black Sea Steppe*. London, 2007.

Davies, N. *Europe: A History*. Oxford, 1996.

Demir, U. "Muhayyel bir Kirim Tarihçisi Kefevî Ibrahim Efendi ve Humbaracıbaşi Ahmed Paşa'nin Rusya'ya Dair Raporu." *Türkiyat Mecmuası* 24 (2014): 23–32.

Demirtaş, H.N. *Açıklamalı Osmanlı Fetvâları*, vols. 1–2. Istanbul, 2011–12.

DeWeese, D. *Islamization and Native Religion in the Golden Horde: Baba Tükles and Conversion to Islam in Historical and Epic Tradition*. University Park, PA, 1994.

Düzbakar, O. "Divorce and Types of Divorce at the End of Seventeenth-century Bursa." *Journal of Family History* 41, no. 2 (2016): 118–130.

Ergene, B. "Evidence in Ottoman Courts: Oral and Written Documentation in Early-Modern Courts of Islamic Law." *Journal of the American Oriental Society* 124, no. 3 (2004): 471–491.

Ergene, B. (ed.). *Judicial Practice. Institutions and Agents in the Islamic World*. Leiden and Boston, 2009.

Ergene, B. *Local Court, Provincial Society and Justice in the Ottoman Empire: Legal Practice and Dispute Resolution in Çankırı and Kastamonu (1652–1744)*. Leiden and Boston, 2003.

Ergene, B. "On Ottoman Justice: Interpretations in Conflict (1600–1800)." *Islamic Law and Society* 8, no. 1 (2001): 52–87.

Ergene, B. "Why Did Ümmü Gülsüm Go to Court? Ottoman Legal Practice between History and Anthropology." *Islamic Law and Society* 17, no. 2 (2010): 215–244.

Ergene, B. and A. Kaygun. "Spouse Selection and Marital Mobility in the Ottoman Empire: Observations from Eighteenth-Century Kastamonu." *Historical Methods: A Journal of Quantitative and Interdisciplinary History* 45, no. 1 (2012): 3–20.

Ergene, B. and A. Berker. "Wealth and Inequality in 18th-Century Kastamonu: Estimations for the Muslim Majority." *IJMES* 40, no. 1 (2008): 23–46.

Establet, C. and J-P. Pascual. *La gent d'État dans la société ottomane damascéne. Les 'asker à la fin du XVIIe siécle*. Damascus, 2011.

Eszer, A. "Die *Beschreibung des Schwarzen Meeres und der Tatarei* des Emidio Portelli d'Ascoli O.P." *Archivum Fratrum Praedicatorum* 42 (1972): 199–249.

Eszer, A. "Giovanni Giuliani da Lucca O.P. Forschungen zu seinem Leben und zu seinen Schriften." *Archivum Fratrum Praedicatorum* 37 (1967): 353–468.

Eszer, A. "Missionen im Halbrund der Länder zwischen Schwarzem Meer, Kaspisee und Persischem Golf: Krim, Kaukasien, Georgien und Persien." In *Sacra Congregationis De Propaganda Fide Memoria Rerum 1622–1972*, edited by J. Metzler, vol. 2: 1700–1815, 421–462. Rome, 1971.

Eszer, A. "Missionen in Randzonen der Weltgeschichte: Krim, Kaukasien und Georgien" in *Sacra Congregationis De Propaganda Fide Memoria Rerum 1622–1972*. Edited by J. Metzler, vol. 1, part 1: 1622–1700, 650–679. Rome, 1971.

Eszer, A. "Neue Forschungen zur Geschichte der II. Krim-Mission der Dominikaner (1635–1665)." *Archivum Fratrum Praedicatorum* 41 (1971): 181–239.

Evracı, M.H. "The Role of the Crimean Tatars in the Ottoman-Safavi War (1578–1639)." *Historical Yearbook* 4 (2007): 153–160.

Faizov, S. "Znachenie nasledia Husaina Faizkhanova v oblasti krymsko-tatarskoi arkheografii dla izuchenia istorii Krymskogo yurta i russko-krymskikh otnoshenii." *Faizkhanovskie chtenia* 2 (2005): 146–151.

Faroqhi, S. *Approaching Ottoman History*. Cambridge, 1999.

Faroqhi, S. (ed.). *The Cambridge History of Turkey: The Later Ottoman Empire, 1603–1839*. Cambridge, 2006a.

Faroqhi, S. "Crisis and Change, 1599–1699." In *An Economic and Social History of the Ottoman Empire*. Vol. 2: *1600–1914*, edited by H. İnalcık and D. Quatert, 411–622. Cambridge, 2000.

Faroqhi, S. "Guildsmen and Handicraft Producers." In *The Cambridge History of Turkey*. Vol. 3: *The Later Ottoman Empire, 1603–1839*, 336–355. Cambridge, 2006b.

Faroqhi, S. "Political Activity among Ottoman Taxpayers and the Problem of Sultanic Legitimation (1570–1650)." *JESHO* 35, no. 1 (1992): 1–39.

Faroqhi, S. "Social Mobility and the Ottoman 'Ulema in the Sixteenth Century." *IJMES* 4 (1973): 204–218.

Finkel, C. *The Administration of Warfare: The Ottoman Military Campaigns in Hungary, 1593–1606*. Vienna, 1988.

Fisher, A. *Between Russians, Ottomans and Turks: Crimea and Crimean Tatars*. Istanbul, 1998.

Fisher, A. *The Crimean Tatars*. Stanford, 1978.

Fisher, A. "G.A. Sanin, Otnoshenia Rossii i Ukrainy s krymskim khanstvom v seredine XVII veka, Moskva 1987. [The relations of Russia and Ukraine with the Crimean Khanate in the middle of the seventeenth century, Moscov, Nauka 1987] (Book review)." *American Historical Review* 95, no. 2 (1990): 546.

Fisher, A. A Precarious Balance: Conflict, Trade, and Diplomacy on the Russian-Ottoman Frontier. Istanbul, 1999.

Fitzgerald, T.J. "Murder in Aleppo: Ottoman Conquest and the Struggle for Justice in the Early Sixteenth Century." *Journal of Islamic Studies* 27, no. 2 (2016): 176–215.

Fotić, A. "Non-Ottoman Documents in the Kadis Courts (Mōloviya Medieval Charters): Examples from the Archives of Hilander Monastery (15th–18th C.)." In *Frontiers of Ottoman Studies: State, Province and the West*, edited by C. Imber, K. Kiyotaki, and R. Murphey, vol. 2, 63–73. New York, 2005.

Frazee, C.A. *Catholics and Sultans: The Church and the Ottoman Empire 1453–1923*. Cambridge, 1983.

Gerber, H. "Social and Economic Position of Women in the Ottoman City, Bursa, 1600–1700." *IJMES* 12 (1980): 231–244.

Gerber, H. *State, Society, and Law in Islam: Ottoman Law in Comparative Perspective*. New York, 1994.

Gierowski, Józef Andrzej. "Krym w Polityce Wersalu w latach 1704–1709." In *Węgry–Polska w Europie Środkowej. Historia-Literatura. Księga pamiątkowa ku czci Profesora Wacława Felczaka*, edited by A. Centarowicz, C.G. Kiss, and I. Kovács, 86–92. Cracow, 1997.

Ginio, E. "Coping with the State's Agents 'from Below': Petitions, Legal Appeal, and the Sultan's Justice in Ottoman Legal Practice." In *Popular Protest and Political Participation in the Ottoman Empire: Studies in Honor of Suraiya Faroqhi*, edited by E. Gara, M.E. Kabadayi, and C.K. Neumann, 41–56. Istanbul, 2011.

Ginio, E. "Jews and European Subjects in Eighteenth-Century Salonica: The Ottoman Perspective." *Jewish History* 28 (2014): 289–312.

Ginio, E. "Neither Muslims nor Zimmis: The Gypsies (Roma) in the Ottoman State." *Romani Studies – 5th Serieş* 14, no. 2 (2004): 117–144.

Ginio, E. "Patronage, Intervention and Violence in the Legal Process in Eighteenth-Century Salonica and Its Province." In *Law, Customs, and Statute in the Muslim World. Studies in Honor of Aharon Layish*, edited by R. Shaham, 111–130. Leiden and Boston, 2007.

Gradeva, R. "On the Judicial Functions of Kadi Courts: Glimpses from Sofia in the Seventeenth Century." *Wiener Zeitschrift zur Geschichte der Neuzeit* 5, no. 2 (2005): 15–43.

Gradeva, R. "On Judicial Hierarchy in the Ottoman Empire: The Case of Sofia, Seventeenth—Beginning of Eighteenth Century." In *Dispensing Justice in Islam: Qadis and Their Judgements*, edited by. M.K. Masud, R. Peters, and D.S. Powers, 271–298. Leiden and Boston, 2006.

Gradeva, R. "Orthodox Christians in the Kadi Courts: The Practice of Sofia Sheriat Court, Seventeenth Century." *Islamic Law and Society* 4, no. 1 (1997): 37–69.

Greene, M. "An Islamic Experiment? Ottoman Land Policy on Crete." *Mediterranean Historical Review* 11 (1996): 60–78.

Greene, M. *A Shared World: Christians and Muslims in the Early Modern Mediterranean*. Princeton, 2000.

Gülsoy, E. *Girit'in Fethi ve Osmanlı Idaresinin Kurulması, 1645–1670*. Istanbul, 2004.

Haivoronskii, Oleksa. *Pobediteli dvukh materikov*, 2 vols. Simferopol, 2007–2009.

Hammer-Purgenstall, J. *Geschichte der Chane der Krim unter Osmanischer Herrschaft vom 15. Jahrhundert bis yum Ende 18. Jahrhundert*. Vienna, 1856.

Hegyi, K. "The Terminology of the Ottoman-Turkish Judical Documents on the Basis of the Sources from Hungary." *Acta Orientalia Academiae Scientiarum Hungaricae* 18, nos. 1–2 (1965): 191–203.

Heyd, U. *Studies in Old Ottoman Criminal Law*. Oxford, 1973.

Humphreys, S. "Law as Discourse." *History and Anthropology* 1 (1985): 241–265.

Hungarian-Ottoman Military and Diplomatic Relations in the Age of Süleyman the Magnificent. Edited by G. Dávid and P. Fodor. Budapest, 1994.

Imber, C. *Ebu's-su'ud: Islamic Legal Tradition*. Edinburgh, 1997.

Imber, C. *The Ottoman Empire, 1300–1650: The Structure of Power*. New York, 2002.

Inalcık, H. "Adaletnameler." *Belgeler* 2, nos. 3–4 (1965): 49–145.

Inalcık, H. and D. Quatert (eds.). *An Economic and Social History of the Ottoman Empire*, vol. 2: *1600–1914*. Cambridge, 2000.

Inalcık, H. "Introduction to Ottoman Metrology." In *Studies in Ottoman Social and Economic History*, edited by H. Inalcık, 311–348. London, 1985.

Inalcık, H. "Kalgay." *Islam Ansiklopedisi*. Edited by A. Adıvar et al., 6:505–522. Istanbul, 1967.

Inalcık, H. "The Khan and the Tribal Aristocracy. The Crimean Khanate under Sahib Giray I." *Harvard Ukrainian Studies* nos. 3–4 (1979–80): 445–466.

Inalcık, H. "Kirim Hanlığı Sicilleri Bulundu." *Belleten* 140 (1996): 170–189.

Inalcık, H. "Power Relationships between Russia, the Crimea and the Ottoman Empire as Reflected in Titulature." In *Passé turco-tatar. Présent soviétique. Études offertes à Alexandre Bennigsen*, 175–211. Paris, 1986.

Iskhakov, D. *Ot srednevekovykh Tatar k Tataram novogo vremeni*. Kazan, 1998.

Iskhakov, D. "Seidy v pozdnezolotoordynskikh tatarskikh gosudarstvakh." *Tatarica* 1 (1997–98): 42–95.

Iskhakov, D. *Tursko-tatarskie gosudarstva XV-XVI vv.* Kazan, 2009.

İslamoğlu-İnan, H. *State and Peasant in the Ottoman Empire: Agrarian Power Relations and Regional Economic Development in Ottoman Anatolia During the Sixteenth Century.* Leiden and Boston, 1994.

Itzkowitz, N. "Eighteenth Century Ottoman Realities." *Studia Islamica* 16 (1962): 73–94.

Ivanics, M. "Der Bündnisplan zwischen dem Chan Gazi Giray II. und dem Fürsten Sigismund Báthory aus dem Jahre 1598." In *Hungarian-Ottoman Military and Diplomatic Relations in the Age of Süleyman the Magnificent*, edited by G. Dávid and P. Fodor, 183–198. Budapest, 1994a.

Ivanics, M. "Die Şirin. Abstammung und Aufstieg einer Sippe in der Steppe." In *The Crimean Khanate between East and West (15th–18th Century)*, edited by D. Klein, 27–44. Weisbaden, 2012.

Ivanics, M. "Entstehung und Quellenwert der Krimtatarischen *Tiyiş* Defters." *Acta Orientalia Academiae Scientiarium Hungaricae* 47, nos. 1–2 (1994b): 115–122.

Ivanics, M. "Formal and Linguistic Peculiarities of 17th Century Crimean Tatar Letters Addressed to Princes of Transylvania." *Acta Orientalia Academiae Scientiarum Hungaricae* 29, no. 2 (1975): 213–224.

Ivanics, M. "Macaristan'daki Kırım Tatarlarına Ait Vesikaları." In *VIII. Türk Kongresi II. Cilt'den Ayrıbasım,* 423–426, 1049–1053. Ankara, 1981.

Ivanics, M. "Posolstva krymskikh tatar pri Venskom dvore v 1598–1682 gg. (iz istorii krymsko-tatarskoi diplomatii XVI-XVII vv.)." In *Turcica et Ottomanica. Sbornik statei v chest' 70-letia M.S. Meiera*, edited by I.V. Zaitsev and S.F. Oreshkova, 226–237. Moscow, 2006.

Ivanova, Svetlana. "The Divorce between Zubaida Hatun and Esseid Osman Aga: Women in the Eighteenth-Century *Shari'a* Court of Rumeli." In *Women, the Family, and Divorce Laws in Islamic History*, edited by A. Sonbol, 112–125. Syracuse, 1996.

Jankowski, Henryk. *A Historical-Etymological Dictionary of Pre-Russian Habitation Names of the Crimea.* Leiden and Boston, 2006.

Jennings, R. "Kadi, Court and Legal Procedure in 17th Century Ottoman Kayseri." *Studia Islamica* 48 (1978): 133–172.

Jennings, R. "Limitations of the Judicial Powers of the Kadi in 17th Century Ottoman Kayseri." *Studia Islamica* 49 (1979): 151–184.

Jennings, R. "Women in the Early 17th-Century Ottoman Judicial Records: The Shari'a Court of Anatolian Kayseri." *JESHO* 18 (1975): 53–114.

Jobst, K.S. *Die Perle des Imperiums. Der russische Krim-Diskurs im Zarenreich.* Konstanz, 2007.

Johansen, B. "Legal Literature and the Problem of Change: The Case of the Land Rent." In *Islam and Public Law*, edited by C. Mallat, 29–47. London, 1993.

Johansen, B. "Signs as Evidence: The Doctrine of Ibn Taymiyya (1263–1328) and Ibn Qayyim al-Jawziyya (d. 1351) on Proof." *Islamic Law and Society* 9 (2002): 168–193.

Kamps, I. and G. Singh (eds.). *Travel Knowledge: European "Discoveries" in the Early Modern Period*. New York, 2001.

Kançal-Ferrari, Nicole. *Kırım'da Kalan Miras. Hansaray*. Istanbul, 2005.

Kara, G. (ed.). *Between the Danube and the Caucasus: Oriental Sources of the History of the People of Central amd South-Eastern Europe*. Budapest, 1987.

Keenan, E. "The Yarlik of Ahmed-Khan to Ivan III: A New Reading." *International Journal of Slavic Linguistics and Poetics* 11 (1967): 32–47.

Kellner-Heinkele, B. "Who Was 'Abdulghaffar el-Qirimi? Some Notes on an 18th Century Crimean Tatar Historian." *Journal of Asian History* 32, no. 2 (1998): 145–156.

Kemper, M., A. von Kügelgen, and D. Yermakov (eds.). *Muslim Culture in Russia and Central Asia from the 18th to the Early 20th Centuries*, edited by M. Kemper. Berlin, 1996.

Kermeli, E. "Caught in Between Faith and Cash: The Ottoman Land System of Crete, 1645–1670." In *The Eastern Mediterranean under Ottoman Rule: Crete, 1645–1840*, edited by A. Anastasopoulos, 17–48. Rethymno, 2008.

Khazanov, Anatoly. "Muhammad and Jenghiz Khan Compared: The Religious Factor in the World Empire Building." *Comparative Studies in Society and History* 35, no. 3 (1993): 461–479.

Khoury, D.R. "The Ottoman Centre Versus Provincial Power-Holders: An Analysis of the Historiography." In *The Cambridge History of Turkey*. Vol. 3: *The Later Ottoman Empire, 1603–1839*, edited by S. Faroqhi, 135–156. Cambridge, 2006.

Khodarkovsky, M. *Russia's Steppe Frontier: The Making of a Colonial Empire, 1500–1800*. Bloomington, IN, 2002.

Khoroshkevich, A. *Rus i Krym. Ot soiuza k protivostoianiu. Konets XV- nachalo XVI vv.* Moscow, 2001.

Kılıç, R. *Osmanlı'da Seyyidler ve Şerifler*. Istanbul, 2005.

Kırımlı, H. *Geray Hanedanı Mensuplarının Rumeli'ne İskanı*. Paper presented at International Congress of Ottoman Social and Economic History. Sofia, 2017.

Kizilov, M.B. "The Black Sea and the Slave Trade: The Role of Crimean Maritime Towns in the Trade in Slaves and Captives in the Fifteenth to Eighteenth Centuries." *International Journal of Maritime History* 17, no. 1 (2005): 211–235.

Klein, D. (ed.). *The Crimean Khanate Between East and West (15th–18th Century)*. Wiesbaden, 2012a.

Klein, D. *'Das Chaos der Welt' Ein krimtatarischer Blick auf die Zeit um 1700* in *Şehrâyîn. Die Welt des Osmanen, die Osmanen in der Welt Wahrnehmungen, Begegnungen und Abgrenzungen/Illuminating the Ottoman World: Perceptions, Encounters and Boundaries. Festschrift Hans Georg Majer*, edited by Y. Köse with collaboration of T. Völker, 157–172. Wiesbaden, 2012b.

Klein, D. "Tatar and Ottoman History Writing: The Case of the Nogay Rebellion (1699–1701)." In *The Crimean Khanate between East and West*, 125–146. Wiesbaden, 2012c.

Kochegarov, K. "The Moscow Uprising of 1682: Relations Between Russia, the Crimean Khanate, and the Polish-Lithuanian Commonwealth." In *The Crimean Khanate Between East and West (15th–18th Century)*, edited by D. Klein, 59–73. Wiesbaden, 2012.

Kołodziejczyk, D. *The Crimean Khanate and Poland-Lithuania. International Diplomacy on the European Periphery (15th–18th Century): A Study of Peace Treaties Followed by Annotated Documents*. Leiden and Boston, 2011.

Kolovos, E. "Beyond 'Classical' Ottoman Defeterology: A Preliminary Assessment of the Tahrir Registers of 1670/1671 Concerning Crete and the Aegean Islands." In *The Ottoman Empire, the Balkans, the Greek Lands: Towards Social and Economic History. Studies in Honor of John C. Alexander*, edited by E. Kolovos, P. Kotzageorgis, S. Laiou, and M. Sariyannis, 201–235. Istanbul, 2007.

Kortepeter, C.M. *Ottoman Imperialism During the Reformation: Europe and the Caucasus*. London, 1972.

Kotzageorgis, P. and D. Papastamatiou. "Wealth Accumulation in an Urban Context: The Profile of the Muslim Rich of Thessaloniki in the Eighteenth Century on the Basis of Probate Inventories." *Turkish Historical Review* 5 (2014): 165–199.

Kravets, M. "Blacks Beyond the Black Sea: Eunuchs in the Crimean Khanate." In *Slavery, Islam and Diaspora*, edited by B.A. Mirzai, I.M. Montana, and P.E. Lovejoy, 21–36. New York, 2009.

Kravets, M. "From Nomad's Tent to Garden Palace: Evolution of a Chinggisid Household in the Crimea." *Toronto Studies in Central and Inner Asia* 7 (2005): 47–60.

Królikowska, N. "Crimean Crime Stories: Homicide and Bodily Harm Cases During the Reign of Murad Giray (1678–1683)." In *The Crimean Khanate Between East and West*, edited by D. Klein, 109–123 Wiesbaden, 2012.

Królikowska, N. "Praworządny jak Tatarzyn? – stosunki prawne w Chanacie Krymskim na podstawie miejscowych ksiąg sądowych z XVII i XVIII wieku." *Czasopismo Prawno-Historyczne* 65, no. 1 (2013a): 121–142.

Królikowska, N. "Ród Jaszławskich przed sądem chana Murada Gireja. Przyczynek do dziejów mirzów krymskich." In *Od Ałtaju po Syberię*, edited by E. Siemieniec-Gołaś and J. Georgiewa-Okoń, 115–120. Cracow, 2010.

Królikowska, N. "Sąd rady chańskiej w czasach Murata Gireja (1678–1683)." In *Studia z dziejów i kultury ludów tureckich. Badania polskich turkologów prezentowane podczas I i II Konferencji Turkologicznej: Poznań 2007 i Warszawa 2008*, 161–171. Warsaw, 2013b.

Królikowska-Jedlińska, N. "Foreigners in Front of the Crimean Khan's Courts in the Seventeenth and Eighteenth Centuries." *International Crimes and History: Annual International and History Journal* 16 (2015): 139–154.

Królikowska-Jedlińska, N. "Social Standing, Living Conditions and Reliogiosity of Slaves from the Territory of the Commonwealth in the Crimea in the 17th Century."

In *Osmanlı Devletinde Kölelik: Ticaret–Esaret–Yaşam*, edited by Z. Güneş Yağcı, F. Yaşa, and D. İnan, 269–296. Istanbul, 2017.
Kunt, M. *The Sultan's Servants: The Transformation of Ottoman Provincial Government (1550–1650)*. New York, 1983.
Kurat, A.N. *Topkapı Sarayı Müzesı Arşivdeki Altın Ordu, Kırım ve Türkistan Hanlarına ait Yarlık ve Bitkileri*. Istanbul, 1940.
Kurz, M. *Das sicill aus Skopje. Kritische Edition und Kommentierung des einzigen vollständig erhalten Kadiamtsregisterbandes* (sicill) *aus Üsküb* (*Skopje*). Wiesbaden, 2003.
Kurz, M. "Gracious Sultan, Grateful Subjects: Spreading Ottoman Imperial *Ideology* throughout the Empire." *Studia Islamica* 107, no. 1 (2012): 96–121.
Lambton, A.K.S. "Mongol Fiscal Administration in Persia." *Studia Islamica* 64 (1986): 79–99.
Lambton, A.K.S. "Soyūrg͟hāl." *Encylopaedia of Islam, New Edition*. Edited by P.J. Bearman, Th. Bianquis, C.E. Bosworth, E. van Donzel, and W.P. Heinrichs. Brill online 2017.
Lane, G. *Daily Life in the Mongol Empire*. London, 2006.
Lashkov, F. "Arkhivnyia dannyia o beilikakh v Krymskom khanstve." *Arkheologicheskii S'ezd: Trudy* 6, no. 4 (1889): 96–110.
Lashkov, F. "Istoricheskii ocherk Krymsko-tatarskogo zemlevladeniia." Part 1, *ITUAK* 21 (1894): 59–89; part 2, 22 (1895): 35–81; part 3, 23 (1895): 71–117; part 4, 24 (1896): 35–71; part 5, 25 (1896): 29–88.
Lashkov, F. "K voprosu o kolichestve naseleniia tavricheskoi gubernii v nachale 19 stoletiia." *ITUAK* 53 (1916): 158–176.
Lashkov, F. "Statisticheskaia svedeniia o Kryme, soobshchennyia kaimakamami v 1783 godu." *ZOOID* 14 (1886): 91–156.
Lemercier-Quelquelay, C. "Les Expéditions de Devlet Giray contre Moscou en 1571 et 1572 d'après Documents des Archives Ottomanes." *CMRS* 13 (1972): 555–583.
Lemercier-Quelquejay, C., Gilles Veinstein, and S. Enders Wimbush (eds.). *Passé turco-tatar. Présent soviétique. Études offertes à Alexandre Bennigsen*. Paris, 1986.
Loenertz, R. "Le origini della missione secentesca dei Domenicani in Crimea." *Archivum Fratrum Praedicatorum* 5 (1935): 261–288.
MacLean, G. *The Rise of Oriental Travel: English Visitors to the Ottoman Empire, 1580–1720*. New York, 2004.
Majer, H.G. (ed.). *Das osmanische "Registerbuch der Beschwerden"* (*Şikāyet defteri*) *vom Jahre 1675*, Vienna, 1984.
Majewski, R. *Cecora 1620*. Warsaw, 1970.
Manz, B.F. "The Clans of the Crimean Khanate." *HUS* 2 (1978): 282–309.
Marcus, A. *The Middle East on the Eve of Modernity: Aleppo in the Eighteenth Century*. New York, 1989.

Masters, B. "Christians in a Changing World." In *The Cambridge History of Turkey: The Later Ottoman Empire, 1603–1839*, 272–279. Cambridge, 2006.

Masud, M.K. "Adab al-qāḍī." *Encyclopaedia of Islam, THREE*, edited by K. Fleet, G. Krämer, D. Matringe, J. Nawas, and E. Rowson. (Brill online 2017).

Matthee, R. "Poverty and Perseverance: The Jesuit Mission of Isfahan and Shamakhi in Late Safavid Iran." *Al-Qantara* 36, no. 2 (2015): 463–501.

Matuz, Joseph. "Qalga." *Turcica* 2 (1970): 101–129.

May, M. "Jewish Criminal Law and Legal Procedure." *Journal of Criminal Law and Criminology* 31, no. 4 (1940): 438–447.

Mihneva, R. "The Muscovite Tsardom, the Ottoman Empire and the European Diplomacy (Mid-Sixteenth – End of Seventeenth Century)." *Études Balkaniques* 34, nos. 3–4 (1998): 99–128.

Mihneva, R. "The Muscovite Tsardom, the Ottoman Empire and the European Diplomacy (End of Sixteenth Century – Beginning of Eighteenth Century (On the 'Center,' 'Periphery' and 'Europe' in the Transition to Modern Times)). Part 2." *Études Balkaniques* 36, no. 3 (2000): 41–54.

Mihordea, V. "Raportuile Moldavei şi Ţării Româneşti cu Tătarii în secolele XVI–XVIII." *Revista de Istoria* 32, no. 6 (1979): 1069–1095.

Moačanin, N. *Town and Country on the Middle Danube 1526–1690*. Leiden and Boston, 2006.

Morgan, D.O. "The Great Yasa of Chingiz Khan and Mongol Law in the Ilkhanate." *BSOAS* 49 (1986): 163–176.

Morgan, D.O. *The Mongols*. Oxford, Malden, and Carlton, 2007.

Muhamedyarov, S. and I. Vásary. "Two Kazan Tatar Edicts (Ibrahim's and Sahib Girey's Yarliks)." In *Between the Danube and the Caucasus*, edited by G. Kara, 181–216. Budapest, 1987.

Munck, T. *Europa XVII wieku (1598–1700). Państwo, konflikty i porządek społeczny*. Warsaw, 1998.

Murphey, R. *Exploring Ottoman Sovereignty: Tradition, Image and Practice in the Ottoman Imperial Household, 1400–1800*. Auckland, 2008.

Nekrasov, A. "Zhenshchiny khanskogo doma Gireev v XV–XVI vv." In *Drevneishie gosudarstva vostochnoi Evropy*, edited by T.M. Kalinina, 213–221. Moscow, 2000.

Novoselski, A. *Borba Moskovskogo gosudarstva s tatarami v pervoi polovine XVII v*. Moscow, 1948.

O'Brien, C.B. "Russia and Turkey, 1677–1681: The Treaty of Bakhchisarai." *Russian Review* 12, no. 4 (1953): 259–268.

Ochmański, J. "Michalon Litwin i jego traktat o zwyczajach Tatarów, Litwinów i Moskwicinów z połowy XVI wieku." *Kwartalnik Historyczny* 83, no. 4 (1976): 765–783.

Ortaylı, I. "Türkiye'de Kırımlı Aydınlar." In *Sanatı, Tarihi, Edebiyatı ve Musikisiyle Kırım*, edited by O. Aslanapa, 58–64. Ankara, 2003.

Ostapchuk, Victor. "Crimean Tatar Long-Range Campaigns: The View from Remmal Khoja's History of Sahib Gerey Khan." In *Warfare in Eastern Europe, 1500–1800*, edited by B.J. Davies, 147–171. Leiden and Boston, 2012.

Ostapchuk, Victor. "The Publication of Documents on the Crimean Khanate in the Topkapı Sarayı: New Sources for the History of the Black Sea Basin." *HUS* 6, no. 4 (1982): 500–528.

Ostapchuk, Victor. "The Publication of Documents on the Crimean Khanate in the Topkapı Sarayı: The Documentary Legacy of Crimean-Ottoman Relations." *Turcica* 19 (1987): 247–276.

Othman, A. "*And Amicable Settlement Is Best*: Sulh and Dispute Resolution in Islamic Law." *Arab Law Quarterly* 21, no. 1 (2007): 64–90.

Özdem, Z. *Kırım Karasubazar'da Sosyal-Ekonomık Hayat (17. Yüzyil Sonlarından 18. Yüzyil Ortalarına Kadar)*. Ankara, 2010.

Öztürk, Y. *Osmanlı Hakimiyetinde* Kefe: *1475–1600*. Ankara, 2000.

Özyetgin, M. "On the Use of the Title 'Beg' Among the Turks." *International Journal of Central Asian Studies* 11 (2006): 156–170.

Pamuk, Ş. *A Monetary History of the Ottoman Empire*. Cambridge, 2000.

Papp, S. "Die Inaugurationender Krimkhane durch die Hohe Pforte (16.–18. Jahrhundert)." In *The Crimean Khanate Between East and West (15th–18th Century)*, 75–90. Wiesbaden, 2012.

Parveva, S. "Rural Agrarian and Social Structure in the Edirne Region During the Second Half of the 17th Century." *Études Balcaniques* 3 (2000): 55–90.

Paydaş, K. "Moğol ve Türk-İslam Devletlerinde Suyurgal Uygulaması." *Bilig* 39 (2006): 195–218.

Peirce, L. *The Imperial Harem: Women and Sovereignty in the Ottoman Empire*. Oxford, 1993.

Peirce, L. *Morality Tales: Law and Gender in the Ottoman Court of Aintab*. London, 2003.

Peters, R. *Crime and Punishment in Islamic Law: Theory and Practice from the Sixteenth to the Twenty-first Century*. Cambridge, 2005.

Petrushevsky, I. "The Socio-Economic Condition of Iran under the Il-Khans." In *The Cambridge History of Iran*. Vol. 5: *The Saljuq and Mongol Periods*, edited by J.A. Boyle, 494–524. Cambridge, 1968.

Pochekaev, R. "Kırım Hanı Murat Giray'ın Adli Reformu." *Belleten* 75 (2011): 571–578.

Podraza, A. (ed.). *Wielka historia świata*, vol. 7 – *Świat w XVII wieku*. Cracow and Warsaw, 2005.

Powers, P. "Evidence." *Encyclopaedia of Islam, Three*, edited by K. Fleet, G. Krämer, D. Matringe, J. Nawas, and E. Rowson (Brill online 2017).

Rebstock, Ulrich. "A Qāḍī's Errors." *Islamic Law and Society* 6, no. 1 (1999): 1–37.

Repp, R.C. "Courts of Law, Ottoman." *Encyclopaedia of Islam, Three*, edited by K. Fleet, G. Krämer, D. Matringe, J. Nawas, and E. Rowson (Brill online 2017).

Riazanovsky, V. *Fundamental Principles of Mongol Law*. Bloomington, IN, 1965.

Riza, S. "Islam's Fourth Amendment: Search and Seizure in Islamic Doctrine and Muslim Practice." *Georgetown Journal of International Law* 40, no. 3 (2009): 702–806.

Rosen, L. *The Anthropology of Justice: Law as Culture in Islamic Society*. Cambridge 1989.

Rozen, Minna. "The Ottoman Jews." In *The Cambridge History of Turkey*. Vol. 3: *The Later Ottoman Empire, 1603–1839*, 256–271. Cambridge, 2006.

Sanin, G. *Otnoshenia Rossii i Ukrainy s krymskim khanstvom v seredine XVII veka*. Moscow, 1987.

Sartori, Paul. *Vision of Justice: Sharia and Cultural Change in Russian Central Asia*. Leiden and Boston, 2017.

Savory, Roger M. (ed.). *Introduction to Islamic Civilization*. Cambridge, 2000.

Schurmann, H.F. "Mongolian Tributary Practices of the 13th Century." *Harvard Journal of Asiatic Studies* 19 (1956): 304–389.

Schütz, E. "The Tat People in the Crimea." *Acta Orientalia Academiae Scientiarum Hungaricae* 31 (1977): 77–106.

Semerdjian, Elyse. *"Off the Straight Path": Illicit Sex, Law and Community in Ottoman Aleppo*. Syracuse, 2008.

Seyyityahya, Narimaan. "Istoricheskaia proza w krymskotatarskoi literature XV–XVIII vv." PhD dissertation. Crimean University, Simferopol, 2005.

Seyyityahya, Narimaan. "Proiskhozhdenie Seiida Mukhammeda Rizy (k voprosu o meste ego 'Semi planet' sredi proizvedenii krymskoi istoricheskoi prozy XVIII veka)." *Kultura Narodov Prichernomora* 44 (2003): 35–41.

Seyyityahya, Narimaan. "Uchebnyi iz Karasu Abdul'gaffar Kyrymi i ego istoricheskoe cochinienie." In *Choban-zade. Sbornik materialov I krymskoi mezhnunarodnoi konferentsii. Belogorsk (Karasubazar), 23–25 maja 2012* g. Edited by A.R. Emirov, 222–242. Simferopol, 2013.

Seyyityahya, Narimaan. "Voennye deistvia v Krymu v 1735–1736 gg." *Qasevet* 33 (2008): 40–49.

Shaham, R. *The Expert Witness in Islamic Courts: Medicine and Crafts in the Service of Law*. Chicago and London, 2010.

Shamiloglu, U. "The Qaraçı Beys of the Golden Horde: Notes on the Organization of the Mongol World Empire." *Archiwum Euroasiae Medii Aevii* 4 (1984): 283–297.

Shamiloglu, U. "Tribal Politics and Social Organization in the Golden Horde." PhD dissertation, Columbia University, 1986.

Skorupa, D. *Stosunki polsko-tatarskie 1595–1623*. Warsaw, 2004.

Smirnov, N. *Rossia i Turtsia v XVI–XVII vv*. 2 vols. Moscow, 1946.

Smirnov, V. "Tatarsko-khanskie iarlyki iz kollektsii Tavricheskoi Uchenoi Arkhivnoi Kommissii." *ITUAK* 54 (1918): 1–19.

Smirnov, V. *Krymskoe khanstvo pod verkhovenstvom Otomanskoi Porty do nachala XVIII veka*. St. Petersburg, 1887.

Smith, John M. "Mongol and Nomadic Taxation." *Harvard Journal of Asiatic Studies* 30 (1970): 46–87.

Sneath, D. *The Headless State: Aristocratic Orders, Kinship Society, and Misrepresentations of Nomadic Inner Asia*. New York, 2007.

Soysal, Abdullah Zihni. "Emine Sultan Biyim." *Emel* 52 (1969): 37–38.

Spring, E. *Law, Land, and Family: Aristocratic Inheritance in England, 1300 to 1800*. Chapel Hill, NC, 1993.

Spuler, B. *Die Goldene Horde*. Wiesbaden, 1965.

Spuler, B. *Die Krim*. Berlin, 1944.

Stilt, K. *Islamic Law in Action: Authority, Discretion, and Everyday Experiences in Mamluk Egypt*. Oxford, 2011.

Syroechkovskii, Vladimir. "Mukhammed-Gerai i ego vassaly." *Uchenye zapiski Moskovskogo Gosudarstvennogo Universiteta im. M.V. Lomonosova* 61, 2 (*Istoria*) (1940): 3–71.

Tamdoğan, I. "Sulh and the 18th Century Ottoman Courts of Üsküdar and Adana." *Islamic Law and Society* 15, no. 1 (2008): 55–83.

Tezcan, B. "The Ottoman *Mevali* as Lords of the Law." *Journal of Islamic Studies* 20, no. 3 (2009): 383–407.

Trepavlov, V. *Istoria Nogaiskoi Ordy*. Moscow, 2001.

Trepavlov, V. *Sibirskii iurt posle Ermaka: Kuchum i Kuchumovichi v bor'be za revansh*. Moscow, 2012.

Tuğ, B. *Politics of Honor in Ottoman Anatolia: Sexual Violence and Socio-Legal Surveillance in the Eighteenth Century*. Leiden and Boston, 2017.

Turan, A.N. "Kırım Hanlığı Kadı Sicilleri Hakkında Notlari." *Türk Kültürü İncelemeleri Dergisi* 9 (2003): 1–16.

Turan, A.N. "Sudebnyie reiestry krymskovo khanstva (posle ich obnaruzheniia)." *Kultura narodov prichernomoria* 30 (2002): 90–93.

Turcica et Ottomanica. Sbornik statei v chest' 70-letia M.S. Meiera. Edited by I. Zaitsev, S. Oreshkova. Moscow, 2006.

Upton, A.F. *Charles XI and Swedish Absolutism, 1660–1697*. Cambridge, 1998.

Ürekli, Muzaffer. *Kırım Hanlığının Kuruluşu ve Osmanlı Himayesinde Yükselişi*. Ankara, 1989.

Ursinus, M. *Grievance Administration (Şikayet) in an Ottoman Province: The Kaymakam of Rumelia's 'Record Book of Complaints' of 1781–1783*. London and New York, 2005.

Usmanov, M.A. *Zhalovannye akty Dzhuchieva ulusa, 14–16vv*. Kazan, 1979.

Uzunçarşılı, I. *Osmanlı Devletinin İlmiye Teşkilatı*. Ankara, 1984.

Vasil'eva, O. "Krymsko-Tatarskie Rukopisnye Materialy v otdele rukopisei Rossiiskoi Natsional'noi Biblioteki." *Vostochnyi Sbornik* 5 (1993): 37–45.

Veinstein, G. "La révolte des mirza tatars contre le khan 1724–1725." *Cahiers du monde russe et soviétique* 12, no. 3 (1971): 327–338.

Veinstein, G. "Les Tatars de Crimée et la second election de Stanislas Leszczyński." *CMRS* 11, no. 1 (1970): 24–92.

Veinstein, G. "Missionaires Jésuites et agents français en Crimée au début du XVIIIe siècle." *Cahiers du monde russe et soviétique* 10, nos. 3–4 (1969): 414–458.

Vel'aminov-Zernov, V. *Issledovanie o Kasimovskikh tsariakh i tsarevichakh*. 4 vols. St. Petersburg, 1863–67.

Vernadsky, G. "The Scope and Contents of Chingis Khan's Yasa." *Harvard Journal of Asiatic Studies* 3 (1938): 337–360.

Vesolovskii, N.I. "Ob izdanii kadiaskerskogo sakka." *ITUAK* 54 (1918): 276–278.

Vinogradov, Alexander. "Rod Sulesha vo vneshnei politike Krymskogo khanstva vtoroi poloviny XVI v." In *Turkologicheskii Sbornik. 2005 – Turskie narody Rossii i velikoi stepi*, 26–72. Moscow, 2006.

Vinogradov, Alexander. *Russko-krymskie otnoshenia. 50-e-vtoraa polovina 70-kh godov XVI veka*, vols. 1–2. Moscow, 2007.

Vogel, F.E. "Siyāsa." *Encylopaedia of Islam, New Edition*, 9:693–696. Edited by P.J. Bearman, Th. Bianquis, C.E. Bosworth, E. van Donzel, and W.P. Heinrichs. Leiden: Brill, 1997.

Wakin, J.A. *The Function of Documents in Islamic Law*. Albany, NY, 1972.

Williams, B.G. *The Crimean Tatars: The Diaspora Experience and the Forging of a Nation*. Leiden and Boston, 2001.

Yaşa, F. "Bahçesaray (1650–1675)." PhD dissertation, University of Sakarya, 2017.

Yaşa, F. "Kırım Hanlığı'nda Köleliğin Sosyal ve Mali Boyutları." *Gaziantep University Journal of Social Sciences* 13, no. 3 (2014): 657–669.

Yılmaz, Fehmi. "On Sekizinci Yüzyılın İkinci Yarısında Kırım'da Gayrimüslimler." *Osmanlı Araştırmaları* 33 (2009): 237–268.

Zaitsev, I. *Astrakhanskoe khanstvo*. Moscow, 2004.

Zaitsev, I. "'Istoria tatarskih hanov, Dagestana, Moskvy i narodov Desht-i Kipchak' Ibrahima b. Ali Kefeli." In *Desht-i Kipchak i Zolotaia Orda v stanovlenii kultury evraziiskih narodov*, 95–102. Moscow, 2003.

Zaitsev, I. *Krymskaia istoriograficheskaia traditsia XV-XIX vekov*. Moscow, 2009.

Zaitsev, I. "The Structure of Giray Dynasty (15th–16th Centuries: Matrimonial and Kinship Relations of the Crimean Khanate)." In *Kinship in the Altaic World: Proceedings of the 28th Permanent International Altaistic Conference,* Moscow 10–15 July 2005. Edited by E.V. Boikova and R.B. Rybakov, 341–353. Wiesbaden, 2006.

Zajączkowski, A. "Dyplomatyka Złotej Ordy i Krymu z XV w. (nowe materiały z archiwum tureckiego)." *Przegląd Historyczny* 37 (1948): 217–222.

Zarinebaf, F. *Crime and Punishment in Istanbul, 1700–1800*. Berkeley, 2010.

Ze'evi, D. "The Use of Ottoman Sharīʿa Court Records as a Source for Middle Eastern Social History: A Reappraisal." *Islamic Law and Society* 5, no. 1 (1998): 35–56.

Zetterstéen, K.V. *Türkische, tatarische und persische Urkunden im Schwedischen Reicharchiv*. Uppsala, 1945.

Zilfi, M.C. "Elite, Circulation in the Ottoman Empire: Great Mollas of the Eighteenth Century." *JESHO* 26, no. 3 (1983a): 318–364.

Zilfi, M.C. "The Ilmiye Registers and the Ottoman Medrese System Prior to the Tanzimat." In *Contributions à l'histoire économique et sociale de l'Empire ottoman*, edited by J.-L. Bacqué-Grammont and P. Dumont, 309–327. Leuven, 1983b.

Zilfi, M.C. "The Ottoman Ulema." In *The Cambridge History of Turkey*. Vol. 3: *The Later Ottoman Empire, 1603–1839*, edited by S. Faroqhi, 209–225. Cambridge, 2006.

Zilfi, M.C. *The Politics of Piety: The Ottoman Ulema in the Post-Classical Age* (*1600–1800*). Minneapolis, MN 1988.

Zilfi, M.C. "Women and Society in the Tulip Era." In *Women, the Family, and Divorce Laws in Islamic History*, edited by A. Sonbol, 290–303. Syracuse, 1996.

Index

The index covers pp. 1 – 223 excluding footnotes, tables, appendices and words: Black Sea, Crimea/Crimean, Giray(s), Islam, *kadı*, *kadıasker*, Muslim, Ottoman, *sicils*, Tatar(s), as well as Crimean Khanate, Murad Giray and Ottoman Empire as they appear throughout the text. Individuals appearing as parties in cases or registered as legal or case witnesses were not listed with exception of the key officials of the Crimean Khanate like the vizier, *kadıasker* or mufti.

www.ingramcontent.com/pod-product-compliance
Ingram Content Group UK Ltd.
Pitfield, Milton Keynes, MK11 3LW, UK
UKHW021421091026
15624UKWH00010B/341